BECOMING THE MATH TEACHER YOU WISH YOU'D HAD

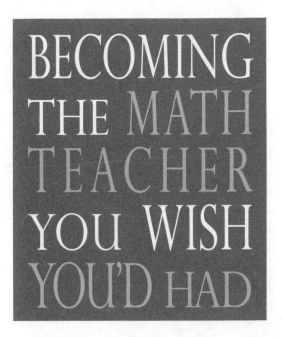

BECOMING THE MATH TEACHER YOU WISH YOU'D HAD

IDEAS AND STRATEGIES FROM VIBRANT CLASSROOMS

TRACY JOHNSTON ZAGER

FOREWORD BY **ELHAM KAZEMI**

Stenhouse
PUBLISHERS

Stenhouse
P U B L I S H E R S
w w w . s t e n h o u s e . c o m

Credits

Figure 5.1: Photo courtesy of Cindy Gano

Figures 5.3 and 5.4: Photos courtesy of Judy Hill

Figures 6.17 and 6.18: Courtesy of Dan Meyer, CC-BY-3.0

Figure 7.1: Photo courtesy of Christopher Danielson

Figure 7.2: Photo courtesy of Dan Anderson

Figure 7.3: Photo courtesy of Dan Meyer, CC-BY-3.0

Figure 7.16: Photo courtesy of Christopher Danielson

Figure 8.2: Photo courtesy of Annette Young

Figures 9.9 and 9.10: Photos courtesy of Andrew Stadel

Figure 9.14: Photo courtesy of Joe Schwartz

Figures 10.3, 10.8, 10.9, and 10.10: Courtesy of Angela Turrou and Wendy Moulton

Figure 11.10: Courtesy of Andreas Stylianides and NRICH

Figure 12.13: Courtesy of Christopher Danielson and Stenhouse Publishers

Figure 12.14: Photo courtesy of Andrew Gael

Library of Congress Cataloging-in-Publication Data

Names: Zager, Tracy, 1972-

Title: Becoming the math teacher you wish you'd had : ideas and strategies
   from vibrant classrooms / Tracy Zager.

Description: Portland, Maine : Stenhouse Publishers, [2016] | Includes
   bibliographical references and index.

Identifiers: LCCN 2016018738 (print) | LCCN 2016023270 (ebook) | ISBN
   9781571109965 (pbk. : alk. paper) | ISBN 9781625311283 (ebook)

Subjects: LCSH: Mathematics--Study and teaching. | Mathematics
   teachers--Training of. | Effective teaching.

Classification: LCC QA11.2 .Z34 2016 (print) | LCC QA11.2 (ebook) | DDC
   510.71--dc23

LC record available at https://lccn.loc.gov/2016018738

Cover design, interior design, and typesetting by Lucian Burg, LU Design Studios, Portland, ME

Manufactured in the United States of America

PRINTED ON 30% PCW
RECYCLED PAPER

23 22 21 20 19   9 8 7 6 5

Dedication

For my mom and my girls.
Don't ever let anyone take math away from you; it's yours!

Contents

FOREWORD

*I*t can take moments, sometimes years, to know the good fortune that befalls us when we cross paths with another person. Tracy Zager was one of my first students at the University of Washington when I began my career as a math educator. It took only a few moments to recognize Tracy as a bighearted soul with large ideas and boundless energy. And what a joy it is for me, fifteen years later, to have the honor of introducing readers to her book. Readers, be warned: you are about to fall in love.

Tracy writes, "Good math teaching begins with us." With those six words, she invites you on a journey through this most magnificent book of stories and portraits where you will find new friends: Sofia, Fawn, Dan, Richard, Pierre, Sylvia, Vi, Daina, Shawn, and many more. This book turns on its head the common misconception of mathematics as a black–and–white discipline and of being good at math as entailing ease, speed, and correctness. You will find it full of color, possibility, puzzles, and delight. What's more, you will find it widening your community of teachers and colleagues.

Let yourself be drawn in. On this journey, linger in the classrooms, in the math problems, in the stories of mathematicians you encounter. Wonder about and plan for what you will try next in your classroom. Follow, too, Tracy's leads and suggestions and get better connected to other teachers around the country and the globe who are opening up their classrooms, sharing their struggles and their insights, and helping us become the mathematics teachers we wish we'd had. One of the biggest challenges to growing as teachers is overcoming the barriers to real collaboration with others. What does good teaching look like? How can we know if we don't get to be in one another's spaces, if we don't get to share our decision making and see how different decisions play out, if we don't get to continually learn new content together?

What does doing mathematics entail? Each chapter in this book is organized around the real work of doing mathematics in classrooms by students and teachers and as practiced by research mathematicians. I hope you will find ways to help students learn more about the lives of real mathematicians such as Daina Taimina in Chapter 8. Tracy has given us a great gift of weaving stories of mathematicians alongside stories of teachers and students doing mathematics. These stories are accessible and make real that mathematics is about reasoning and proof but also about making connections, rising to a challenge, taking risks, and making mistakes. Her vivid classroom dialogues help us see these same practices in action with young children.

When the pages of the manuscript arrived in my mail, I was amazed by its length. Its size is really a reflection of Tracy's heart, her passion for young children's ideas, and her belief in the power of teachers. I don't want you to think that you have to take it all in at once—although, it's quite likely that you won't want to put this book down. It's not speed that matters, right? Take your time; invite a colleague or a few to read it with you. Revel in the treasures each chapter offers and let it inspire your own curiosity about children's mathematical ideas. That's what this book is about. Your copy will become dog-eared, taped, scribbled on, and referenced over and over again.

We become who we are through the stories we tell. No doubt this book will help you tell many new stories about yourself and your students. Making mathematics a subject that all children and teachers love is completely within our reach.

Elham Kazemi, professor, math education,
University of Washington

ACKNOWLEDGMENTS

Early on in my research, when I knew I had something to say but wasn't exactly sure what, I took up residence in the classrooms of Heidi Fessenden, Shawn Towle, Jennifer Clerkin Muhammad, and Deborah Nichols. Day after day, they allowed me to get inside their heads so I could understand their thinking and make their instructional decisions transparent. Over time, I figured out how to articulate just why I was so darned happy in their classrooms, and my table of contents was born.

Heidi, Shawn, Jen, and Deb, you are the four anchors and inspirations of this book. I am honored to have you as colleagues and now dear friends. I tried my hardest to write a book worthy of each of you. I hope you like it.

I'm also honored to share the teaching and thinking of Julie Clark, Annie Fetter, Andrew Gael, Ann Gaffney, Cindy Numata Gano, Kristin Gray, Sheryl Horton, Aimee Krauss, Peter Liljedahl, Chris Luzniak, Linda Melvin, Dan Meyer, Fawn Nguyen, Katie Norton, Mark Pettyjohn, Max Ray-Riek, Mary Beth Schmitt, Joe Schwartz, Justin Solonynka, Andrew Stadel, John Stevens, and Becky Wright. Thank you all for trusting me with your work and for the work you do for kids every day. Deep bow.

Dozens more teachers, mathematicians, coaches, researchers, principals, and professors helped me write this book, whether they know it or not. Each of the scores of teachers who allowed me to visit his or her classroom is in here somehow. Each person who stood talking to me outside our cars in a cold, dark parking lot; met me at the crack of dawn for an early breakfast or after work for a quick coffee; shared ideas with me in the hallways of conferences; talked or Skyped with me late into the night after teaching and parenting all day; organized visits for me; or gave me feedback on drafts is part of this book. I am enormously grateful. Special thanks to Alexandra Fagan, Jenny Jorgensen, Rudy Morales, Marisa Peralta, Mary Beth Schmitt, and Annie Shah for helping me with my field research and lending me your colleagues.

Amie Albrecht, Virginia Bastable, Zachary Champagne, Christopher Danielson, Reuben Hersh, Allison Hintz, Robert Kaplinsky, Elham Kazemi, Danny Bernard Martin, Rachel McAnallen, Dan Meyer, Kassia Omohundro Wedekind, and Rebeka Eston Salemi each helped me by reading partial drafts or discussing specific sections of this book. Thank you for your keen eyes and pointed questions. You made me so much smarter. Joan Carlson has read every word of this manuscript, sometimes twice. Joan, your feedback was indescribably helpful. Thank you!

Principal Kate Lucas and the entire team of educators at Rollinsford Grade School have been amazing partners. You helped me translate the big ideas I had for this book into meaningful, practical professional development for busy teachers. I love working with you!

My online math community is the professional learning community of my dreams and pushes my thinking every day. I'm particularly indebted to those tweeps and bloggers already mentioned, plus Brian Bushart, Graham Fletcher, Mike Flynn, Simon Gregg, Ilana Horn, Chris Hunter, Mike Lawler, Chris Lusto, Kate Nowak, Michael Pershan, and Malke Rosenfeld, all of whom have helped me wrestle with essential ideas that made their way into these pages. Christopher Danielson began as my ambassador to the Math-Twitter-Blog-o-Sphere (#MTBoS) and quickly became a treasured critical friend and colleague. I look forward to making sense of math, writing, and parenting together for a long time. Thank you also to the Casco Bay Math Teachers' Circle and the lovely people who make up the Association of Teachers of Mathematics in Maine, our National Council of Teachers of Mathematics affiliate, for letting me play math with you and for helping me become a better teacher.

On the first day of math methods at the University of Washington in 2001, Elham Kazemi stood in front of my cohort of preservice teachers and said, "I have the privilege of introducing you to the fascinating world of young children and mathematics." My life has never been the same since. Thank you, Elham, for your guidance, friendship, and leadership then and now. Professionally, I am deeply honored by your foreword and feel so lucky to learn with you. Personally, I'll tell you that you made me cry good tears.

I will always be grateful for my years teaching at Ordway Elementary in Washington State, especially because I was put out in the portables with Terri Peterson and Suzy Peters, two veteran teachers, mentors, and partners in crime. Terri knows how much I wish I could share this phase of my teaching with Suzy, who died suddenly right before I started this work. I sometimes imagine what Suzy's face would look like after reading a passage. I'm hoping for twinkly eyes, rather than a *meh* or a mischievous raspberry. I like to imagine her curled up with the book and a pad of sticky notes, under a blanket from Montana, empty red sneakers tucked beneath her chair, jotting down ideas to try for next year. "Next year!" Suzy and Terri would cry every June, as they reflected on their years and decided what to do differently and better in the future. You taught me—through the power of your examples—what phrases like *professional development* and *continuing education* really mean.

In November of 2011, I talked with Toby Gordon about doing some part-time work for Stenhouse Publishers. After chatting for a while, she said, "What about you? What about you writing a book?"

"About what?"

"Well, that's up to you; it's your book! What do you have to say?"

So began a collaboration and dear friendship for which I am immeasurably grateful. Thank you, Toby, for taking a chance on me, for your endless support, and for helping me figure out what I have to say. It is my great honor to work with and learn from you as a writer and an editor.

The whole Stenhouse team has been phenomenal, and I can't imagine writing for anyone else. I am in awe of the work and integrity of Dan Tobin, Jay Kilburn, Chris Downey, Louisa Irele, Grace Makley, Lucian Burg, and everyone in production, marketing, editorial, and operations. Thank you all! The book is beautiful. I hope it was worth the wait.

The wait was long. During the writing of this book, both my mother and I were diagnosed with breast cancer. I want to thank Stenhouse for being so supportive and patient during our treatment. I am eternally grateful to our medical teams for saving our lives and to our community for making our lives bearable during their saving.

My family has been my rock throughout treatment and the writing of this book. My husband's parents, Robin and Al Zager, made work trips possible, took the kids while I was in chemotherapy, and were understanding when I took my laptop and snuck off to community libraries, coffee shops, hotel lobbies, and even a slopeside yurt to work during family trips. My parents, Susan and Jim Johnston, took care of little kids and big dogs more than any retired couple should have to, giving weekends, afternoons, evenings, whole weeks. They cheered me on and believed in me. My mother's personal history with mathematics was the original and lasting motivation for this book. I remember saying, "If I write a good enough book, I will change your mind about math!"

My daughters, Maya and Daphne, shared their math thinking with me, hugged me a lot, and fed the dogs so I could write. Kids, I hope, with time, you'll more fully understand why I was so busy during the writing of this book and be proud of me. In many ways, I wrote it for you and your teachers.

And Sam, my partner and teammate, thank you for having faith in me and in this idea. You showed me what support looks like.

READING *BECOMING THE MATH TEACHER YOU WISH YOU'D HAD*

This book is long because it's chock-full of ideas to discuss and strategies to try. There are many ways to read it successfully:

- From start to finish
- In sections
- As a collection of standalone mini-books that can be read in any order
- On your own
- In a book study group or professional learning community
- With a colleague
- As part of a larger professional development course
- As part of a math methods course

There is no wrong way, as long as reading it is useful to you.

It may help you to know that, as I wrote the book, I thought of its structure in terms of months and seasons. The thirteen chapters are the months that make up five larger seasons. For example, taking risks, making mistakes, and being precise are a season. Intuition, reasoning, and proof are a season. You might choose to read a season at a time, pausing between seasons to allow sufficient time to try strategies and connect ideas.

{ Chapter 1: Breaking the Cycle
{ Chapter 2: What Do Mathematicians Do?

{ Chapter 3: Mathematicians Take Risks
{ Chapter 4: Mathematicians Make Mistakes
{ Chapter 5: Mathematicians Are Precise

{ Chapter 6: Mathematicians Rise to a Challenge
{ Chapter 7: Mathematicians Ask Questions
{ Chapter 8: Mathematicians Connect Ideas

{ Chapter 9: Mathematicians Use Intuition
{ Chapter 10: Mathematicians Reason
{ Chapter 11: Mathematicians Prove

{ Chapter 12: Mathematicians Work Together and Alone
{ Chapter 13: "Favorable Conditions" for All Math Students

Study Guide, Further Resources, and Communication with Tracy

There is a robust collection of free resources for you at stenhouse.com/becomingmathteacher, including the following:

- Online resources to support, deepen, and expand upon the ideas in each chapter. There are videos of classrooms in action, articles, blogs, and curated references and tools.
- A detailed study guide for facilitators, coaches, and instructional leaders. I've thought about how I—as a coach—would use this book with teachers. I've suggested (1) fruitful places in the text to pause and discuss, (2) activities to do together in your professional learning community, and (3) places where you might put your book down and go try something specific with your students, along with how you might share what you learned with your colleagues.

However you choose to proceed, I hope you'll share your learning with me as well. You can find me on Twitter at @tracyzager, or by using the hashtag #becomingmath. I have posts organized by chapter at my blog, tjzager.com, where I invite you to talk with other readers and with me. I'll moderate discussions, read comments, and respond to ideas and questions. I'll provide a place for you to talk about the results of any ideas you try. I'll also post current information about online discussion groups and forums as I hear about them, and plan to drop in whenever I can. I'm grateful that modern technology makes it possible for us to collaborate across space and time, and I look forward to learning together with you wherever and whenever we might meet.

BREAKING THE CYCLE

Several years ago, I was out to breakfast with some members of my extended family when a mathematical question came up. Out of the corner of my eye, I saw my then sixty-something mother go pale. Her eyes filled with terror. I moved us through the moment as fast as possible, but asked her about it later that day, when we were alone and I knew she felt safe.

"I was terrified. I had no idea what they were talking about, and I was so afraid I'd look dumb in front of everyone."

My mom has always described herself as "bad at math" or "not a math person," even though she ran several successful small businesses. She managed the payroll, ordering, expenses, taxes, and books—and they were actually books: wide paper ledgers with long columns of handwritten figures. In one business, she and her partner designed and manufactured maternity clothing. I grew up in the studio where they created patterns and measured, blocked, and calculated yardage, scaled up and down for different sizes. In later years, she built a successful stable from the ground up, pacing off fence lines, designing the indoor and outdoor spaces, setting prices, and analyzing costs and revenue. In her last business, she and my father worked together. He designed homes, so my mother learned to visualize three-dimensional spaces from two-dimensional blueprints, and she learned web design in the early days of the Internet.

My mom has worked with math all her life. She has phenomenal number sense, especially, and delights in balancing her checkbook to the penny. Yet, she froze if I asked for help with my math homework. When I pointed this contradiction out to her, she said, "What I do isn't math; it's money! That's entirely different!"

Curious about this distinction between what she did every day and what she counted as "math," I asked my mom, "What is math?"

"Math is when they hand you a sheet of paper, and it has a word problem you don't understand on it."

She talked about nightmarish problems involving trains leaving Chicago and New York. She talked about procedures she was supposed to memorize even though she didn't know where they came from. She talked about teachers who treated girls as if they didn't belong in math class. And most of all, she talked about her father.

My grandfather was a self-taught engineer and a generous person, but he was also a rigid thinker and an authoritarian parent. When my mother was in algebra, he made math a battleground between the two of them. She kept asking *why*, and he kept telling her *how*. She remembered him yelling, "You don't think right!" My mom sighed to me and said, "I had no room. There was never any room for me to figure things out or understand. I just had to learn his process, his way."

After a lot of listening, I started to understand the sources of my mother's negative feelings about math. Mostly, I wanted her to learn the difference between *mathematics* and *math class*, because her terrible experiences in math class—at home and at school—have very little to do with mathematics as it really is. I began telling her about math as I've come to know it, including the creativity, curiosity, play, puzzling, and attention to detail essential to the field. We talked about her work over the years and how I've always seen her as a problem solver who uses the tools and habits of mind of mathematicians. Finally, I asked, "Did it ever occur to you that your dad might have been wrong? That maybe your dad was the one who didn't understand what math really is? He had such an impoverished view of math, as nothing more than steps and procedures. Maybe he wasn't the authority on the subject you thought he was when you were twelve?" Her eyes grew wide in shock at the idea.

The following week, my parents were shopping for a new TV. The salesperson explained that TVs are shaped differently than they used to be: the aspect ratios are now 16 by 9 instead of 4 by 3. My mom excitedly told me that she didn't freeze up at the math word *ratio*; instead, she stayed in the moment and thought about what he was saying. She drew rectangles in the air for me as she explained that the 4:3 TVs of her childhood were closer to a square because four and three are closer together, but the new 16:9 ones are stretched out and shaped more like movie theater screens, with one side almost twice as long as the other. She'd observed that change in her daily life, and now had the mathematical language to describe what she'd noticed. And then she said, "The best part was, I thought, 'This is math, and I understand it because I can do math! The name for what I do is math!'"

Over the next few weeks, she told me story after story like this. Her transformation was delightful to witness. After some time, I asked her to tell me what these changes meant for her. She immediately said, "It's not my fault." For all those decades, she thought there was something wrong with her. She believed her father when he said she didn't think right, and his words became part of her self-concept. It makes me cry every time I think about it. Being "bad at math" was such a part of her identity that she renamed the math she did well as something else. This isn't math; it's money. Or cooking. Or business. Or design. Or crafts. Now, she saw what a shame it was that she'd spent so long thinking math was remote, rigid, and intimidating, when really it is everywhere, and exciting.

Mostly, though, she's felt terrific ever since. More confident. Not limited. Happy.

My mom was sixty-six when she changed the way she thought about math.

What Happened in Math Class?

What does my mother's story have to do with teachers? A lot. Most of us came through the same school system and societal treatment of math my mom did, often with the same results. As Deborah Schifter and Cathy Fosnot put it, teachers are "the products of the system they are being asked to change" (1993, 13). Although some teachers had great experiences as students and retained a deep love for mathematics, they were the exceptions. For example, just 7 percent of preservice teachers used positive language to describe their experiences as math students (Jackson and Leffingwell 1999). The other 93 percent of respondents had more of a mixed bag, and at least some of their dominant memories were negative.

Many teachers suffered through such negative experiences in math class they developed math anxiety, and they experience physiological symptoms such as heart palpitations, sweaty palms, upset stomach, or a desire to flee when presented with a mathematics problem. In the most robust study, Rachel McAnallen (2010) found that 33 percent of elementary school teachers have math anxiety. When McAnallen asked teachers when their math anxiety started, they shared painful memories:

> "Timed fact tests in second grade—I would get so nervous I would freeze and/or wet my pants!"

> "I remember being in elementary school and thinking I had done well on my 'morning papers' and then I would get them back with big red Xs next to each problem and I'd feel really bad. I don't remember a teacher ever sitting down with me to try and figure out what I was doing wrong."

> "A teacher ridiculed me for my inability to perform long division at the blackboard in third grade."

"Growing up, math was considered a 'male' attribute."

"My ninth-grade math teacher played favorites and separated the smart kids, or 'gurus' as she called them, from the not-so-smart kids. It was very obvious I was one of the not-so-smart kids."

"Algebra completely threw me. I couldn't figure it out to save my life and a really mean teacher humiliated me."

Our experience as math students is relevant because we default to teaching how we were taught. A math methods class and the occasional professional development workshop are small potatoes compared with enduring thousands of hours of dreary teaching as students (Fennema and Nelson 1997; Lortie 1975; Schifter 1996; Schifter and Fosnot 1993; Stigler and Hiebert 1999). By the end of our schooling, we held deeply entrenched beliefs about what math is, based on our accumulated experiences in math class, and we've had few opportunities to examine and question those beliefs in the years since.

Excepting the occasional bright spot, a typical North American math class involved memorizing a litany of rules. Our days were filled with pages of calculations, timed tests, procedures that worked according to incomprehensible codes (do I add across or flip and multiply, bring down the zero or line up the decimal points?), "real-world" problems that didn't have anything to do with our real worlds, and, above all else, a singular right method to follow or else we were marked down. We watched our teachers demonstrate and explain procedures—some well, some not so well—and tried to replicate those procedures through repetitive exercises. We heard correct answers praised and mistakes criticized. Our tests were hung from the bulletin board, with percentages written in red for the world to see. Day after day of worked examples, night after night of computing problems 1 to 31 odd for homework, we learned what math was. This is how math feels. This is what it means to teach math. This is the script.

Over the past several decades, researchers have created an enormous body of literature detailing the shortcomings of this script because we are not getting the results we want (e.g., Stigler and Hiebert 1999). From the National Council of Teachers of Mathematics' *Principles and Standards* to the Common Core State Standards for Mathematical Practice, we now have guidance and encouragement to establish a different culture in our math classes, one built around sense-making, conceptual thinking, and fluency. Wonderful. The problem, though, is we've skipped a step. We moved right into a new way to teach math, without addressing teachers' personal histories with and understanding of mathematics. Sure, there has been some professional development about new ways to teach math, but it's usually more focused on the program than on the people teaching it.

Anyone who has been in schools for a while knows that programs come and go. The people, though, are the heart of education. We would get a lot more bang for our professional development buck if we invested in people first, so that's the approach I'm taking here. You'll notice throughout this book that I avoid arguments about curriculum and standards. They are hugely important, but whatever curriculum and standards we are using, in whatever type school, at whatever grade level, good math teaching starts with us. The more we know and enjoy math the way it really is, the more we will be able to bring that positive affect and deep knowledge into our math classes and teaching. We will make good instructional decisions with the resources we have and the contexts we are in, and, over time, we will get better and better at this incredibly challenging and rewarding job.

What Is Mathematics?

Remember my mother's definition?

Math is when they hand you a sheet of paper, and it has a word problem you don't understand on it.

My mother defined mathematics based on her reality—her lived experiences in math class. We all do this. If you were lucky enough to have math teachers who valued your ideas, you probably think of math as a place where your ideas matter. If, as is more likely, you experienced speed drills in math class, you probably inferred that speed matters in mathematics.

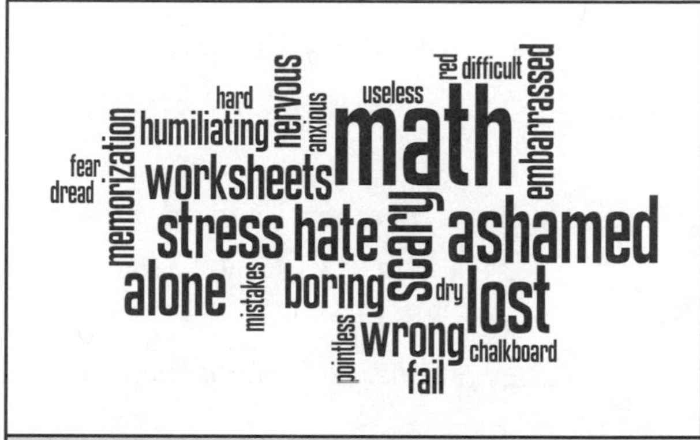

To figure out what mathematics really is—separate from my personal experiences as a student—I have turned toward the professionals for guidance. I've spent several years befriending mathematicians, reading their writings, and diving into the history of the field. Early on, I noticed a dramatic difference between the language we typically associate with math in our society and the language mathematicians use to describe their work. Consider the differences between Figures 1.1 and 1.2, in which I informally gathered words from teachers' and mathematicians' writing about math.

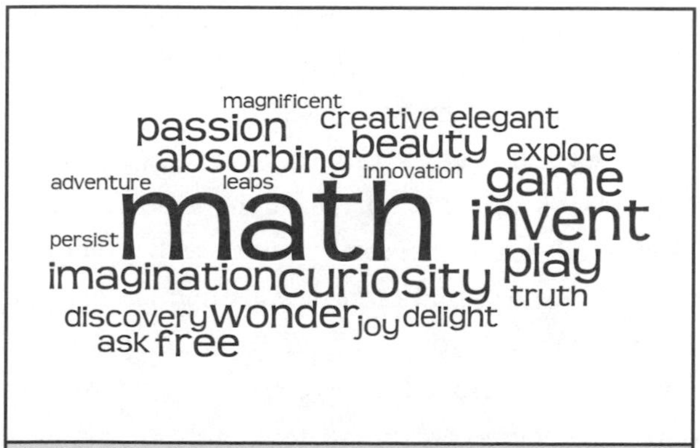

Admittedly, these images describe the extremes of a continuum, and I expect most of our personal mental maps about mathematics fall somewhere in between. Nevertheless, these images make it clear that school math classes have very little to do with mathematics. We experienced a sad

Figure 1.1 *Words many teachers use to describe their experience as math students*

Figure 1.2 *Words mathematicians use to describe mathematics*

distortion of a lovely subject, and we missed out on most of the good stuff. My Algebra II class had nothing in common with the world described by mathematicians:

> *It is impossible to be a mathematician without being a poet in the soul.*
>
> —Sofia Kovalevskaia

> *Pure mathematics is the world's best game. It is more absorbing than chess, more of a gamble than poker, and lasts longer than Monopoly. It's free. It can be played anywhere— Archimedes did it in a bathtub.*
>
> —Richard J. Trudeau

> *The true spirit of delight . . . is to be found in mathematics as surely as poetry.*
>
> —Bertrand Russell

> *The life of a mathematician is dominated by an insatiable curiosity, a desire bordering on passion to solve the problems he is studying.*
>
> —Jean Dieudonné

> *All mathematicians share . . . a sense of amazement over the infinite depth and the mysterious beauty and usefulness of mathematics.*
>
> —Martin Gardner

> *The way of mathematics is to make stuff up and see what happens.*
>
> —Vi Hart

> *The true joy in mathematics, the true hook that compels mathematicians to devote their careers to the subject, comes from a sense of boundless wonder induced by the subject. There is transcendental beauty, there are deep and intriguing connections, there are surprises and rewards, and there is play and creativity. Mathematics has very little to do with crunching numbers. Mathematics is a landscape of ideas and wonders.*
>
> —James Tanton

One of my favorite metaphors about mathematics comes from mathematician Reuben Hersh in his book *What Is Mathematics, Really?* (1997). Hersh borrowed the construct of sociologist Erving Goffman, who talked about ideas of "front and back." For example, in a restaurant, the dining room, with its orderly tables and neatly arranged cutlery, is the front. The kitchen, with chefs barking orders, food splattering, creativity, and chaos, is the back. In a theater, the front is the stage, where costumed, made-up actors deliver well-practiced lines. Backstage, though, are rehearsals, crew, makeup artists, directors, stagehands, costume designers, and so on. If you've ever looked at needlepoint, you know the front is a matrix of neat, even stitches, but the back is a tangle of knotted, frayed threads. If you start to look around with this idea in mind, you'll see fronts and backs everywhere.

Hersh argued that mathematics has a front and a back, too:

> The front and back of mathematics aren't physical locations like dining room and kitchen. They're its public and private aspects. The front is open to outsiders; the back is restricted to insiders. The front is mathematics in finished form—lectures, textbooks, journals. The back is mathematics among working mathematicians, told in offices or at café tables.
>
> Front mathematics is formal, precise, ordered, and abstract. It's broken into definitions, theorems, and remarks. Every question either is answered or is labeled: "open question." At the beginning of each chapter, a goal is stated. At the end of the chapter, it's attained.
>
> Mathematics in back is fragmentary, informal, intuitive, tentative. We try this or that. We say, "maybe," or "it looks like." (1997, 36)

I love this passage and think about it a lot. So many of us have bought into the myths about the front of mathematics, that it's "formal, precise, ordered, and abstract." But we have missed out on the back, where the passion, curiosity, dead ends, gut feelings, drama, collaboration, and magic happen. In the upcoming chapters, you and I will begin to understand how the back works. When we understand it ourselves, we can teach it to our students. There is a place in math for all of us. If the front was never your style, you might be surprised by how you feel about the back.

Making Math Class More Like Mathematics

Moving forward, my goal is to close the gap between math as it is taught and math as it is. It will be hard work, but we can intentionally and deliberately rewrite the script for math class. I believe in teachers, and I know we can rise to this formidable challenge! We can learn how to teach better than we were taught and thereby break our cultural cycle of negativity around math. To help us, I'll be approaching this work from the three angles I've found most productive in my coaching.

First, I will continue to introduce you to mathematicians and their habits of mind so we can add depth and authenticity to our understanding of mathematics. The dusty and impersonal version of math we were taught—heavy on algorithms but devoid of stories—left out the best parts. Therefore, I will pepper brief glimpses of mathematicians throughout our classroom work so we can develop a feel for how math is really created, discovered, and invented by living, breathing people with real feelings, biases, and desires.

Second, and this is the bulk of the book, I will bring you with me into classrooms where teachers teach math in the spirit of the mathematicians' word cloud (Figure 1.2). These experienced teachers have benefited from excellent professional development, coaching, university partnerships, professional learning communities, conferences, book studies, and reflective practice. Through hard work and classroom experimentation, they have developed specific teaching techniques that can help the rest of us learn *how* to teach math better than we were taught, as well as *why*. I looked for teachers in a wide variety of settings—urban, suburban, and rural; different grade levels; more and less linguistically and ethnically diverse; public and private; high- and low-socioeconomic status; and so on. I have been picky on your behalf, selecting the most practical, replicable, and worthy teaching techniques I could find. I'm hoping many of them will resonate with you, and you'll be inspired to try them in your own teaching context.

Third, I will give you opportunities to engage with mathematics. As mathematician George Pólya articulated, our personal relationships with the disciplines are an essential part of our teaching:

> To teach effectively a teacher must develop a feeling for his subject; he cannot make his students sense its vitality if he does not sense it himself. He cannot share his enthusiasm when he has no enthusiasm to share. (1963, 1)

It's essential that you take an active role in this journey. That's the only way to make real and lasting change. You'll need to examine past experiences, think deeply about new ideas, and be willing to explore mathematics with an open mind so you can reconnect to the little kid inside you who once loved playing around with patterns and numbers.

This is a safe place to do such brave things.

And so, to begin!

WHAT DO MATHEMATICIANS DO?

"*I* like math, but I'm not very good at it."

"When I have to do math fast, like on a test or something, I have trouble."

"No one in my family can do math. We don't have the math gene."

"I suck at math. I always get it wrong."

During my travels through dozens of math classes, I've been gathering examples of student talk about math. Sometimes I interview students, but most of the time I overhear them making these offhanded, revealing comments to one another. When I look through the long list of statements I've gathered, there is an unmistakable pattern. Students have a firmly established, deep-rooted working definition of what it means to be "good at math," and it goes something like this:

Being good at math means you answer the teacher's questions fast, right, easily.

I beg to differ. Oh, how I beg to differ! This definition is skewed toward the student who has a strong working memory, follows directions, and remembers algorithms: the plug-and-chugger. Certainly, being a fast and accurate calculator is nice, but it's not the same thing as being good at math. We teachers have been overvaluing the plug-and-chugger for decades, even though these attributes aren't particularly valued in mathematics. For example, mathematician Paul Lockhart wrote, "Many a graduate student has come to grief when they discover, after a decade of being told they were 'good at math,' that in fact they have no real mathematical talent and are just very good at following directions" (2009, 31).

Throughout this book, we'll explore the habits of mind that are authentic to and important in mathematics so we can teach those dispositions to our students. As we move through the big ideas, mathematicians' stories, and classroom case studies, our own working definitions of what it means to do math and be good at math may change dramatically. I want to start by sharing ideas and resources for how—and why—to open the same conversation with your kids soon.

Let's get right in the classroom and meet our first exemplar teacher.

Deborah Nichols, first and second multiage, Rollinsford, New Hampshire

"Did you ever realize that math was more than black marks on paper?"

Debbie Nichols has been teaching the same grade levels in the same sunny classroom for thirty-five years. She works in Rollinsford, a former mill town set in the gentle hills of southeastern New Hampshire. The mill is now finding a second life as an artists' colony, but the town's overall population is in decline, and currently sits at about 2,600 residents. Rollinsford Grade School is correspondingly small, with approximately 120 students in kindergarten through sixth grade.

Deb teaches nineteen first and second graders in a multiage setting. One student is Indonesian and speaks Bahasa Indonesia at home. The other eighteen students are white and speak English at home. The needs of Debbie's students are such that she has a full-time paraprofessional in her classroom. Deb has a long history of teaching math in a warm, engaging way and was recognized for her work with a Presidential Award for K–6 Mathematics Teaching in 2006, among other honors. She is a soft-spoken, curious, gentle teacher who builds a community of kindness and trust. It is a joy to watch her lean in and listen to students' ideas.

Taking on "This is easy."

The first time I visited Deb's classroom, she had assigned a challenging problem that involved a paragraph of text and a large graphic. I watched as students furrowed their brows, read the directions, and studied the picture. Everyone looked ready and eager to figure it out, and got right to work. A minute or two later, something changed. In pockets around the room, table group by table group, individual students said, "Oh! This is *easy!*"

Imagine for a moment you're the student sitting next to the student who read the problem quickly and announced it was *easy* while you were still trying to get your bearings. What happened to your interest in the problem? Your confidence? Your focus? Well, the same thing happened with these kids. When Andrew announced it was easy and started writing, Emily stopped thinking about the problem. She looked nervously at Andrew, looked back at her own paper, and lowered her pencil.

I see the same body language in classrooms all over the country, in all grades. I can almost see thought bubbles over the heads of a room of eighth graders. A few of the bubbles say, "This is *easy!*" while others say, "Everybody else understands and I don't. I hate math." Students cede mathematics to their classmates who get it first and get it right without breaking a sweat.

Debbie and I talked after class and decided to take this issue on. We planned to start the next class with a discussion about language that was interfering with the lively, inclusive, safe math classroom she wanted to create.

Deb: We wanted to talk today about some words that we heard last time. We heard these words: *easy, hard, slow, fast, right, wrong.* Can you talk to me about what it feels like when people are using words like *easy, hard, slow, fast, right, wrong*?

Sophia: I don't really think it's fair if they say it's easy, because some people don't think it's easy. Like, I don't think it's easy that much.

Deb: OK, so if somebody else is saying, 'That's easy,' what does it feel like to you?

Sophia: I feel sad.

Deb: You feel sad. Does anybody else feel the same way Sophia feels?

(Several hands went up, including Serena's.)

Deb: Serena, talk to me about why.

Serena: Because it sometimes hurts a little bit.

Ricky: Because like, they're saying words, they're saying that it's so easy, and you feel sad that you can't do it and they can.

Kenlee: Sometimes it's easy and sometimes it's not to different people.

Lydia: Well, you could say that it's easy, like, in your head so nobody hears it.

Deb: Oh, so you think that's a strategy that will help some people not feel uncomfortable and help you feel confident? What else do you think we could do when we go to work today that would not make people feel like they're not capable?

Jules: Say this is easy in your head so you don't make people feel that way.

Deb: What if it slips out? What if we forget and it just slips out?

Andrew: You could just say sorry.

Clint: Well, you shouldn't just say that it's easy, because it might make people feel like they don't know any questions and they don't know math.

Deb: What words could we use?

Lydia: Maybe if you think that's easy then you could just say "That's hard."

Deb: Do you think you should say something that you don't believe?

Lydia: No, but then it would make people feel better.

Deb: But what about you? Are you lying to yourself?

Ricky: Yeah. If you say the opposite of what you think, it's lying.

Gregory: We should try and keep it in our head, what we say. Like say it in our head.

Deb: Do you think talking about math is important?

Gregory: Yes, but saying easy, or not easy, you should just say it in your head.

Deb: What words could we say out loud?

Gregory: You could say this is fun.

Deb: You could say it's fun. But what if it wasn't fun to somebody else? What if it was drudgery?

Gunther: You could say nothing.

Deb: You could say nothing, but math talk is good. So what do we do?

Clint: You could just say it was right. You could just say, like, "Nice job on your math so far." You could compliment them.

Deb: Hmm. You could. I want to tell you from my own experience, like when we were in an exercise group in the afternoon and somebody said, "Good job, Mrs. Nichols," and I am thinking to myself, it's *not* a good job. I know I can do better than this. And I almost don't want them to say those words to me, because I don't think that they're real. So how do we make our words *real* and mean something, without hurting somebody?

Such an important question, for math class and life!

Deb and I continued to watch, listen, and talk with students and with one another over the next several sessions until the patterns became clear. Of the six thorny words we'd named—*easy, hard, slow, fast, right, wrong—easy* was our biggest issue in this particular class. We kept watching it shut students down. Deb and I knew that math problems are neither easy nor hard by any objective measure—the level of difficulty is always relative and always personal—so we wondered exactly what students were trying to say when they told one another, "This is easy."

We found two dominant usages. Sometimes they said, "This is easy" to mean, "I already know how to do this." In other words, they'd had previous opportunities to make sense of the mathematics involved. More accurate language might be:

"This is familiar to me."

"I used to struggle with this kind of math, but now I can do it."

"I've practiced this before."

"I know something that I can use here."

"I feel confident about this kind of math."

"I have experience with similar problems."

What I saw that first day in Deb's room was different, though, because that problem involved mathematics that was unfamiliar to everyone. We noticed that, when students face something novel or challenging, they use "This is easy" as shorthand for "I just made some sense out of this":

"This seemed hard at first, but I think I can do it!"

"Oh! Now I understand the question!"

"I see a way to start."

"I have an idea to try."

"I think I've figured out what this graph means."

"I see what's going on here!"

Deb's students brainstormed these phrases, which Deb posted as an anchor chart. We talked about feeling confident or figuring something out as good, satisfying feelings and a big part of why math and puzzling are so rewarding. At the same time, we talked about the language we use and how we can unintentionally affect our friends and classmates. We wanted students to encourage one another, and we added some supportive messages such as "I see a path, and you will too!" or "I believe in you." Deb's students—especially her students who were not yet confident in math—responded positively to these conversations, and we watched them engage more in math class.

We also saw students' empathy grow. I particularly loved it when students were adding on the hundreds chart and Jules announced, "This is *so* easy." A few minutes later, Deb asked students to subtract. Clint said, "This is easy, peasy, lemon squeezy," and Jules looked crushed. When students met on the rug at the end of class, Jules raised her hand and said, "I felt a little sad when Clint said, 'This is easy, peasy, lemon squeezy,' because it wasn't easy for me! The beginning was kind of easy, but when we got to the twenty-six part, it kind of got hard." I pointed out that she'd said "This is *so* easy" just a couple of problems before. Her mouth opened and her eyes widened in recognition and surprise. When I asked her about it later, she said, "Now I know how it feels, and I'm not going to say it anymore!"

"What does it mean to be good at math?"

We were certainly glad to see students more aware of their language in math class, and the climate and class community were improving. It was clear, though, that students still thought being good at math meant being fast and right without much trouble. Before addressing these underlying beliefs, we wanted to understand them more, so we opened a new discussion.

Deb: What does it mean to be good at math?

Lydia: Listen to directions and do what's right.

Ricky: You know a lot of facts.

Carl: Being good at math is practicing math.

Gloria: You try hard and don't give up.

Sophia: You answer the questions.

Kenlee: Being a good math person means listen to directions and do the right thing.

Jules: It means, even if you get stuck, use materials.

Deb: And materials are?

Jules: Like rulers or Unifix cubes . . .

Deb: What do we call those?

Students: Tools.

Jules: Last time I got stuck, I used Unifix cubes, and it helped me.

Deb: That's a really important one. Can we come back and talk about that some more later? What does it mean to be good at math?

Andrew: Try your hardest.

Sara: I think you should try your best even if you don't know the answer.

Serena: When you're smart.

Deb: So you're saying they are smart. What else, Serena? How are you good at math? How is somebody good at math? (Wait time.) Can anybody help her?

Sophia: By trying to learn a lot and paying attention.

Ricky: To be good at math, you study it a lot.

Deb: You study what?

Ricky: Math.

Deb: Tell me what math is.

Ricky: Math is . . . (Trails off.)

Deb: Aha! We're getting down to the real question. What is math?

Ricky: Math is, like, numbers you add together to make a different number.

Deb: Math is adding. What else?

Students shared aloud:

"Subtraction."

"Times."

"Division."

"Square roots."

"Doing stuff that makes sense."

"Groups."

(After an initial flurry, students were quiet.)

Sophia: It can also be used with letters and numbers. I don't really know how to use letters yet but I know you can use letters.

Gloria: Math is you can have these sheets of paper and it has math on the board. And also, math can be learning how to write sheets of paper.

Kenlee: I don't know. Wait. Math is infinity.

Deb: Infinity. Tell me about that.

Kenlee: Well, numbers are infinity and they don't stop. So, numbers, and how much bigger they get, they still won't stop.

Deb: Why?

Kenlee: I don't know.

Deb: It's OK not to know. Did you know that? It's perfectly OK not to know.

Clint: Math is everything.

Deb: Math is everything. Tell me more.

Clint: Like you could say a dog plus a dog is two dogs . . . or five letters plus six letters is eleven letters.

Deb: Are you saying that maybe you could be doing math in everything? That there's math in everything?

Clint: Yeah.

Karly: Math is something that could actually help you because when you grow up you need to buy food for yourself and stuff. If you don't know math, you can't really tell how much money it is.

Serena: Math is doing papers.

Nate: Math is patterns. Number patterns and A, B, C patterns.

When we teach science or history, we usually spend at least some time talking about what science and history *are*. In math, though, we generally just start "doing it," without talking about what "it" really is. Without ever being introduced to the discipline of mathematics, our students built ideas from their experiences at school and at home: math must be adding, subtracting, multiplying, dividing, infinity, money, doing what's right, listening to directions, trying hard, being smart, using tools, writing numbers and letters on sheets of paper and the board. We heard some promising things in their answers. Some students had the ideas of perseverance and resourcefulness, which are certainly big parts of math. There was an awful lot missing, though.

In a later conversation about math, we learned another important piece: most students saw math as something external to them. They thought the only way to learn math was to be taught it by someone who knew more, usually a teacher in school. They didn't think children had the power to figure math out for themselves and thought students arrived in school knowing no mathematics. I gave them one study and one story to chew on during this revealing conversation.

Edgar: I was thinking about it in my head, and I think my question is, what about a two-year-old kid? How are you gonna know patterns or math? Are you going to teach everyone that?

Deb: I'm thinking this is what I heard: What if you were a two-year-old kid, or you had a two-year-old kid, and how are they going to learn patterns, or how am I going to teach them math?

(Edgar nodded.)

Deb: Wow, great question. How would you teach a young child about math? Let's take some think time.

(Think time.)

Tracy: I think he said the young child would *have* to be taught those things, and I'm wondering if that's true? If two-year-olds have to be taught, or if they can figure some things out on their own?

Deb: What do you think about that?

(Think time.)

Jules: Well, wait until they are a little bit older?

Tracy: Do you think they're too young to do math?

Jules: (Nodding.) Wait until they are a little bit older or try to get their attention.

Nate: What about a kid that doesn't know nothing?

Gloria: You could get little teeny books and help them read and then go on and on for math and reading.

Kenlee: I have one about patterns, that when kids are young, like two years old, I would let them use colored blocks and I would try to show them a way to do something and see if they could do what I could do, and I would be doing a pattern, so I would see if they could do it.

Ricky: Well, I would give them the basic steps.

Tracy: What are the basic steps?

Ricky: Like basic steps to math, like starting one plus one.

Tracy: Babies know the answer to that.

Students: What?!

Tracy: They did a study where they showed babies two things together, and then they put a screen down. When they lifted the screen back up and there were still two things, the babies didn't react much. But if they lifted the screen up and now there were three things—they'd added something when the screen was down—the babies looked like this. (I made a confused/surprised face.) Because the babies knew the difference between two and three, and they wondered, "Where did that one come from?"

Students: Whoa.

Serena: You could spend most of your time helping the two-year-old.

Nate: But you need to teach them everything you know!

Tracy: I want to tell you a quick story about my daughter when she was two years old. We had a wedding to go to, so we were buying shoes in a shoe store. Have you ever bought shoes and there were those crushed-up pieces of paper in the front of the shoe?

Students: Yeah.

Tracy: Well, there were three of those sitting on the floor. My daughter stared at them for a long time with her brow furrowed, looking really puzzled. Then she said, "Mommy, why are there three?" I asked, "What do you mean?" She said, "There should be two, or there should be four. Why are there three?" What was puzzling my two-year-old daughter?

Gregory: There is only one in each shoe. So if there were four, there would be one in one shoe, and then there would be another one in the second shoe that went with it, and then there would be one in one pair of a shoe and then there'd be another one that went with it, because shoes come in pairs. (He showed four shoes in the air with his hands while he talked.)

Tracy: Shoes come in pairs! So when she found an odd number—when she found three— she thought that was really weird. But listen to this. I had never taught her about odd or even. Ever! So, to me, she was doing what a mathematician does. She was noticing math in the world around her.

Deb: Noticing! Is that part of math? What do you think?

Students: Yes!

Tracy: She was noticing. And she was thinking about what makes sense and what doesn't make sense because have you ever seen anyone with three legs who needs three shoes?

Students: No!

Tracy: No, it doesn't make any sense, right? So my two-year-old daughter asked a question about something she noticed in her world, and it was a *mathematical* question. She was doing math, and nobody was teaching her or telling her how to do it.

Deb: She was doing math while she was trying on shoes!

What Do Mathematicians Do? A Mini-Unit

Debbie and I knew we were doing too much telling. We felt the best next step was to launch a short investigation around these essential, related questions of what math is, what mathematicians do, and what it means to be good at math. We decided to gather resources that would introduce these first- and second-grade students to real mathematicians so they could draw their own conclusions. We wanted to see what would happen to their working definition of math, and whether we could get beyond "Math is you can have these sheets of paper and it has math on the board."

Because we were making this unit up as we went along, it took several days. I have since used it with teachers in my role as a coach and have found it's easy to condense into shorter, highly effective professional development activities. Deb and I both think that, alongside plenty of rich problems, this investigation into what mathematics is and what mathematicians do would be an ideal way to build a positive math culture and define math productively in the first days or week of school.

Using Picture Books to Introduce Students to Mathematicians

With both students and teachers, I wanted to start with a comfortable, familiar format: high-quality children's literature. I scoured through picture-book biographies of mathematicians and stories about great moments in math. Many of the books were disappointing. They emphasized the life stories and intimidating brilliance of famous mathematicians but didn't illuminate the process of math or the habits of mind of the mathematicians. I did find four picture books I thought were very good, though, and we decided to spend two class sessions with them:

> *On a Beam of Light: A Story of Albert Einstein* by Jennifer Berne (2013)
>
> *Blockhead: The Life of Fibonacci* by Joseph D'Agnese (2010)
>
> *The Boy Who Loved Math: The Improbable Life of Paul Erdős* by Deborah Heiligman (2013)
>
> *Infinity and Me* by Kate Hosford (2012)

The first day, I read *On a Beam of Light* to the whole class. The pictures are approachable and fun, and the emphasis of the book is on what Einstein loved to do: imagine, question, wonder, figure, read, notice, observe. There is a fabulous picture of Einstein daydreaming while riding his bicycle: he imagined riding right off the earth's surface and into the air, just like the kids in *E.T.* In the picture, his eyes are wide and he is completely absorbed in his thought experiment. He wondered what would happen if he rode his bicycle along a beam of light? That daydream led to years of study of physics at or near the speed of light and, ultimately, Einstein's theories of relativity and the famous equation $E = mc^2$.

Debbie's students had wonderful observations and questions prompted by the book. A few examples:

> "Wait, does science have math in it?"
>
> "He's having fun!"
>
> "I think he's thinking about what he's doing . . . not anything else but what he's doing."
>
> "He's dreaming . . . daydreaming!"
>
> "He's imagining, again!"

"He was mindful."

"He's so curious!"

During our discussion about Einstein's imagination, I decided to connect back to our earlier conversation.

Tracy: Do kids imagine a lot?

Students: Yeah!

Tracy: I think kids imagine *a lot*. And I think mathematicians imagine *a lot*. And this is why I think of all kids as mathematicians. But, I listened to you last week when Ms. Nichols asked, "What is math, and what do you do in math?" and I heard a lot of things about paper—you do answers on paper. We do figure out answers on paper in math sometimes, but we also pretend we're riding on a beam of light, on our bicycles, in space. This is math too!

Deb: I'm listening to what we talked about last week and what you came up with today and they're different. I'm wondering, did you ever realize that math was more than just numbers or black marks on paper? Did you know you could say all these things about math?

Students: No.

Deb: You didn't know that, but now, it's kind of opening up, and there is a lot more to math!

After our read-aloud and discussion, we broke up into groups and took a math walk around the school to wonder, to notice, and to ask questions. Students still tended to look for written numbers and obvious patterns, but groups also explored the math of the vending machine, the tiles on the wall and floors, the safety instructions in the kitchen, the ceiling of the gym, a patchwork quilt, stacks of chairs on a trolley, a census form, a graph, a map, a timeline, and so on. Each group took pictures on an iPad and shared observations afterward. Debbie emphasized student questions and wonders, saying, "You were wondering? Is that doing math?"

Throughout this work, we added students' observations to our ongoing anchor chart about math (Figure 2.1). Deb recorded in a different color each day, and we could see that we'd come a long way from their earlier vague, teacher-pleasing replies (in dark green), to powerful verbs (in red), such as *wondering, figuring, questioning, imagining, noticing*. We started our next session by looking over the chart together.

Deb: Who in here thinks they're a mathematician?

(About half the hands went up.)

Jules: Even if you don't go into a career as a mathematician, you can still think like one and be smart like one.

Clint: I really like math, and I wonder a lot about math.

Ricky: I like math because it's a career.

Deb: Tell me more. What kind of career could you have?

Ricky: Teaching math.

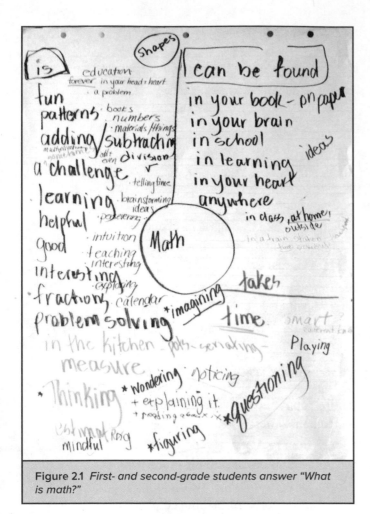

Figure 2.1 *First- and second-grade students answer "What is math?"*

Atticus: I think, just like art in the book *Ish*, you can do math anytime, anywhere.

Deb: Do you think someone could be math-ish?

Atticus: Yeah.

Deb: Who feels like, "I'm not math-ish, and I'm not a mathematician," and tell me why you have these feelings?

(About one-third of the hands went up.)

Sophia: I don't practice. I can still write down math on paper.

Deb: What about the wondering, questioning part?

Sophia: Not really.

Kenlee: I have a hard time. Sometimes I have a hard time and get stuck on something, and I don't know what to do.

Ricky: When I'm being pressured to do math, I'm not really good at it.

Atticus: I'm kind of with Ricky about being pressured. Sometimes I feel like I need math in my life, and sometimes I don't want to have anything to do with math right now.

Deb: Why?

Atticus: Sometimes when I'm relaxed, my mom wants me to do math and it stresses me out.

Serena: I don't think I'm a mathematician because sometimes I don't get math. Like, sometimes I don't get subtraction. Sometimes I use my fingers and sometimes I use materials, but I don't really understand it.

Tracy: I'm thinking about what Kenlee, and Ricky, and Atticus, and Serena are saying, and I'm thinking about the book we read about Einstein last time. Did Einstein get stuck sometimes?

Students: Yes.

Tracy: What did he do when he got stuck?

Kenlee: He put the problems to the side and did something else, like sail in his boat or play the violin.

Edgar: Or eat ice cream!

Tracy: That makes me think about something that happened last week. I was at a math circle for teachers, and we were working on a problem in partners. The leader asked us to share our work, and we weren't ready. My partner and I said, "We need more time," so the leader waited until we were ready. I've been thinking about that a lot. I'm comfortable, now, as an adult, saying, "I need more time," or "I need to work with someone else to understand this," or "I need some help," but I don't think I knew how to say those things as a kid. Maybe we could work on you learning how to say what you need so you could be successful in math? You could say, "I need to take a break from this problem and come back to it."

Ricky: Yeah, and then we could try again!

Tracy: Sure! Also, Serena, I think that what you're saying about subtraction is really important. I think you could learn how to *do* subtraction so you could calculate problems. But what I'm hearing is that you want to *understand* subtraction. Subtraction is a really big idea, and we use it to mean many different things, and you want to make sense out of it for yourself. You want to understand it, not just do it, and that's a very mathematician-y way to learn. I think you're thinking like a mathematician.

Deb: Whoa, Serena!

(Serena smiled broadly.)

After this opening, we gave short book talks about the three other picture books—*Blockhead, The Boy Who Loved Math,* and *Infinity and Me*—and allowed students to choose the book that most interested them. We each took a book and read it to our small groups, who then shared out afterward.

The first and second graders had a range of observations, from the illustrations to the math involved to learning about the mathematicians as people. The group reading *The Boy Who Loved Math* noticed how social Erdős's math world was and how he connected mathematicians and their ideas to each other. The group reading *Infinity and Me* had many questions about the idea of infinity and the different ways the girl tried to visualize infinity in the book. And the group reading *Blockhead* was fascinated that mathematics can describe what we see in nature. We'd brought in pinecones and sunflower heads, and they spent quite a while studying them (Figure 2.2). One student said, "There are so many spirals, and spirals are his math, we found out!"

Bringing Math into the Present Day—Online Resources

Debbie and I were starting to make real progress unseating students' prior ideas about mathematics and adding new ones. Several students who had not been as engaged with math initially, such as Serena, Gloria, Emily, Sophia, and Kenlee, were becoming much more involved and participatory. At the same time, I was growing increasingly worried that students were developing three new misconceptions

Figure 2.2 *Three students read* Blockhead: The Life of Fibonacci.

about mathematicians:

1. Math is historical. It's something people figured out a long time ago. It's finished, and we talk about it in the past tense.
2. Mathematicians are dead, white European men.
3. Mathematicians are socially awkward, "different," or "quirky" geniuses.

We needed to bring math up to the present day, make it worldwide, and show that mathematicians are as diverse as the rest of us (or, at least, if they haven't been so historically, they should be now!). It was time to turn to the web. You can find all the links from this section and throughout the book compiled at our companion website, www.stenhouse.com/becomingmathteacher.

We started with a series of mathematical videos by Vi Hart. Vi is a mathemusician who has made more than one hundred playful short films doing math with things like mashed potatoes and gravy, the theme from the *Harry Potter* films, and doodling elephants. We chose three videos to start.

In the first 2:10 video we chose, *How to Snakes*, Vi plays with several packages of plastic, segmented snakes, which she says "writhe with potential." She breaks them into pieces, shapes them into fractals, looks for patterns in the colors, experiments with how they can and can't turn, and builds them into a huge mass of Hydra monsters. In a couple of minutes of open-ended exploration, she draws from a wide range of mathematical ideas.

After the video, we asked students to turn, talk, and share one thing they loved, and then answer our question: *Was she doing math?* Student answers were fascinating. They universally loved the video, but many students didn't think she did any math. A typical response was, "She's not doing math; she's playing!" After listening to one another's answers, they decided she might have done a little math after all because she wrote some things down on paper, looked for a pattern, and counted.

We played the second video, a 2:28 segment called *Binary Hand Dance*. In this irreverent video, Vi counts in binary on her fingers and then dances the binary digits of pi. She dips each finger into a different color of paint and creates visual art by counting. The film is set to a thumping beat, and the kids pronounced it "awesome." This time, students wondered aloud if playing might be part of math.

In the third video, a 4:52 segment called *Math Improv: Fruit by the Foot*, Vi says, "So I saw these fruit by the foots, or fruit by the feet, or maybe fruits by the foots? Anyway, I figured they had mathematical potential so I decided to just record myself playing with them." She unrolls three of them and explores Möbius strips, Borromean rings, frieze patterns, and lots of symmetry. The students were completely pumped by this point, especially when Deb pulled out adding machine tape and packages of fruit by the foot for the kids to explore themselves.

Debbie demonstrated playing with the materials and wondering, and then we talked a little about our expectations. Before releasing students to their sticky, sweet math, Deb made her management expectations clear: wash hands before starting in case you end up eating the candy; use a "messy mat" to keep your table clean; talk in soft voices so we could hear one another's ideas. We also wanted to make our mathematical goals clear to students:

Deb: Can mathematicians wonder and try out things and not know what's going to happen?

Students: Yes!

Deb: Do you think mathematicians have to try things out? And what if they fail? What if I wreck it?

Students: Try it again! It's OK.

Tracy: Is that what she did in the video? Did anyone notice if she tried anything that didn't work out so well?

Students: Yeah! The cube.

Tracy: And then she tried to take the paper off and what happened?

Jules: It made a big sticky mess.

Deb: Who wants to try?

Students: Me!

Deb: Wait, mathematicians are playful?! Do they think and wonder?

Students: Yes!

Atticus: (Quietly) I don't want to do it; it's too hard.

Tracy: I just heard Atticus say something. I think I heard you say, and tell me if I got it right, I think you said, "I don't want to try to make a Möbius strip because it looks too . . ."

Atticus: Hard.

Tracy: I wonder if there's a right way or a wrong way to play around with this stuff today?

Ricky: There is no right way, and there is no wrong way.

Tracy: And I wonder if someone tries to do a Möbius strip and it all gets sticky and they're trying to cut and don't cut in a straight line, if that's OK?

Andrew: It doesn't matter what you make.

Tracy: Are you making some fancy project that everyone needs to look at?

Students: No.

Deb: Can you wonder on your own like I did?

Atticus: I'll try.

Deb: You'll try! Yay!

Tracy: Atticus, I want you to remember that we just saw a mathematician try some things and some of them didn't work out for her.

Deb: Can teachers try, too? I want you to know, in my whole life, I've never done this before.

Several students clearly enjoyed the open-ended time and used it to muck around with Möbius strips (Figure 2.3) and investigate the patterns in their candy. They declared it "the

Figure 2.3 *A second grader with her interlocking Möbius strips*

best day *ever*," because math was so fun. A couple of students, however, were unsettled by this freedom. "I don't know how to do it right," they said. "I don't know what I'm supposed to do next." There were a few tears, even though we repeatedly reassured students that there was no "right" way to explore with these materials, and we had no expectations for any sort of outcome or product. They had never explored like this in math and were not sure how to please their teachers or do what they were supposed to without a clear-cut assignment. We supported these students individually and then put our heads together during planning time.

Deb and I felt as though we were on to something but needed to keep going. Students needed to know that math was more than answering someone else's questions. We decided we would continue to show them short films of mathematicians playing, exploring, asking, engaging in thought experiments, and wondering, especially with everyday objects students might recognize, and then we would ask students to find math in the world around them. Deb thought giving students more ownership might remove their anxiety about pleasing teachers or exploring "the right way." Debbie also profiled this work in her communication home, trying to establish positive math talk with families.

Over the next week, Deb showed at least one brief math video every day during snack. We looked hardest for films that showed problem posing—not just problem solving—and involved the element of mathematical play. You can find the complete list of links at www.stenhouse. com/becomingmathteacher. We showed brief videos from these sites:

- *Numberphile* (numberphile.com) is consistently marvelous. We showed students a video about the mathematics of the Rubik's Cube.
- *Math Munch* (mathmunch.org) is a wonderful teacher-run website with tons to explore. A favorite feature is the "Q&A" portion of the website, where the teachers regularly interview working mathematicians. Students can submit questions for those interviews. They also have an extensive video, game, and applet collection to surf. We showed students an interview with mathematician Nalini Joshi.
- Neil deGrasse Tyson, director of the Hayden Planetarium in New York City, is passionate about math and science education for kids. We showed a *NOVA ScienceNOW* video about a thought experiment in which Tyson journeys through the center of the earth, as

well as a *StarTalk* interview called "How to Become an Astrophysicist."

- Students loved "The Mathematics of Juggling" from *Scientific American*.
- We chose two *TED Talks*: Karl Schaffer and Erik Stern explored the relationship between the "science of dance and the art of math" in "Teaching Math Through Movement," and Margaret Wertheim discussed the mathematics of coral and climate change in "The Beautiful Math of Coral."

Finding Math in Our World

After several glimpses of mathematicians at play and at work, we asked students to look for math at home over the long weekend and to bring something in for a gallery walk. Tuesday morning, students were jumping all over themselves to share what they'd found. We made them wait a few more minutes in order to watch a video of my children describing the results of their math hunt (available at stenhouse.com/becomingmathteacher).

Deb's students were excited to meet my kids, and listened carefully as Maya (six) and Daphne (four) described the math they saw in tissue boxes, sticks, leaves, Rubik's Cubes, floral prints, rocks, woven napkins, knitting, and music. For example, Maya wondered about the offset veins on a maple leaf. She asked whether the number of veins on each side of the central stem was the same, even though the branching veins weren't symmetric. She said, "I thought it would be interesting to play around with it. . . . Since they're not even, it would kind of be a little bit of fun to figure out if there was exactly the same number on both sides." She counted, discovered there were ten veins on each side, and cheerfully announced her results. She *asked and answered her own question through math*, which was perfect modeling for Debbie's class.

After the video, Deb's students were charged up and took turns naming their objects. They had brought in a tube of toothpaste, a slotted pancake turner, a beater from an electric mixer, a bowl, dried macaroni, a calendar, a field guide to animals, a bag of glass beads, a few measuring cups, several rulers, a tire pressure gauge, cardstock with a chevron and grid pattern, a mini-muffin tin, an empty tissue box, a large quilt made out of baby clothes, a miniature pumpkin, a foam puzzle block with a jigsaw edge, a whisk, a soccer ball, and a clipped recipe from a magazine. Stellar! Deb placed a few objects at each table group and gave students a chart to record their thinking. Our young math detectives then moved around the room, hunting for the mathematics in these everyday objects (Figure 2.4).

We saw a range of mathematical thinking. Some students looked only for numerals or color patterns, while other students started to explore geometric ideas. For example, during the share-out, Emily raised her hand to talk about the soccer ball (Figure 2.5).

Figure 2.4 *Students finding math in everyday objects*

Figure 2.5 *"The shapes have different numbers."*

Emily: There's different numbers of the lines. The shapes have different numbers. When you count the lines to them, they have five and then six.

Tracy: Can you come up and point to what you're talking about?

(Emily pointed to a hexagon and counted its six sides.)

Tracy: So this shape was a six? (Emily nodded.)

Ricky: That's an octagon.

Tracy: Actually, a closed shape with six straight sides is a hexagon. And, Emily, you also said there was one that was a five?

(Emily pointed to a pentagon and counted five.)

Tracy: And that one has five sides. That's called a pentagon.

Ricky: They're the same.

Tracy: What's the same?

Ricky: It's really just part of it. They both share it. (Pointing to a side.)

Tracy: Oh, they share a side?

Ricky: Yeah.

Tracy: I wonder how they can share a side, but then be different shapes? And it still all fits together. When this was put together, there aren't any extra spots and there are no holes, are there?

Students: (perplexed) No . . .

Serena talked about the quilt in Figure 2.6.

Serena: Well, I found a faster way to count the little squares. There are five on each row so I counted by fives and went 5, 10, 15, 20, 25, 30.

Deb: So you decided that you're going to count 1, 2, 3, 4, 5, and, because they line up, you can go, 5 . . .

Students count chorally: 5, 10, 15, 20, 25, 30.

Deb: Wow! Look at the muffin tin. Can you do that with the mini-muffin tin (Figure 2.7)?

Figure 2.6 *"Well, I found a faster way to count the little squares."*

Serena: Yes.

Deb: What did you count by?

Serena: You can count by four this way, and you could count by three this way, or you could count by sixes.

Deb: Ah! Can you count by twos?

Serena: Yes.

Deb: So a lot of different ways to count!

When Deb and I debriefed, what was most interesting to us was which students were highly engaged in this activity and which students were a little more passive. We both noticed that the students who typically had their hands up in more traditional math classes—who wanted to call out the answer to known-answer questions—were quieter during this share-out. Conversely, students who tended to hold back in math class—who lacked confidence and had described themselves as "not a mathematician" a few class sessions earlier—were highly engaged, talkative, and expressive.

Figure 2.7 *"You can count by four this way, and you could count by three this way, or you could count by sixes."*

For example, Emily and Serena, the two students I just quoted, had been two of the quietest and most tentative math students in other sessions, but both were animated and involved during the everyday objects lesson. I was particularly happy to see Emily notice the different shapes and tiling on the soccer ball. She generally struggles in math, almost never raises her hand, and tries to fly under the radar, but here she volunteered to share something she observed. It was something nobody else had seen, and the rest of the class learned from her. It was a brief moment, but it felt like a powerful one for Emily. Similarly, Serena is the student who said she doesn't feel like a mathematician because she doesn't "get" subtraction, and here she was discovering how to skip-count rectangular arrays. The ownership and math power in her language especially pleased me: "Well, I found a faster way to count . . ."

I wasn't worried that the students who lead in more typical math classes—the classes that favor the quick mental processor with a good memory—took a backseat in this lesson. They were listening carefully, and those students get frequent validation. I was thrilled, however, to see the creative, thoughtful, observant, tentative students rise to the occasion. If I had to sum it up in a line, I'd say they started to think, "Maybe there's a place in math for me, too."

In a country that has fallen prey to the myth that some people are "math people" and some people aren't, it felt really good to help a class of kids consider that math might just be for all of us. It's a much bigger tent than we think.

The Relationship Between What Mathematicians Do and What We Do in Math Class

Debbie kept this meta-conversation going, even as she shifted the work of the class into other areas of mathematical content. She periodically asked students to talk or write about the discipline of mathematics, and they added to and revised their definitions as they learned more. She valued multiple perspectives and approaches to mathematical ideas and gave status and respect to different types of thinking in her math class. She put up a "Wonder Wall" and found room for students to pose their own mathematical questions sometimes, not just answer someone else's. She used this early work in the fall to introduce students to mathematics, set the tone for her math class, and create a safe place for all her learners. Over the year, we thought back to these fall days, mucking around with big questions, and were certain it was time well spent.

I can't emphasize this point enough: this mini-unit has to connect to the rest of math class. It makes no sense to spend a few days developing a definition of doing mathematics that includes powerful words, such as *notice, wonder, imagine, ask, investigate, figure, reason, connect,* and *prove,* and then switch back to downloading procedures through "I do, we do, you do" demonstrations, guided practices, and drills. Students won't buy it, either. They're smart, and they learn more from our actions than our words. If we want students to build this complex, authentic understanding of the discipline of mathematics, they need to engage in these wonderful verbs as they learn new mathematical content throughout the year. In every subsequent chapter, we'll focus on a different element of this challenge so that we can teach students to do real mathematics within today's classroom realities.

MATHEMATICIANS
TAKE RISKS

Mr. Duncan (pseudonym) was my eighth-grade algebra teacher. I would describe him as a methodical but uninspired math teacher, and we marched through the book learning procedures and mnemonics. I vividly remember the day he taught us the "rule" that any number raised to the zero power equals one, written $a^0 = 1$. I had been fairly comfortable with exponents up until then, thinking they were a nifty notation for writing big numbers. I had been taught to think of 2^4 as shorthand for two multiplied by itself four times: $2^4 = 2 \times 2 \times 2 \times 2 = 16$. Raising two to the zero power, however, was a new idea, and I was having trouble imagining it.

I sat in the back row of the class, wondering whether 2^0 should equal zero, because it was two multiplied by itself zero times. Or maybe it should equal two, because it was a two nobody seemed to do anything to? No matter how I looked at it, though, I couldn't figure out where a one would come from. I raised my hand for help. My conversation with Mr. Duncan went something like this:

"I don't understand where the one comes from."

"It comes from this rule I just taught you, $a^0 = 1$."

"But why is that the rule? It doesn't make sense to me."

"Because that's the rule."

"I could kinda see the answer being zero, or a, but how do we get a one? There's no one in the problem. It feels like you pulled it out of thin air."

(Irritated.) "It comes from the rule."

"But how can one be the answer for any value of a? How can $5^0 = 1$ and $20^0 = 1$ and $1000^0 = 1$? I don't see how all those problems can be equal, and why are they all equal to one? What does one have to do with anything?"

(He sounded truly exasperated now.) "You're right. Any number raised to the zero power is one. That's the rule you need to memorize."

"But..."

At this point, my classmates joined my teacher. The popular kid I had a crush on said, "Give it up, Tracy! Who cares?" A chorus followed him, and everyone started laughing, including Mr. Duncan. This was eighth grade. I gave it up, pretending to laugh on the outside.

On the inside, I was angry. I was a good student trying to understand. At the time, I felt like Mr. Duncan tried to shut me down, and it worked: I stopped raising my hand in class. In hindsight and as a teacher, though, I think I understand Mr. Duncan's behavior better. My guess is he didn't know the answer to my question. He had been taught to memorize exponent rules, just like he was now teaching us. Rather than seeing my curiosity as an opportunity to go deeper into the mathematics and build real understanding—mine and his—he likely perceived my questioning as a public challenge to his expertise and authority. He was standing at the front of the class, trying to save face. Shutting me down wasn't his goal, I'm sure (or at least I hope!), even though that was the effect of his actions.

When I listen to teachers talk about their experiences as math students, a story similar to mine often emerges: they were (1) trying to understand a math concept, so (2) they asked their teachers (or parents) a lot of questions until (3) the teachers (or parents) ended the discussion with a thud:

> "Because that's the rule."
>
> "You just need to memorize it."
>
> "I know it's confusing, but you need to learn it."
>
> "Stop worrying about why. This is how you do it."
>
> "It's in the book; that's why."

These sorts of responses certainly lead to negative feelings about math. Students feel confused, baffled, incompetent, frustrated. Terrible! In addition to all that, though, these sorts of moments contribute to a pervasive, damaging myth about mathematics as a discipline, which is that *obedience* is ultra-important. We're just supposed to quiet down and abide by the rules. If we follow the teacher's procedures, lining everything up and doing the steps in order, we'll get the correct answer, right?

The thing is, obedience is unmathematical. Mathematicians, as a group, are a ragtag bunch of rebels. They push boundaries, ask questions, take risks, test conjectures, try new things, and are relentlessly passionate about pursuing meaning. As mathematician Paul Lockhart (2009, 31) put it:

> Math is *not* about following directions, it's about making *new* directions.

Mathematicians are most excited by problems that have no known answers, steps, or "right ways to do it." These problems are called *unsolved*, or *open*, problems, and they drive the field. By seeking to understand what is not yet understood, mathematicians discover and invent new techniques, models, tools, ideas, connections, and structures. Their goal is to create new mathematics, not to replicate, practice, or regurgitate existing methods, and they certainly have no answer key!

For mathematicians to tackle open problems, they must take risks. They need to be bold enough to try novel approaches, including far-fetched ones that have a high likelihood of failure, because new thinking is what's needed to solve a problem that's been stumping everybody else. It takes a certain amount of gumption to say, "Newton died unable to solve this problem, but I think I'll give it a go."

Mathematicians head into uncharted territory without maps, intentionally walking away from the familiar and the known, hoping to forge new trails somewhere interesting. In short, mathematicians have moxie. Consider the terms of praise they reserve for the most important solutions to the most captivating problems: *innovative, breakthrough, surprising, daring, revolutionary, creative, beautiful, subversive, elegant, imaginative!* A far cry from the forced compliance of "Because that's the rule you need to memorize," aren't they?

Perhaps you're thinking that pluck, innovation, and risk taking apply only at the frontiers of mathematics and only to research mathematicians? After all, we're not inventing any new math in school, are we? Don't we just teach "the basics"?

The answer is no, thank goodness!

Risk Taking Among Young Mathematicians

Imagine a young girl walking on a sidewalk, counting her steps on her way home from first grade. Once she gets to fifty, she decides to switch and count down instead of up. As she approaches zero, her stride slows, but she still has more steps to take. Her jaw drops as she wonders whether there are numbers on the other side of zero. She can almost see them stretching out in front of her. She may not know their conventional name, but she has just had the same epiphany the great Indian mathematician Brahmagupta had in the seventh century when he invented negative numbers. Don't let our society's acceptance of these radical ideas take anything away from the breakthrough that girl just made! She is thinking like a mathematician, daring to wonder about limits and possibilities, and her ideas are delightful.

When students generate real mathematical understanding, they are creating math anew. Each time a child has an aha! moment about place value, makes a connection between fractions and division, or discovers rotational symmetry in a flower, that child is reinventing mathematics. Whether or not other mathematicians have had the same idea before is *completely irrelevant to that student*. The inverse relationship between addition and subtraction may be settled mathematics to us, but it's an open problem for every single young mathematician we teach.

For our young mathematicians to tackle open problems, they must tinker with mathematics, make leaps, ask questions, share their ideas, and handle frequent failures in math class, and we must make them feel safe and encouraged to do so. Mathematician James Tanton (2012) said, "Math is being able to engage in joyful intellectual play—and being willing to flail (even fail!)." As educators, we must teach students how to engage in joyful intellectual play, flail, and even fail as they muck around with math, because that is how they will construct new mathematical understanding for themselves.

I often hear teachers commiserate that their students won't take risks, won't try anything new, won't start a problem if they can't see a short, clear path from the start to the finish. When conversation shifts toward what we do to encourage risk taking in the math classroom, however, I hear a lot of messaging strategies and not much else:

> "I *tell* my students that the only way to learn something new is to try."

> "I *tell* my students that I make mistakes all the time."

> "I *tell* my students that taking risks is part of learning."

These messages are all well and good, but it's going to take a lot more than spoken messages and inspiring posters to teach students how to take mathematical risks, especially if they've already been socialized into a culture of passive obedience in mathematics. It's going to take *teaching. Actions. Instructional strategies.* If we want students to line up quickly and quietly, we must teach them how. If we want students to take quality notes, we must teach them how. And if we want students to take risks in math class, we must teach them how!

In this chapter, we'll learn from three teachers who have developed specific instructional strategies to teach them how:

- We'll visit Heidi Fessenden and see how she values and highlights risk taking publicly as part of teaching mathematics.
- We will analyze student work samples from Cindy Gano to see how she uses brief, specific, written feedback to encourage risk taking.
- We'll look at how Shawn Towle establishes a classroom culture that is *both* rigorous and safe, and see how he leverages his leadership to support students while they take risks.

Heidi Fessenden, second grade, Boston, Massachusetts

Valuing Risk: "Other people might be inspired by Alvin's example."

When I first met Heidi Fessenden, she had been teaching at Young Achievers Science and Math Pilot School in the Boston Public Schools for ten years. Ninety-six percent of the students are black and Latino and live primarily in the Dorchester and Mattapan neighborhoods of Boston. More than 80 percent of Young Achievers students receive free and reduced lunch. The faculty has a shared emphasis on inquiry, especially in math and science, and emphasizes experiential education and scientific habits of mind.

On the fourth day of math in September, and my first time in her classroom, I observed Heidi teach students the *Today's Number* routine from TERC's *Investigations in Number, Data, and Space* (2008). In this routine, the teacher chooses a number of the day and asks each student to generate several equations about that number. Heidi chose *Today's Number* because it would help her meet several goals in one lesson. She wanted to give students a rich opportunity to play with numbers and ideas, gather useful formative assessment about her new class, set norms and expectations for math for the year, and teach students how to have productive mathematical discussions.

Heidi chose the number 10. She modeled a bit on the chart paper before sending students off to work independently and then gave students several minutes to write lots of equations. After this quiet work time, students left for physical education class—scheduled right in the middle of math block—and Heidi flipped through her students' work to see what she noticed. When the class returned, Heidi asked students to gather on the rug and look at Alvin's *Today's Number*, which she placed under the document camera.

> Heidi: This is the work of one student. What I want you to do is to look at this work and see what you notice. You're going to have to look at it really closely to see what you notice. I'm going to use the sticks (popsicle sticks with student names for random calling), so you don't have to raise your hand. Everyone should be looking, and everybody should be thinking. Just so you know, this is Alvin's work. See what you notice about his work.

Heidi repeated each equation orally and recopied them because she was having focus trouble with her projector. Alvin's work looked like Figure 3.1. "That's as far as he got. The last one he didn't finish. What do you notice? Don't raise your hand, just look at it and see what you notice about his work. Lily, put your hand down and think." (Heidi waited for more than two minutes while students thought.)

> Heidi: Alicia, What did you notice?
>
> Alicia: I noticed that you put checks.
>
> Heidi: No, *I* didn't put checks! Why do you think *he* put checks, Alicia?

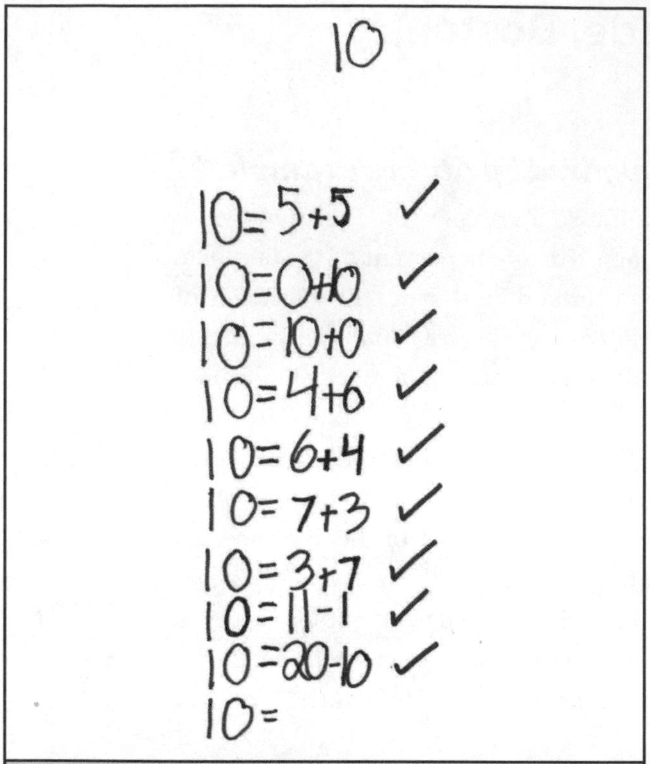

$$10$$

$$10 = 5 + 5 \quad \checkmark$$
$$10 = 0 + 10 \quad \checkmark$$
$$10 = 10 + 0 \quad \checkmark$$
$$10 = 4 + 6 \quad \checkmark$$
$$10 = 6 + 4 \quad \checkmark$$
$$10 = 7 + 3 \quad \checkmark$$
$$10 = 3 + 7 \quad \checkmark$$
$$10 = 11 - 1 \quad \checkmark$$
$$10 = 20 - 10 \quad \checkmark$$
$$10 =$$

Figure 3.1 *Alvin's equations about 10*

Alicia: To make sure he did it correct.

Heidi: You think he double-checked them to make sure he thought they were right? Do you want to tell us why you put checks, Alvin?

Alvin: I checked them.

Heidi: So you went back and checked them? Malcolm, what do you notice?

Malcolm: That he didn't make them too messy.

Heidi: OK, I want you to think about the math. What did you notice about the math? You're right; he kind of organized his paper.

(Everyone was quiet for thirty seconds while Malcolm thought.)

Malcolm: Um. He um. He changed the numbers. Um, like he changed it left to right and right to left.

Heidi: What do you mean by that?

Malcolm: Like 7 + 3 and 3 + 7.

Heidi: I'm going to ask someone if they can repeat what you said. Octavia, can you repeat what Malcolm just said?

Octavia: (Silent.)

Heidi: Malcolm, say it again, 'cause what you said is really important. Everybody listen because I think Malcolm is peeking into Alvin's brain, and he's making a guess about what was going on in Alvin's brain, and Alvin will tell us if Malcolm was right.

Malcolm: That he changed the numbers right to left and left to right.

Heidi: So give us an example.

Malcolm: So, see like 7 + 3 and 3 + 7.

Heidi: 7 + 3 and then 3 + 7. So you're saying that this was left to right and then here he did it right to left?

Malcolm: Yes.

Heidi: So he turned it around. Alvin, were you thinking about numbers like that when you did this? Were you thinking about putting them together? Putting the ones that go together together?

(Alvin shrugged.)

Heidi: No? When you wrote 7 + 3, did you then think, "Oh, I know, if 7 + 3 equals 10, then 3 + 7 equals 10?"

Alvin: I already knew it.

Heidi: You already knew it. So it's kind of a habit? Does anybody know a name for this? Mabel?

Mabel: Turn-around facts.

Heidi: These are called turn-around facts. Can I write that here, Alvin?

Alvin: Yeah.

Heidi: Does anybody see another turn-around fact? (Eight seconds of wait time.) Jaleesa?

(Jaleesa murmured.)

Heidi: I can't hear you. Speak up!

Jaleesa: 10, 0, 10, and then 0, 10, 10.

Heidi: Is this what you're looking at? 10 = 0 + 10 and 10 = 10 + 0? Is that what you said?

Jaleesa: Uh-huh.

Heidi: Does anybody see another turn-around fact? Naomi?

Naomi: 4 + 6 and 6 + 4.

Heidi: Mm hmm. Alvin was being really organized when he did this! Does anybody notice anything else about Alvin's work? I'm going to take two more observations. Deandre? What do you notice, Deandre?

(Twenty-eight seconds of wait time.)

Heidi: Are you thinking?

Deandre: Could you come back to me?

Heidi: Mm hmm. Tabriya, what do you notice?

Tabriya: He did a really good job.

Heidi: Why? Be specific with your feedback.

(Tabriya was silent.)

Heidi: Can I say one thing that I noticed? Alvin, tell me if you think I'm right. I thought probably 5 + 5 was something you knew pretty quickly, right? And then he did 10 + 0 and 0 + 10 and you probably knew those in a snap, right? And then he did 4 + 6 and 7 + 3, those turn-around facts—I bet he knows those pretty well. And *then*, I thought, he'd try to do some harder ones. I thought, oh, he decided he'd do some subtraction, which is harder. And so, after he wrote a bunch that he knew, he decided to *challenge* himself and put some equations that were harder to figure out. Did I get it right, Alvin?

Alvin: Yeah.

Heidi: Do you think that Alvin was concentrating on math for all of the math time, or do you think he was doing other stuff?

Class: Math the whole time.

Heidi: He did nine and a half equations, and he didn't have that many minutes! So that probably means he was concentrating all the time, right?

Alvin: Yeah.

Heidi: So other people might be inspired by Alvin's example next time.

During class, I noticed several remarkable things about this interchange:

- The length of wait time Heidi used. She made it clear with her actions that **she wants deep thinking, and values thoughtfulness more than speed**. Take a minute to contrast Heidi's facilitation with more typical math teaching, in which the students who raise their hands quickly are the exalted ones. Heidi was setting a new and different tone by explicitly valuing student thinking and encouraging varied, thoughtful answers.

- **She engaged students with mathematical thinking**, not appearances or answers. When students looked at check marks or neatness, Heidi redirected them to the mathematics. Substance matters in this class.

- Heidi was **teaching students how to have a discussion** about math by holding students accountable for listening to one another and by expecting specificity in their language (Chapin, O'Connor, and Anderson 2009). It was only the fourth day of school, so the discussion didn't flow fantastically yet. No matter. Students need time and instruction to adjust to these expectations for productive mathematical discussions. Heidi was laying the groundwork here.

- Above all, Heidi was **explicitly teaching students to challenge themselves and take risks in math class**. I could easily imagine a different teacher chiding Alvin for not completing the list of turn-around facts for 10 because he skipped 8 + 2. Instead of saying, "Oops, I think you missed one," Heidi ended the lesson by publicly praising Alvin for moving beyond what he already knows and trying some harder problems he probably didn't know when he started. By telling students they might be "inspired" by Alvin's example of challenging himself, she made it clear to her students that she wants them to stretch.

I left Heidi's room and made my way to the Amtrak station. On the train ride home, I worked Heidi's choices over and over in my mind. I found myself backing up and thinking about how we choose student work to share. I have a short list of criteria: a strategy I'm hoping will emerge, an organizational approach I'd like to catch on, a juicy mistake that will help us all think more deeply, a surprising result, a useful representation, an efficient way to keep track. What Heidi taught me was to add risk taking to that short list. If risk taking matters in mathematics, I should value it by looking for examples to highlight publicly in the large group.

I was curious whether Heidi thought about her choice in a similar way, so I e-mailed and asked her to tell me about her instructional decision to select Alvin's work to share. Heidi took the time to provide an incredibly thoughtful context about Alvin as a student and about her choices as his teacher. I am grateful to her, and this peek into her brain is worth reading and sitting with in its entirety.

We knew even in the summer that he was a tricky kid, because he was highlighted on our class list, which meant his first-grade teachers recommended a home visit for him. (About ten of our kids were recommended for home visits because they are either very shy or have learning challenges or behavior problems.) His mom missed or canceled three home visits before we made it happen, which was a clue to me that his life may be somewhat chaotic. Then he got to school the first day and told us pretty quickly that he hates school and refused to participate. I imagined that he had had pretty negative experiences (despite having great teachers in K and 1) with school, probably because he really struggles academically. If a student won't even say their name on the first day, my first guess is anxiety, even though he didn't project nervousness at all—he projected opposition. But that is a very familiar guise to me.

When we did his home visit last Saturday, he and his mom talked to us about how he can't sleep well. He said his room is too dark and he sees scary things. We suggested a nightlight. Again, that made me think he is a scared little guy. I don't know enough about his life to know why.

In terms of selecting his work to share, I honestly didn't get to look at many kids' work in much detail. But I wanted to take a peek at his because I noticed how he went to work alone on the rug (his choice), and he worked so intently there. Interestingly, in the whole-class introduction to Today's Number, *I really couldn't tell if he was following the conversation at all. But he knew exactly what to do when he got his paper. So I was curious what he had done during that time working alone. Then when I saw it, I was impressed—he didn't just copy equations off our class chart, he wrote down things he knew himself, and I could see a pattern in his thinking (the turn-around facts). Also, because of my sense of him being anxious, I thought that trying some subtraction at the end seemed like a risk he was taking—it seems likely to me, although I'm not yet sure, that he doesn't automatically know that $11 - 1 = 10$ and $20 - 10 = 10$. Subtraction is much more challenging than addition.*

So I wanted to check out his work, and then I saw that he had done a few mathematically important things: 1. He used turn-around facts. 2. He took a risk and challenged himself. 3. Less important, because we had done this on the class chart, he used subtraction. (Some years it has been rare that students use subtraction in this exercise.)

It was perfect to see this, because it wasn't a stretch to highlight his work—there were truly mathematically valuable things he had done, that other kids could learn from, and I really want him to start the year off by establishing an identity for himself as a kid who works hard and is academically successful.

One thing I heard Annie [Heidi's coteacher] say to him over and over again the other day during writing was, "I don't care if your work is perfect or 'right.' I just care that you try your hardest." She said it a number of times, and he really worked on his writing for her that day—he worked so hard that when it was time to stop, he didn't want to, and he asked to work on it more later that day and then he took it home to keep working on. That is really powerful stuff for a kid who has felt disconnected from school in his first years. I guess that is a message we both really want to convey to the whole class—that working hard, and taking risks, is what matters . . .

That is my attempt to answer, in a roundabout way, your question about why I highlighted Alvin's risk taking. Mostly, above all, I wanted him to feel acknowledged as a thinker, and I wanted to affirm him doing something a little scary, academically. At the same time, of course, I wanted to present that as a way to approach math, and learning, in general, to everyone in the class.

Heidi also sent me some thoughts about Alvin from his first-grade teacher, who reflected:

The thing that makes me most sad about Alvin is that there is very little that he gets excited or enthusiastic about academically. Even the really cool expeditionary learning stuff we do, he doesn't seem to really care about. I just feel like he's sort of sad all the time—at home, at school, and he's just sort of making it through each day because school is so hard for him. He has very, very low self-confidence and has cried to me several times, saying he's stupid.

I've thought a lot about Alvin, about Heidi's decisions, and about the language she used to describe what she did. The more I think about it, the more impressed I am with Alvin's risk. He did something that is hard for everyone: he left the sure and comfortable ground of things he already knows and ventured out into the unknown. The fact that he did it as a student with negative feelings about school and a lot of anxiety is even more striking. I find my thoughts drifting back to Heidi's comment at the end: "Other people might be inspired by Alvin's example next time." She was talking to her students, of course, but I see no reason to limit it there. What about us teachers?

I decided to let myself be inspired by Alvin's example in a concrete way. I sat down with a piece of blank paper and wrote the number 10 on top, shown in Figure 3.2. Like Alvin, I started by writing some things I already knew about 10. It's a good way to make that big piece of blank paper a lot less intimidating. And then, thinking about Alvin's example, I planned to follow my thinking wherever it took me without worry. I would take some risks and just think aloud with my pen as I went.

I certainly could have gone in different directions, playing with multiplication, division, or subtraction instead of addition, but I had no goal in sight, other than to play with the number 10, to see where that took me, and to be inspired by Alvin's example!

Now it's your turn. If you want to teach your students to take risks like mathematicians do, like Alvin did, it's helpful for you to put yourself in their shoes by engaging in your own low-stakes mathematical explorations. Indulge in your own thinking for a bit. Grab a blank piece of paper, write the number 10 on the top, and play. Nobody will look at your work. Nobody will correct it, evaluate it, judge it, or comment on it. This is for you. Somewhere inside you is a child who used to play with numbers, patterns, and shapes. Reconnecting with your inner mathematician will improve your teaching and benefit your students, and it will also benefit you.

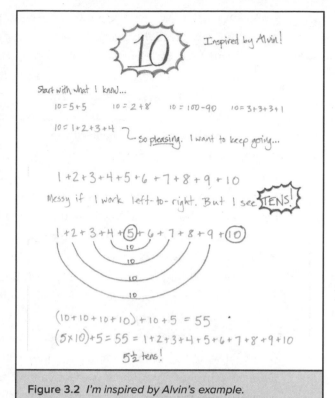

Figure 3.2 *I'm inspired by Alvin's example.*

Like Alvin, you can start with what you know about 10, and then go from there. You may hit dead ends; you may find a pattern you like; you may notice something new. There is no right or wrong here, just a chance to take a risk and play with numbers for a few minutes. If he can do it, surely, so can we.

If you did it, how do you feel? Nervous, irritated, resentful, wary, intrigued, excited, joyful, free? Whatever you feel, it's OK. I'd like to humbly suggest you consider feeling proud of yourself if you tried it out. And if you didn't try it this time, you can always go back and try it later, when you're ready to take a mathematical risk.

Cindy Gano, first and second grades, Accelerated Progress Program, Seattle, Washington

Individual Written Feedback: "I know you like a good challenge, so . . ."

I asked Cindy Gano how she encourages students to take risks in math, and she told me she has had a lot of success using individualized written feedback to urge students to push their mathematical thinking in a supported way. Cindy teaches a first- and second-grade split at Thurgood Marshall Elementary, one of two host schools for Seattle's Accelerated Progress

Program (APP). APP is a citywide, self-contained public school program for students who qualify as having highly capable needs. Cindy's students travel to school from a range of central and southern Seattle neighborhoods. Sixty-four percent of her students are white; 27 percent are of Chinese, Japanese, or Asian Indian descent; and 9% are black. About one-third of her students are first-generation Americans.

The APP service delivery model has students going both faster and deeper, and students generally work two years ahead of the standard curriculum. At some point in first or second grade, Cindy said her students "hit the area where it's not easy for them anymore." Most of these precocious students have skated through math until now, easily impressing everyone without much effort. In Cindy's class, the harder curriculum catches up with them, and they have to learn how to try. As Cindy told me, "There have been some tears," as students learn how to "overcome the challenge, and work, and study."

All students need to learn how to overcome challenges and work and study. High-achieving students often have the hardest time with these lessons, especially if they have bought into the myth that being smart means school is easy and the only mistakes you make in math are careless errors. There has been some powerful recent research about these associations, much of it following psychologist Carol Dweck's seminal studies in New York City Public Schools (2006). I want to take just a minute to give you a few highlights of her work for three reasons. One, it's gripping! Two, I hear the word *smart* used in math classes all the time, and its usage is something to reconsider. Three, we'll get much more out of looking at Cindy's choice of words in her written feedback by having this brief context.

Here's the experimental setup: Dweck and her team pulled fifth-grade students out of class individually and gave them a relatively easy test of nonverbal puzzles to solve. All the students did fairly well on the test. One-half of the students were told, "You must be smart at this," while the other half were told, "You must have worked really hard."

Dweck and her researchers wanted to see the effect of this single line of praise on student choices and performance, so they did three follow-up tests:

1. They gave students a choice on the next problem. Students could take another test similar to the one they'd just finished, or they could take a harder test. Researchers promised students they would "learn a lot" from attempting the more challenging puzzles. The majority of the students who were praised for their smarts on the first puzzle chose the easier problems, but 90 percent of the students who were praised for effort chose the more challenging problems (Bronson and Merryman 2009, 14).

2. In a subsequent round, all students were given an extremely challenging problem—so challenging that all students failed to solve it. The students who had been praised for effort handled failure and struggle well. "They got very involved, willing to try every solution to the puzzles. Many of them remarked, unprovoked, 'This is my favorite test.'" The students who had been praised for intelligence were much quicker to melt down. Dweck said, "Just watching them, you could see the strain. They were sweating

and miserable" (Bronson and Merryman 2009, 15).

3. After this round of induced failure, all students were given a test with puzzles at the same level of difficulty as the first test. Students who had been praised for their effort improved their scores by about 30 percent. Students who had been praised for their smarts did worse than they had at the beginning, with their scores falling by about 20 percent.

Dweck's research teaches us that, no matter how benevolent our intentions, when we tell students a problem will be easy because they are smart, kids fill in the corollary messages and start worrying. If answering right means you're smart, then answering wrong means you're dumb. If finding work easy means you're smart, then having to try means you're dumb. Students decide it's better to play it safe, not take the risk, and keep looking smart rather than risk looking dumb, right? Except, wrong. Really, really wrong.

Most of Cindy's students have been praised for their smarts and arrive thinking they're smart because math is easy for them and they don't often make mistakes. Cindy breaks this myth down and explicitly teaches them that success in her class does not mean perfection or coasting; rather, it means taking risks and embracing challenges. She uses this language during instruction and emphasizes it in written feedback.

For example, Cindy has students work with a *Number of the Day*, which is basically the same routine as Heidi's *Today's Number*. Cindy's students write in spiral notebooks, though, which Cindy collects. She writes brief comments after each session—just a phrase or two. Cindy tailors these comments to individual students, highlighting risk taking when she sees it and giving specific, encouraging nudges to students when she doesn't. I've selected three sets of before and after pictures so you can see how students initially play it safe but eventually learn how to take risks with Cindy's regular guidance. In each case, it's important to look deeply at the student's work. What's going on in the math? What do you notice about Cindy's feedback in response to the math?

Emily

Emily's first example is typical of her fall entries (Figure 3.3). She found a great pattern but kept going with it ad nauseam, rather than generalizing it or moving on to something new, like Alvin did. She tried to impress her teacher with quantity, so

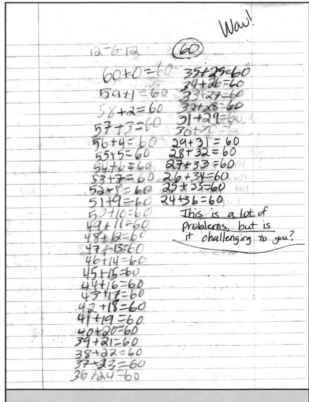

Figure 3.3 *Emily's work in September*

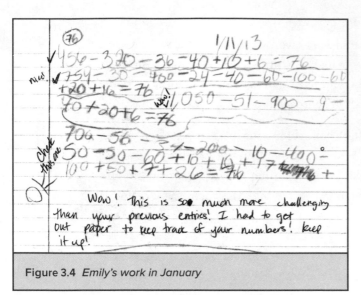

Figure 3.4 *Emily's work in January*

Cindy emphasized quality.

In mid-January, Emily finally took a big chance (Figure 3.4). Cindy responded to Emily's risk positively and encouraged her to keep going. Also, Cindy noted the mistake Emily made but didn't make a big deal out of it. She certainly didn't say, "Go back to easier problems until you're 100 percent accurate, and then try these harder ones again." Cindy expects that, if students are working at the leading edges of their understanding, they are going to make mistakes. She is teaching students to take those mistakes in stride and to continue on.

Charlie

Charlie was doing a good job challenging himself with addition and subtraction in September (Figure 3.5). Cindy encouraged him to carry on and gave him a nudge toward incorporating multiplication.

By December, Charlie was regularly using lots of multiplication and was ready for a new challenge (Figure 3.6). Cindy continually adjusts her feedback based on what she knows about these students individually, so students stay in the learning zone.

Joseph

In September, Cindy was really encouraging Joseph to push himself (Figure 3.7). Look how he responded (Figure 3.8)!

By March, Joseph had incorporated negative numbers into his work and continued to explore new and interesting mathematics (Figure 3.9).

As I read through a class set of student notebooks, I compiled examples of the language Cindy uses. Notice how she gives clear, specific guidance on what it means to challenge yourself when needed.

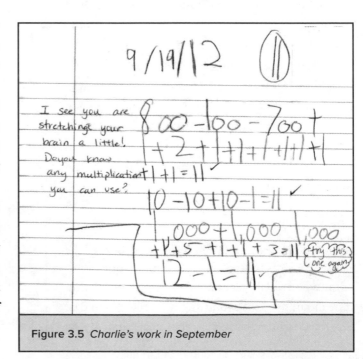

Figure 3.5 *Charlie's work in September*

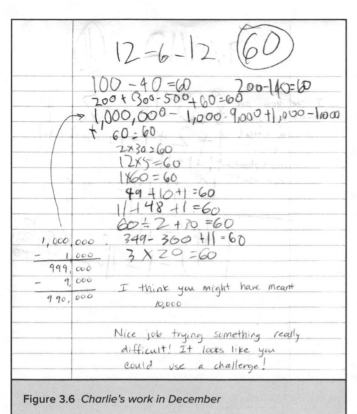

$12 = 6 - 12$ ⑥⓪

$100 - 40 = 60$　　　$200 - 140 = 60$
$200 + 300 - 500 + 60 = 60$
$1,000,000 - 1,000 \cdot 9,000 + 1,000 - 1000 + 60 = 60$
$2 \times 30 = 60$
$12 \times 5 = 60$
$1 \times 60 = 60$
$49 + 10 + 1 = 60$
$1 + 48 + 1 = 60$
$60 \div 2 + 30 = 60$
$349 - 360 + 11 = 60$
$3 \times 20 = 60$

$$\begin{array}{r} 1,000,000 \\ -\quad 1,000 \\ \hline 999,000 \\ -\quad 9,000 \\ \hline 990,000 \end{array}$$

I think you might have meant 10,000

Nice job trying something really difficult! It looks like you could use a challenge!

Figure 3.6 *Charlie's work in December*

---

⑩　9/18/12

$100 \times 10 - 1,000 + 10 = 10$

Nice! $180 - 10 - 10 - 10 - 10 - 10 - 10 - 10 - 10 - 100 + 10 = 10$

I know you like a good challenge so see if you can start with a number that doesn't end with 0.

9/19/12　　　　⑩

$41 - 30 = 11$ ✓　You got this pattern down!
$81 - 70 = 11$ ✓　Try some things out of
$51 - 40 = 11$ ✓　your comfort zone ☺
$21 - 10 = 11$ ✓
$91 - 80 = 11$ ✓

Figure 3.7 *Joseph's work in September*

1/11/13　　　　　⑦⑥

$3,994 - 1 - 2,900 - 1093 + 25 + 25 + 25 + 1 = 76$

This is more like it! Remember that you are a second grader who likes a challenge!

Figure 3.8 *Joseph's work in January*

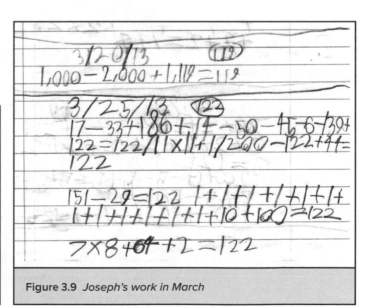

3/20/13　　⑩⑨

$1,000 - 2,000 + 1,118 = 118$

3/25/13　　⑫②

$17 - 33 + 186 + 14 - 50 - 45 - 6 - 39 + 22 = 122$　$11 \times 11 + 1/200 - 122 + 44 = 122$

$151 - 29 = 122$　$1 + 1 + 1 + 1 + 1 + 1$
$1 + 1 + 1 + 1 + 1 + 1 + 10 + 100 = 122$

$7 \times 8 + 64 + 2 = 122$

Figure 3.9 *Joseph's work in March*

Written comments for students who are playing it safe:

- *It's time to bump it up a notch.*
- *This is a lot of problems, but is it challenging to you?*
- *I bet you can do much more complicated problems now!*
- *Can you challenge yourself even more? Try starting with really big numbers and subtracting to reach the number.*
- *I see you know turn-around facts! For a challenge, try starting at 50 and subtracting back to the number of the day.*
- *Can you use larger numbers? This is a wonderful start!*
- *Is + 20 − 20 challenging to you? I am wondering if you could add steps that challenge your brain where you have to think about the numbers.*
- *You have a lot of good ideas and I know you could use a bigger challenge.*
- *I know you like a good challenge, so try starting with a number that doesn't end with 0.*
- *You got this pattern down! Try some things out of your comfort zone.*
- *I can see that you really like playing around with numbers! For your challenge, I would like you to try getting up to those high numbers and then get back to the number of the day without using ×0. Good luck!*

Written comments for students who are taking risks:

- *I see you are really bumping it up today! Woohoo!*
- *Wow! This is so much more challenging than your previous entries! I had to get out paper to keep track of your numbers! Keep it up!*
- *I see that you have really taken on the challenge and are trying harder problems! Good for you!*
- *Way to push your thinking!*
- *I circled the two that were the most challenging.*
- *I see you really like to challenge yourself!*
- *I see you are stretching your brain a little! Do you know any multiplication you can use?*
- *You're really on the right track of trying some harder problems!*
- *This is more like it! Remember that you are a second grader who likes a challenge!*
- *You have really stepped it up a notch!*
- *Good try! You are trying such challenging numbers. I think they are hard to keep track of. What can you do to help keep track of your totals?*

Many teachers are comfortable giving individual, written feedback in literacy, but we don't often think to use it in math. The progress students are making with Cindy makes me wonder if more of us should try this technique. Her students are clearly striving to meet her high standards, at least in part because of her thoughtful and targeted language. Thinking back to Dweck's research, it's clear Cindy uses her comments to encourage effort and risk taking, rather than to praise right answers and correct mistakes. The word she uses most is *challenge*, and I've never seen the words *smart* or *easy* in one of her notebooks. Over time, students have adjusted to her expectations of stretching their brains, taking risks, and seeking challenges as a fundamental part of doing mathematics.

Shawn Towle, eighth grade, Falmouth, Maine

Support in the Vulnerable Moment: "You've got a whole room full of not sure. No worries. We'll help."

Shawn Towle used to teach middle school math in a traditional, procedural way before high-quality professional development exposed him to more fulfilling and successful methods. He has evolved into an extraordinary math teacher and serves as a district, state, and national leader. In 2009, Shawn was awarded a Presidential Award for Excellence in Mathematics Teaching, grades seven to twelve.

Shawn teaches in Falmouth, a seaside town and middle-class suburb of Portland, Maine. Falmouth was ranked "The Top City to Live and Learn" by *Forbes* magazine in 2011, largely because the school system is considered excellent while the cost of living is reasonable. Racially, 94 percent of the middle school students are white, 5 percent are Asian, and the remaining 1 percent are black. Four percent of students qualify for reduced-price lunch.

Shawn's students say he is strict, and they're right. He holds students to incredibly high mathematical and behavioral standards. What's clear to them and me, however, is that Shawn's high standards and expectations are supportive and aspirational: he expects a lot from all of his students because he knows they are all worthy. Shawn is particularly passionate about teaching his students with special educational needs, and I've watched them grow in leaps and bounds in the respectful, challenging environment Shawn cultivates.

From the first day, Shawn makes it clear students will be exploring new territory, changing their minds, muddling through confusion, and working together as they make sense of mathematics. Shawn sets this tone through (1) explicit instruction and discussion of norms and culture and (2) leadership. For example, Shawn starts the year by randomly grouping students and asking them to analyze quotations that support a growth mindset and productive learning environment (Figure 3.10). He revisits these ideas and norms regularly, connecting them to students' work.

As for Shawn's leadership by example, when a student asks a brave question, she has a fierce protector and advocate in her teacher. When a student is teetering on the edge of whether to try, risk, or share an incomplete idea, Shawn steps in with just enough firm encouragement

> "A closed mind is a dying mind" - Edna Ferber, Pulitzer Prize - winning novelist.
> If you're not open to new ideas your mind will never grow or learn.
>
> "To have a great idea, have a lot of them."
> I chose this because I understand it, you can have many good ideas, but together it can be a great idea!
>
> "Most people don't recognize opportunity because it comes disguised as hard work."
> I chose this quote because I thought that you have to always work hard for what you want.
>
> "You can't solve math problems unless you are willing to talk to yourself." - Carol Findell, Boston University
> I chose this because I can understand that it means you have to help yourself understand the problem, and you have to work with yourself.

Figure 3.10 *Eighth-grade team journal entry in response to provocative quotations about learning, effort, and mathematics*

that students usually tip toward taking the chance. If a student is contemptuous or mocking of another student's effort, Shawn responds instantly and unforgettably. I've never seen a student make that mistake twice in Shawn's room. After the first few weeks of school, Shawn's eighth-grade students—whose heightened social awareness can present a significant impediment to risk taking—are standing up, trying new ideas, revising their thinking, and sharing their wondering publicly.

For example, one morning in October, Shawn's students were working on a problem comparing the areas of similar triangles. As Shawn circulated, several students said they were shaky on this problem, so Shawn decided to take it up in the large group.

Before we jump into the lovely mathematical thinking Shawn's students did, we need to start with the problem. One of the most important habits a math teacher can develop is to *do the problem first, always.* We engage with the mathematics ourselves before talking about it, teaching it, or looking at any student work for these reasons:

- Playing with the problem ourselves activates our identities as mathematicians. Just like reading teachers need to read and writing teachers need to write, math teachers need to do math.
- Noticing which mathematical concepts and techniques come into play while we work focuses our thinking on content. Rather than jumping right to planning activities students will *do*, we spend time thinking about the mathematics students may *learn*.
- Exploring the problem helps us anticipate different approaches and strategies students may try, as well as preconceptions and misunderstandings we expect to emerge. We'll be much more present in classroom discussions—and much more able to follow students' thinking—if we've dug into the problem ahead of time. A passive reading of solutions in the teacher's guide can't compare.

Let's establish the habit of playing with the problem first and carry it forward from here. Shawn uses *Connected Mathematics Project*, and this problem is adapted from the second edition of *Looking for Pythagoras* (Lappan et al. 2009). Students had the representation of similar right triangles in Figure 3.11 and were asked, *How are the areas of the triangles related?*

There's no need for you to remember any equations or rules to get started on this question, although feel free to use them if you do remember them and think about the problem that way. You can also play around with your pencil or trace and cut out these shapes so you can estimate how much bigger the triangle on the left is than the one on the right. It might help to think about the question as how many little triangles can fit inside the bigger triangle? Perhaps estimate first and then try?

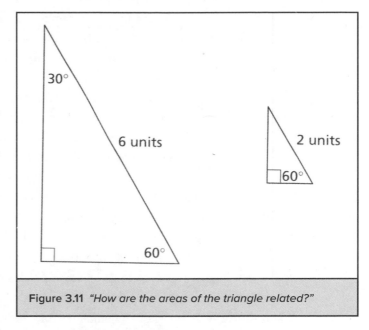

Figure 3.11 *"How are the areas of the triangle related?"*

Once you've worked on the problem, put your teacher hat back on and reflect on what mathematical content and practices you used. What strategy appealed to you? Do you see any other ways to solve it? Where might students go with this problem, and where might they get confused?

When Shawn felt his students had had enough time to engage with the problem and were ready to discuss it, he moved to a sidewall of the classroom and gathered their attention:

Shawn: There's a question about number 28. There was a question about how the areas compare. Somebody needs some convincing. I need someone to get us started on it.

(Nobody raised a hand at first.)

Shawn: Is there a volunteer to try? We will help.

(Lucy tentatively fingered her paper.)

Lucy: I'm not sure . . .

Shawn: You've got a whole room of "not sure," so no worries.

(Lucy stood up and headed to the document camera in the front of the room.)

How did Shawn convince Lucy to take a risk? Take a closer look at his language:

"I need someone to get us started on it."

"Is there a volunteer to try? We will help."

"You've got a whole room of not sure, so no worries."

This is what it sounds like when a teacher supports students to share their incomplete, partially formed, or tentative thinking. Shawn wasn't begging or pleading in his tone; rather, he was calm and confident, encouraging and expectant. By using *us*, *we*, and *whole room*, he framed the class as a collective and the work on this problem as a joint effort. With a statement like "We will help," Shawn was making his expectations clear to the rest of the class: their job was to listen to their classmate supportively and help when needed.

Bolstered by this support, Lucy rose and walked to the front of the room. She explained her thinking with clarity. She exuded confidence in herself as a mathematical thinker, even when she wasn't entirely convinced of her own answers. Students asked her questions as she went, and she fielded them directly. Shawn stayed quiet, leaning against the heater by the windows, until she finished leading the class through her solution.

Lucy approached the problem in an algebraic way. She used relationships she'd learned about different kinds of right triangles to calculate the side lengths. She then used the Pythagorean theorem and the formula she knew for the area of a triangle to calculate the areas of both of these triangles. The area of the larger triangle turned out to be $9\left[\frac{\sqrt{3}}{2}\right]$ square units, and the area of the smaller triangle was $\frac{\sqrt{3}}{2}$ square units. Lucy compared these two expressions and concluded, "So, ultimately, I would say the area of this triangle is nine times the area of this triangle."

Lucy's mathematics were solid, and her explanation was clear to people who were familiar with what she knew, but it went by very fast. Shawn waited a few moments before asking, "Comments or questions for Lucy?"

The discussion revealed that some students had followed Lucy's thinking, but several were confused. Shawn knew he had to put this learning back on his students and give them a chance to make sense out of it individually, in pairs, or in small groups. He said, "Can you take a few minutes to try that out? Lucy's claiming the area of the bigger one is nine times the area of the smaller one. Can you try and see?"

At their table groups, students got right to work trying to prove or disprove Lucy's claim. Lots of them used diagrams, some used scale factors between the two triangles, and some used equations to work through Lucy's solution on their own. Shawn slowly moved around the room, sitting down and joining each table as a member of the math discussion. He did a lot of listening with his chin in his hand and his head cocked to one side. After several minutes, when students seemed set to discuss the problem in the large group again, Shawn asked Megan's group to share their work. They had carefully fit smaller triangles inside the larger one, using a geometric representation to demonstrate that Lucy's algebraic approach was correct (Figure 3.12). Students could actually *see* the nine from Lucy's solution. Megan's thinking and picture were so clear and compelling that the class applauded at the end.

When I step back and think about the trajectory of this ultimately successful lesson, I see three crucial moments wherein its success or failure hinged on students' taking mathematical risks. First, students needed to feel comfortable expressing that they were unsure about the triangles problem, rather than pretending they understood and masking their confusion. Second, a student needed to share a tentative solution with the whole class to get the conversation started. Lucy's bravery here was essential. Third, students needed to get their arms around Lucy's solution, experimenting with different approaches until they had proven or disproven it. Many students were confused by her explanation, but they plunged ahead anyway, trying to make sense of what she had done. Nobody shut down, gave up, or checked out. Megan's group took a particularly big mathematical gamble by using spatial relationships (geometry) to test numeric relationships (algebra). That's innovative thinking.

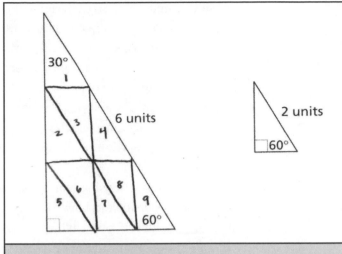

Figure 3.12 *Students' geometric representation showing the relationship between the triangles' areas*

In most eighth-grade math classes, students avoid risks by refusing to try. They'd rather doodle on their binder and count on the "smart kids" in the class to do the problem. I've never seen a student withdraw like that in Shawn's room. Even if students are not quite sure where they're headed when they start a problem, they start. They pick up their pencils, lean forward, and give it a try. If their first attempt doesn't work, they think some more, maybe talk with a peer, get some tools, and try it again a different way. We often talk about *word attack* in literacy; I think of this trait as *problem attack* in math.

Shawn explicitly and implicitly teaches problem attack every day. He teaches students to get comfortable with confusion as they muddle their way toward a solution or grapple with a concept, because that is the nature of doing mathematics. He teaches students to speak up when they don't understand, not just when they do. Through strong leadership, he creates a cultural expectation that students will try, especially when they don't know. And, by explicitly supporting students during these moments of vulnerability, he normalizes and defends mathematical risk.

Problem Selection—Making Room for Mathematical Risk Taking

There's an important common feature to these three stories from Shawn's, Cindy's, and Heidi's classrooms, and it has to do with the problems they assigned. In each case, there was some openness in the problem. There was room for students to take mathematical risks.

When we assign problems that have a single, closed path from start to finish, we've eliminated the possibility that students will take mathematical risks. There's nothing to try if everything is prescribed. At that point, the only kinds of risks available to students are *social risks,* like raising hands or speaking up in class. Social risks are important, and we need to create safe climates where students will participate. They are not the same as mathematical risks, however, and mathematical risks are essential for learning.

A mathematical risk involves attempting some mathematics without being certain of the outcome. It might involve asking a question, taking a stab at a different strategy, working with unfamiliar numbers or operations, looking for a relationship, or imagining an alternate scenario. If we want students to take mathematical risks, we must choose tasks with potential. Problems that have multiple entry points, a range of solution paths, more than one answer, or different interpretations make it possible for students to experiment with their ideas and make decisions.

The benefits of choosing rich tasks will be a recurrent theme throughout this book. We'll take a deeper look at how to open problems in Chapter 6, "Mathematicians Rise to a Challenge." For now, I hope you'll start turning a critical eye toward the problems you assign. Are there any opportunities for students to take mathematical risks?

Reacting to the Unexpected

Mathematician Melanie Wood told me this story:

> In kindergarten, I remember playing with some number flashcards with the one-digit numbers on them, sorting them into odd and even, and discovering some of the properties of odd and even numbers (like an even number plus an even number was an even number). But I was then required to put them away because I had already passed the "one-digit number" test and was supposed to be working on more "advanced" number things.

This is a classic example of a teacher—unintentionally, I'm sure—squashing a student's risk taking. Melanie was supposed to use the tools in one, narrow way, and the teacher limited her to that one option, rather than encouraging Melanie's exploration and mathematical play. From the teacher's point of view, it's understandable that she was focused on students finishing their assignments and moving through her planned progression. What we need to remember, though, is that students' mathematical risks will often catch us by surprise. Many won't be in our lesson plans. We can hope they come, but we won't know when, from whom, or about what. We

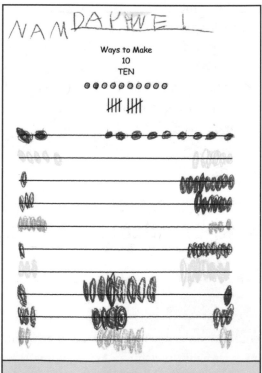

Figure 3.13 *A kindergarten problem with openness leads to a mathematical risk.*

need to recognize and encourage these students' risks anyway, even if we're caught off guard.

For example, when my younger daughter, Daphne, was in the fall of her kindergarten year, her teacher, Katie Norton, e-mailed me a picture of her work (Figure 3.13).

Students were working with a giant abacus, which has ten colored beads on each string. Katie created this simple, brilliant sheet so her students could represent their combinations to ten: 1 + 9, 2 + 8, and so on. When Katie created the assignment, she assumed students would use two addends per line.

Katie was surprised and delighted by Daphne's symmetric solutions on the last three lines: (1, 8, 1), (3, 4, 3), and (2, 6, 2). Daphne dared to wonder what would happen if there were three addends. Rather than saying, "No, Daphne. You are supposed to make two groups on each line. Try to find all the ways," Katie congratulated Daphne for taking the assignment in an unexpected direction. Yes, the two-digit combinations to 10 are extremely important, but so are risks, mathematical play, and students' own ideas. Teaching math is much more rewarding when we are open to being pleasantly surprised by our students' thinking.

Making It Safe

I began this chapter by arguing that we've historically overvalued obedience in math class, when we really need to value risk taking. Let's look at classroom practices through this lens:

PROMOTING OBEDIENCE	ENCOURAGING RISK
Emphasis on obedience and rigidity—students have to do it the teacher's way or the textbook's way. Memorization of different algorithms is a big part of math. Example language: *Where do we always start when we add?* *You can't subtract a bigger number from a smaller number, so you have to borrow.* (Think about how this particular refrain sets students up for confusion when they get to negative numbers later.) *I marked you down even though you got the right answer because you skipped a step.* *What's the rule about adding fractions?* *Everybody trade your 100 for 10 tens.*	It is recognized and celebrated that there are different ways to approach problems. It is also understood that not all solutions work equally well, and rich discussions can grow out of evaluating different methods for efficiency, clarity, aesthetics, accuracy, usefulness, and flexibility. Example language: *Did anybody look at this problem in a different way?* *I want to be able to follow your thinking, so be sure to show your work in a way somebody else can understand.* *That's an interesting approach, and it worked for you with this problem. Do you think it will always work?* *Let's all try to solve a problem using Max's method so we can see if we understand the way he did it.* *Oh, you thought about it using a pattern!*
Notation, procedures, and uniformity are paramount.	Thinking and understanding are paramount.
Students are expected to follow the teacher.	Students are expected to build new understanding from what they already know, guided by the teacher.

PROMOTING OBEDIENCE	ENCOURAGING RISK
Students speak up in class when they know the answer.	Students speak up in class when they have a question, notice something, have an idea, make a conjecture, agree or disagree, build on a classmate's thinking, would like help, or have an answer.
Teachers demonstrate methods and students reproduce them.	Teachers guide and support students as needed as students solve problems. Teachers help students interpret their work and uncover connections between ideas.
Conventions are treated as commandments and are taught and tested to excess, leading to the perception that math is all about rules, notation, procedures, and obedience. Examples: *Fractions in which the numerator is bigger than the denominator are "improper" and must always be converted to a mixed number.* *Your answer isn't finished if it has a square root sign in it.*	Conventions are described accurately as habits mathematicians have agreed on so they can communicate with one another. They are sometimes arbitrary, and they are not that important. They are not the substance of mathematics. Sometimes improper fractions are much clearer, especially when they are in an equation, so mathematicians often work with them. For example, it is much clearer what is multiplied by x in $\frac{9}{2}x$ than it is in $4\frac{1}{2}x$. $\sqrt{3}$ is more precise and easier to write than 1.73205080 . . .
Students are taught to accept rules, procedures, and methods without question.	Students are encouraged to make sense out of mathematics in an active way and to push the boundaries of their thinking. They should only accept a claim if they are satisfied by a convincing mathematical argument. If their questions lead to new thinking for the teacher, that's a bonus.
Students are sometimes teased or humiliated when they are confused or make mistakes.	Students are encouraged when they are confused or make mistakes. Students are *never* teased about their thinking. *No* sarcasm or humiliation.
Smart and *easy* are common words. Speed is overvalued. *This problem will be easy for you because you're such a smart class!* *Wow, that was fast! You must be smart!*	*Challenge* and *try* are common words. It's understood that doing good math takes time. *This problem is really interesting, so let's take our time and dig into it.* *I have a great challenge for us today!* *Nice job this morning. I saw you trying really hard, especially when you realized your answer didn't make sense and you went back to figure out what was happening.*

PROMOTING OBEDIENCE	ENCOURAGING RISK
Students are passive.	Students are explicitly encouraged and supported to take risks. *"You might be inspired by Alvin's example." "I see you really like to challenge yourself." "Is there a volunteer to try? We will help."*
Students are expected to do exactly what they are supposed to, according to the assignment, and stay within those constraints.	Teachers expect that students will come up with surprising, unexpected, novel ideas. Teachers expect and welcome these unexpected thoughts and encourage students to try out their ideas.

Herbert Kohl (1992) wrote a marvelous essay some years back called "I Won't Learn from You!" in which he talked about the role of a safe climate for learning. Kohl showed that, if a student felt embarrassed or humiliated by a teacher, the student would devote his intellect to "not-learning" what that teacher was trying to teach in order to save face, dignity, and self-image. I think that's what happened to so many of us in math class. We felt vulnerable when we didn't know because *learning something publicly is taking an emotional risk*. It's showing our soft underbellies. How teachers and classmates responded to that exposed vulnerability affected how we felt about school, the subject, and ourselves.

I have visited many classrooms that use wonderful prosocial curriculum, start the day with a welcoming morning meeting, teach reading in an approachable and welcoming way, and then math class feels like it might as well be the year 1953. Kids still watch each other sweat through board work and teachers still needle kids for making "stupid mistakes." In short, we're continuing to give math anxiety to whole new generations of kids.

In Heidi's, Cindy's, and Shawn's classrooms, however, students are expected and encouraged to take mathematical risks. When they do, they are supported, celebrated, and defended. Students are socialized into a mathematical culture in which questioning, innovating, and attempting are highly valued.

Teaching math this way is the honest thing to do because mathematicians are bold and brave risk takers, and we need to convey that idea to kids. A cautious, fearful, obedient, or passive mathematician will not be a mathematician for long. Let's introduce students to risk taking as part of doing math, and let's encourage them to challenge themselves, try new ideas, expose their misunderstandings, and question openly in the safe math climates we create.

MATHEMATICIANS MAKE MISTAKES

*A*s long as people have been looking up, we've wondered how planets and stars move through the night sky. Copernicus, Galileo, and Kepler each brought us significantly closer to understanding celestial motion, but none of them could model the orbits with accuracy. Sir Isaac Newton broke through in 1687, when he invented the math (calculus) and physics (gravity, laws of motion) to describe the orbits of the Sun and Earth, or the Earth and Moon, or any other two-body system. This was an enormous accomplishment, but Newton's curiosity wouldn't let him stop there. He wondered if he could add just one more body so he could model the Sun, Earth, and Moon. Unfortunately, the three-body problem turned out to be much harder. Accurately modeling their motion involves at least eighteen variables, including the position, velocity, and acceleration of each object at any given moment. Newton was able to define the problem, but couldn't solve it and died stumped.

About 200 years later, a thirty-one-year-old French mathematician, Jules-Henri Poincaré, took on the still-unsolved three-body problem. With the cockiness of youth, he promised a solution in a highly publicized mathematics contest. Poincaré was an intuitive mathematician who liked to wonder about big ideas, but he disliked calculating. He decided to approach this messy problem using a strategy we teach our students: solve a simpler problem. Instead of identifying the locations of the bodies with precision, he made small approximations that simplified the math. His innovative and imaginative solution caught the eye of the judges, and he won the prize.

As his solution went to press, however, Poincaré discovered he had made quite a mistake. It turned out those tiny approximations made massive differences when everything started moving. Instead of modeling a stable three-body orbit such as a star, a planet, and a moon, his three bodies would quickly fly apart from one another and hurtle off into space or turn and crash right into one another. Oops.

Poincaré became even more interested in the problem once he realized his methods were flawed. How could such small differences in the setup of the model create such large-scale effects? He had inadvertently discovered an entirely new branch of mathematics, which we now call *chaos theory*. You might have heard of the classic chaos theory example: the *butterfly effect*, whereby a butterfly flapping its wings in China during the formation of a weather system can affect the size and trajectory of a tornado in the United States. In other words, small variations in the initial conditions of a system are amplified and lead to big changes in the outcome. Anyone who plays sports knows this phenomenon to be true: a tiny change in your stance, position, or even the blades of grass under the golf ball can mean the difference between hitting the green or dropping a ball in the water. Chaos theory is now an important and accepted field of mathematics with applications in geology, biology, physics, computer science, sports, meteorology, economics, engineering, finance, and philosophy, and it all came about because of a mistake!

Poincaré's story might be especially public and dramatic, but it's not uncommon. Mathematicians are precise and strive toward perfection, but they also understand that mistakes are vital. A mistake leads to a furrowed brow and a new question, which often lead to really good mathematics. Mathematician Louis Auslander described the guidance of his beloved thesis adviser, Shiing-Shen Chern, who taught him this valuable habit of mind:

> Somehow he conveyed the philosophy that making mistakes was normal and that passing from mistake to mistake to truth was the doing of mathematics. And somehow he also conveyed the understanding that once one began doing mathematics it would naturally flow on and on. Doing mathematics would become like a stream. (Yau 1988)

"Passing from mistake to mistake to truth [is] the doing of mathematics." Indeed. That might be a quote to write on a sticky note and put somewhere you'll see every day. It's true for advanced mathematicians, and it's true for our young mathematicians as well. The process of learning math is messy. Students often lurch through a bunch of misunderstandings while they try out different ideas and actively make sense of mathematics. And—this is a biggie— how we respond to those mistakes is often what separates a negative math classroom from a positive one.

To clarify, there is a big difference between a small computation error and a teachable, interesting, juicy mistake. It is, of course, essential that we teach students how to avoid, check for, and correct computation errors and that we expect students to be precise. In Chapter 5, we'll take a look at several excellent teaching strategies for handling errors in positive, efficient, and appropriate ways. In this chapter, we're talking about mistakes that reveal conceptual misunderstandings.

As a child, I don't remember a big distinction between errors and misunderstandings. The message I internalized was that making mistakes meant I was lazy, careless, stupid, sloppy, or inattentive. Most people I have interviewed for this book, including mathematicians, remember feeling bad about being wrong in math class. We were taught to feel ashamed of mistakes and to aim for the perfect 100 percent.

When I listen to master math teachers, however, they have an entirely different approach to mistakes:

- Shawn Towle eagerly told me, "Now, I know I've got a really good mistake we can talk about!" when a student exposed confusion.
- Marisa Peralta described a student's mistake as "lovely" and said she was "delighted" when it came up.
- Heidi Fessenden and I listened to two students try to formulate an incorrect conjecture. She turned to me afterward and said, "Wasn't that fascinating?!"
- In Jennifer Clerkin Muhammad's fourth-grade class, students arguing about conflicting answers came to her to appeal their cases. She replied, "That's a great dilemma!" smiled, and sent them back to work.
- Justin Solonynka said, "What's really exciting is when a mistake is made, but it seems logical. There's some kernel of truth to it, where, as the teacher, I can say, 'Oh! I see what they're thinking! I see where that's coming from!'"
- One of Debbie Nichols's students changed his mind partway through his explanation because he realized his approach was flawed. Debbie hugged him and told the class, "He is doing *the best* kind of learning right now!"

These math teachers know mistakes are golden opportunities for students to examine and refine their mathematical thinking. To convert these potential learning opportunities to actual learning, these educators teach students how to react to mistakes. It is a rare student who arrives knowing how to turn mistakes—of any kind, in any aspect of life—into productive learning and growth. If we want students to learn from mistakes, we need to teach them how. I wonder if there is a more important disposition we can teach?

Our goal is a three-part one:

1. To teach students to take mistakes in stride.
2. To teach students to keep going when they realize they've made a mistake! They need to get to the bottom of their misunderstandings with tenacity, determination, and curiosity until they understand exactly why their reasoning was flawed.

3. To teach students to make the most of the knowledge and experience they gained by figuring out their mistake. Now they can develop better reasoning and improved methods that yield correct results.

This process is incredibly important, so let's look at an example to bring it to life.

Julie Clark, fifth grade, Talented and Gifted Program, Traverse City, Michigan

"She creates an environment where everybody can speak their mind about math."

In her seventeen years of teaching, Julie Clark has taught every grade from first through eighth and has led teacher workshops for Western Michigan University and TERC. Julie is now the elementary math teacher for Traverse City's Talented and Gifted (TAG) program. Starting in fourth grade, students who qualify for the district-wide program are transported to Central Grade School, a historic building in Old Towne Traverse City, just a few blocks from the shores of Lake Michigan. Math is accelerated in the TAG program, so fourth graders use fifth-grade *Investigations*, and fifth graders use sixth-grade *Connected Mathematics Project* curriculum. Class sizes range from twenty-one to thirty. In this particular fifth-grade section, Julie's twenty-one students were 81 percent white, 14 percent Asian, and 5 percent Latino. When I met them, they were a few months into their second year with Julie.

When she introduced me to her class, Julie shared the story of my mother in the electronics store from Chapter 1. In it, my mom was figuring out the difference between a 4:3 aspect ratio (historic TVs) and a 16:9 one (new TVs). Julie's class was working with ratios, so she pulled this example from the book to explore:

Julie: In the very opening chapter, she actually had ratios. Isn't that cool? That's what we're doing! The ratios she had in her book were 16 to 9 and 4 to 3. So, here's my question. I want you to think before you talk, and I want you to just look at it for yourself, and I want to know, are those equivalent ratios? Take a minute. (She wrote the ratios on the projector and gave students quiet think time.)

$$16:9 \qquad\qquad 4:3$$

Remember: do the problem yourself first! Are these ratios equivalent? Why or why not? What do you anticipate students might think? Why?

Julie: Take a minute and talk at your table.

During this minute, students jumped into debating whether the ratios were equivalent and why. The level of student engagement was high, and students passionately argued their points. Julie circulated and listened in. Most students thought the ratios were not equivalent, but there was some debate. In particular, at Soledad's table, three of the four students thought the ratios were not equivalent, but Soledad was not convinced. After one minute, Julie brought the students back together to talk.

> Julie: So what's interesting is when I looked at this with my other section of fifth graders, it was almost 50–50. Half the class thought yes and half the class thought no. I was curious to see how you guys would approach it. I've got a lot of people that are confident in their answer, and I've got some people who are kind of on the fence. And so I want to hear some thoughts on what are you reasoning through? Soledad, you were kind of thinking things through. Can I call on you? What are you working through right now?

> Soledad: Well, of course, if you were actually doing it, 3 can't go into 16 and make 4, but it's still . . . it's 4 to 3, and it can also be 16 to 9, but it's kind of hard to explain.

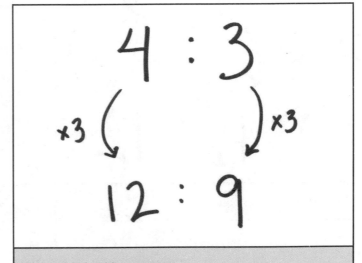

Figure 4.1 *Caleb's argument*

> Julie: So, I heard you say that 3 doesn't go into 16, but I want you to think about with ratios, remember that . . . if it's sixth grade it has to go to sixth grade, and if it's seventh grade it has to go to seventh grade? (Julie was referencing an anchor problem they had solved earlier in the unit.) Remember, with ratios, order matters. Does that change your thinking at all?

> Soledad: Yeah. That's what I was thinking at first . . . (She trailed off, thinking.)

Soledad was obviously working something through but wasn't able to articulate it yet. Julie gave her some time to think and to listen to other perspectives on the problem.

> Julie: Does someone else want to give me their reasoning?

> Caleb: What I thought was that 3 times 3 equals 9, so 4 times 3 would have to equal 16 for it to work.

> Julie: So you're saying it works? They're equivalent?

> Caleb: No. I'm saying it does *not* work because 4 times 3 does not equal 16.

> Julie: OK, so Caleb is saying that if we did this, 3 times 3 is 9, and we're making that 3 times bigger, then what would have to happen here, Caleb? (Pointing to the 4 in 4:3.)

> Caleb: You would have to times by 3 again.

> Julie: OK, to keep your proportion the same?

> Caleb: Right.

> Julie: And what's that?

Students: 12.

Julie: (Recording Caleb's thinking as shown in Figure 4.1.) So can 12 to 9 be the same as 16 to 9?

Students: No.

Julie: They can't be equivalent. Does anyone else have a thought on that so there's some more evidence that we're looking at? Ingrid, what are your thoughts?

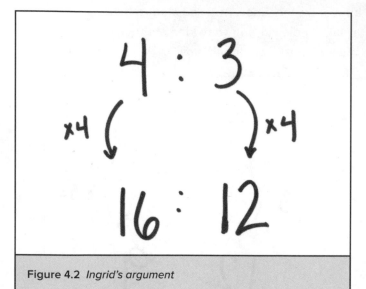

Figure 4.2 *Ingrid's argument*

Ingrid: I kind of did the same but opposite as Caleb. They have to be either both multiplied by the same thing, both by 3 or both by 4. They just *have* to be multiplied by the same number.

Julie: So you're saying if we went the other way, if you multiplied by . . .

Ingrid: 4 . . .

Julie: (Recording Ingrid's thinking as shown in Figure 4.2.) If we multiplied by 4, then this one would be 16, but this would also have to be times 4, which would be 12.

Julie: So you're saying that either of those would be equivalent ratios (connecting 4:3 to 12:9 and 16:12), but this one is not (pointing to 16:9). OK. Vivian?

Vivian: I noticed that nine-sixteenths isn't three-fourths. Like three-fourths would be twelve-sixteenths.

Several students said, "Oh!" listening to Vivian. Thinking about equivalent fractions was a different way to look at the problem and helped students make a connection. We can write Vivian's statement this way:

$$\frac{9}{16} \neq \frac{3}{4} \quad \text{because} \quad \frac{3}{4} = \frac{12}{16}$$

Three different students had now made three different, compelling arguments to explain why the ratios were not equivalent. Throughout this discussion, Soledad was listening carefully and concentrating intently. Julie moved the class deeper into the problem by sharing the TV context, but Soledad was still thinking about why she initially thought the ratios were equivalent. She raised her hand and brought the class back to the relationship between the ratios:

16:9   4:3

Soledad: Of course, you're not multiplying them by the same number, so they're *not* equivalent. But, still, you *are* doing 3^2 and 4^2.

There were audible gasps in the room, including Julie's and mine. Several students said, "Oh!" and, "Oh, yeah!" Suddenly, many of us understood why the ratios looked like they *should* be equivalent. The numbers 3 and 9 and 4 and 16 are associated in our minds because each set is that special type of factor and multiple: they're squares. No wonder our intuition is a little fooled by this problem!

Julie: I'm so glad you brought that up! It would be fun to investigate whether you can square ratios!

I was struck by Soledad's handling of her mistake and what the interchanges revealed about the climate Julie has created. Soledad started the lesson as the lone voice of dissent at her table group. Julie asked her to share her thinking with the whole class, right in the midst of her confusion, which she did. Soledad then spent seven or eight minutes listening to other approaches to the problem, realizing she was wrong, and working hard to figure out her mistake. Finally, she insisted on seeing her confusion all the way through to resolution—to the source of her mistake—and shared that thinking with her peers.

What Soledad did is exactly what we want all students to do. She took her mistake in stride, and then dug as far down as she needed to go to make sense out of this problem. Her confusion and resultant thinking helped move the whole class forward, mathematically. The class was now in deep, conceptual territory where students were building meaningful understanding of what ratios and proportions are and what they are not. Students even came in during recess to explore and test conjectures about squaring ratios.

I stopped by Soledad's table to ask her about making mistakes in math class:

Tracy: Soledad, I would love to know what it was like to have your whole table think it was one thing and you thought it was something else.

Soledad: Well, that happens sometimes, and now I see why I was wrong. And sometimes that happens, and sometimes I'm wrong, and sometimes I'm right, but I mean, I respect that they have different answers than me.

Tracy: What does it feel like, to be the only one arguing for something? Are you comfortable with that? Do you feel like it takes bravery, or does it feel normal?

Soledad: It feels kind of like . . .

Susie: That's just part of math. (With a smile.)

Soledad: Sometimes you might be afraid if it's a popular person, and they're not thinking at all, but, really, if they come up with an answer and that's what they think, and if I come up with an answer and that's what I think, then we can come up with different answers. Whoever gets it right and whoever gets it wrong . . . really, it feels kind of normal. It's not like it's out of the ordinary.

Tracy: What do you think Ms. Clark has done to make it feel normal, to make you feel safe to do that?

Soledad: Well, she creates an environment where everybody can speak their mind about math. She won't say, "One centimeter is equal to one millimeter and that's it. You can't say anything about it and I'm right." She knows that we are all going to make mistakes and that's OK because we are here to learn.

Tracy: And if it turns out you're wrong about something?

Soledad: Well, I just learn from it.

Tracy: Awesome. Were your tablemates respectful when you had a different idea?

Soledad: Yeah.

Tracy: What language did they use?

Soledad: Susie said, "I say 'no,' but I see *why* you said that."

Tracy: Oh! Who taught you to say that, Susie?

Susie: Ms. Clark has us, when somebody has an answer, if you think it's wrong, you have to say *why* you think it's wrong, and also why you think *they* think it's right. At first, I thought it was right, too, so I kind of thought why she was thinking it was right.

Tracy: Oh, so you were trying to understand her thinking?

Susie: Yes.

Tracy: Great job. Soledad, I was really interested when you pointed out they're square numbers. I had never noticed that before. I think maybe that's why half the other class and lots of kids in this class looked at it right away and thought they were equivalent, because those four numbers are kind of family. They relate to each other. So that was a new way for me to think about that problem, even though it's in my book! So, thank you. Do you think it works to square ratios?

Soledad: No, because squaring different numbers makes it so you're multiplying them by different numbers, and the proportion doesn't stay the same.

Language That Creates Safety

Let's step back and look at the language in this classroom, starting with excerpts from Julie:

"I was curious to see how you guys would approach it."

"I've got a lot of people that are confident in their answer, and I've got some people who are kind of on the fence. And so I want to hear some thoughts."

"What are you reasoning through?"

"You were kind of thinking things through. Can I call on you? What are you working through right now?"

"Does someone else want to give me their reasoning?"

"Does anyone else have a thought on that so there's some more evidence that we're looking at? Ingrid, what are your thoughts?"

"I'm so glad you brought that up! It would be fun to investigate whether you can square ratios!"

I notice:

- Julie *started the conversation by asking for thoughts and reasoning.* She certainly gets to the answer, and correct answers matter in her class, but she frames discussions around reasoning and mathematical arguments, rather than answers alone. Instead of launching this discussion by asking, *What did you get?* or asking a yes/no question like, *Are they equivalent?* and then trying to work backward to students' thinking, Julie told them she was curious about their approaches, thinking, and reasoning, and opened with, *I want to hear some thoughts. What are you reasoning through?* There is a huge difference in tone and emphasis between those opening questions. Ever since visiting Julie, I've set myself a goal to launch with a thought-oriented opening question, rather than an answer-focused one, when discussing problems with classes. The small change in language is a specific, tangible goal for myself, but it's really transforming the tone of the discussions. Something to try, perhaps?

- Julie frames *thinking as an ongoing process.* "Thinking things through" and "working through" are phrases she uses regularly. Finishing the problem and circling the answer is *not* the end of the thinking. Because of her emphasis, students—even those who answered the question correctly from the beginning—stayed engaged, gained new insights, and made new connections throughout the discussion, adding depth to their understanding. Nobody checked out.

- Many of her questions are *open ended,* which pave the way toward quality discussions. *Does someone else want to give me their reasoning?* is an invitation for students to contribute fully to the conversation, rather than to fill in the blank at the end of a cloze-style math question.

- Julie is *purposeful about students sharing methods and strategies.* She gathers different approaches to problems so students can benefit from hearing each other's perspectives, and so she can hear what students are thinking. She continues collecting ideas until students have enough evidence to make connections and draw conclusions and stops once they do. Students are not talking for the sake of talking.

- Julie's *posture, language, and facial expressions* (sincere interest, smiles, intense listening, approachable body language) remained encouraging throughout the discussion. She is genuinely curious about students' thinking and about mathematics, and that curiosity sets the tone for the class. She does more than expect active listening; she models it.

- Julie creates situations in which students engage in *productive struggle.* She does not rescue students from mistakes or help too much. She knows that students must work through the mathematics to become patient, resilient problem solvers and capable mathematicians.

Let's turn to Julie's students' language:

"Now I see why I was wrong."

"Sometimes that happens, and sometimes I'm wrong, and sometimes I'm right."

"I respect that they have different answers than me."

"If they come up with an answer and that's what they think, and if I come up with an answer and that's what I think, then we can come up with different answers."

"Whoever gets it right and whoever gets it wrong . . . really, it feels kind of normal."

"That's just part of math."

"She creates an environment where everybody can speak their mind about math."

"We are all going to make mistakes and that's OK because we are here to learn."

"And if it turns out you're wrong about something?" "Well, I just learn from it."

"I say 'no,' but I see why you said that."

"Mrs. Clark has us, when somebody has an answer, if you think it's wrong, you have to say why you think it's wrong and also why you think they think it's right."

"At first I thought it was right too, so I kind of thought why she was thinking it was right."

These students have internalized some really important understandings about doing mathematics:

- Different people will sometimes come up with different answers, and then they'll need to do some reckoning.
- Mistakes are part of learning, and their job is to learn.
- It's essential to figure out *why* flawed reasoning was flawed.
- They need to understand other people's thinking, not just their own.
- Disagreeing does not mean disrespect.
- Part of doing math is "speaking your mind" about math.

Soledad is a student who has stayed with me, long after I returned home from Traverse City. She was the only Latina student in the class, and a girl, and the lone voice of dissent during a phase of school in which students think about social standing a lot. As the discussion continued, evidence mounted that her initial answer was wrong. Yet, she was perfectly comfortable and confident speaking out and stuck with the problem until she was satisfied. I want all our students to share Soledad's attitude to learning from mistakes, in math class and in life.

Soledad was a few months into her second year with Julie when I met her, so Julie's classroom climate and norms had really penetrated and solidified. Soledad had seen Julie handle hundreds of student mistakes constructively and knew from experience that making mistakes and learning from them is normal. Passing from mistake to mistake to truth is the doing of mathematics, right?

Let's turn to a different classroom to see another example of a teacher handling mistakes constructively, this time by squeezing lots of learning out of a good mistake by taking it up with the whole class. A few students made the mistake, but she gave all students the opportunity to seek truth from it.

Heidi Fessenden, second grade

"Ayoka's mistake is such an easy one to make, and I knew many kids would make it."

We met Heidi in Chapter 3, "Mathematicians Take Risks," in which we saw her support Alvin when he tried something new. This example is from a few months later. Students were constructing rectangular buildings from snap cubes and then calculating the total number of cubes in the buildings. Students were using the mathematical language of *rows* and *columns,* as well as the everyday language of *rooms* on each *floor* of a *building.* Mathematically, Heidi was nudging students toward skip-counting rectangular arrays and developing early ideas of multiplication by looking at the number of cubes per row, the number of rows, and the total number of cubes. She was also building early foundations of algebra, especially functions, by giving students opportunities to notice, to explore, and to extend patterns as the buildings gained and lost floors.

For this lesson, students were working with buildings that had five rooms on each floor. Heidi held up a building with three floors and asked students what they knew about the building (Figure 4.3):

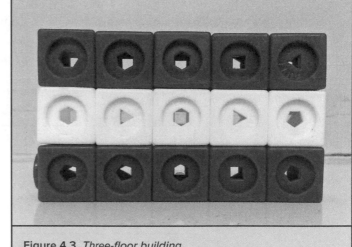

Figure 4.3 *Three-floor building*

> Mabel: There's three rows, and there's five cubes in each row.
>
> Heidi: I want someone to tell us what Mabel just said. Mabel, call on someone who can repeat what you just said.
>
> Alicia: Mabel said there are three floors and there are five rooms, five cubes, on each floor.
>
> Heidi: Alicia, do you want to call on someone to tell us something else? (Alicia called on Malcolm.)
>
> Malcolm: When there are two floors in the building, there are ten rooms.
>
> (As he talked, Heidi smiled and pointed to a posted sentence frame: *When there is one floor*

in the building, there are ___ rooms. When there are two floors in the building, there are ___ rooms.)

Heidi: Wiggle your thumb if you think he's right, if you agree. He said, "When there are two floors in the building, there are ten rooms."

(Most students wiggled their thumbs.)

Heidi: We're going to hear from one more person. Malcolm, will you choose the person? (He called on Jaleesa.)

Jaleesa: I have something to add about what he said. It's about if you had more. If you had more, you could just count by fives to try to figure it out. Instead of making a whole bunch of stairs, that will take a long time, you could just count by five if you knew it was five.

Heidi: Would you say to us what you would say if you were counting? (Pointed to each row as Jaleesa counted, and then gestured to each imaginary row in the air above the building as Jaleesa kept going.)

Jaleesa: I would just say 5, 10, 15, 20, 25, 30, 35, 40, 45, 50, 55, 60, 65, 70, 75, 80, 85, 90, 95, 100.

Heidi: Whoa! Does anyone want to respond to that? Jaleesa, would you choose someone who hasn't spoken yet? (Jaleesa called on Jackie.)

Jackie: I want to add to something to what Jaleesa said. It has fifteen. It has three columns.

Heidi: When they go this way (gesturing at the rows), are they rows or columns?

Jackie: Columns.

Heidi took a minute to review the difference between rows and columns, including acting out columns holding up buildings and shuffling side to side to make rows. Once Jackie was clear on rows and columns and all students had another chance to review the terminology, Heidi turned students' attention toward a table she'd written on chart paper:

# OF FLOORS	# OF ROOMS
1	5
	10
3	15
	20
5	

10	

Heidi: So, take a look at this. This is a table about this building. Some of the numbers are left out of this table. So let's just look at the table and see what you can tell us about this building from looking at the table. Joseph, I'm going to call on one other person, and then I'm going to call on you to tell me one thing you know from looking at the table. Luella, tell me one thing you know from looking at the table.

Luella: When there are two floors in the building, there are ten rooms. (Heidi filled in the missing 2 in the second row of the chart.)

Heidi: Joseph?

Joseph: When there are five floors in the building, there are twenty-five rooms.

Heidi: Wow, Joseph is already filling in our chart. (Heidi filled in the missing 25 in the fifth row of the chart.)

Heidi called on Ayoka, who came to the front, picked up a marker, and filled in all the remaining blanks like this:

# OF FLOORS	# OF ROOMS
1	5
2	10
3	15
4	20
5	25

10	30

Heidi: Let's have everybody take a look at the chart and see if you agree or disagree with what Ayoka did.

Ayoka: I agree with myself because 5, 10, 15, 20, 25, 30 and 1, 2, 3, 4, 5. (Pointing down each column as she talked.)

Heidi: Two people have something they want to say about what Ayoka did.

(Wait time. Hands steadily went up.)

A few students: I agree.

Heidi: You agree with Ayoka? OK. (Smiling.)

(Another student shook her head.)

Heidi: Oh. Some people disagree with Ayoka. (Smiling.)

Ayoka: I did it right!

Heidi: She did it right, she says. (Smiling.)

One of the most important things Heidi did here was to keep her face, body language, voice, and words neutral. Students are used to teachers hinting at which answer is correct, either by changing tone, squinting at errors, smiling only at correct answers, or giving all manners of winks and nudges. We want students to determine whether the math is correct by engaging with the mathematics, not eyeing the teacher for clues. Experienced math teachers have mastered the art of keeping their faces curious and interested—but neutral—so students can't use them as answer keys. As Heidi said, "I like to look for opportunities to engage my students in dialogue about math disagreements. If they don't know what I think is the 'right answer,' they have to pay attention to the different arguments and think about what makes sense to them, and that is exactly what we want math students to be doing!"

Jackie: I understand that she . . . I agree . . . I agree with her because this is kind of counting by ones (points to the 1, 2, 3, 4, 5, 10 column), and this is counting by fives (pointing to the 5, 10, 15, 20, 25, 30, column).

Heidi: OK, you agree with that. Does anyone see anything they disagree with? Jackie told us one thing she agreed with. Does anyone see something they disagree with?

Malcolm: When there are 10 floors in the building, there are 50 rooms.

(Heidi raised her eyebrows in surprise and looked around the room for reactions. Students signaled with their hands, some agreeing and some disagreeing.)

Heidi: OK, so what are we going to do? Ayoka says if there are 10 floors, there are 30 rooms, but Malcolm says if there are 10 floors, there are 50 rooms. Naomi, what do you think?

(Heidi added Malcolm's answer and a question mark to the bottom of the chart.)

10	30? 50?

Naomi: I agree with 30, not with 50, because if you count by fives . . . count by ones . . . if you count by ones . . .

(Heidi pointed to the floors column of the chart.)

Heidi: Here?

Naomi: Yes. So 1, 2, 3, 4, 5 . . .

Heidi: So, we got up to five. What happens after five?

(Naomi pointed to the side of the chart.)

Heidi: You want me to go here?

Naomi: Yes.

Heidi nodded in recognition because she had done an example like this with her class before. To the right side of the table, she wrote the missing floors in an inset.

# OF FLOORS	# OF ROOMS
1	5
2	10
3	15
4	20
5	25

6	
7	
8	
9	

10	30? 50?

Heidi: So what would happen then, Naomi? We were at twenty-five when we got to five, so how did you get thirty for ten?

(Naomi was thinking intently, and then her face lit up as she figured the problem out.)

Naomi: She thought it was six!

Heidi: She thought it was six! Do you remember the space? Yesterday, we talked about the space, where we skipped a bunch of numbers? So if we counted by fives, let's do it altogether.

(Heidi pointed at the number of floors—1, 2, 3, 4, 5, 6, 7, 8, 9, 10—as students counted by fives.)

Students: 5, 10, 15, 20, 25, 30, 35, 40, 45, 50.

(Heidi was standing with her finger pointing at 10.)

Heidi: So what did we get to when we counted by fives all the way to ten floors?

Students: Fifty!

Heidi, to Ayoka: What do you think? (Heidi cocked her head to the side and put her hand to her chin, with pure curiosity on her face.)

Ayoka: No.

Heidi: You still think it's thirty?

Ayoka: Yes.

Heidi: Do you want to use some cubes and see what you think? See if you can build it? Or, Ayoka, it might be faster to draw a picture. Do you want to draw a picture?

Ayoka: Yes.

Heidi: Do you want to do it on paper or on the board?

Ayoka: On the board.

Heidi: OK. I'll make you some space. We're going to go on, OK, and you can draw it and report back to us.

Heidi had wondered if Ayoka was confused by the conventions issue of the blank space in the chart, the math version of an ellipse in writing. She spent a little time exploring the convention of the table to see whether that cleared things up. Naomi was also confused but was able to work through the problem in the moment. Ayoka, though, was unswayed by the work Heidi did with the class and still believed the ten-story building would have thirty rooms.

Heidi knows her students' personalities well and told me, "Ayoka is stubborn and does things very quickly without stopping to think. I don't think she was really hearing, or making sense of, what other kids were saying. She just wanted to be right! If I told her she was wrong, she would hate that! But taking her seriously, listening to her, and letting her keep working on it would make her feel important. It was more likely she would find her own mistake and own it."

All students need opportunities to make sense of their mistakes for themselves and own the resultant learning. For Ayoka, who is fantastic, bold, and spirited but sometimes confrontational or defiant, it is especially important that her teachers give her opportunities to learn from her mistakes with dignity.

Heidi moved on with the class, introducing a lesson in which students were building different-shaped buildings with five rooms on the first floor. Ayoka worked hard on her drawing, but rather than draw a rectangular array with straight lines, she drew each room individually. By the time she finished her building, it was cockeyed and very hard to read. She counted the floors and announced, "I got 70!" She went back and counted again, this time saying, "I got 60!" Heidi checked in with her and said, "I want you and Malcolm to work on this together."

At this point, Heidi gave Ayoka cubes as well. The problem had started with an abstract chart. When Ayoka was confused, Heidi suggested she draw, because drawing the building is one step less abstract than using a table. When Ayoka still wasn't figuring her mistake out, Heidi removed another layer of abstraction and gave her the concrete tools, as well as the support of a peer. The two kids got to work together, drawing, building, and sometimes arguing.

Heidi's scheduled math time was divided by specials, so students had to pause their work and head to gym. During her planning time, Heidi looked over Ayoka and Malcolm's work, thought about the lesson and how many students had agreed with Ayoka, and decided to have the whole class investigate this problem. When I asked Heidi about her decision later on, she wrote:

I wanted to dig into the convention of the table in a way that would make the students really think about what it meant. Ayoka's mistake is such an easy one to make, and I knew many kids would make it. I wanted them to understand what that space in the table meant, that it was something to slow down and pay attention to. I thought if we spent more time on it, thinking critically about it, that would help cement it, instead of rushing through. If I just explained it to them, they might not remember what it meant. But if we had a discussion involving a disagreement, it was more likely to make sense to them, and they were more likely to remember it later.

Also, looking for patterns, the way Ayoka did, is an important math skill. That's what you do in algebra—you see a pattern and you use it to figure out what will happen later. This is a basic skill that I wanted to focus on, and Ayoka and Malcolm's disagreement was the perfect opportunity to highlight it.

Heidi took up this problem both because of what Ayoka did wrong and what she did right, didn't she?

Heidi reproduced the table on a piece of paper, leaving the bottom half blank for student work. When students returned from gym, she gathered them on the rug:

Heidi: I was thinking a lot about the conversation we were having before gym. We were talking about how many rooms this building would have when it had ten floors. Ayoka thought it would have thirty rooms, and a lot of kids agreed with her. Right? Can one person tell me why do you think that a building like that with ten floors might have thirty rooms? Who can tell us one reason?

Mabel: Because it says 5, 10, 15, 20, 25, 30.

Heidi: Who wants to respond to Mabel? Mabel, pick someone. (Mabel picked Jaleesa.)

Jaleesa: I know it was fifty because sometimes five and ten have something in common. Like they always, they not always, like sometimes they always like together like after 5 is 10 and 5 plus 5 is 10, and 5 and 10 have a lot in common. I mean, yeah, 10 and 5 have a lot in common.

That is a word-for-word transcription, and a perfect example of how hard it can be to follow a student's thinking! Watch carefully to see how Heidi handled it:

Heidi: So, are you agreeing with Mabel, or are you disagreeing with Mabel?

Jaleesa: I'm disagreeing with Mabel. Well, I know that it goes 5, 10, 15, 20, 25, 30, but I'm disagreeing with her.

Heidi: So, say again what you're thinking about five and ten have a lot in common. Did you use something you know about five floors to figure out ten floors?

Jaleesa: Yeah. Because 5 plus 5 equals 10, and 50 plus 50 equals 100.

Heidi: So you did this 5, and you said 5 plus 5 is 10, right here. (Pointed to the 5 and 10 in the number of floors column, then wrote 5 + 5 = 10 underneath the table.)

# OF FLOORS	# OF ROOMS
1	5
2	10
3	15
4	20
5	25

10	30? 50?

$$5 + 5 = 10$$

Heidi: And then you said . . .

Jaleesa: 50 plus 50 equals 100.

Heidi: Where did you get the 50 from?

Jaleesa: That 50, where the 30 is. (Pointed to the "30? 50?" cell of the table.)

Heidi: OK. How does that 50 connect to this? (Pointed to 5 + 5 = 10.)

Jaleesa: Fifty connects to 10 because 50 plus 50 equals 100. One hundred has 10 in it, so that's how I knew that it's going to be 50.

(Heidi thought for several seconds, formulating her next question. She also wrote 50 + 50 = 100 on the board.)

Heidi: How did this (pointed to 5 + 5 = 10 and 50 + 50 = 100) help you get that 50? (Pointed to "50?" in the chart.)

Jaleesa: Because if you erase the zero inside of the 100 it's 10, and if you erase the zero in the two 50s it would be 5 + 5 = 10.

(Heidi waited for several seconds before turning to the whole class.)

Heidi: What do you guys think? Do you understand what Jaleesa said?

(A few students nodded.)

Heidi: I don't understand it yet.

I love this moment! Heidi engaged Jaleesa for a long time, asking a series of clarifying questions to try to understand her thinking. Heidi told me later, "I didn't dismiss her because I didn't understand her, or brush past what she was saying. I have faith that she is making sense. That's a cornerstone of my teaching—that kids are always making sense for themselves." Heidi showed so much respect for Jaleesa by trying to make sense, too.

In this case, it's really hard to understand Jaleesa's thinking. She had some ideas about this problem, place value, and the relationships between numbers, but exactly what those ideas were was not clear. She may have gotten the right answer because she was thinking about doubling and has some intuition about what five and ten really do have in common but doesn't know how to explain it. Or, she may have found the right answer because this particular example involved 5, 10, and 50, and 50 was already on the board. What if the building had four cubes per floor and nine floors? Would her method work? And what, exactly, is her method, anyway?

Heidi has the security to admit when she doesn't know or isn't following a student's thinking. She was not at all concerned about "looking dumb," even with me as a (then, relatively unfamiliar) guest observing her. It's important to recognize that *all* math teachers get confused sometimes, either when we're trying to solve a problem ourselves or when we're trying to follow a student's unfamiliar or convoluted thought process. Through her example, Heidi teaches us how to handle these inevitable moments. She is focused, but relaxed and comfortable splashing around in these murky waters. She is confident she and her students can wade through confusion and emerge on the other side, hopefully with new understanding and insights about math, and about the ways her students think about math.

By sticking with Jaleesa and admitting when she didn't understand, Heidi modeled the grappling we need students to do, along with the perseverance we want. The sentence, "I don't understand it yet," is a fantastic one: *yet* might be the most powerful word in all of education. How meaningful for students to see their teacher work to understand!

Heidi: I don't understand it yet. (To Jaleesa) Do you want to call on someone?

Tabreeya: About Jaleesa's thing? I understand that she used 5 plus 5 equals 10.

Heidi: To get here, right? This is 5 floors and this is 10 floors, and 10 is a double of 5.

5	25

10	30? 50?

Tabreeya: Yeah. And I think it's 50, because I counted on my fingers by fives.

(Long wait time while Heidi thought.)

Heidi: Jaleesa said that 10 is 5 plus 5. Right? Can you use that? If you use this 5 to get this

> 10, is there anything you can do with this number (pointed to 25), to find out what goes here? (Pointed to the cell with "30? 50?" in it.)
>
> Jaleesa: I can use 25 to get to 50 because, if I already know that's 25, and then, if I take away the 2 and put the 5 from 25 and put a 0, then it's going to be 50.

Ah! Now things are a little clearer. It's still not evident how Jaleesa solved the problem, but we can tell she has significant misunderstandings. By staying with Jaleesa, involving the class, and asking more questions, Heidi was able to work these misunderstandings toward the surface. Ayoka isn't the only student who needs more time with this problem:

> Heidi: Mm hmm. I see. OK. All right. I think it probably will help you guys figure it out if you either build the building, or you write down how many there are on each floor. Ayoka thinks there are thirty rooms when there are ten floors, and Malcolm thinks there are fifty rooms when there are ten floors. You've got to figure out, who do you agree with? So, what I did was I made this table on this piece of paper, and then I asked this question: "How many rooms will there be if the building has 10 floors?" There's some space for you to figure it out. I want you to try to figure it out without the cubes. See if there's something you can do with numbers to figure it out without the cubes. See, do you agree with Ayoka, or do you agree with Malcolm? Or maybe you don't agree with Ayoka or Malcolm! Maybe you think it's something else. You might draw rooms, you might write words, you might write numbers that you used to count, you might write equations. I don't know. But I'm going to ask you to work on this for about seven or eight minutes, and then I'm going to ask you to show somebody sitting near you what you did, and what you're thinking about, and who you agree with.

Students were highly engaged as they got to work. Heidi circulated, seeing which students attempted the problem more abstractly and which students she should direct toward manipulatives. After working independently and then sharing with a partner, students returned to the rug to discuss their findings. Heidi had three students share their approaches, demonstrating a nice range of strategies.

Alicia counted by fives:

1	5
2	10
3	15
4	20
5	25
6	30
7	35
8	40
9	45
10	50

Jackie drew a star to represent each room, and then counted the stars by ones. She said she found thirty rooms in all. She and Heidi looked at her paper, and Jackie had only counted six floors. Heidi nudged her toward more efficient strategies such as drawing a grid instead of stars (Figure 4.4), so she could keep track more easily.

Luella doubled twenty-five and solved it by breaking it into pieces:

$$20 + 20 = 40$$

$$40 + 5 = 45$$

$$45 + 5 = 50$$

Students wanted to discuss *how* Luella solved 25 + 25, but Heidi pushed them to discuss *why* Luella would want to double 25 in the first place. She asked, "What was the reason?" She returned to the picture she'd drawn during Jackie's share. When Hafiz pointed them out, Heidi highlighted the two 5-by-5 arrays so students could better see how Luella used doubling (see Figure 4.5).

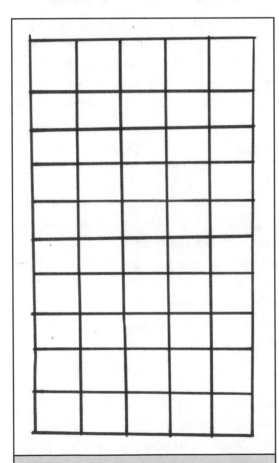

Figure 4.4 *Heidi's representation of a ten-story building with five rooms on each floor for Jackie*

Figure 4.5 *Heidi helped students see Luella's doubling strategy with this representation.*

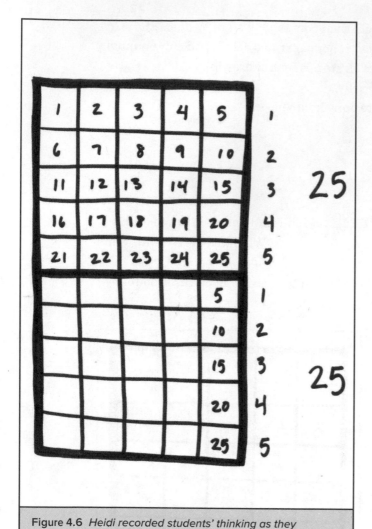

Figure 4.6 *Heidi recorded students' thinking as they connected numbers with the visual representation of the building.*

Several students had lightbulbs go off when they looked at the picture, and they discussed it actively. In particular, Winifred said, "I know why she doubled 25! This is 25 and this is 25 (pointing to the two halves of the picture), so she did 25 + 25 = 50." As Winifred counted, Heidi labeled her representation with numbers (Figure 4.6).

I was especially pleased to see Jaleesa and Ayoka highly engaged in this discussion, mulling over the mistakes they made, and the new approaches they'd just seen.

Responsive Planning—Students' Mistakes as Teacher's Guides

When Ayoka first made her mistake, Heidi had a choice to make. She could sweep the mistake under the rug and carry on with the day's lesson, or she could investigate it. She opted to investigate it and see whether she could clear it up by addressing the conventions of the table. When Ayoka was unconvinced, Heidi gave her an opportunity to make sense of the problem a different way. When Heidi saw Ayoka still struggling with the problem and thought about other students who had agreed with her, she decided to give the whole class the opportunity to explore this mistake.

During that exploration, Jaleesa also revealed significant misunderstanding, and Jackie lost track of the problem. Taken together, these three mistakes ended up driving Heidi's math instruction for the day. By the end of the lesson, after many twists and turns, several students understood quite a bit more about the relationships between the number of rooms per floor, the number of floors, and the total number of rooms. They were building foundations of patterns, multiplication, and algebraic functions.

Of course, not all students had figured out the problem by the end of the discussion. Heidi collected their work and looked through it in a quiet moment so she could think about next steps. If just a few students were confused, she could work with them individually. If there was a really interesting mistake, or patterns among the misunderstandings she saw, she could use those examples as her next teaching opportunity. For all students, she needed to think about a new problem to pose so students could apply this session's learning. Perhaps Luella's reasoning would catch on among those who were ready. Alicia's skip-counting method was a good next step for students such as Jackie who were still counting by ones. Students definitely needed another crack at this sort of problem to cement their understanding and improve their methods.

Math teachers generally have plenty of guides for planning, including standards and curriculum. Student mistakes can be the most valuable planning guides around; however, if we turn toward rich mistakes, invest time to understand them, and give students meaningful opportunities to make sense. We respect students as mathematical thinkers and guide them responsively as they move from mistake to mistake to truth.

Making Mistakes and Equity

On the first school day one September, I observed a group of five eighth-grade students working through a challenge in Shawn Towle's classroom. One boy, Dash, brushed his Justin Bieber hair to the side and made a joke. Maisie, the only girl in the group, twirled her long hair around her fingers and giggled. They settled down to work, trying to find all the ways they could pack twenty-four cubes into a rectangular box. Maisie didn't seem particularly confident but was holding her own. She threw out an idea about the factors of twenty-four being involved.

"I think they're all going to be factors of 24. Like, 8 by 3 and 6 by . . . um . . . ugh. I still don't . . . know my multiplication facts." Maisie cocked her head to the side, flipped her hair, and said, "I'm so bad at math." She slumped lower in her chair and quieted down.

A few minutes later, Dash and another boy were trying to reconcile their different results. Dash found his mistake and said to his group, "I'm wrong." He looked at his work again. He nodded, "You're right. I'm sorry. You were right all along. OK, cool." He seemed perfectly comfortable making a mistake in public.

I approached the two of them and said to Maisie, "I noticed something. When you made a mistake, you said you were bad at math, but when he made a mistake, he just moved on."

Dash said, "She *always* does that! The PE teacher was on her about that in volleyball the other day. She always says she's bad at things when she messes up!" Maisie agreed and told me she had to work on not putting herself down.

Driving home, I found myself remembering one of my early teaching observations. In the late 1990s, I taught extracurricular science to children in a range of schools. I noticed a consistent pattern when working with first and second graders and electrical circuits. Pretty much everybody had trouble connecting wires to bulb holders because the alligator clips were difficult for little hands to open. Almost every girl who struggled to connect her wire sighed, looked down, and mumbled, "I can't do it." Almost every boy who struggled to connect his wire grew irate, shoved his circuit at me and said, "Mine's broken! You gave me a broken one!" These are generalizations, to be sure, but there was a clear pattern to me. So often, when girls and women make mistakes, they let the mistakes define their identity: "I'm so bad at math." "I suck at this." "I can't do it." "I'll never get it."

Many boys also struggle with making mistakes, and there is certainly a gender story with boys and math. If society says that boys are good at math, how is the boy who struggles at math supposed to feel? Nevertheless, in our culture, boys seem to have more freedom to make mistakes. They're entitled to fail and expected to dust themselves off, learn something, and keep going. If girls and women are going to succeed in science, technology, engineering, and mathematics (STEM), they are going to have to learn how to be wrong.

Fear of looking stupid by making mistakes can play an outsized role for students of color and emergent bilingual students. For example, black mathematician Fern Hunt, who was a trailblazer when she earned her PhD in 1978, spoke about her relationship with mistakes in an interview for Claudia Henrion's book *Women in Mathematics: The Addition of Difference* (1997, 219):

> Willingness to look bad, to be wrong, is very difficult . . . Things would have happened a lot faster if I had been more confident about that. It took a very, very long time, and I'm definitely better than I was, but I still have reticence. You can't really make good things happen unless you make a certain number of mistakes. And you might as well go through them right away.

Dr. Hunt went on to talk about the additional pressure she felt as a black woman:

> If you make a mistake, then some people are likely to say, "Well that just goes to prove how stupid 'they' are." That's unendurable. Nobody wants to add to the stereotype.

Unendurable. I first came across this passage quite some time ago, but that heartbreaking word has stayed with me ever since. It so completely describes the enormous pressure she was under, and the aching burden we must lift from our students. We must make misunderstanding, struggle, confusion, and mistakes more than endurable; they need to be familiar states of being. When we approach student confusion in a positive way and explore student mistakes in an emotionally safe climate, like Julie and Heidi do, we can teach students this much larger life lesson of working right through the mistake to the learning on the other side. Dr. Hunt described how hamstrung she was by her fear of making mistakes. We must remove this limitation, especially on our math students who are most susceptible to stereotype threat.

Incidentally, I happened to visit Shawn's class on the very last day of that same school year in June, 180 classes after I first watched Maisie and Dash work together. As I headed down the hallway to drop off my visitor's badge after class, I found myself walking alongside Maisie. I asked her about that early mistake, which she remembered clearly. She laughed, embarrassed by her reaction, or maybe by her early flirtations with Dash, who had lost his appeal by June. I asked Maisie if she still felt the same way when she made mistakes in math class. She said, "No, not at all. Now I just make a mistake, figure out what went wrong, learn from it, and move on." She smiled at me. I was heartened by the change in her after just one year in a positive math classroom. I wished her luck. She smiled, and I watched her head off down the hallway, ready for high school.

MATHEMATICIANS
ARE PRECISE

*B*rian Conrey, director of the American Institute of Mathematics, described what it feels like to do mathematics:

Part of it is trying to do something that nobody has done before. In that sense you're an adventurer, an explorer, and you get to go somewhere maybe that nobody has been, and so you certainly have that kind of a feel about it. There's also the feel of being an artist. While you're doing math you feel like you're being creative and you're trying to combine things in a new way and get a different perspective on things or see things in a new light, so there's definitely part of that. And it's part science, just the exactness and the precision and being careful and paying attention to details and making sure that everything goes right, and there's a certain amount of satisfaction in that. I think when you combine all these things together, it produces something fairly amazing. (Cherniwchan, Ghassemi, and Keating 2009)

I love that Conrey talked about the adventurous and creative aspects of mathematics, which have largely been absent from our classrooms. It is far beyond time to embrace investigation, curiosity, and dynamism as essential components of math teaching. Contrary to what articles about "the math wars" would have us believe, however, correct answers matter in the inquiry-based math classroom. We must end the false dichotomies of process and product, of constructivism and correctness. Math without inquiry is lifeless, but math without rigor is aimless. There is no tension between teaching students how to solve problems accurately and efficiently and teaching students how to formulate conjectures, critique reasoning, develop mathematical arguments, use multiple representations, think flexibly, and focus on conceptual understanding.

As Professor Conrey described, attending to detail is an essential and wonderful element of mathematics, making math class a perfect opportunity to develop students' mental discipline. In this chapter, we're going to look at a series of classroom examples so you can gather positive, supportive strategies to teach this habit of mind. Once you build a framework for thinking about mathematical rigor, you'll notice that every teacher in this book demands clear, clean, and correct mathematics from his or her students.

Before we jump into classroom examples, I want to bring a little precision to this word, well, *precision*. The writers of the Common Core State Standards chose the phrase "attend to precision" for Mathematical Practice Standard 6, and it's a meaningful phrase if we're using precision in the colloquial sense. In science, precision has a narrower definition, referring to the "repeatability" of results. To give a full picture of how good their results are, scientists and mathematicians draw from a whole host of terms, which are sprinkled throughout the Common Core practice and National Council of Teachers of Mathematics process standards. They're important, and we need to understand them to grasp this disposition of mathematicians. Here are the biggies—a bunch of related ideas with subtle but important distinctions:

- **Accuracy**. How close are we to the true answer(s)? In school, accurate is usually what we mean when we say "correct."
- **Appropriateness**. How good of an answer do we need? Will an estimate do, or do we need something more exact? Conversely, is our answer artificially exact? Can we realistically space carrot seeds 1.82 centimeters apart? Can we have "4 remainder 5" vans? Does this answer make good common sense? What's the context?
- **Specificity**. Details matter in problems and answers. What units are we using? What are the scales on those axes? Which kinds of numbers will work in this function? Did the question specify what shape the containers need to be? Be exact.
- **Clarity**. What do you mean? Students need to be clear about terms, explanations, and representations so others understand their conjectures, questions, and arguments. Clarity is where appropriate use of math vocabulary, logically sequenced explanations, and organized written work come into play. Can you show us where Luis's apples are in

your representation? What do you mean, "I timesed it"? Can you please label your graph so we know what you're talking about?

- **Rigor**. Did you question your assumptions? Did you adopt other perspectives? Did you look for other solutions? Did you try to prove yourself wrong? Did you verify your results by solving the problem a different way?
- **Thoroughness**. How careful and focused is your work? How disciplined and thoughtful is your reasoning? Did you take your time? Did you think about the question carefully before getting started? Are your answers and supporting arguments complete? Did you reread the question to make sure you answered it fully? Have you overlooked anything?

In this chapter, I will share several instructional strategies for setting and teaching high standards for mathematical precision while upholding our cultural values of mathematical risk taking and sense making. The first group of examples will help you raise the levels of thoroughness, rigor, clarity, and specificity in your classroom, so you'll get better math out of your kids. The second group of examples includes four different instructional strategies for teaching students how to check for errors and produce accurate, appropriate work.

Part 1: Strategies to Raise Expectations

How can we convey the expectation that young mathematicians do high-quality mathematics? These four examples offer some ideas.

Shawn Towle, eighth grade

Thoroughness: "How will you know you've found them all?"

Shawn's students were working on the question, *How many ways can you pack twenty-four cubes into a rectangular prism?* from the *Connected Mathematics Project's Filling and Wrapping* unit (Lappan et al. 2009). Shawn led by asking them, "How will you know you've found them all? How will you prove to someone else that you've found them all?" He gave students cubes and a table (similar to the one on the next page) to organize their thinking and let them at it.

Please take a moment to play with the mathematics first. How many solutions do you think there are? What are they? What kind of math came up when you started making sense of this problem? Where will the kids go with it?

At one table group, two students were working together:

Johnny: I think it has something to do with the factors of twenty-four.

Nick: Maybe . . .

Johnny: See, like 8 by 3 by 1. Eight times 3 times 1 is 24. I think they're all going to multiply to 24.

Nick kept building.

LENGTH (IN.)	WIDTH (IN.)	HEIGHT (IN.)	VOLUME (IN.³)	SURFACE AREA (IN.²)	SKETCH

A few minutes later, I stopped by and looked at their work. They had written down and sketched these cubes:

8 × 3 × 1

4 × 6 × 1

12 × 2 × 1

24 × 1 × 1

6 × 2 × 2

4 × 2 × 3

Nick was still building and trying other solutions. Johnny was sure they were finished and was busy calculating surface areas.

Tracy: How will you know when you've found them all?

Nick: We'll never know.

Johnny: No, we've found them all. We're done.

Nick: But there must be a seventh solution. There's a place for it.

Ryan: (Walked over from another table.) Do you guys only have six options? Is that all of them? Is that correct?

Johnny: Yeah.

Nick: We don't know.

Ryan: I think there are six, because what you do is you go through the factors of twenty-four, and then you have to break them down."

Nick: "Yeah, we used the factors, too, 1, 2, 3, 4, 6, 8, 12, 24.

Johnny: There are only six ways.

Ryan: Yeah. So what you do is you start with 24 × 1 × 1, and then you break down the 24. If you have 4, you break that down some more, until you can't break it down anymore.

Johnny: Right. So you only had six options too?

Ryan: Yeah. There are only six ways to multiply the factors to twenty-four. (Walked back to his table.)

Meanwhile, Nick continued to try to find more solutions.

Nick: "Let's see, 3 × 3 × 1?

Johnny: It won't work.

Nick: I know it doesn't multiply to 24, but 3 is a factor of 24. (Tried to build it.) It doesn't work. It's only 9 cubes. What about 8? Did we do all the possible ones with 8?"

After an additional twenty minutes or so, Nick said, "I can't find anymore. I really think we found them all. I started with one, then two, and went in order, so I know. I'm sure of it."

The *Connected Mathematics Project* and Shawn did something so simple yet so brilliant with this lesson: they provided a table with more rows than solutions. If the table had six rows, students would have written their six solutions and moved on, sure they'd found them all because they'd filled in the whole chart. Because there were seven spaces, however, students stuck with the problem for a much longer time, looking for that seventh solution. When they finally decided there were only six, either by looking at factors like Johnny and Ryan, or by building like Nick, it was *because they were mathematically certain they'd found all the possible solutions, not because the worksheet was filled out.*

The materials we use can lead students to an answer and hint to students when they're done. By providing ambiguous materials, Shawn was teaching his students to be thorough: to solve the problem until they were convinced it was complete. As a result, students persevered and engaged in much higher-quality mathematics. They moved from guess-and-check answers to thinking about *why* there could only be six solutions, and why a seventh solution was impossible.

This is a simple strategy to implement with any curriculum. Next time you provide written materials to students, check to see whether you're inadvertently telling students when to stop thinking. Are there quick tweaks you can make that will teach students to finish a problem because the mathematics is complete, rather than because the paper is filled out? The changes might be as easy as adding some rows, columns, or blanks, or, better yet, substituting plain paper or a whiteboard for a provided worksheet.

Cindy Gano, first and second grades

Raising the Rigor in Games

We met Cindy in Chapter 3, where we learned how she encouraged students to challenge themselves through written feedback. She is constantly looking for ways to teach her advanced students to slow down and go deeper, rather than grabbing the first thought or most obvious solution and moving on. She often modifies games and routines to support these goals with students. In this case, Cindy took the common strategy of asking students to extend a pattern and ramped up the rigor.

Once per week, as a warm-up, Cindy will post a partially completed pattern like this:

————, ————, 84, ————, ————,

Cindy asked students to come up with a solution that would fit the pattern. She then asked students to discuss one another's patterns to see whether they agreed or disagreed. Once students had the routine down, Cindy added depth. She gave students a few minutes to develop patterns individually. She then asked each table to discuss their patterns and choose one to present to the class. The twist was that Cindy told her students she hoped each table would share a *different* pattern. She asked, "Can you find a pattern you don't think any other table will think of?"

What Cindy saw was the number of students choosing the obvious patterns, such as adding or subtracting 1, 2, or 10, really dropped, and students developed much more creative solutions. For example, rather than lots of students copping out with solutions such as 81, 82, 83, 84, 85, 86, students stretched themselves into patterns such as -84, 0, 84, 168, 252. The first week, they were thrilled when, out of seven tables, they only had one duplicate. They couldn't wait for their next chance to see whether they could develop seven unique solutions, which they did for the problem:

————, ————, 48, ————, ————,

As you can see in Figure 5.1, as the rigor rose, so did students' creativity. And so did the number of mistakes! I particularly love the mistakes with negative numbers from table groups Africa (Af) and North America (NA), which are worth exploring in depth. There's another nice mistake in Antarctica's (Ant) pattern. And what connections might come from comparing Europe (Eu) and South America's (SA) work?

Cindy capitalizes on the opportunity to teach students to check for accuracy while being rigorous. She told me, "What I do is have the class check the patterns. They have to check a pattern that was not their own, and say 'I agree with the pattern because . . .' or 'I disagree with the pattern because . . .' People can also say, 'I would like to amend the pattern by changing _____ to _____ because _____.' Anyone can amend a pattern, so that has been helpful." Cindy is teaching students to go deeper and then revisit their work until they develop correct, rigorous, and interesting solutions.

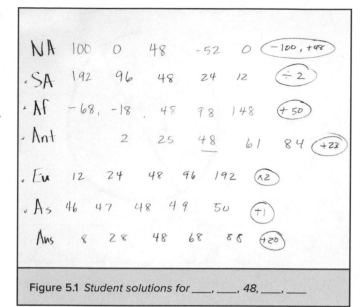

Figure 5.1 *Student solutions for ___, ___, 48, ___, ___*

What I like best about this example from Cindy is it shows that we can teach rigorous math without creating every task from scratch. We can keep some existing tasks and improve them. Are there games you play or routines you use in which you can make small tweaks that ramp up the rigor? Students tend to grab the obvious solution and move on. How can you encourage them go deeper?

Shawn Towle, eighth grade

Clarity and Specificity: Demanding Precise Language

I've observed Shawn many times, and I have never left without recording a moment in which he emphasized precise language. He holds students accountable for their language every day, not because he is some math-grammar snob, but *because he is interested in what his students think and wants to understand exactly what they're saying.* If we view math language this way—as a communication goal—we can see that vocabulary and terminology are always attached to a context and problem, not stand-alone facts to memorize. If we structure our math classes so students talk, discuss, reason, and argue, then the need for clear and exact language will emerge naturally. Shawn takes advantage of these teaching opportunities in the moment, in context, so students really learn and remember the meaning of the terms. Some examples from my transcripts:

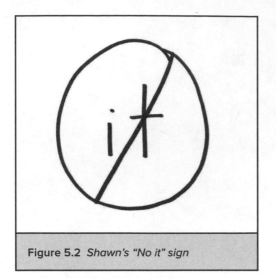

Figure 5.2 *Shawn's "No it" sign*

Max: Looking at the graph, it looks like it went up by three every time.

Shawn: Excellent. I'm so glad you said that. Let me direct your attention to the little whiteboard. What does it say on the little whiteboard? (See Figure 5.2.)

Students: No *it*.

Shawn: We've eliminated use of the word *it*, like, "It goes up," or "It goes down." I'm fair game, too. You can catch me if I slip. Here's the context in which you can't use *it*: "As it increases, it increases." Do you know what I'm talking about? Or, "As time increases, it increases." Do you know what I'm talking about?

Students: No.

Shawn: How many things have we got up there?

Students: Time, area...

Shawn: We're going to call variables by their names so we know what we're talking about.

❀ ❀ ❀

Shawn: How did you count?

Lydia: Length times width.

Shawn: And what would you call a length?

❀ ❀ ❀

Shawn: What's the perimeter of your hexagon?

Sally: Five.

Shawn: Five what?

Sally: Five inches.

Shawn: Inches is good. Why five?

❀ ❀ ❀

Shawn: I'm just curious what that half means. Half of what?

❀ ❀ ❀

Jena: I knew I didn't have to figure out the area of triangle B because it's exactly the same as triangle A, just flipped over.

Shawn: Tell us more about that.

Jena: Well, this side matches this side, and this side matches this side, and this side matches this side. And the angles are the same, too.

Shawn: There's a fancy math word for that. Did you use it?

Jena: Congruent?

Shawn: Exactly. (Turns to class.) Talk about that word at your table for a minute to make sure you understand it.

(After table discussion.)

Shawn: Let's have one representative from each table tell us what you talked about. What does *congruent* mean, and how does that word help us here?

Shawn certainly teaches vocabulary outright—when the need for the word *congruent* first arose, he taught students the word—but he takes precise language a step further by focusing on how these words help us communicate. The high standards Shawn holds don't feel arbitrary, because his motivations are to empower students to express themselves and to help students understand one another.

Justin Solonynka, seventh and eighth grades, Abington, Pennsylvania

Specificity: "I don't think it's actually countless..."

Justin Solonynka has been teaching math for eighteen years. For the past five years, he has taught at Abington Friends School, an inclusive, independent Quaker school in Pennsylvania. Justin is passionate about mathematics and good math teaching and brings tons of energy and enthusiasm to his classroom. In this lesson, Justin was teaching twelve seventh-grade students who were 42 percent white, 33 percent black, and 25 percent Asian.

Justin showed students his two-year-old daughter's toy, an *All Aboard Train Puzzle* (Marc Boutavant, Chronicle Books). He read them the blurb on the back of the box: "It says, on the back, that there are twelve two-sided puzzle pieces, and children will adore the imaginative art and quirky characters on both sides of each puzzle piece, making it possible to arrange the puzzle *in countless ways*."

Justin paused and then said: "I don't think it's actually *countless*."

Students quickly wondered how many possible ways the train could be arranged (Figure 5.3). Do yourself a favor and watch the delightful three-minute video he and his class made. You can find *How to Arrange a Train (a counting problem)* by AbingtonFriendsVideo on YouTube at tinyurl.com/trainmath or linked at www.stenhouse.com/becomingmathteacher.

Figure 5.3 *Students working on the* All Aboard Train Puzzle

What you'll see in the video is the students are incredibly perplexed (in the best possible sense of the word!) and animated as they make sense of the question together. Actually, students' enthusiasm and engagement were so contagious that the video was picked up by Upworthy and went viral. A few months later, the puzzle company sent Justin a new, circular puzzle that's much more challenging to count because of the interchangeability of the pieces (Figure 5.4). He and his students, now in their eighth-grade year, created a sequel video at tinyurl.com/aroundworldmath.

In this second video, you can see Justin's students working together, asking questions, trying different models, using problem-solving strategies, and sticking with an extremely difficult problem for a long time. I particularly enjoyed hearing Justin ask them, "Do you have a decent theory here?" His students responded with a resounding, "No!"

Then they kept going.

Math vocabulary and definitions are often taught in boring ways, but Justin shows us that the meaning of a word can launch a great investigation. What is or is not _____ (a circle, a factor, possible, infinite, countable, a fraction, average) can be a provocative question that leads to a great debate. Next time you're wondering how to hook students with a concept, you might consider whether a single, specific word can help you create an authentic mathematical experience for your students.

Part 2: Four Classroom Strategies to Teach Students to Check for Errors

Let's turn to the elephant in the room for precision—math errors! It is our responsibility to teach students to look out for and catch errors in their own work and in one another's work. In these four examples, you'll see teachers hold students to high standards of accuracy and reasonableness while teaching students generalizable strategies to catch errors in the future.

Figure 5.4 *Justin and his students discuss the* Around the World Train Puzzle.

Jennifer Clerkin Muhammad, fourth grade, Dual Language Immersion, Boston, Massachusetts

"Estimation to the rescue!"

Jen has been teaching fourth grade at the Joseph J. Hurley K–8 School since 2001 and was named one of Boston's Educators of the Year in 2012. Tucked in Boston's South End, the Hurley is a vibrant public school where all students learn all subjects in Spanish and in English through dual-language immersion. Jen and her Spanish-teaching partner, Rudy Morales, alternate weeks with their two sections of fourth graders. Seventy-three percent of Hurley students are Latino/a, 19 percent are white, 5 percent are black, and the remainder identify themselves as multiracial. Sixty-seven percent of the students have a first language that is not English, and 72 percent qualify for free or reduced lunch. There are twenty students in each section.

Jen has an approachable, engaging style and uses humor, slang, voice, and lots of personality in her teaching. I've observed four sections of students over two years, and the level of on-task behavior in her classes always stands out. Jen's management is excellent, her expectations are high, and students work hard for her. She particularly loves teaching math, and her students adopt her enthusiasm and interest quickly, even if they don't arrive with it.

A dominant theme in Jen's room is that she pushes students to think about reasonableness for *every problem, every day.* She asks a steady drumbeat of questions, such as "Does that make sense? Is that reasonable? Does that match your estimate? Is that what you expected?" Regarding estimation, Jen has picked up on an important disconnect, which is that, although teachers often suggest students estimate as a strategy to check their work, students generally don't estimate unless they're explicitly instructed to, especially when they are working a little outside their comfort zones. Jen and I talked about this pattern after a division lesson.

> Every year, estimation is such a hard sell. And I get it. It reminds me of myself in high school. I'd write my final draft of my paper, but we were supposed to have a first draft, so I'd go back and write a pretend first draft, defeating the whole purpose! Estimation is so similar. It's supposed to be—not a chore—but something that really helps you! At certain times, it's all you need, and other times, it's all you have time for, and it always helps you think about reasonableness.
>
> In fourth grade, with division, sometimes all common sense goes out the window. As soon as paper and pencil get involved, it's all about getting that answer, and they stop thinking about reasonableness. So, I've been trying to push the kids to think about what makes sense or not.
>
> When I started seeing answers that were way off, even though we had spent so

much time working on "Does this make sense or not?" I was seeing that, what we were practicing, they weren't actually putting to use. They weren't actually applying that. I told them: "You are actually getting a lot better at estimation. My next step for you is to have estimation be something that you naturally do and becomes a habit for you, because you're not going to have that teacher next to you or that kid next to you who says, 'Um, that's wrong,' or 'Um, that doesn't make sense.' You're going to have to do that for yourself."

I'm sure many of us relate to what Jen described, because we see students forget all about estimation, even if they have practiced it moments before, as soon as they are asked to calculate a problem exactly. Jen wanted to close that gap and convince students that making an estimate is a good use of time, even when they are solving for a "real" answer. She took advantage of a teaching opportunity during her division unit.

Warm Up: "I think _____ is unreasonable because _____."

As she often does, Jen started the lesson with a number talk that was entirely focused on reasonableness. She had a student, Ethan, lead the discussion, and he posted the problem:

$$6739 \div 47$$

Students had nothing in their hands and were asked to estimate the answer. (Make sure to take a few minutes and estimate it yourself, so you'll be able to follow the dialogue and understand the errors.)

After a good amount of think time, Ethan asked students to write their estimates on mini-whiteboards. He walked around the room and recorded estimates, which he then projected. The estimates ranged from 130 to 6,700:

130, 150, 155, 300, 597, 500, 1524, 2350, 2600, 750, 6700, and 372.

Ethan pointed to Jen's posted sentence frame, which read:

"I think _____ is unreasonable because _____."

Ethan asked students to write about any answers they thought were unreasonable, making sure to explain why. He then called students together for a discussion. Some example statements:

- "I think 6,700 is unreasonable because if you did 6,000 × 40 that already equals 240,000."
- "I think 2,350 is unreasonable because I already know that if you do 2,350 × 40, that's going to be way too big."

- "Anything less than 120 is unreasonable because 120 × 50 = 6,000, so it's going to be too small."

This was a particularly choice piece of dialogue between two students:

Dylan: I think that 150 and all numbers higher than 150 are unreasonable because I think 20 × 50 is 1,000. Wait. Is that right? Let me think about that. (Dylan looked at his own whiteboard, *not* his teacher.) Yeah. That's right.

Ethan: What do people think about what Dylan said? I'm not sure about that. I got 155 because I know that 100 × 47 is 4,700, and 50 × 47 is about 2,300, and I think that gets you somewhere pretty close. That would get you approximately 7,000 and that would get you pretty close.

Dylan: Oh . . .

An important aspect of the "I think _____ is unreasonable because _____" routine is that students never calculate the exact answer. They whittle away at their collected solutions, narrowing down to an increasingly reasonable range of estimates. Once the outliers are struck and the remaining estimates seem reasonable, Jen moves them on to a new problem. If we want students to internalize estimation as an important habit, we need to let it stand sometimes, rather than always positioning it as subordinate to exact calculations.

Making the connection explicit: "That should make her say, 'What?! Hold up!'"

After this warm-up and focus on reasonableness, students worked for thirty minutes on their own, in pairs, or in small groups solving challenging, multistep, paper-and-pencil, multiplication and division word problems. When Jen brought students back together to debrief, she intentionally *connected* the importance of estimation between the two parts of the lesson, rather than leaving estimation compartmentalized in its own, stand-alone exercise. For example, students were working on 3,998 × 7. Take a second to solve it yourself.

Noemi: I made an estimate and I got 28,000, but when I did the work, I got 3,028, so I knew something was wrong.

Jen: Ooh, let's talk about that. A lot of you get annoyed with me when I make you estimate, but this is a perfect example of how estimation really can come to the rescue! OK, let's look at your work. So, Noemi, I think you were saying, you had initially made an estimate? You had rounded this to 4,000?

Noemi: Yes.

Jen: Did a lot of you end up rounding 3,998 to 4,000?

Students: Yes, because it's so close. It's only two away.

Jen: Because you noticed that 3,998 is only 2 away from 4,000. So you knew, 4,000 × 7 is what?

Students: 28,000.

Jen: 28,000. So you knew, the answer would be bigger than 28,000, or smaller than 28,000?

Students: Smaller.

Jen: Why?

Dashani: Because you rounded *up* to 4,000.

Jen: OK, so she knew it was going to be approximately 28,000, but a little smaller. And what did you end up getting, Noemi?

Noemi: 3,028.

Jen: 3,028. And what do you think she said to herself?

Students: "Huh?!" "What?!" (Said with smiles and animation.)

Jen: Right! That should make her say, "What?! Hold up!" (Said with humor and expression.)

A proud Noemi spent a few minutes showing students where she'd made her mistake and how her estimate helped her catch it. Jen stretched out her arms and said, "Hey, estimation to the rescue, right?" Students nodded in agreement.

Jen uses humor, theatrics, and everyday language to show students how to have an animated internal conversation—and thereby stay engaged with the mathematics—all the way through the problem. Just like in reading, students need to monitor their work and see whether it makes sense. When they make an error that yields an unreasonable answer, they should hear a voice inside their heads say something like, "Whoa, whoa, whoa! Wait a second!" Jen acts this voice out. I've heard her say, "You should be thinking, 'Wowzers!' or 'That's cray cray!'"

None of these expressions are ever said in a critical or edgy way. Jen's classroom is exceptionally safe and welcoming, and students laugh a lot in math, partly because Jen models this kind of talk around her own mistakes in class. She'll say, "Hold up, Ms. Muhammad, that doesn't make any sense! Totally cray."

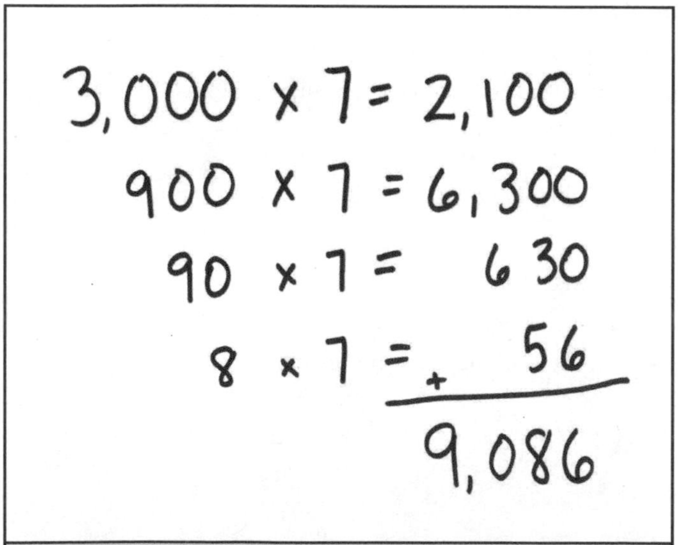

While they were on the subject, Jen shared another example of a student who had trouble with the same problem, 3,998 × 7 (see Figure 5.5):

Jen: I wanted to show another example in which estimation—checking your work for reasonableness—can come to the rescue. (In this case, Jen rewrote a student's work on the whiteboard and shared the example anonymously.) Does anyone see anything up there . . . any red flags up there . . . that say,

$$3{,}000 \times 7 = 2{,}100$$
$$900 \times 7 = 6{,}300$$
$$90 \times 7 = 630$$
$$8 \times 7 = \underline{+ 56}$$
$$9{,}086$$

Figure 5.5 *A student's solution to 3,998 × 7*

"That doesn't make sense! Oh my goodness, that doesn't make sense!" (Said in a comic, panicked voice, with arms waving.)

Eddie: That should be 21,000 instead of 2,100.

Jen: I agree, but why doesn't this make sense?

Annie: It's ten times smaller than it should be.

Jen: But how did you even know that it should have been ten times bigger? How does this one stick out and say, "That doesn't even make sense! That's unreasonable!" (Pointing to $3,000 \times 7 = 2,100$.)

Joseph: I think, because you took $3,000 \times 7$, and 2,100 is already *below* 3,000 before you start multiplying. You should think, "That's the craziest answer ever!" It doesn't make sense that it's smaller than what you started with.

Mateo: And also, 900×7 is 6,300, which is bigger than 2,100, even though 900 is less than 3,000 and they're both being multiplied by 7.

Jen: Do you hear what they're saying? This number is smaller than this one, and you're multiplying both by 7, so how can this answer be bigger than this one? (Pointing to 900 and 3,000, then 2,100 and 6,300.) And if you did one group of 3,000, it's already bigger than 2,100, so that doesn't make sense. Again, I think this person knew that, but sometimes we *all* make silly mistakes, which is why you want to go back and look for these silly mistakes! Capisce?

Two powerful strategies to take away from these examples:

1. **Weave estimation throughout all of math**. Estimation is not a content area to be taught in isolation. Asking students to ballpark *every* problem before, during, or after calculating can help them build powerful thinking muscles, and as Jen said, keep common sense from flying out the window when they pick up their pencils. Demonstrating how estimation can help us catch mistakes, like Jen did with these two examples, can help convince students that estimation is useful and not just something to do because the teacher requires it.

2. **Externalize what students' internal dialogue should sound like** so they learn how to check for reasonableness, self-monitor their math to see if it makes sense, and catch errors. Jen uses a variety of expressions (*That doesn't make sense! Wowzers!*), and images (red flags, numbers jumping out) to teach students how they should react to their work when it doesn't pass a sanity check. The active, animated, internal dialogue she is modeling is so much more desirable than what we've historically taught students to think inside their minds (1 plus 3 plus 6 is 10, put down the 0 and carry the 1). Students who are having an active conversation with the mathematics will produce higher-quality, more accurate work, and they'll enjoy themselves a heck of a lot more.

Heidi Fessenden, second grade

Buddy Checks: *"That's not what I got."*

Heidi wanted to build students' precision and accuracy in a positive way, so she developed a peer system called *Buddy Checks*. When I first saw that she was using a peer system, I was intrigued. On the one hand, it's always easier to catch a mistake in someone else's work. On the other hand, I was skeptical because I've seen many ineffective peer conferences, especially in writing workshop. Peer work feels good and appeals to us but takes specific instruction to be effective. My skepticism vanished after witnessing this exchange between Mabel and Tabreeya about Mabel's work (Figure 5.6). Mabel drew a correct representation of 46 + 36, but originally wrote 55 as her answer. She gave her paper to Tabreeya to buddy check.

Tabreeya: Wait a minute, Mabel, this has to be more than 55. See? 10, 20, 30 . . . (Tabreeya was pointing to Mabel's long rod drawings, symbolizing tens.)

Mabel: Oh! (She began counting again, starting with the tens of the 46.) 10, 20, 30, 40. (She skipped over her ones, and moved to the tens from the 36, but counted them by ones.) 41, 42, 43, 44 . . .

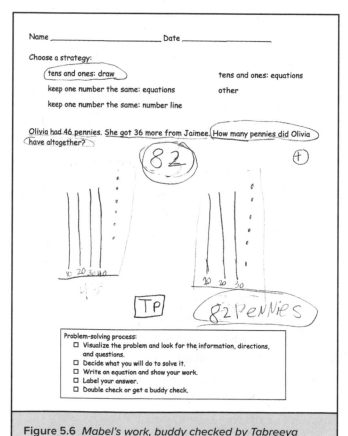

Tabreeya: Wait a minute, Mabel, those are tens.

Mabel: Oh! (This time, Mabel correctly counted all the tens first but had trouble counting the ones.) 10, 20, 30, 40, 50, 60, 70, 71, 72, 73, 74, 75, 76, 77, 78, 79, 50, 51, 52.

Tabreeya: The number after 79 is 80, not 50 . . .

Mabel: Oh yeah! (She went back to the beginning.) 10, 20, 30, 40, 50, 60, 70, 71, 72, 73, 74, 75, 76, 77, 78, 79, 80, 81, 82. There are 82 pennies.

Tabreeya: I agree with you. Nice job!

When Heidi saw what Tabreeya had done for her partner, she asked her to sign her name on a poster on the board, which was labeled: *Buddies help each other find mistakes. I helped a buddy!* There were several student signatures on the poster.

During the close of this lesson, I caught a glimpse of how Heidi had taught students to do *Buddy Checks* so effectively. Heidi gathered students on the rug and posted Mabel's work. Mabel and Tabreeya chimed in as Heidi told

Figure 5.6 *Mabel's work, buddy checked by Tabreeya*

students what happened. Heidi then emphasized why Tabreeya had been so helpful to Mabel:

Heidi: Do you see what I noticed about what Tabreeya did? Tabreeya didn't say to Mabel, "Mabel, it's not 52, it's 82!" She didn't *tell* her. She said, "Mabel, I don't think it could be in the fifties, because I see at least 7 tens." She said something like that. So, she didn't tell Mabel the answer, but she did what a coach does, right? Coaches don't tell people exactly what to do, but they help them figure it out. Coaches don't do it for you. Coaches help *you* figure out how to do it. So Tabreeya did a really good job doing that for Mabel. Not telling her the answer, but asking her a question or pointing something out to get her to think about it in a different way.

Jaleesa did something similar for Ayoka. Do you know what Jaleesa said to Ayoka? All Jaleesa said was, "Ayoka, that's not the same answer I got." So then Ayoka went to check it again. And did you find a mistake?" (Ayoka smiled and nodded.) And she found a mistake, and she fixed it.

Heidi's focus on coaching, rather than on correcting, creates a climate in which students check one another's work for errors without anxiety or stress. Tabreeya helped Mabel figure out each of her three mistakes and then signed off on her work. Mabel checked Tabreeya's work in return and helped Tabreeya clarify what her answers were. Both students were happy throughout. Same with Jaleesa and Ayoka, and other pairs I watched.

When I asked Heidi about *Buddy Checks*, she explained that her approach grew out of her work as a trainer for Tools of the Mind, and its emphasis on self-regulation:

> *What I learned was, it is always easier to check other people than it is to check yourself . . . As you practice regulating other people, you learn the skills you need to regulate yourself. So, with Buddy Checks, the idea was to have kids check one another's work for errors with the theory that learning to check other people's work (and really pay attention to it, rather than just a cursory glance) would help them learn to do that for themselves, with their own work. During tests, for example, I would tell them to buddy check their own work—to really imagine it was someone else's work and they were checking it.*

Buddy Checks ultimately teach students to regulate their own math and monitor for mistakes. Heidi demonstrates that, with an initial investment and some explicit teaching (including strategies like role playing, fishbowls, and sharing examples), we can teach students how to help one another with precision in a constructive, supportive way. The payoff is big, because students teach one another effectively, learn to catch errors (each other's and their own), and develop healthy attitudes around creating precise mathematics.

Jennifer Clerkin Muhammad, fourth grade

Catching Common Errors: Adaptations of My Favorite No

Jen watched a Teaching Channel video called *My Favorite No*, which featured middle school teacher Leah Alcala sharing a routine she created. You can find it here: www.teachingchannel. org/videos/class-warm-up-routine or linked at www.stenhouse.com/becomingmathteacher. Leah has eighth-grade students solve a problem on an index card as their daily warm-up. She collects their work and does a quick sort into *yeses* and *nos*. Leah chooses her favorite mistake, rewrites it so the student's identity is anonymous, and has her class analyze it. What's exciting about *My Favorite No* is Leah has students start with positives:

> I say it's my favorite "no" because I want the kids to first of all recognize what they're about to see is wrong. And, I want them to recognize that there's something good in the problem, like there's a mistake, but it's my favorite "no" because it showed some good math . . . We always talk about what's right first. So that if it's any student's work, they are like, "Oh, I did do that right. There's a mistake, but the mistake didn't ruin the whole thing."

Jen liked Leah's approach of having students look for positive aspects first and then doing error analysis. She kept that idea but has been experimenting with Leah's protocol to make it a more flexible instructional strategy. So far, Jen has used *My Favorite No* for warm-ups, to launch impromptu discussions when useful mistakes came up in the middle of class, and as a structure for group shares to close lessons. She has used it as a quick way to hear what students are thinking, as a vehicle to emphasize strategies she wants kids to try, and certainly to address common sources of error. Jen has also experimented with a written version to use as a formative assessment. We'll look at two brief examples of Jen using *My Favorite No* to get a sense of how we can adapt this teaching strategy for different purposes.

"The reason I chose this one was because I saw a lot of kids having a similar issue with place value."

Jen's students had just started a unit focused on adding and subtracting with large numbers and were starting to develop strategies that would be efficient and accurate as the numbers grew. After an opening discussion in which Jen refreshed students' memories about strategies they'd discussed the day before, students set to work. She circulated among the students, working with them individually or in small groups, looking for patterns among solutions. She was pleased to see most students approaching the problems in logical ways (adding up in chunks, using landmark numbers, subtracting chunks, etc.) but noticed several students had trouble keeping track of place value.

Because students were engaged and working while Jen was circulating, she had time to be thoughtful about what kind of share she wanted to use to close the lesson. Should she ask a student to introduce a particularly efficient strategy? Should she choose a student to share a representation or organizational strategy she wanted to encourage? Should she do some error analysis? On this day, Jen opted for a *My Favorite No*, because she saw several students making similar errors, and she wanted to address them early in the unit. At the same time, Jen looked for a representative error that would emphasize important positive elements. She copied a student's work onto a whiteboard and set it to the side until she was ready to have a closing discussion. The problem was 10,000 – 73.

Think about how you'd solve 10,000 – 73 first. Would you subtract, or would you turn it into a missing addend problem by saying 73 + ____ = 10,000? Would you use column subtraction and cross out all those zeros, or have you learned another strategy? How did you approach it, and where are the natural places students might make mistakes?

Jen shared the work in Figure 5.7.

Jen: Check out this work. Remember, it does not matter whose this is. All you're going to know is that this is wrong, but there are a lot of good things here. Before we talk about what we disagree with, we're going to talk about what we do agree with. Let me give you a minute to check out this student's work, and then we will discuss.

(Think time.)

Jen: Give me a thumbs-up if you have had a chance to look at this student's thinking and are ready to talk about it. Give me a raised hand if you would like more time.

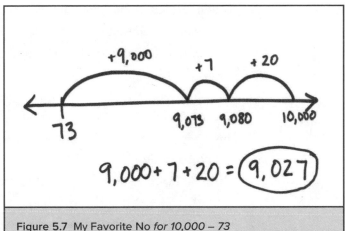

Figure 5.7 My Favorite No *for 10,000 – 73*

(Some of each.)

Jen: I'll give you a little more time.

(Think time.)

Jen: OK, who can tell me something that this student did very well?

Adam: Can I ask a question about something they did?

Jen: Not yet. First, we're going to look for things we agree with.

Janella: The person starts with a big number to add on.

Jen: So you appreciate that this person started with a big chunk. OK. What else did this student do well?

Alwan: I like that they, um, got one thing right about the equation, which was the 9,000. So they thought about the 9,000.

Jen: Do you guys know what he's saying? Can someone explain?

(No hands.)

Jen: OK, I don't either. Do you want to try to explain that again?

Alwan: I think that the 9,000 is the thing that they did right.

Jen: So you're saying that part of the answer is right?

Alwan: Yeah.

Jen: Let's try, right now, to not focus on the answer, which we know is wrong, because otherwise this wouldn't be called, *My Favorite No*. Let's try, right now, to focus on what we like about what this student did.

Tina: I like how, when they did from 9,073, they added 7 to get to a landmark number to make it easier for them.

Jen: So you liked this jump right here, because when you added the 7 to this, you landed on an easier, friendlier, landmark number? (Pointed to 9,073 + 7 = 9,080.) Anyone agree with that?

(Students signed that they agreed.)

Jen: Yeah, I liked that too. What else? This student did a lot of great things.

Susie: I like how this student showed their work on a number line and how that makes it a bit clearer.

Jen: You like this representation. It's pretty clear.

Alwan: I like that he has an equation.

Jen: Can I ask you about the size of the jumps? The way this person showed it on the representation?

William: I think that, if they want to get close, I think jumping so much as 9,000 is a good jump.

Jen: I agree. It was a good first move to get to 10,000. One thing that I noticed is that the 9,000 looks way bigger than the 7. Now, obviously if the 7 were this big, the 9,000 would be even bigger, but notice that the 20 is larger than the 7 and smaller than the 9,000. Sometimes I see kids, and adults, make their 10 this big (drew a jump in the air) and their 3 this big (drew a bigger jump in the air) and their 1,000 this big (drew a tiny jump in the air).

By this point in the conversation, Jen and her students had identified several strengths of this work. This student:

- used a number line as an organized representation.
- represented the jumps so that the size of the jump related to the size of the numbers.
- used landmark numbers.
- started by adding a large chunk, which is a more efficient strategy.
- wrote an equation.

When Jen and I talked about *My Favorite No*, she told me she always looks for an example that has five or six redeeming qualities she wants to emphasize in discussion. Some students still want to zoom in on the mistake right away, but Jen is teaching them to slow down, look closely, and really see the math. In this case, students generated five important positives. Now it was time to turn to the mistake.

Jen: So, what happened here? Why did this student end up with the wrong answer? I'm going to listen around because I see so many hands, and then I'll call on a few of them, but talk at your tables first. Where did this student go wrong?

(Students had animated discussions at their tables about the student's errors. Jen checked in with a few tables, asking, "What did you find?")

Jen: So, the reason I chose this one was because I saw a lot of kids having a similar issue with place value, getting a little bit confused with whether the 8 was worth an 800 or an 8 or an 80. These numbers are pretty big, so that's going to happen right now, right? We just started this unit, so that's OK. So, I heard a bunch of kids saying it, but who would like to articulate where this student went a little astray?

Janelly: They got confused with the place value. They forgot the hundreds place.

Jen: So, tell me specifically what happened.

Janelly: So, where it says 9,000, right next to the 9.

Jen: OK, so can you really orient me? Which part, this, or this? Which number?

Janelly: 9,080.

Jen: OK, so let's focus in here. Tell me what went wrong. (Circled 9,080.)

Janelly: Because 80 plus 20 equals 100, and they said it equals 10,000. They forgot the 900.

Jen: So what is 9,080 plus 20?

Students: 9,100.

Jen: So we didn't really land on 10,000; we only landed on 9,100. How much more do we have to go?

Students: 900.

Mark: If you take away 20 from 10,000, it would be 9,980.

Jen: That's an interesting way of thinking of it, Mark. He's saying, if you were checking your work, and you said, "Let me start with the 10,000 and go backward 20 . . ." Let me write that down, Mark, thank you. (Wrote 10,000 – 20.) Think in your brain for a second, what would you land on if you subtract 20? Maggie, I know you were working on this one earlier.

(Think time.)

Jen: What would you land on?

Students: 9,980.

Jen: It wouldn't be 9,080, it would be 9,980. Interesting. Thank you.

"This student got a little mixed up about what seven represented."

Jen was enjoying the discussions that came out of *My Favorite No*, but she was concerned about the students she wasn't hearing from. Were they following the math? The conversations? So often, we sense that the students are with us because the *students who talk* are with us. Jen wanted to hear from everyone, so she created a written version she could use as a formative assessment. Figure 5.8 is an example of a fourth grader's analysis of a peer's work.

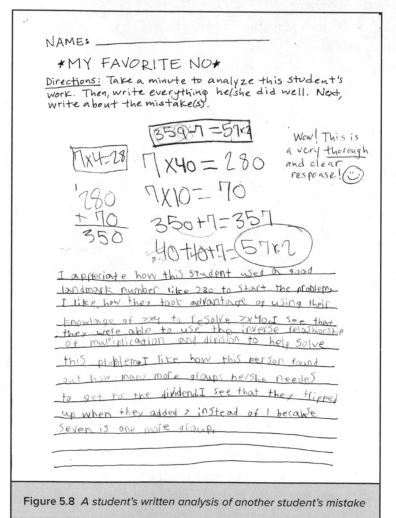

Figure 5.8 *A student's written analysis of another student's mistake*

Other students revealed important math misconceptions in their writing. For example, one student wrote, *One thing that this kid did wrong is that there is no sign of the use of division.* That comment is worth an individual, follow-up conversation. What does this student think about the relationship between multiplication and division?

Jen noticed a large group of students turned in work that was extremely hard to follow, so much so that she wasn't able to determine whether the kids didn't understand the math or didn't know how to write a clear analysis. She decided to back up and teach students how to write a *My Favorite No*, both so her students would learn how to write an argument and so she would be able to assess their mathematical thinking. Jen chose a new mistake and had students work through it as a class and discuss it in small groups until she thought students had a good handle on the math involved. Jen then taught a writing-in-math class, where she helped students structure their analyses with sentence frames and transitional phrases (Figure 5.9).

Students each wrote an individual *My Favorite No* about this problem, and Jen gave them feedback about both their math and writing. Overall, she noticed that students' writing was much more logical after the writing lesson. Since then, Jen has been able to get what she is after with this tool: powerful glimpses into her kids' mathematical thinking.

Jen has developed *My Favorite No* into a systematic structure for an occasional, written, formative assessment. Used this way, it can help us gather valuable insights about our students' thinking that can inform our instruction, guide our conversations with kids, and help us decide best next steps for different students. What's not to like?

Shawn Towle, eighth grade

Whole-Class Critiques: "This is free feedback day. We're going to help you."

Shawn's students worked in teams, and then individually, on a *Connected Mathematics Project* summative performance assessment in which students were given a data set and then asked to create a mathematical model. The context for the problem was a painting job, and students were given a few values for the painted area after different amounts of time. Students were asked to model the data graphically and algebraically, and then critique their own models. It was expected that students' answers would vary, depending on how they modeled the problem. If you're an elementary school teacher, I know this example is from a math problem you wouldn't use. Pay attention to the structure of the whole-class critique anyway, because it is a format that transfers well to younger students working on substantial math tasks, challenges, and projects.

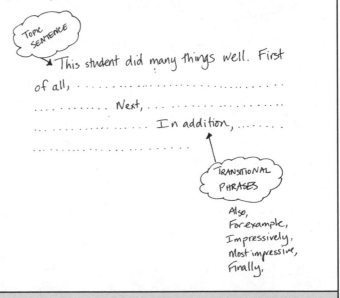

Figure 5.9 *Jen taught students how to structure their written analyses.*

The day before the assignment was due, Shawn devoted the entire class period to critiques, discussion, and reflection. Any student could bring his or her work to the front of the room and project it. The rest of the students and teacher asked questions, made comments, and caught errors and omissions. The authors then had a chance to revise and edit their work based on the feedback, if they so chose. For example:

Shawn: Anybody have feedback on Matt's graph?

Greta: On his axes, he should have area (1,000 sq. ft.), and for time he should have hours.

Shawn: Excellent catch. We have to know how we're measuring time, and how we're measuring area. Because, otherwise, what does an area of three mean? That's one piece of feedback for you to do with what you will.

The critique structure works well because it is beneficial for the student in front—they get feedback and can improve their project—but it also benefits everyone. After Greta pointed out the units weren't labeled on Matt's graph, several students picked up their pencils and added units to their graphs, too.

Another positive feature of the critique is that students discover the communication reasons behind some conventions because they have trouble understanding their classmates' work. For example, Brian's graph had two big issues. One, he put his graph on notebook paper instead of graph paper, so everything was a little off. Two, rather than putting a scale on his x-axis, he only put the given data values and didn't space them accordingly. Brian had done terrific work algebraically, and his model was a better fit than most students', but his peers had trouble reading his graph. Take a look at Figure 5.10, adapted from Brian's work, to see what was happening mathematically.

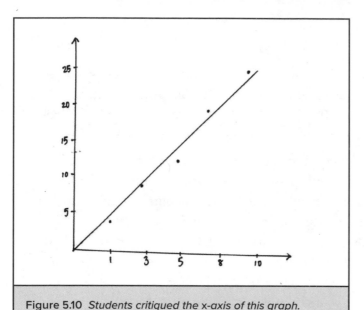

Figure 5.10 *Students critiqued the x-axis of this graph.*

Annie: The bottom line goes 1, 3, 5, 8, 10. It's not equal distance between each of the numbers.

Kara: Annie, what are you saying?

Annie: It goes from 0 to 1 to 3 to 5 to 8 to 10. The difference between 0 and 1 is 1, but the difference between 8 and 10 is 2.

Brian: Oh, I did that because those were the numbers in the data set.

Shawn: Do you think that matters?

Annie: Yeah.

Charles: Me, too. His numbers are equal distances apart, but they aren't a scale because the numbers don't go up evenly. Where he has 3 should really be 2. Where there's a 5, there should be a 3.

Annie: Even though he calculated his equation correctly, the graph is really hard to read because the slope looks different. That's confusing for someone trying to understand his work.

Kara: Oh, I see what you're saying. People probably won't even look at the numbers on the axis because they'll assume they're spread out evenly. Then they will be kind of . . . misled . . . because the slope looks steeper than it really should.

(Brian was nodding throughout their discussion.)

Brian: I totally see what you guys are saying. I will draw my graph again tonight.

Shawn picked up the graph paper versus notebook paper question.

Shawn: What do you think I should do, at this point, if people submit graphs that aren't on graph paper?

Students: "Have them redo." "Throw them out."

Shawn: Throw them out?! You think I should just throw them away?

Students: (Heatedly.) "Don't count them." "Tell them to do it again." "Throw them out."

Shawn: OK, graphs not done on graph paper is a redo? Or partially done? Or am I throwing them out?

Millie: Throw them out! They should be on graph paper. You told us that from the beginning.

Shawn: I have a student over here suggesting that I shouldn't let you redo them because you know better, basically.

Ryan: Yes! There is no excuse. We know they're supposed to be on graph paper.

Shawn: There's a reason for that, and the reason is kind of what we're seeing here. Graph paper costs a little more because it is quadrille; so all those spaces are exactly the same size. Notebook paper is only lined in one direction, so it is hard to be exact, and graphs never come out quite right. I think you've given me good advice. I will not accept graphs done on notebook paper. I think the consensus was I shouldn't even let you redo it. I'm good with that.

These kids care about precision, don't they? Other examples of feedback:

Maggie: When you're labeling the sides of your graph, you need to say what it is.

Shawn: So you need to say what unit of measure of your variable is?

Michael: Tick marks would make your graph easier to read, so I can tell if the number is on the line or the space between.

Shawn: Tick marks would be a nice touch. You could add them if you like.

Julie: Your title, "How does the area change as the time increases?" should be something like, "As the area increases, how does the time change?"

The feedback often exposed students' misunderstandings, so Shawn was able to revisit concepts as needed. For example, Julie's comment led to a terrific discussion around a central idea of the unit: independent and dependent variables. In another section, some students realized they weren't sure how to compare their predicted and actual values, so they asked peers for help. Students also debated the merits of using given data points, best-fit lines, or equations to answer the questions, which provided a nice chance for students to differentiate between the known data and the constructed mathematical models and appropriate uses for each. Students led each of these discussions, with Shawn asking clarifying questions and providing guidance as needed. The class was nearing the end of the unit and naturally reviewed and synthesized concepts during their conversations, while also attending to detail. Much like authors during a writing critique, these young mathematicians received feedback on content, style, and conventions.

I was thrilled by the quality of thinking that came out of these whole-class critiques and wondered why we don't do them more often in math class. Some of us might use critiques in other subject areas but didn't realize we could apply them in mathematics, especially if our curriculum tends toward repetitive, procedural, cut-and-dry math. If we assign rich math tasks to students, though, and allow them to go into fewer, better problems in real depth, their math work becomes complex and interesting. They have authorship and ownership and a real need for constructive criticism.

We will revisit critiques in Chapter 12.

Misguided Approaches to Precision: Timed Fact Tests, Elimination Games, Public Comparisons, and Speed Drills

The following excerpt from NCTM Past President Cathy Seeley's *Faster Isn't Smarter* paints such a familiar picture for me.

> *The second hand hit 12 and the teacher said, "Begin!" The boy I was sitting next to ground out a few answers. He was gripping his pencil so hard that it broke in the process. It seemed an eternity, but finally the three minutes were up. I looked at the boy's paper. He had not come close to finishing, and the few answers he had so painstakingly attempted to write were wrong . . .*

> *The teacher collected the papers and handed out a puzzle-type worksheet for the students to complete while she graded the tests. The puzzle worksheet was on the same facts the students had just seen on the test. I sat quietly as the same boy now used his broken pencil to calmly and correctly complete all the facts on the worksheet. He got the correct answer to the puzzle, put down his pencil, and got out a book to read. A few minutes later, the teacher read the names of the students who had passed the timed test. Of course, the boy seated next to me was not on the list . . .*

> *Some students respond well to competitive and timed situations, thriving on the pressure to bring out their best; others have quite a different reaction. This particular boy received a clear message that some students are good at math and some are not—and he knew which group he was in. He also was prevented from finishing the test, something that causes some students tremendous frustration. Furthermore, the teacher was led to believe, incorrectly, that this student did not know his multiplication facts. Consequently, and perhaps worst of all, the boy was placed in a special group to receive remediation on low-level arithmetic, robbing him of the opportunity to move into more interesting problems and engaging work. (Seeley 2009, 94)*

I've seen it in classrooms so many times, and I've read it in dozens of teachers' math autobiographies. Adults often refer to timed fact tests, elimination games such as *Around the World*, public "star charts" for fact mastery, and speed drills such as *Mad Minutes* as the beginning of math anxiety or math hatred. And yet, these practices continue. I spend much of my time visiting classrooms, and I see new students developing math anxiety every day, one minute at a time, whether the speed drills are on traditional worksheets or embedded in flashy apps on iPads.

So why do we use these techniques? The noble reason is surely that we want our students to know their math facts automatically. There's a lot of sense to this goal: as the problems get more complicated, students can easily lose track of their thinking if they have to calculate each fact anew. We want older students to use their working memories to handle increasingly complex mathematics, not to figure out 8 + 7 again, thereby forgetting where they were in a multistep problem.

The problem is research shows that timed tests, speed drills, and competitive elimination games are not effective tools for teaching, learning, or assessment (Boaler 2014). They do not give valid assessment data, they do not help many students learn their math facts, and they reliably cause math anxiety. A few examples from the literature:

> Instead of helping children develop fluency at computation and become more efficient at problem solving, these policies have produced students that rely more on rote memorization and have increased the level of anxiety in young children by making mathematics a high-risk activity. This tends to produce more adults with "math anxiety" and discourage children who understand the concept but work a little slower. It also may explain some of the disparities between girls and boys regarding attitudes toward mathematics and why minorities tend to perform poorly on mathematics achievement tests . . . We do know that adding time requirements to tasks does increase anxiety, decrease accuracy, and create a negative attitude toward the subject matter. (Geist 2010, 25–26)

> Overall, math anxiety causes an "affective drop," a decline in performance when math is performed under timed, high-stakes conditions, both in laboratory tests as well as educational settings. This means that math achievement and proficiency scores for math-anxious individuals are underestimates of true ability. (Ashcraft and Moore 2009, 197)

> We found no anxiety effects on whole-number arithmetic problems when participants were tested using [untimed] pencil-and-paper format. But when participants were tested online (i.e., when they were timed as they solved the problems mentally under time pressure in the lab), there were substantial anxiety effects on the same problems. (Ashcraft 2002, 182)

Leaders in math education like Jo Boaler and John Van de Walle have written at length about the effects of these practices on our students:

> Second graders from across the achievement spectrum described the tests as making them feel "upset" and "unhappy" and that they are "terrible at math." Timed tests have been given to young children in school districts in the United States with the best intentions, but with negative consequences for many years ... Beyond the fear and anxiety, timed tests also convey strong and negative messages about math, suggesting that math ability is measured by working quickly, rather than thinking deeply and carefully—the hallmark of high-level mathematical thinking. The ideas students develop about math in elementary school are critical for their future in the subject ... I would argue that this particular policy—of giving young children timed math tests—is one of the clearest ways schools damage children, and we now have evidence of the extent of the damage. (Boaler 2012)

> When under the pressure of time, students get distracted and abandon their reasoning strategies. Students also develop anxiety, which works against learning mathematics ... You may have experienced bulletin boards that show which students are on which step of a staircase to mastering their multiplication facts. Imagine how the student who is on Step 3 feels when others are on Step 6. Or imagine the negative emotional reaction to public competition with flash cards for the half who didn't win. Adults often refer to the competitions with flash cards as the moment they started to dislike mathematics, specifically reflecting on a game called *Around the World,* in which one student is pitted against another with the loser sitting down. It is great to celebrate student successes, but avoid public comparisons between students. (Van de Walle et al. 2014, 2:147)

A dear friend of mine (and an amazing teacher) experienced just what Van de Walle described:

> My first-grade teacher put a chart on the wall with our names on it. We were able to get a gold star next to our name if we got every answer correct on our daily math quiz, a silver star if we missed one, and a red or green star if we got two wrong. At the end of the week, we could get a prize if we got five gold stars next to our names. I had no attitude about math until this system. I absolutely wanted all gold stars and a prize. My math skills took a nosedive. One day I got a quiz back and instead of a star I got a frowny-face. After this point, I woke up every morning with a stomachache. When the math quiz came out, my palms got sweaty, I used to see white—like actually blank out, I couldn't remember anything. My heart rate soared. I actually remember these physical sensations from when I was six years old. I dreaded school. Flash cards used to send me running out of the room at home... *Once a teacher publicly or privately shames a student that student's learning is in danger. Children will not learn when they are in this danger zone. Those damn charts and that frowny-face shut me down when I was just six years old.*

Why are these techniques still around? There are three main reasons. First, timed tests are included in some popular curricula. Second, some parents argue that flash cards and timed tests worked for them and want their children to learn the same way. Most of all, though, we use them because we tend to teach how we were taught. Even if we believe we weren't taught very well, and even if we think different methods are better, we still tend to teach how we were taught (e.g., Cohen 1990; Raymond 1997).

I know, because I used to give timed fact tests, have my kids play *Around the World*, and use *Mad Minutes*, too. I tried to soften the edges by having students track their own progress so they were competing against themselves, not one another. The truth is, though, they were still timed tests, and I now know they were torture for some of my students. Obviously, torture and anxiety were not my intention! I was trying to help my kids, so I used the only methods I knew. I deeply regret it now and am adding my voice to the chorus of math educators who say it's time for timed math tests, speed drills, star charts, and elimination games to go the way of the dunce cap and paddle.

So what do we do instead? First, let's think about what we want instead. A conversation with my daughter, Maya, comes to mind. When she was in first grade, she was working on the problem 9 + 7, which certainly counts as a basic math fact we want a first grader to learn. She thought out loud for me so I could record:

Maya: The first way I think of to solve it is to use doubles. I've noticed that, if I'm adding two numbers that skip a number in between, I can just double the middle number. Like, it goes, 7, 8, 9. So, for 7 plus 9, I can double 8 and get 16.

Tracy: Whoa. Why does that work?

• Maya: Really what I'm doing is taking one from the bigger number and giving it to the smaller number to make them the same. So, if I take one from the 9 and give it to the 7, 9 minus 1 is 8 and 7 plus 1 is 8. That's how I can make them both 8, and that's a double I know.

Tracy: I see. Will that always work?

Maya: I think so. I've tried it with lots of numbers, and it's worked every time. Like, 26 + 24 is 50 because 20 plus 20 is 40 and 6 plus 4 is 10 and 40 plus 10 is 50. If I do the doubling thing, I can take 1 from the 26 and give it to the 24 so they're both 25s, and 25 plus 25 is 50. Same answer.

Tracy: Hmm. That's cool. What if you hadn't figured that out? Do you know another way to figure out 9 + 7?

Maya: Well, I could give 1 to the 9 instead. So, I could take 1 from the 7 and give it to the 9 to make it 10 + 6. I know 10 + 6 is 16. Making a 10 makes it a lot easier.

Tracy: Would you use a strategy like that with bigger numbers? Like, what if the problem were 29 + 7?

Maya: Yeah, I think I'd take 1 from the 7 and give it to 29 to make 30 plus 6, which is 36. But

Mommy, I thought of another way to solve 9 + 7.

Tracy: What's that?

Maya: Someone could use double 7, and then add 2. 9 is 7 plus 2, so 9 plus 7 is the same as 7 plus 7 plus 2. Seven plus 7 is 14, and 14 plus 2 is 16. It's a double plus two.

Tracy: It is, isn't it.

Maya: But, Mommy, I don't really solve 9 plus 7 any of those ways anymore. Now I just know it by heart.

Tracy: How do you think you know it by heart? How did that happen?

Maya: Well, I think I solved it all these different ways lots of times, and the answer was always 16 no matter how I solved it. So, after I while, I just remembered that 9 plus 7 is 16.

Maya and I have been playing with mathematical ideas and numbers all her life, and it shows in her thinking. She is strategic. She has moved from direct modeling through counting strategies and derived fact strategies to invented algorithms like incrementing, combining the same units, and compensating, as described in Carpenter et al. (2014). She now has her addition and subtraction facts committed to memory, but she has never seen a flash card or a stopwatch. She is mastering them because she understands and uses numbers frequently, and she still enjoys math. That's what we want.

Many students need extra repetition and practice to develop fluency. No problem—there's still no need to break out the timer! There are tools and strategies we can use that build understanding *and* automaticity and don't turn students off math. Here are several resources for developing students' number sense, counting strategies, reasoning strategies, and, eventually, fact automaticity:

- *Children's Mathematics: Cognitively Guided Instruction* by Thomas Carpenter et al. (2014). This is an indispensable guide to students' mathematical thinking and how it develops. I couldn't teach elementary mathematics without it.
- *Teaching Student-Centered Mathematics* by the late John Van de Walle et al. (2014). Each grade-band book contains numerous examples of developmentally appropriate instruction for basic fact mastery that support students' reasoning.
- *Mastering the Basic Math Facts: Strategies, Activities, and Interventions to Move Students Beyond Memorization* by Susan O'Connell and John SanGiovanni (2011a and b). There are two volumes: one for addition/subtraction and one for multiplication/division. I recommend these books often because they meet a clear need for teachers. The authors share thoughtfully sequenced games, strategies, practice ideas, visualization tools, ideas for using manipulatives, literature connections, and meaningful assessment strategies that will help you build students' automaticity while deepening their understanding of the big ideas.
- *Number Talks*, originally developed by Kathy Richardson and Ruth Parker, are a wonderful way to build deep number sense in all grade levels. A quick Google of

"number talks" will bring you a range of articles, titles, and resources for structuring short sessions that build number sense and fluency. *Number Talks* by Sherry Parrish (2010) and *Making Number Talks Matter* by Cathy Humphreys and Ruth Parker (2015) are excellent books.

- Mental math fluency and number sense are key components of building automaticity. *Number Sense Routines* by Jessica Shumway (2011) includes several terrific ideas.

- There are many games that develop automaticity with conceptual understanding and without time pressure. For addition and subtraction, *Shut the Box* is a personal favorite. *Prime Climb* is a good board game for students working with all four operations. The best app I've seen so far is *DreamBox*, which builds deep understanding through the use of powerful mathematical models.

- *Talking Math with Your Kids*, an e-book, blog, and Facebook feed by Christopher Danielson, is a great resource to give parents who want to support their children's math learning but don't know what to do besides drill, tricks, and algorithms. Educating parents about mathematics and high-quality math teaching has to be part of our work.

Now is a great time to replace anxiety-inducing and ineffective methods with techniques that are both supportive *and* effective. Number facts recall is important, and practicing math facts is essential to build students' automaticity. How lovely that we now have resources and options to teach students basic facts in positive ways! Given the direct, causal link between the traditional practices and math anxiety, changing this one part of our practice will bring down our wildly high national rates of math anxiety and have an enormous, beneficial effect on our current and future students.

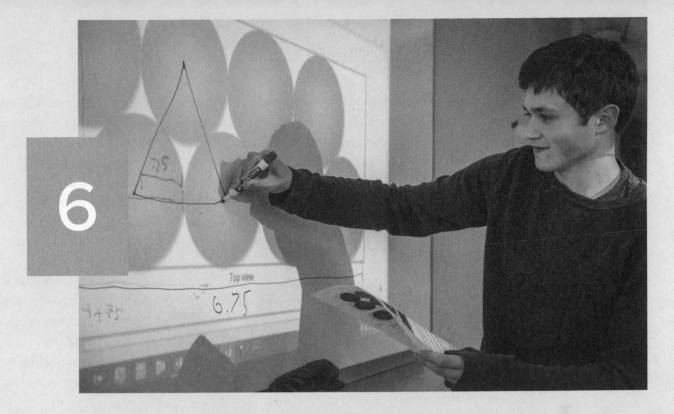

6

MATHEMATICIANS RISE TO A CHALLENGE

One of the theorems we teach in eighth grade is $a^2 + b^2 = c^2$, where c is the length of the hypotenuse of a right triangle in Euclidean space, and a and b are the lengths of the other sides. The Babylonians, Mesopotamians, Indians, and Chinese all independently discovered this relationship, but the theorem bears Pythagoras's name because he and his followers are thought to have been the first to prove it. It's a beautiful example of how lasting rigorous proof is in mathematics: we still use the same proof today, approximately 2,500 years later, because it is still true!

In 1637, French mathematician Pierre de Fermat took up one of the natural questions that rises out of the Pythagorean theorem. He wondered whether the equation would be true for exponents greater than 2. Are there any numbers a, b, and c, where $a^3 + b^3 = c^3$? What about $a^4 + b^4 = c^4$? Or, more broadly, $a^n + b^n = c^n$, where $n > 2$? Fermat wrote in the margins of his copy of *Arithmetica* that no solutions were possible for any n greater than 2. He cryptically noted, "I have discovered a truly marvelous demonstration of this proposition, which this margin is too narrow to contain." And then he died. The nerve!

Fermat wrote many notes in his margins, and later mathematicians dealt with each in turn. This particular conjecture was the last one that hadn't been proved or disproved, so it became known as Fermat's Last Theorem. For more than 350 years, mathematicians tried and failed to prove Fermat, and it became one of the most famous unsolved riddles in history, which made it completely irresistible.

"Mathematicians just love a challenge. They love unsolved problems," said Andrew Wiles, the mathematician who ultimately proved Fermat was right (Singh 1997, 146). Wiles first learned of Fermat's Last Theorem when he was ten years old. "I knew from that moment that I would never let it go. I had to solve it" (6).

Wiles held onto this secret childhood dream while studying several different aspects of mathematics. More than twenty years after Wiles first discovered Fermat, he learned that a colleague had made a breakthrough that opened a possible—although by no means certain—path to the proof. Wiles remembered, "I was electrified. I knew that moment that the course of my life was changing . . . It meant that my childhood dream was now a respectable thing to work on. I just knew that I would never let that go. I just knew that I would go home and work on [it]" (Singh 1997, 205).

And work he did. For the next eight years, Wiles devoted himself to this single problem. The path was long and hard, and there was no guarantee of resolution, but he was consumed by this beautiful challenge. With passion and persistence, he worked. When he needed to learn about an unfamiliar branch of mathematics, he learned it. When he was lost or stuck, he kept going. Wiles described grappling with a big mathematical problem as a long, fumbling journey through a dark, unexplored mansion, punctuated by the occasional breakthrough:

> One enters the first room of the mansion and it's dark. Completely dark. One stumbles around bumping into the furniture, but gradually you learn where each piece of furniture is. Finally, after six months or so, you find the light switch, you turn it on, and suddenly it's all illuminated. You can see exactly where you were. Then you move into the next room and spend another six months in the dark. So each of these breakthroughs, while sometimes they're momentary, sometimes over a period of a day or two, they are the culmination of, and couldn't exist without, the many months of stumbling around in the dark that precede them. (Singh 1997, 236–237)

Wiles delighted in the stumbling around: "I enjoyed the private combat. No matter how hard it had been, no matter how insurmountable things seemed, I was engaged in my favorite problem. It was my childhood passion, I just couldn't put it down. I didn't want to leave it for a moment" (Singh 1997, 265).

Ultimately, Wiles had the satisfaction of solving the problem he loved so much: "When doing math there's this great feeling. You start with a problem that just mystifies you. You can't understand it, it's so complicated, you just can't make head nor tail of it. But then, when you finally resolve it, you have this incredible feeling of how beautiful it is, how it all fits together so elegantly" (Singh 1997, 146).

How can we help our students taste this kind of satisfaction? How can we teach them to rise to a worthy challenge, to grapple with confusion, to focus, to persist, to develop strategies for when they're stuck, and to keep working toward gratification, even if it's delayed or never comes? How can we bring these dispositions of mathematicians into our math classes? Let's look at some strategies to teach students to be puzzlers who stick with it.

Jennifer Clerkin Muhammad, fourth grade

"Ooh . . . a challenge . . . cool . . ."

Jen often starts her class with statements like: "I know you all are really itching for a challenge today." Her students respond with eager nods and smiles, even cheers. Did they start out trying to please their teacher and meet her expectations? Maybe. But over the course of a school year, students internalize her approach to challenges. In one of the simplest, most effective teacher strategies out there, Jen frames being challenged as a positive, always.

For example, early in the year, a student said a problem was challenging. Jen rubbed her hands together and said, "Ooh . . . a challenge . . . cool!" Her students laughed and adopted the phrase as a common refrain. Now, every time she says the word *challenge*, her students rub their hands together like a Bond villain and say, "Ooh . . . a challenge . . . cool!"

Jen's phrasing might not seem like a big deal, but it's such a contrast to the language I often hear in classrooms. What messages do we send with comments like these?

"I need you to work hard in math, and then we'll do something fun."

"These problems are pretty hard. If you can't do them, that's OK. I'll help you."

"I know math isn't everybody's thing. We're almost done."

Language matters. Let's frame challenge as a good thing in our classrooms.

That said, using enticing language about challenges falls flat and rings false unless we *actually* immerse our students in interesting, perplexing, puzzling mathematics. If we want to teach kids to be tenacious problem solvers, we need to look at the quality of our problems.

Dan Meyer and the Math-Twitter-Blog-o-Sphere (#MTBoS)

"Math class needs a makeover."

In 2010, then high school teacher Dan Meyer gave a *TED Talk* called "Math Class Needs a Makeover," www.ted.com/talks/dan_meyer_math_curriculum_makeover. It has since gone viral, with millions of views. I would consider it a must-watch video for any math teacher at any grade level, because it prompted an incredibly important and still ongoing conversation about curriculum and math teaching. I strongly suggest you stick a bookmark here and go watch it now if you haven't seen it yet. You'll get much more out of this discussion if you do.

Wasn't that great?

In the talk, Dan made a compelling argument that students lack initiative, perseverance, and retention because they spend most of their time plugging in formulas without understanding the mathematics. We're not teaching mathematical reasoning or worthwhile problem solving when we use heavily scaffolded, prescriptive curricula; we're just teaching students how to decode textbooks and worksheets and write down answers.

Our goal isn't to help students get answers to problems in our math textbooks, however; our goal is for students to learn mathematics by working on problems (Daro 2013). To help students learn mathematics, Dan suggested teachers and curriculum writers should "be less helpful." He was critiquing a specific kind of (ultimately not very helpful) help: the hinting, cueing, prescribing, breaking down, demonstrating, and enabling we do to get our students to write correct answers on worksheets, whether or not they understand the mathematics.

So what should we do instead? If guiding our students through prescriptive problems isn't teaching them much mathematics, what would?

Dan argued that we should demand better curriculum and design better tasks. We need rich problems about intriguing, perplexing mathematics, crafted thoughtfully, based on what we know about how students learn. We need to devise and facilitate tasks that compel students to make sense of mathematics. Ultimately, we need better curriculum than most of what's currently available. This is, of course, a much bigger challenge than already overworked classroom teachers can meet individually. We do have collective power, however, and we should use it to press publishers and administrators for better math curriculum.

In what little planning time we do have, we can be more intentional about how we use the curriculum we are handed. When is it good to go as is? When should we adapt or improve on it, and how? When should we toss it altogether and swap out specific lessons for something better? How do we know what's better and where to find it? The answers to these questions must be guided by our pedagogical goals. The object of curriculum makeovers is not to hide the mathematics in a fun game or restructure student work so computers can correct it or remove manipulatives so math takes less time to clean up or assign something because it looked cute on Pinterest. Our curricular goal must be to put student learning at the core of problem solving. As Dan said, "Ninety percent of what I do with my five hours of prep time per week is to take fairly compelling elements of problems . . . from my textbook and rebuild them in a way that supports math reasoning and patient problem solving."

Fortunately, there is a shareable, accessible, free record of how Dan and his peers improve and create better curriculum: they've been blogging about it for years. Other teachers joined in the conversation, and the online math community has grown in leaps and bounds ever since. Through blogs, Twitter, shareable documents, virtual file cabinets, free webinars, and self-organized conferences, teachers post lessons, student work, improved tasks, and teacher-created problems. The culture of the online professional learning community affectionately known as the Math-Twitter-Blog-o-Sphere (#MTBoS) is to share resources with one another for free and to solicit feedback, recognizing that the input of our colleagues is one of the best resources we have. I've included several examples of curriculum makeover blogs and information about ways to join the thriving conversation online at www.stenhouse.com/becomingmathteacher. I encourage you to explore them. We have so much to learn together!

To get you started, here's a middle school example of how to transform a dreary textbook problem into a perplexing challenge for students.

Fawn Nguyen, eighth grade, Somis, California

"When I let students own the problem"

I've been reading Fawn Nguyen's blog for years because her writing is beautiful, and I learn something about math teaching with every post. "When I Let Students Own the Problem" is a favorite. Look for it at fawnnguyen.com/let-problem/.

Fawn started by sharing the problem in Figure 6.1 from her textbook with her Mesa Union School students.

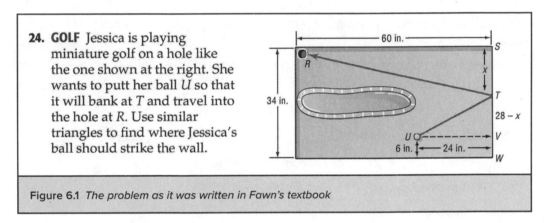

24. GOLF Jessica is playing miniature golf on a hole like the one shown at the right. She wants to putt her ball U so that it will bank at T and travel into the hole at R. Use similar triangles to find where Jessica's ball should strike the wall.

Figure 6.1 *The problem as it was written in Fawn's textbook*

Fawn wrote:

> Stuff like this makes my heart sink . . . There is essentially nothing left in this problem for students to explore and figure out on their own. If anything, all those labels with numbers and variables conspire to turn kids *off* to math. Ironically even when the problem tells kids what to do (*use similar triangles*), the first thing kids say when they see a problem like this is, "I don't get it." *They say they don't get it because they never got to own the problem.*

Fawn thought the underlying mathematical elements of this problem were promising, so she decided to give it a makeover. Right off the bat, she wanted to reduce the text load to make the problem less off-putting and more accessible to all students. That dense paragraph of text is a real barrier to entry for many students, so she got rid of it.

Fawn decided to remove the labels and numbers also. Without the measurements, students couldn't jump to plucking numbers, calculating, or randomly guessing which formula to use. They'd have to think instead, especially about what information would help them solve the problem. When we hand students everything they might need to solve a problem right alongside the problem, we rob them of this essential part of the thought process. By separating the question from the given information, Fawn gave her students a chance to decide what information was important (e.g., angles, distances, that the ball had to go around the water) and what information was not important (e.g., the player's name, the color of the ball, if the water had a bubbling fountain in it). An added bonus of Fawn's decision to delete the measurements was, if students decided they needed them, they'd have to figure them out for themselves.

Fawn passed out blank paper and directed each student to draw a blob and two dots such that each student created a miniature-golf hole that would require a bank shot. Fawn wanted students to create unique problems so they would have more ownership over their work. A second benefit was that students would have opportunities to think more generally about the mathematics of similar triangles if they analyzed the solutions to a set of related problems. They could make connections and look for patterns across their work, rather than just calculating the answer to problem number 24, checking it in the back of the book, and moving on to the next.

Fawn's students jumped right in. Because the problem was challenging, they naturally turned toward one another to think it through. Fawn listened in as her students worked. She heard:

"The angle that the ball hits the border and bounces back out must be the same."

"Because we're talking about angles, something about triangles."

"This is like shooting pool."

"Right triangles."

"Similar right triangles."

"Do we need to consider the velocity of the ball?"

"This is hard."

"I can't figure out how to use the right triangles."

"Similar *right* triangles because that'll make things easier."

"Even though it's more than one bounce off the edges, I'm still just hitting the ball one time."

"I think I got this."

"I have an idea."

"Wish my golfer is Happy Gilmore."

Fawn was happy to see her students engaged in such meaningful struggles with the mathematics, so she tried not to be too helpful. When Fawn's students asked her for validation, she redirected them to the challenge and to the mathematics:

> One student drew hers in quickly and asked, "Is this right?" I replied, "I'm not sure, but that's my challenge to you. You need to convince me and your classmates that the ball hitting the edge *right there* will bounce out and travel straight into the hole. Does it? What can you draw? What calculations are involved?"

She didn't want to rob students of the opportunity they had to learn mathematics by stepping back in and prescribing solution methods. And there was no need! As you can see in the examples of student work on Fawn's blog, her students solved the problem in a variety of ways, using measurement, proportion, similar triangles, midpoints, symmetry, different construction techniques, and a lot of trial and error. As Fawn said:

> Imagine none of this thinking and sharing would have occurred if I had given them problem number 24 in the book. Half of my kids were still struggling and working to find the correct bank shot(s), but they were *given* the chance to struggle. And none of them said, "I don't get it."

Elementary Math Curriculum Needs a Makeover, Too: The Mittens Problem

What's the equivalent of an overwritten, prescriptive textbook problem in elementary school? Let's look at a first-grade problem (Figure 6.2).

The mittens problem is similar to Fawn's golf problem in that the prescriptive steps, visual clutter, and a huge text load are enough to shut students down before they even start. Student thinking has been scaffolded right out of this problem.

If you were expected to teach this problem as part of a school- or district-adopted curriculum, what would you do? This would be my thought process, based on what I've learned from Dan, Fawn, and the rest of the Math Twitter-Blog-o-Sphere, as well as my work with kindergarten through sixth-grade teachers who use a variety of curricula.

Figure 6.2 *The mittens problem*

First Things First: What's the Math Here?

The very first question needs to be about the mathematics at the heart of the problem. To decide whether a problem is worthwhile or interesting mathematically, we need to start with the mathematical content of the problem.

"What's the math here?" is a surprisingly complicated question for this problem because there are a few possible responses. Are we counting things that come in groups to develop a foundation for multiplication? Are we trying to teach the problem-solving strategy of make a table? Are we identifying arithmetical patterns? The lesson in the teacher's guide and the student worksheets have *Look for a Pattern* draped across the top in big letters. The handouts include several more problems that boil down to multiplication, for example, "There are 4 boxes. Each box has 5 crayons. How many crayons are there in all?" For each of these problems, however, the kids are told to use a table and look for a pattern to find their answers. As a teacher, I find the objective of this lesson murky, which is ironic because the problems and curriculum are so prescriptive. So, what do I do? I dig into the problem more deeply, either on my own or with colleagues, focusing on what mathematics would come into play if the kids were allowed to think it through themselves.

To my way of thinking, at its core, this problem is a multiplication problem. Mittens come in pairs, so they create a reasonable context for counting items that come in equivalent groups. I'm not sure why anyone needs to know how many total mittens are needed, but I can live with that. Mittens seem like a fine thing for kids to count because I want students to build intuition with pairs, counting by twos, and doubling. I also know that simple multiplication and division word problems are important in the early grades and help build students' understanding of number (Carpenter et al. 2014, 71).

I'm not at all inclined to use the problem-solving strategies of make a table or look for a pattern to solve this problem, though. If there were 180 kids going out to winter recess and you wanted to know how many mittens they needed in all, would you draw a 2 by 180 table and start filling it in? 1, 2, 3, 4, . . . , 179, 180? And then 2, 4, 6, 8, . . . , 356, 358, 360? Would you recommend that strategy to someone you like?

The table shows the patterns in the numbers nicely, but looking for patterns in the solutions for varying numbers of kids is *not* the same thing as using a table to *solve* the problem. Although the curriculum writers might want to tick off multiple goals with this problem, and a few students who are ready for more abstract reasoning might actually create a table, it's a stretch to direct all first-grade students to solve this problem by making a table and looking for a pattern.

I might consider creating a table *after* students have made sense of the problem to see whether they find the repetition and regularity. What if there were three kids? Five kids? Ten kids? That would be a nice follow-on exploration that would help students notice the structure in the mathematics and develop the kind of pattern-seeking and algebraic thinking we want. But I'm not going to lead with a table, and I won't require students to solve this problem using a table. I want kids to build on what they already know and figure out how to solve problems themselves. I want them to own their thinking.

Is This Problem a Good Fit for the Math I Want to Teach?

Now that I've figured out what the math in this problem really is, I can make an informed choice about whether I should teach it. If my goal were to teach students to count things that come in equivalent groups as early work with multiplication and I had been directed to teach this curriculum, I would pick the three or four best questions (out of the fourteen problems in this packet) and make them over, discarding the rest. I'd opt for much less repetition and much more thinking: *fewer, better problems.*

If my goal were to teach the problem-solving strategy of make a table, however, I would not use the mitten problem. Instead, I'd look for a problem in which a table would truly come in handy. Combination problems create the intellectual need for organizational strategies such as tables and lists. For example, "How many ways are there to make twenty cents?" is a first-grade problem that cries out for a systematic strategy to try combinations and to keep track of solutions. The mittens problem doesn't. I'd make a substitution.

Similarly, if I wanted to teach "look for a pattern" as a problem-solving strategy, I'd swap out the mittens for a more suitable problem.

If I'm Using This Problem, How Can I Make It More Perplexing?

Let's say I've decided to use the mittens problem as an early multiplication problem but want to make it better. In this case, the curriculum has provided numerous steps, directions, representations, text, and even the answer, which remove all possible thinking and interest. Students are more focused on filling out the worksheet—or shutting down—than on asking any questions or making sense. I would remove all those scaffolds. If a student needs a picture to solve this problem, she can draw one. If anyone wants to make a table, he can write one. Do we really need to tell anyone, "Each child has two hands?" Students do not need to be commanded to count kids by ones and hands by twos. Let's have more respect for our students than this.

When I take all the prescriptive elements out of the problem, I'm left with this slim little question on a large page with ample room for student work:

> Four kids want to play in the snow. How many mittens do they need?

Is this question perplexing to a first grader? Contextually, it or may not be. Mathematically, though, it is. Primary students have to do a lot of grappling to figure out number and operations. This problem gives them a chance to make sense of numbers that are growing in an interesting way. For every one child, we need two mittens. The cognitive work to extend that relationship is worthwhile. It's the beginning of multiplicative reasoning.

How Do Kids React?

For my first field test, I corralled my two daughters and asked them my pared-down question. I read the problem to Daphne, who was four at the time. She nodded, thought for a minute, and

Figure 6.3 *"One kid"*

Figure 6.4 *"Two kid"*

Figure 6.5 *"Three*

then looked down at her hands. She stuck out a pair of fingers in her right hand and said, "One kid" (Figure 6.3).

She stuck out a second pair from her left hand and said, "Two kid" (Figure 6.4).

She went back to her right hand, put out two more fingers, and said, "Three kid" (Figure 6.5).

Then she returned to her left hand and stuck out the last pair. "Four kid" (Figure 6.6).

Once all the kids were accounted for, she counted the fingers that were sticking out: "1, 2, 3, 4, 5, 6, 7, 8. They need eight mittens, Mommy" (Figure 6.7).

I asked her why she'd stuck out two fingers at a time, and she explained, "Because each kid needs two mittens." It turned out I didn't need to spell anything out for her. All on her own, Daphne used her fingers to create an appropriate direct model of the problem.

Maya, who was six at the time, read my revised problem herself. She said, "Well, mittens come in pairs. For every kid, there are two mittens. So, to figure out how many mittens I need for four kids, I can just double four. They need eight mittens." Beautiful. Left to her own devices, she took this problem to multiplicative scaling, which had been overwritten right out of the curriculum's version of the problem.

The teacher who shared this problem with me said her class really struggled with it. She asked four students to stand up and model the problem, and all students were able to solve it. They had no idea how to fill out the table, however, so her math class involved lots of questions like these:

"Where are we supposed to write . . . ?"

"What are we supposed to put in the boxes . . . ?"

"What do they mean when they say . . . ?"

"Is this right?"

"I don't get it."

Some students were confused, frustrated, and detached. Other kids cracked the code and filled out the whole packet, but weren't able to answer any probing questions about their work.

Figure 6.6 *"Four kid"*

Figure 6.7 *"They need eight mittens, Mommy."*

The teacher, who was required to implement this curriculum with "strict fidelity" in its first year, was taking copious notes about what she wanted to improve as soon as she was allowed.

Debbie Nichols, first and second grades

"A picture popped up in my head…"

I wanted to take the revised problem to a different class and see what would happen. Debbie kindly offered to have her students take a crack at it. I gave her three versions of the problem with increasingly "unfriendly" numbers of kids (4, 9, 13), so all her students would have to do some figuring out, whether or not they had learned their basic math facts.

I asked Debbie how the problems were received. She said, "When I was giving directions, students were on their knees, ready to grab it and run." She said there was a general sense of "Let me at this!" Students' questions included:

"Can we do more than one?"

"Can we start with any one we want?"

"Can we do all three?"

"Can we draw pictures?"

Debbie's answer to all these questions was "Yes!"

Throughout the session, students were engaged and purposeful. Nobody was hesitant, and nobody was frustrated. Having the three versions was effective because some students worked on one the whole time, while others solved all three.

The next time I visited, Deb and I sat together and looked through her students' work. We saw a lovely range of early multiplication strategies. Nobody used concrete tools, but students' representations ranged from more concrete to representational to abstract or sometimes included elements of all three. We gathered lots of information we would have missed with worksheets because, "when children fill out worksheets, they do not have to organize their thoughts on paper. When they are given a blank sheet of paper with only the problem written at the top, they have a chance to organize their thoughts and decide how to externalize them on paper" (Kamii and Housman 2000, 26). Organizing and externalizing thoughts is essential for kids, but it's also fantastic for teachers. In its original, fill-in-the-blank form, this problem didn't yield any useful, actionable, formative assessment for teachers because we couldn't see how students were thinking. In contrast, we learned quite a bit by looking at the madeover student representations. We created an even fuller picture of how students were thinking by observing them while they worked and having conversations with kids during and after the session. Taken together, these products, observations, and conversations helped us learn what kids were thinking and plan where to go next.

I am gaga over this student's explanation:

Well how I figured out the ansor was that whene Mrs. Nichols said 4 kids wanted to play in the snow a picher poped up in my head and it was a picher of 4 kids and every one has 2 hans and so I figurd out the answer was 8 and I caonted by 2's.

When we removed the line-art drawing from the original curriculum, we gave students room to have their own "pictures pop up in their heads." Visualizing the scenario is an integral part of making sense. How can children make sense if we always hand them the image already prepared? Look at the range of pictures that popped up in different children's heads in Figures 6.8, 6.9, and 6.10.

The student who created Figure 6.11 is thinking a little more abstractly about this problem. She drew her thirteen circles and counted them by ones to figure out the number of kids. Then she went back to the beginning and tapped each circle twice, counting, "one–two, three–four, five–six . . ." until she had counted twenty-six mittens. It's exciting that she had each circle represent two different units at one time—kids and mittens—which reveals a lovely developing understanding of multiplication. In a spectacular display of how not-linear learning mathematics is, she drew an abstract picture and then counted all the parts of her model by ones. Her thinking is in transition, and it's exciting!

Four kids want to play in the snow.
How many mittens do they need?

Figure 6.8 *A concrete, detailed direct model of the mittens problem*

Thirteen kids want to play in the snow.
How many mittens do they need?

Figure 6.9 *A more schematic direct model of the mittens problem that makes it easy to count 13 kids and their mittens*

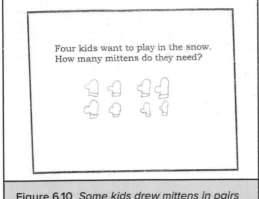

Figure 6.10 *Some kids drew mittens in pairs and skipped drawing the kids.*

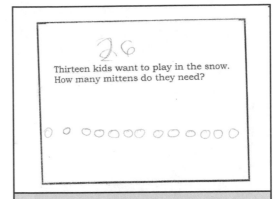

Figure 6.11 *This student touched each circle once and counted to 13 and then went back to the beginning and counted each circle twice to count to 26.*

The student who created the work in Figure 6.12 started to draw a direct model, and then erased it and used a counting strategy instead. She carefully drew nine twos and then skip-counted to find there were eighteen mittens.

One unplanned delight was that some children chose to do all three problems in order of difficulty, so we got to see their thinking grow. For example, the work in Figures 6.13, 6.14, and 6.15 are from a single student. She began with an illustrated direct model where we can see four pairs of mittens (Figure 6.13). In her second problem, she labeled the pairs with numbers and wrote an equation representing repeated addition: $2 + 2 + 2 + 2 + 2 + 2 + 2 + 2 + 2 = 18$ (Figure 6.14). In her third problem, she still drew the direct model, but she skip-counted by twos and wrote those numbers accordingly (Figure 6.15).

That's a pretty amazing progression within a matter of minutes. Even though the numbers became more challenging, she had figured out the structure of the problem and was able to extend her reasoning.

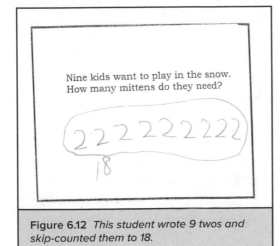

Figure 6.12 *This student wrote 9 twos and skip-counted them to 18.*

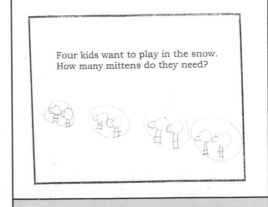

Figure 6.13 *This student started by creating a direct model of the problem with 4 kids.*

Figure 6.14 *The same student tackled the 9 kids problem. She still drew a direct model but used repeated addition as well.*

Figure 6.15 *Finally, the same student used skip-counting to solve the problem when there were 13 kids.*

And look at this! One student developed tables over the course of the three problems (Figure 6.16).

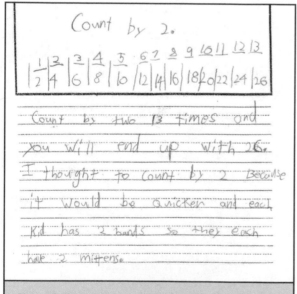

Figure 6.16 *One student invented his own table and used it to keep track of his thinking.*

Low Thresholds, High Ceilings, and Open Middles

When I look over the class set of Debbie's students' representations and think about the mittens problem, I am struck by how well this problem worked for everyone. Debbie teaches a multiage class, so she was looking at the same range of strengths and needs everyone else is, only doubled. Yet, every student in her class was able to access the revised mittens problem and make sense out of it. Nobody cried and nobody sighed. Nobody said, "I don't get it," asked to go to the bathroom, or tried to hoodwink a paraprofessional into doing the work for them. They were too busy thinking about the mathematics of the problem and representing it in pictures, numbers, and equations.

In contrast, the original mittens problem, as published, sent some kids in a tailspin of frustration, while other kids were bored. A much narrower group of students was able to access it.

So what was it about our makeover that made this problem work for more kids?

One way to think about what we did is to borrow a lovely image from Seymour Papert (1980). Imagine this problem is a room, and all students need to enter it through a doorway. If we want all our students to be able to succeed, we can *lower the threshold* in the doorway and the floor in the room so students have fewer barriers to get inside and get started. In this case, removing the massive text load, the prescriptive directions, the table, and the representation lowered that threshold and removed obstacles to entry.

We also want to make sure the students in the room are not constrained, banging their heads, unable to stretch. We want to *raise the ceiling* so there are fewer limits on students' thinking. We want to create problems that will flow right into deeper investigations for students who are ready. For example, the student who developed the table in the mittens problem could be encouraged to keep going and see where those thoughts lead him. Similarly, my daughter, Maya, and I were walking the dogs about a week later when she said this:

> Maya: I've been thinking about the mittens problem. If 4 kids need mittens, you need 8 mittens. If 10 kids need mittens, you need 20 mittens. If 100 kids need mittens, you need 200 mittens. See, it's always doubling. There are 2 mittens for each kid, so the number of mittens will always be double the number of kids.

How's that for Common Core Standard for Mathematical Practice 8, "look for and express regularity in repeated reasoning"? After we played around with doubling a little more, I asked a new question:

> Tracy: Let's think about it a different way. If you have ten mittens, how many kids can wear mittens?
>
> Maya: Five kids.
>
> Tracy: How did you figure that out?
>
> Maya: Um . . . I . . . well . . . what I think I did is . . . I . . . minus doubled.

Minus doubled might be my favorite coinage ever. Maya needed to create a phrase to mean the *opposite of doubling*, and she did!

Thinking back to the class that solved the problem as it was originally written in the curriculum, I can assure you that none of them came back a week later and said, "I've been thinking about the mittens problem, and . . ." The problem was finished when the worksheet was done because the ceiling on this problem was so low.

Dan Meyer (2014) has given us another helpful image for thinking about ways to make over problems so they work for more students. He thinks about the problem-solving path from the beginning, through the middle, to the end in terms of whether it is *open* or *closed*. In the original mittens problem, the beginning, the middle, and the end were all prescribed, so the path looked like Figure 6.17.

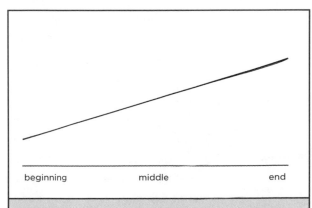

Figure 6.17 *A problem with closed beginning, middle, and end*

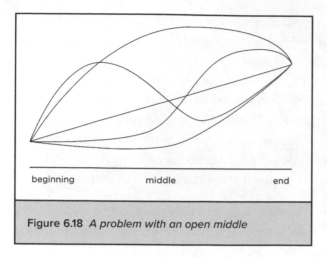

Figure 6.18 *A problem with an open middle*

All students, regardless of how they might think about the mathematics, were expected to march along this singular path in lockstep and arrive at the same destination. This problem was completely closed. No wonder implementation was so difficult.

Dan values problems with an open middle, which he visualizes as Figure 6.18. You can see that students start with the same question and are trying to get to the same answer, but they have multiple solution paths available to them in between. In an eighth-grade problem, students might make a table, draw a graph, or try to solve a problem algebraically. In a fourth-grade problem, students might draw a picture, use a number line, make an array, solve a related problem, break the problem into chunks, use a strategy such as doubling-and-halving, or contextualize a problem with a story. And in a first- or second-grade problem, students might draw or build a direct model, use counting strategies, use what they know to figure out what they don't know, or think about the properties of the operations, as we saw above.

In other words, students have decisions to make in an open-middle problem. These are meaningful, mathematical decisions. They are not decisions about whether to write in colored pencil or pen, or whether to work at your desk or on the rug. They are decisions about which problem-solving strategy to try, which models to use, which representations to create, whether to contextualize or decontextualize, and where to begin and how.

It is enlightening to think about the mittens problem makeover in terms of opening the middle. In its original form, students had no meaningful, mathematical decisions to make because the method was explicitly prescribed: "Make a table to show a pattern. Write the numbers. Count the children by ones. Count the mittens by twos." When I deleted all of that, I put the mathematical decision making back in the hands of the students, where it belongs. Students enjoyed having choices, and we saw them forge multiple paths as they made sense.

In addition, Deb and I added a touch of openness to the beginning and end as well, by providing choice among numbers in the problem and encouraging students to extend the problem into new territory. These multiple access points and options for extensions made it possible for students to surprise us in marvelous ways. A first grader on an Individualized Education Plan for math chose the most difficult problem and nailed it. The student who created the tables—a precocious second grader—started with the smallest numbers, perhaps because he wanted to think about the structure of the problem on the steady ground of $4 + 4 = 8$.

I urge you to experiment with opening the beginning, the middle, or the end of problems and see what results you get. Dan convinced me that the middle is the most essential part to open, so if you're going to pick one, I'd recommend starting there. Thankfully, there's a free tool to help us. Math teachers Robert Kaplinsky, Nanette Johnson, and Bryan Anderson curate and share rich open-middle problems—"challenging math problems worth solving"—at http://www.openmiddle.com/. They organize the problems by both content strand and grade level, from kindergarten through high school. It's a terrific resource, and I recommend it whether you are looking to learn more about what makes for a great task or looking for specific tasks to substitute for weaker problems in your curriculum. As you experiment and play with problem makeovers, you might even find yourself generating problems to submit to openmiddle.com!

When I started thinking about problems in terms of low thresholds, high ceilings, and open middles, my criteria for choosing math problems changed drastically. I want problems that will work for all my students, that have multiple access points and extensions built right into their structure. Hsu, Kysh, and Resek (2007) provided a helpful set of guidelines for analyzing problems to see whether they're rich enough to use in a heterogeneous classroom:

1. The mysterious part of the problem is mathematical.
2. The problem has very little scaffolding.
3. There are many ways to do the problem.
4. Students of different skill levels can learn from this activity.
5. The problem has natural extensions.

When we teach with rich problems with these qualities; when we quit telling kids what tiny, incremental steps to follow; when we drop the *I do, we do, you do* procedural math demonstrations, we create space for students to make mathematical connections, decisions, choices, and risks. We give them the chance to have original thoughts. Math class becomes inclusive and empowering, rather than disenfranchising. Deb's first- and second-grade students show that, when we respect students as mathematical problem solvers and decision makers, they will rise to the challenge beautifully.

Flat Soda

Your turn! Figure 6.19 shows a fourth-grade problem.

How would you make it over?

- What's the math here?
- Is this problem a good fit for that math, or other, interesting math?
- If you were going to teach this problem, how would you revise it?
- Do you see ways to lower the threshold? Raise the ceiling? Open the middle?

Next time you have a planning meeting with your colleagues, you might want to talk through

Follow these steps for each problem.

a. Decide which two numbers need to be multiplied to give the exact answer. Write the two numbers.

b. Estimate whether the answer will be in the tens, hundreds, thousands, or more. Write a number model for the estimate. Circle the box to show your estimate.

c. On the grid below, find the exact answer by multiplying the two numbers. Write the answer.

1. The average person in the United States drinks about 61 cups of soda per month. About how many cups of soda is that per year?

a. _____ * _____   b. _____   c. _____

numbers that give the exact answer | number model for your estimate | exact answer

10s	100s	1,000s	10,000s	100,000s	1,000,000s

Figure 6.19 *How would you make this problem over?*

this problem together. It's a great candidate for a makeover. Or, you could pick a different problem from your curriculum and take a whack at it as a group. We're always smarter together, and makeovers take practice. Once you get the hang of them, though, I expect you'll find that they are effective—and *doable*—even within our ridiculous time constraints for planning.

Productive Struggle Versus Destructive Struggle

I want to dig a little deeper into why I put all this makeover stuff in a chapter about challenge and perseverance. The big idea is we want to create conditions for students to engage in "productive struggle" or "productive failure" and active sense-making, because that's when they learn (e.g., Kapur 2010, 2014). From NCTM's *Principles to Actions*:

> Effective teaching of mathematics consistently provides students, individually and collectively, with opportunities and supports to engage in productive struggle as they grapple with mathematical ideas and relationships. (2014, 48)

This term *productive struggle* captures both elements we're after: we want students challenged *and* learning. Not all struggle is productive! R. Jackson and Lambert (2010) clarified the differences between destructive and productive struggles:

PRODUCTIVE STRUGGLE	DESTRUCTIVE STRUGGLE
Leads to understanding	Leads to frustration
Makes learning goals feel attainable and effort seem worthwhile	Makes learning goals feel hazy and out of reach
Yields results	Feels fruitless
Leads students to feelings of empowerment and efficacy	Leaves students feeling abandoned and on their own
Creates a sense of hope	Creates a sense of inadequacy

We want students challenged, not frustrated; leaning forward, not slumping down. To get students in that sweet spot, we need to design problems that will require them to wrestle with the mathematics, and then we teachers need to be less helpful than we've been historically:

> Teachers sometimes perceive student frustration or lack of immediate success as indicators that they have somehow failed their students. As a result, they jump in to "rescue" students by breaking down the task and guiding students step by step through the difficulties. Although well intentioned, such "rescuing" undermines the efforts of students, lowers the cognitive demand of the task, and deprives students of opportunities to engage fully in making sense of the mathematics. (NCTM 2014, 48)

I see this rescuing every day. As long as learners are engaged in productive struggle, even if they are headed toward a dead end, we need to bite our tongues and let students figure it out. Otherwise, we rob them of their well-deserved, satisfying, wonderful feelings of accomplishment when they make sense of problems and persevere.

Productive Struggle, Be Less Helpful, and Special Education

In my experience, the tendency to "rescue" children when they hit snags in their mathematics is especially true and problematic for students with special needs. How do we resolve the tension between wanting all students to engage in productive struggle with the fact that some students need more support?

The first and most essential step is to reexamine what we mean by modifications and accommodations. The most common versions I see are (1) breaking the problem down into smaller steps for students and (2) teaching students tricks, rules, algorithms, or procedures to implement so they can get an answer. There are big problems with both.

The problem with the break-it-down approach is, if an educator (classified or certified), breaks down the problem and directs what to do for each step, then the educator is the person who has done the problem solving, thinking, and learning. The student is left to implement the educator's strategies, whether or not he understands them. The next time the student works with similar mathematics, he won't be any wiser, because he wasn't allowed to do any thinking.

As for teaching tricks and rules, this approach is also shortsighted and ineffective (Burns 2000). Jean Behrend (2001) described the downside in her case study of a student she named Dan, a third grader who received math education in the resource room. In this case, Dan was adding columns of numbers by lining them up on the left, so he wrote *6 + 21 = 81*. Behrend figured out why:

> Over the years, Dan had been taught an extensive set of rules, including count the dots on the numbers, start with the ones, line the numbers up, do not subtract a larger number from a smaller number, and carry the 1. Because he did not understand why the rules worked, he applied them indiscriminately. Even though Dan had reasonable number sense, his reliance on the rules interfered with his mathematical understanding. He blindly accepted the rules, almost as if he had no expectation that mathematics should make sense. (39)

When she thought about what to do next, she could see the appeal of giving Dan a new rule, but she could see the long-term downside as well.

> I could have used a quick fix by teaching the rule "Line up the numbers on the right." This rule is often heard in elementary classrooms, especially those for students identified as learning disabled, to "help" the students. Repetition and reminders of the rule may have eliminated the computational mistakes I observed. Teaching the rule, however, would not develop base-ten knowledge nor help the students understand why lining up numbers can be useful in certain methods of computation. In the long run, teaching students to align numbers on the right without understanding the power of combining like units, that is, ones with ones, tens with tens, and so on, could confuse them later. If students just learn the rule that says they should "Line up numbers on the right," they have to learn a new rule to add or subtract decimals: "Line up the decimal points." *Without an understanding of the mathematical relationships, each new situation demands a new rule.* (36–37, emphasis added)

In her research with math students with learning disabilities, Behrend found she needed only one rule: understand the problem.

> This basic strategy of "understand the problem" allowed students to solve a variety of problems without learning new strategies for different types of problems. (2003, 270)

Meaningful accommodations may include giving a student more time, better learning conditions, or different ways to participate. We can support students as they make sense of the question by teaching them to model the action in the problem, use manipulatives, draw representations, or use reading comprehension strategies to make sense. Once a student understands the problem, she can engage in productive struggle to solve it. When she gets stuck, Behrend suggests we redirect her to the conditions of the problem "instead of giving clue words or procedures" (2003, 273). We need to focus on the development of the young mathematicians in front of us and let them focus on the assignments in front of them.

For an in-depth look at productive, supportive, effective math teaching for students with special educational needs, I recommend Judy Storeygard's book and DVD, *My Kids Can: Making Math Accessible to All Learners, K–5* (2009). In the foreword, Deborah Schifter wrote, "The most important message in this book is that *all* children, given appropriate supports, can learn mathematics for *understanding*. This may come as a surprise to those who were taught that the best way to work with struggling students is to break mathematical tasks into small chunks to be memorized. Instead, the key is to find where a student is on solid ground and provide tasks that will help him or her move forward" (viii). Through classroom examples, Storeygard shared several approaches, strategies, accommodations, and modifications that will give all our students access to meaningful mathematics. These strategies are especially important for the paraprofessionals, educational technicians, and classroom aides who are in the trenches but often left out of the necessary collaborations and professional development.

Margin Symbols: "I need _____ to be successful at this . . . "

Students who have been taught to depend on teachers and curriculum for guidance and validation have often learned helplessness. If we're going to give students opportunities to struggle, we need to teach them strategies to try if they get stuck. Years ago, I learned about margin symbols at a workshop and began experimenting with them in my fourth-grade class. The idea is you teach students simple communication icons they can draw in the margins of their work to let you know where things stand. Over time, I developed a set of six symbols that served as both a formative self-assessment and a teaching tool to create resourceful, persistent problem solvers, shown in Figure 6.20.

I love these particular margin symbols for several reasons:

- **The assumption is students will be successful with hard work and good strategies**. None of the choices is, "I can't do this; I quit." If students don't have the

MARGIN SYMBOLS	
!	I've got this and am ready for something new
✓	I'm feeling pretty good about this. It's coming together. I still want to practice a little more
⏱	I need more time to be successful at this.
😊😊	I need to work with a peer to be successful at this.
🌳♪	I need a break to be successful at this. I'll put this problem to the side, do something else, and then come back to it.
✊	I need help from a teacher to be successful at this.

Figure 6.20 *Margin symbols for math class*

concept nailed down just yet, it's clear that all roads still lead to success. They just need to choose a path and keep going. Margin symbols teach perseverance as a disposition.

- **Students learn how to say what they need.** I want my students to recognize their needs and advocate for themselves from early on. Margin symbols can help us give students the language to identify and state their needs. Instead of feeding them cues and hints, we can say, "You're stuck? OK. What would help you?"

- **Margin symbols reflect how problems are solved.** Many students have the misimpression that problem solving means you read the problem and you either know the answer or you don't. The truth is mathematicians spend most of their time in between knowing and not knowing: thinking, solving, getting stuck, getting unstuck, trying again. They take all the time necessary, and they talk to peers or consult experts as needed. When they're stuck, they take breaks to get some exercise, do something creative, have a change of scene, and let their thoughts wander. Einstein used to take breaks to talk with colleagues, eat ice cream, ride his bicycle, play the violin, or go to the ocean. I'm no Einstein, but I've figured out more than one chapter of this book when I closed my laptop and took my dogs for a walk in the woods. Why not share this problem-solving strategy with our students?

- **Nobody lingers in boredom or frustration.** Once students are fluent in margin symbols, they can put them on any assignment. If a student feels like she has worked with a concept plenty and really has it inside and out, the exclamation point (!) symbol is an easy way for her to tell me. I can check in with her, make sure she's self-assessing accurately, and encourage her to explore a new idea or go deeper if she is ready. Likewise, if a student is really having a hard time, he can draw the raised hand to let me know he needs teacher help. I can get with him before productive struggle turns to destructive struggle.

- **They enable me to be strategic with assessment.** I can pick a problem or a series of problems tightly aligned to my objective and ask students to let me know how they feel about them. For example, if problem number 2 is an especially good measure of the elements I'm after, I ask students, "Would everyone please give me a margin symbol on number 2?" Then, when I sit with their work, I can see students' mathematics and gain insight about their affects, confidence, and needs at the same time. Individual conferences are ideal and important, but margin symbols are a quick, written version of the same idea.

- **Each concept—and each student—is treated individually.** Margin symbols are a far cry from ability groups, for good reason. One student might cruise through double-digit multiplication but really struggle with seeing symmetry in geometry. A different student might still be working toward efficient addition strategies but knows how to explain his thinking in writing. A third student might be procedurally proficient with fractions but have no idea how to justify what she did. Which of those students is high, medium, or low? The answer is none. Each student has some concepts mastered and is working toward others, because every student has areas of strength to build from and areas that are opportunities for growth. Margin symbols allow students and the teacher to be specific about what the student knows and is able to do and what the student has not yet learned. This level of specificity helps us move past the fixed-mindset world of high, medium, and low to get to a place of truly responsive instruction where we are all honest about what we need to learn.

Developing the Skills and Content Expertise to Challenge Students

In teacher workshops, I sometimes have grade-level teams choose problems to make over. What I've learned from my colleagues is that—like anything worth knowing—learning how to analyze problems takes work and time. At first, thinking through a problem will take quite a while. With practice, though, it gets much faster and easier. It took me no more than ten minutes from start to finish to think through the mittens problem and to create the new documents. I count those ten minutes of a planning period as time very well spent.

What also emerges, however, is that many teachers lack the confidence to critique published curriculum problems. Some of the most common comments I've heard:

"I figure if they're in the book, there must be a good reason."

"The people who wrote the curriculum are math experts, and I'm not. Should I really undo what they've done?"

"I am worried that this stuff is probably in the book because it's going to be on the test in April. If I don't teach them to do problems like this, they might do badly on the test."

That last concern breaks my heart, but it is a sign of the times. Let's tackle it first. I have two responses:

1. None of us became teachers because we cared about that test. We happen to be teaching in a time when policy makers have gone mad for high-stakes testing, but that doesn't mean we should let badly written test questions drive us to teach badly written problems. That's not why I'm here.
2. Even if we do care about the test, the best way to prepare students for it is to teach them how to reason mathematically. In the mittens problem packet, there were fourteen problems, all with identically laid out tables (written horizontally, created for the students). What if the problems on the test are similar, but the tables are vertical? Or students are asked to create the table themselves? Kids who decode worksheets and depend on scaffolds instead of reasoning through the math will be lost.

Don't take my word for it, though. Stanford professor Jo Boaler has researched and written about this issue extensively. In her terrific book *What's Math Got to Do with It?* (2008), she summarized research from a longitudinal study of two demographically matched schools, pseudonyms Phoenix Park and Amber Hill. At Phoenix Park, students engaged in problem-based learning in mixed-ability groups. Teachers taught mathematical methods as needed to help students solve problems. At Amber Hill, teachers used the traditional demonstration, guided practice, independent practice model. According to Boaler's research, students at Phoenix Park generally found math interesting and flexible, whereas students at Amber Hill disliked math and found it tedious and rote.

When it came time for exams, the results were fascinating. "In lessons, the Amber Hill students were often successful, getting lots of questions right in their exercises, but they often got them right, not by understanding the mathematical ideas but by following cues . . . Unfortunately, the same cues were not present in the exams" (Boaler 2008, 76). Students described panicking on the exams when no text-based or teacher-based cues told them which memorized procedures to use. A teacher said, "Students are generally good, unless a question is slightly different to what they are used to, or if they are asked to do something after a time lapse, if a question is written in words, or if they are expected to answer in words. If you look at the question and tell them that it's basically asking them to multiply 86 by 32, or something, they can do it, but otherwise they just look at the question and go blank" (Boaler 1999, 48). If students were able to decide on a reasonable procedure, they often remembered it incorrectly and weren't able to implement it successfully. Even though Amber Hill's math approach was "examination oriented" and Phoenix Park teachers only spent a few weeks preparing students for exams, Phoenix Park students "attained significantly higher examination grades" (Boaler 2008, 77).

Not only that, Amber Hill students said they "would never, ever make use of their school-learned methods in any situation outside school . . . The Amber Hill students thought school mathematics was a strange sort of code that you would use in one place—the mathematics classroom" (79–80). Phoenix Park students, on the other hand, were "confident they would utilize the methods they learned in school" (80). Indeed, when Boaler interviewed students several years later, "The Phoenix Park young adults were working in more highly skilled or professional jobs than the Amber Hill adults" (80–81). As adults, the Phoenix Park graduates described the "ways they used the problem-solving approach they had been taught in their mathematics classrooms to solve problems and make sense of mathematical situations in their lives" (81). In contrast, the Amber Hill graduates felt "their school mathematics approach had prepared them . . . badly for the demands of the workplace" (82).

The evidence is clear, and the results are happy, because we don't have to choose between high-quality math teaching and higher test scores. If we want students to do well on exams and in life, we need to teach them how to reason their way through a problem. Stripping the cues, prompts, and scaffolds out will help us create powerful problem solvers who succeed.

Let's turn to the other issues colleagues bring up about makeovers, which are teacher confidence, expertise, and content knowledge. These are important issues, and we need to deal with them honestly. If we don't have the content knowledge or pedagogical content knowledge to think about the mathematics in a problem deeply and critically, we need to do something about it.

For example, as a fourth-grade teacher, I haven't taught multiplication and division of fractions much, so I haven't been pushed to dig into the content. Because my content knowledge is shakier, I tend to fall back on the algorithms I was taught as a kid. I can calculate the answers, but I don't have great intuition about division of a fraction by a fraction. I don't have powerful visual models in my mind of exactly what's going on there. The keywords I was taught—codes such as *of means multiply*—have misled me more than once. I rely on procedures like inverting and multiplying when dividing, and I have a hunch that there are much more sensible approaches.

So, whenever I'm at a math education conference, I attend sessions about multiplication and division of fractions. I also picked up a few highly recommended books about teaching fractions that have strong fractions content. I read blogs, talk with other teachers on Twitter, and join fifth- and sixth-grade planning meetings so I can learn. Because I realized that I didn't understand the content well enough to teach it powerfully—or for my own satisfaction—I am giving myself the time to make some sense. I am honoring myself as a learner. I still have more to learn, but the understanding is coming, and it's exciting! Doing that work is good for me and will benefit my students as well.

What I've found is that teachers with the strongest math content background are the most willing to say, "I don't understand the math here." For example, a middle school math teacher recently tweeted to thousands of fellow math teachers, "Wait a minute! I just realized I don't understand long division! Why does it work? Help!" I loved that. I love that he recognized where he needed to work on content, and he reached out for help. Other math teachers jumped in the conversation, and they figured it out together.

The math we teach in elementary school includes big, fascinating concepts, worthy of respect and study: cardinality, equality, the number system, operations, zero (Ma 1999). Most of us were not taught those big concepts well, which is why so many elementary teachers say, "I didn't really understand this until I had to teach it." We were given procedures to memorize, like the kids at Amber Hill. Nowadays, we know we should be teaching like the teachers at Phoenix Park. We can't possibly switch from one mode to the other without exploring the mathematical content ourselves, in better and deeper ways than we did as students.

Here are some resources that will help you develop your own mathematical content knowledge and improve your math teaching.

Elementary and Middle School Mathematics: Teaching Developmentally by John A. Van de Walle, Karen S. Karp, and Jennifer M. Bay-Williams (2013, but earlier editions are excellent, too).

Math Matters: Understanding the Math You Teach, Grades K–8, Second Edition, by Suzanne Chapin and Art Johnson (2006).

The CGI series:

Children's Mathematics: Cognitively Guided Instruction, Second Edition, by Thomas P. Carpenter, Elizabeth Fennema, Megan Loef Franke, Linda Levi, and Susan B. Empson (2014).

Extending Children's Mathematics: Fractions and Decimals; Innovations in Cognitively Guided Instruction by Susan B. Empson and Linda Levi (2011).

Thinking Mathematically: Integrating Arithmetic & Algebra in Elementary School, by Thomas P. Carpenter, Megan Loef Franke, and Linda Levi (2003).

The Young Mathematicians at Work series by Catherine Twomey Fosnot and Maarten Dolk (2001).

Both *Investigations in Number, Data, and Space* and the *Connected Mathematics Project* have excellent essays for teachers about content embedded right in the curriculum.

"Ask Dr. Math" is a free program from the good people at the Math Forum. Teachers or students can ask specific math questions and converse with knowledgeable experts. They also have a searchable archive of past questions and answers: mathforum.org/dr.math/.

Your colleagues. Other experts. These print resources are great, but learning and doing math is an ongoing, human endeavor. Talk with other people, in person and online. Take workshops together. Think it through out loud. Honor yourselves as learners.

You can use makeovers as an opportunity to develop your content knowledge, too. If you find yourself stuck at the question, "What is the math here?" there is a chance you might have some new learning to do. Your motivation for doing that learning is because you want to do better for your students than was done for you. But a second, equally important reason is that you deserve to keep learning and growing yourself! Makeovers give you a chance to dig into specific content in short, contained chunks. Over the years, a problem at a time, your mathematical content knowledge will grow and deepen.

As for expertise and mass-marketed curriculum, that's a mixed bag. There is some wonderful curriculum written by thoughtful experts, and there is some unconscionably awful stuff peddled to school districts daily. As your content knowledge and grasp of students' mathematical thinking grow, so will your ability to separate the wheat from the chaff. You'll increasingly be able to keep the good, make over the weak, and junk the terrible. Eventually, you might find yourself creating new and perplexing problems, too, as you deepen your understanding of what makes for a good problem and add to your repertoire of strategies. Starting with makeovers is one of the best, most effective ways I know to build that essential pedagogical content knowledge, and your own expertise, one manageable piece at a time.

MATHEMATICIANS
ASK QUESTIONS

*P*eter Hilton, an algebraic topologist, has said: "Computation involves going from
a question to an answer. Mathematics involves going from an answer to a question."
*Such work requires creativity, original thinking, and ingenuity. All the mathematical methods
and relationships that are now known and taught to schoolchildren started as questions, yet
students do not see the questions. Instead, they are taught content that often appears as a long
list of questions that nobody has ever asked.*

—Jo Boaler, *What's Math Got to Do with It?*

In math classes, students mostly answer someone else's questions and solve someone else's
problems using someone else's procedures. They rarely get to ask their own questions, pose
their own problems, generate their own ideas, explore their own observations, or try out their
own theories. After enduring years of this kind of teaching, once inquisitive little kids evolve
into passive, apathetic teenagers: "Young children have a natural curiosity about the world
in which they live. Unfortunately, this curiosity, particularly with respect to mathematics,

often seems to disappear by the time they reach secondary school" (Knuth 2002, 130). Similarly, Eleanor Duckworth (1987, 5) observed, "What happens to children's curiosity and resourcefulness later in their childhood? Why do so few continue to have their own wonderful ideas?"

This loss of curiosity is alarming across the board, but it's especially concerning for math teachers. It's not possible to do good mathematics—or enjoy it—without being curious, asking questions, seeking out patterns, probing for underlying reasons and structures, wondering, *Why does that happen?* or *What if . . . ?* Curiosity drives mathematics and leads to posing problems in the first place.

I once asked a group of students, "Where do you think mathematicians get the problems they work on?"

There were some shrugs, and then a student volunteered, "Maybe their teachers give 'em to them?"

Another student said, "From the book?"

Alrighty then. Let's ask mathematicians who assigns them problems:

> *The best problems are your own.* You are the intrepid mental explorer; it's your mind and your adventure. Mathematical reality is *yours*—it's in your head for you to explore any time you feel like it. What are your questions? Where do you want to go? . . . Don't be afraid that you can't answer your own questions—that's the natural state of the mathematician . . . What makes a mathematician is not technical skill or encyclopedic knowledge but insatiable curiosity and a desire for simple beauty. Just be yourself and go where you want to go. Instead of being tentative and fearing failure or confusion, try to embrace the awe and mystery of it all and joyfully make a mess. Yes, your ideas won't work. Yes, your intuition will be flawed. Again, welcome to the club! I have a dozen bad ideas a day and so does every other mathematician. (Lockhart 2012, 9–10)

If questioning, curiosity, inquiry, investigation, problem posing, and pattern seeking are so highly valued by mathematicians, then we should value and teach these dispositions in math class. Of course, we'll still need to assign students plenty of problems, but surely we can make at least some room for students to ask genuine mathematical questions, too.

I've chosen several different instructional strategies for infusing curiosity in math class. They all emphasize asking questions, teaching how to ask questions, deemphasizing or delaying answers in order to highlight questioning, and honoring students' wondering. Where these strategies really differ is in the amount of classroom time they take and the scope of the questions they allow you to take on. I'm hoping you'll find the variation in grain size helpful as you think about how to incorporate more questioning in your math classes.

We're going to start off with *101questions,* a resource that makes it possible for us to add mathematical questioning to our roster of warm-up and transition routines in math class. If all you can manage is five or ten minutes one day per week, you can still engage in meaningful curiosity development with *101questions*.

Second, we'll turn to *Notice and Wonder*, which is a beautiful strategy for problem- and lesson-sized teaching. Once you've learned how it works, you'll be able to apply it to tasks of your choice in whatever curriculum you are using. *Notice and Wonder* can help you delay answer getting and encourage sense making.

Third, a natural follow-up to *Notice and Wonder* is to focus explicitly on problem posing, which is an essential part of mathematics that students rarely learn. We'll see what happens when a teacher gives students data and asks them to generate questions.

Fourth, we'll look at building student curiosity and wondering by teaching them to riff off problems. Once they've put in a good amount of work solving a problem, we can encourage students to tweak the conditions, to change some parameters, to wonder *What if . . .* , and to think about implications.

Fifth, we'll look at individual inquiry projects, or independent studies. Given the pressures on teachers to get through curriculum, it's challenging to carve out time for students to pose and pursue their own mathematical questions. Nevertheless, if you can find a few days or weeks—perhaps in those odd partial weeks on the calendar, or toward the end of the school year when everyone could use an influx of energy—independent studies are worth the investment.

Finally, we'll dive into a question-driven inquiry unit in a mathematics classroom. One of Debbie Nichols's students asked, "Are shapes math?" and that question launched a multiweek geometry unit built around students' geometric wonders. I won't share everything they did, of course, but I hope to go into just enough detail to embolden you to teach math as inquiry while still teaching the expected content and practice standards.

101questions (101qs.com)

Take a look at the picture in Figure 7.1. What's the first question that comes to mind?

Don't worry about answering. Just ask! These were some of my questions:

- Do Double Stuf Oreos really have double the stuff?
- Why do Double Stufs have double the stuff but half the f's?
- How many ways do people actually eat them? Twist-off? Dunk? Bite?
- What's the most popular way to eat them?
- Why do people want double the stuff but not double the cookie?

Figure 7.1 *What's the first question that comes to mind?*

Figure 7.2 *What's the first question that comes to mind?*

What about Figures 7.2 and 7.3? What questions come to mind?

These pictures are from *101questions*, a searchable, free, crowd-sourced bank of thousands of perplexing photographs and videos created and curated by Dan Meyer. I encourage you to pause for a moment and go to the website, 101qs.com. First, play! Take a look at the all-time top ten entries. Surf around. I expect you'll find it delightful. Notice if you smile. Which images inspired lots of questions?

When you're ready to put your teacher hat back on, think about how *101questions* could work as an instructional routine in your classroom. You certainly could use it as a warm-up at the beginning of class or the start of school rather than a more traditional *Do Now* or *Math Message*. I can't think of a better way to set the expectation that students should approach math with inquisitiveness and curiosity than starting your lesson with *101questions*. If you have one class of students all day, you might project *101questions* during snack or lunch and encourage kids to discuss their questions with their neighbors. If you have a few minutes at the end of the day or between activities, it makes a terrific transition or closing activity.

One reason this routine is so powerful is the focus on questions, and only questions. How do you think your students would react if they had the opportunity to ask questions without the pressure of finding answers? In my experience, reluctant math students savor the freedom to take risks, to enjoy math, to generate ideas without dread. There is no way to be wrong here, and nobody need think, "I have a good question, but I'm not going to say it because then she'll make me solve it, and I have no idea how."

Figure 7.3 *What's the first question that comes to mind?*

Sometimes students will be so perplexed by their questions they'll be disappointed when you move on without giving them a chance to answer. When was the last time you had that reaction in a math class—"No, wait! What's the answer? I'm dying to know!" How refreshing to be able to say, "I'm sorry, no answers today. We're just asking questions," smile, and move on. Of course, if they want to work on the problem and let you know how it goes, that would be fantastic, too.

A few follow-up questions that will promote discussion during *101questions*:

- What question do you think most people ask?
- What question would you really want an answer to?
- What question would you never want to have to figure out? Why?
- Share your questions at your table. Did anyone else's question inspire you to think of a new question, or add on to theirs?"
- What's a question you heard today that was surprising/interesting/thought provoking to you?
- Did you ask any questions we could figure out using mathematics, if we wanted to?

Annie Fetter, Max Ray-Riek, and the Math Forum

Notice and Wonder

As much as I love *101questions*, we do need to find answers in math class. Lots of them! So how can we maintain the inquisitiveness of *101questions* while teaching problem solving? The thoughtful teachers at the Math Forum invented a lesson structure that meets our needs perfectly. They call it *Notice and Wonder*, and it is one of those simple ideas that makes a huge difference in a classroom.

Max Ray-Riek explained *Notice and Wonder* in detail in his excellent book *Powerful Problem Solving: Activities for Sense Making with the Mathematical Practices* (2013, 42–55). Max included several classroom examples there, and I've linked to a number of additional online resources at stenhouse.com/becomingmathteacher.

The basic structure of *Notice and Wonder* follows:

1. Give students an image or scenario without a question. If you like, you can use problems from your curriculum and obscure or delete the question.
2. Ask them, "What do you notice?" (You might want to use think-pair-shares at each step to increase engagement and thoughtfulness.) Record their noticings so students can see them.
3. Ask students, "What are you wondering?" Record their wonderings.
4. Ask students, "Is there anything up here that you are wondering about? Anything you need clarified?" Pursue any follow-up questions.
5. Once students have had ample time for noticing and wondering, you can either reveal a question you'd like them to solve or have students come up with a question by asking, "If this story were the beginning of a math problem, what could the math problem be?" (46–47)

For example, here is a scenario called Pooling Tips:

Ethan, Fran, and Gloria have summer jobs at the local Dairy Freeze. They collect their own tips and then share them equally. One week Ethan collected $25 in tips, Fran collected $48, and Gloria collected $41.

What do you notice? What do you wonder?

We've all had students who pluck the numbers out of the problem and immediately start doing things to them. "Add! Wait, is this a subtract?" By removing the question from a textbook problem and inserting the time to *Notice and Wonder*, we prolong thinking and delay answer getting. We teach students to slow down and make sense of the situation rather than throw operations at the numbers. In Pooling Tips, students could certainly average the three numbers and figure out what each kid took home. But, if we breathe for a second, we think, what's going in this story? Why isn't Ethan pulling in the money that Gloria and Fran are? Is he working in the back? Is he working fewer days? Is he grouchy? There is such potential for rich conversation and curiosity when we keep the scenario and simply remove the written question.

Annie Fetter used a scenario called Growing Worms with several classes at two different middle schools near Philadelphia and then shared student thinking with me. Let's see a sampling of what kids noticed and wondered about the image in Figure 7.4.

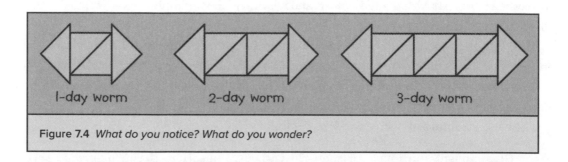

Figure 7.4 *What do you notice? What do you wonder?*

I notice . . .

- The worm is made of shapes.
- It says days and numbers.
- They go from big to bigger to biggest.
- It increases every day.
- It adds two triangles every day.
- They have triangles on the ends.
- The slant always goes in the same direction.
- The worms are made of polygons.
- The two triangles on the end would add to equal a square.
- Each one has a 90-degree triangle.
- There are parallel lines in it.

- There's a pattern. Day 1, there are two triangles in the middle. Day 2, there are four triangles in the middle. Day 3, there are six triangles in the middle.
- Each day has an even number of triangles.
- There are two types of triangles (right and equilateral).
- None of the worms look like worms.
- If you cut every triangle in half, you get the same triangle shape.
- The worms have N shapes inside.
- There is no roundness.
- Each day has an odd number of lines.
- Each day, add five lines.

I wonder . . .

- Why are the squares cut in half?
- How many triangles are there in all three worms?
- What type of worm is it?
- How many triangles will it have on Day 115?
- What is this picture?
- How many boxes get added each day?
- What does this have to do with math?
- How many squares would there be in ten days?
- What's the total number of boxes in all of the worms?
- What day worm is made of twenty triangles?
- What is the pattern going up by?
- Why is there an even number of triangles?
- If there's only a half-day, would you find the same pattern?
- What will we learn by finding out the days or the triangles?
- What polygon would it be if you rearranged the shapes?
- Why are the worms shaped as they are?
- Why are there three examples instead of two?
- Will the worms keep growing infinitely?
- Can you fold all the triangles together to form one?
- What happens if we cut the worm in half?

Wow! Look at how much they see, and what marvelous questions they have about this scenario! I wouldn't have thought of several of the ideas they had. Also, student participation was excellent, and the teachers were struck by how many comments came from students who rarely speak in math class. Expanding math class to encompass questioning—not just answering—can shake up the entrenched patterns and assumptions in your class (Brown and Walter 2005).

The Growing Worms scenario is rich, so student questions ranged from geometry to fractions to growing patterns. Depending on Annie's objective for the lesson, she could then choose one of the student questions or a question she'd prepared ahead of time that would best fit her learning objective. Because students have already done tremendous thinking about the scenario, the shift into problem solving is smooth. Max described the benefits of the *Notice and Wonder* routine this way:

> When students see a *question* in math class, they tend to go into "get the answer quick!" mode. Students often feel pressure and anxiety around having to get the answer, whether it's competitiveness to show their smarts or fear that they won't be able to answer that stops them from engaging. We've found that leaving off the question and just sharing an initial story/scenario/image increases participation from struggling students because there are no right or wrong answers to "What do you notice?" and "What are you wondering?" It keeps speedy students engaged in creative brainstorming rather than closed-ended problem solving. It provides a safe, welcoming opening for students who don't often feel like they have anything to say in math classes—it starts to unsilence their voices! And often, students generate the very question we would have asked through their wonderings; answering a question *they* generated increases all students' engagement. Through wondering, students see that math problems come from their own thinking. (46)

When I introduce teachers to *101questions* or *Notice and Wonder*, they are often on board with the general idea but express concern that students will notice and wonder about all kinds of things that don't have to do with math. There is some truth to this: students are likely to cast the net wide at first, which is great. Generating lots of ideas is part of the process. Over time, you'll probably want to help students focus on mathematical noticings and wonderings with questions like (Ray 2013, 50):

> "Which of these noticings have to do with math?"
>
> "Which of these wonderings could we use math to help us answer/prove?"
>
> "What would a scientist notice? What would an artist notice? What would an athlete notice? What would a mathematician notice?"
>
> "Which of these did you use math to think of?"

"Which of these could we use math to explore more?"

Determining what is or isn't a mathematical question seems worthy of some math classroom time, doesn't it? What questions are inherently mathematical? What contexts can or should be mathematized? Which of those questions are compelling, and which feel like we're trying too hard to make the world sound like a word problem from a textbook? How is math a way to make sense of the world? Let's dig a little deeper into problem posing.

Problem Posing

As we learned in Chapter 2, "What Do Mathematicians Do?" students define math based on its portrayal in society and their accumulated experiences in math class. Becky Wright, an outstanding kindergarten teacher, told me her students arrive believing math only exists within the walls of the math classroom. By age five, they've already internalized a narrow definition of mathematics as answer getting and worksheets in school.

Engaging students in problem posing is one way to add substance and depth to students' definition of mathematics. If students think math is answering someone else's questions on a worksheet, their worldview is rocked a little when we ask students to create the questions themselves. I recently watched this happen in the second-grade classroom of my colleague Sheryl Horton.

Sheryl initially planned to create some interesting problems using the data her students had gathered during a science investigation. Debbie Nichols (who teaches across the hall) encouraged Sheryl to give students the data and ask *them* to write the questions instead. Sheryl was excited by the idea and set to planning.

Sheryl's class had taken a field trip to the fish hatchery and returned with 200 live trout eggs. Along with their fifth- and sixth-grade buddy class, Sheryl's students were monitoring the tank regularly and keeping track of data: How many eggs hatched into alevin? How many eggs were still alive but had not yet hatched? How many eggs and alevin died? As eggs and alevin died, the kids removed them from the tank and fed them to fish in a different, warm-water tank. Sheryl was confident kids understood the story here. After several days with the tanks, Sheryl gave her second graders this challenge:

> The fish hatchery gave us 200 trout eggs. Right now we have 75 live alevin, 25 live eggs, and 20 dead eggs in the tank. What questions could you ask using these data?

After the lesson, Sheryl asked me to visit the class the next day because she was struck by how difficult this challenge was for her kids. They struggled to generate questions, and they didn't seem to understand that different questions might have different answers or not use the same numbers.

When I walked in, Sheryl's students were discussing four questions they'd developed the day before:

- How many things are in the tank?
- How many eggs are there altogether?
- How many things are alive in the tank?
- How many dead eggs or dead alevin have we fed to the fish in the warm-water tank?

Conversation screeched to a halt when Nate asked, "How is this math?"

He was troubled by the whole premise of this activity. When we asked him to say more, he explained that math involves adding or subtracting the numbers in a problem that somebody else wrote. He was not used to thinking about what mathematical questions he might ask about a situation. Sheryl used Nate's comments as a launching point for a larger discussion about what mathematics is and where we can find it. We didn't come close to settling the issue in the large-group discussion, but Sheryl and I both thought we'd given the kids food for thought.

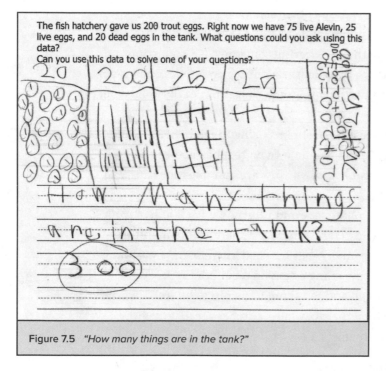

Figure 7.5 *"How many things are in the tank?"*

Providing an opportunity for students to pose problems would be worth the time invested if all it did was lead to this expanding definition of mathematics. Problem posing goes one better, however, because it pushes students into much deeper thinking than most answer getting. I'm thinking particularly of the work of Samuel, shown in Figure 7.5.

Samuel's question was how many things are in the tank? His answer was 300. He told me all about how he added up the numbers in the problem. He represented the numbers carefully and thoughtfully. He'd made an error adding but that was not my immediate concern. My concern was that his answer made no sense with his question.

What was fascinating was that Samuel was able to describe the story of what happened with the fish eggs. They had started with 200 eggs and then some had hatched and then some had died. He'd been there when the dead eggs were physically *removed* from the tank and fed to the warm-water fish. Yet, he *added*. When I asked him why he added, he said, "That's what you do in math problems. See these numbers up here? What you do is you take those numbers and you add them together." When I asked how he could end up with more eggs than he started with if some had hatched and others had died and became fish food, he was clearly puzzled. What he knew from experience didn't match what he thought he knew about math.

If Sheryl had written cut-and-dry problems from this data set, she never would have known how Samuel, Nate, and their classmates were thinking. Imagine the difference if she had asked, "There are 75 live alevin, 25 live eggs, and 20 dead eggs in the tank. How many things are in the tank?" Samuel would have plucked the numbers out, added them together, and probably written the correct answer.

Now, however, Sheryl had learned that lots of her students were getting answers in math without thinking about the question. They were unsure of how to pose a question. And they were not thinking about what makes sense. This was incredibly valuable information that affected her planning going forward. She decided to renew her focus on *101questions* and *Notice and Wonder*, as well as give students many more opportunities to pose problems. She also decided to try one of Debbie Nichols's warm-up routines, which is to post a number and say, "_____ is the answer. What is the question?" Deb's students find this structure challenging initially, but with practice, they grow increasingly comfortable asking mathematical questions.

Riffing Off Problems: Asking, "What If?"

In genuine mathematical activity, answers suggest new questions.
        —Peter Hilton, Derek Holton, and Jean Pederson, *Mathematical Reflections*

Once a problem has been posed or answered, mathematicians often engage in a delightful stage of riffing off the original problem. They might create a related problem, try to break what they've just built, or imagine a slightly different scenario that would yield a problematic result. Mostly, they change the problem's parameters to see how those changes affect the outcomes. I don't often see this sort of play in classrooms, where we tend to treat the answers to problems as endings, rather than beginnings. The analogy in my mind is a car ride: We often treat problems as if they were road trips to single destinations. Once we get where we're going, we don't even look out the window before we turn the car around and head to a new destination. Asking "What if?" instead is like getting out of the car, stretching our legs, and checking out the neighborhood a bit before journeying on. In other words, if we're going to take all that time to drive there, why not have a look around before leaving?

For example, my seven-year-old daughter, Maya, appeared in the kitchen with a problem of her own creation:

> Maya: What if our family had 2,300 people in it? How would we spread them out on the floors of our house so it would be the most even?

I stood, blinking, for a moment, trying to understand the question. She repeated it a few times, and then I switched on my camera and asked Maya to tell me more.

> Maya: If we had 100 children, 200 moms and dads, 400 cousin Nathans, 400 cousin Lilys, 500 Aunt Janas, 400 Uncle Joshes, 200 aunts and uncles, 50 Nanas, and 50 Poppies, we would have 2,300 people in our house.

Tracy: Where did this story come from?

Maya: Me and Daphne were talking about what it would be like to have that many people in our house, and then I started thinking about it.

Tracy: OK . . . And why did you decide to put them evenly on the three floors?

Maya: I wondered, if they all came to stay, how many people would be on each floor, and not just have 2,300 people on the first floor or the third floor or the second floor. Have them spread out evenly. So not have one floor crammed and another floor with just two people on it.

Tracy: (Laughing.) If we have 2,300 people in our house, we're going to be crammed anyway!

Maya: (Laughing.) I know. But this is the least crammed it could be.

This problem is not a problem I would ever write, but it was Maya's problem, and it made sense to her. She had not yet learned division, so she asked for help. We drew a house and dealt out groups of people until we had 766 people on each floor, with two people left over. Maya said, "They have to go in the yard!"

I had a wonderful time doing this problem with Maya and thought we were done, but she was only getting started. She wanted to check out the neighborhood.

Maya: I wonder how it would work out at Maggie's house?

Tracy: What do you mean?

Maya: Well, she has two floors at her house. I wonder if anyone would end up in the yard?

That is what I mean by riffing off a solution! Maya worked on her house problem for a number of different floors, trying to find out when it worked out evenly and when it didn't. While I cleaned up the kitchen, she drew house after house (for example, Figure 7.6). Periodically, she'd call out her findings:

"Mommy, if there are two floors, no one is in the yard! I wonder what would happen with six floors?"

"If someone lived in an apartment building

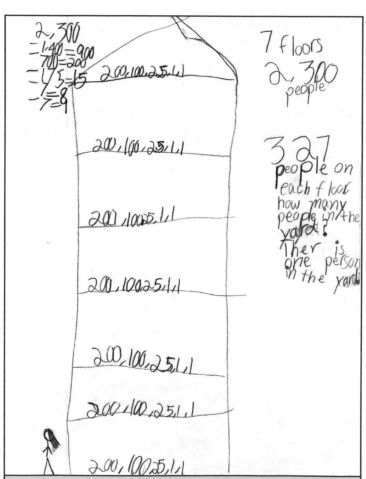

Figure 7.6 *A sampling of Maya's work on her question*

with eight or nine floors, it would be different. If someone lived in a little cottage, it would be different. In the apartment building, there are going to be less people on each floor because the people will be more spread out."

After she had solved the problem for five different numbers of floors, I sat down and talked with her. I had recently read this quote in a thought-provoking article from Knuth, and it was on my mind:

> Mathematical curiosity includes more than simply a desire to learn or to know mathematics. Mathematical curiosity also includes a desire to explore mathematical ideas through posing mathematically interesting problems after one has "finished" a problem. The solution or aspects of the problem can become springboards for further exploration. (2002, 126)

I was conscious of the choices in front of me—much more conscious than I'd ever been before. If I asked her "What did you find out?" or "What did you learn?" I'd be implying that her investigation was finished and that she should summarize it and move on. I decided to open our conversation with a different question, one that might encourage her to springboard to a new exploration:

Tracy: Do you have more questions after doing this? What are you wondering about now? (Her answer was immediate, and made me gasp.)

Maya: Is there a pattern? I think I'm starting to notice a pattern. If it's an odd number of floors, then people are outside. When it was nine floors, five people were outside. When it was three floors, two people were outside. But when it was two floors, zero people were outside. So, maybe there's a pattern?

Tracy: Maybe there is. What will you do to figure out if it will always be true?

Maya: Keep doing it!

Tracy: What would be your next building?

Maya: Four floors! And five floors! I want to know about even and odd. I want to do them all up to ten and then start figuring out if there's a pattern.

I gasped because Maya's ideas were exciting, yes, but mostly I was struck by the massive number of opportunities I've missed with students. I kept wondering how I'd never before asked, "Do you have more questions after doing this? What are you wondering about now?" I'd never encouraged students to wonder "What if?" or to riff on a problem. If I want students to think relationally, to look for underlying structure, and to seek connections, then I need to nurture this type of curiosity. Also, as Christopher Danielson (2013) has taught me, if we have new questions to ask, we have learned something. Asking "What new questions do you have?" can help us assess the most meaningful learning.

Since that conversation with Maya, I have put these questions in my mental speed dial. It's taken conscious effort, but now they're automatic. Students' new questions often leave me gasping, too.

In the case of Maya's house problem, the original problem was her brainchild, and that's great. What was most fun to watch, though, was how she kept toying around with the parameters because she was curious about what would happen. Last I heard from her, she said, "Six floors didn't work. I wonder if that's because three floors didn't work?"

I wonder, too.

Independent Study: Math as a Way to Ask and Answer Your Own Questions

> *The right question at the right time can move children to peaks in their thinking that result in significant steps forward and real intellectual excitement . . . Although it is almost impossible for an adult to know exactly the right time to ask a specific question of a specific child—especially for a teacher who is concerned with 30 or more children— children can raise the right question for themselves if the setting is right. Once the right question is raised, they are moved to tax themselves to the fullest to find an answer.*
> —Eleanor Duckworth, *"The Having of Wonderful Ideas"*
> *and Other Essays on Teaching and Learning*

When I taught in Washington State, I always had a wide range of student needs because I was certified in special education and served as my school's coordinator for students who qualified as having "highly capable" needs (please forgive the fixed-mindset language—this work predated Dweck's *Mindsets*). For example, in my last class, I had thirty fourth-grade students, including nine students with Individualized Education Plans (IEPs) and five students on Individualized Learning Plans for advanced work. I did a lot of meaningful differentiation within heterogeneous groups, which I loved.

At the start of each math unit, I always offered all students the option of taking the end-of-unit assessment. Any student who could demonstrate that he or she already had the concepts and skills was exempt from the unit and free to pursue other mathematics in depth. I had a variety of options prepared, but I always offered independent study as one of the choices. I explained to students that independent studies were a chance for students to pursue their interests mathematically. My ground rules:

1. Choose a question that is interesting to you. It can involve exploring mathematics just for the fun of it. It can involve thinking about something else that interests you in a mathematical way. It just needs to be interesting to you!

2. Tell me your question, meet with me regularly, and use me as a resource. I might not have the answers, but I would be happy to learn alongside you. Use other resources, too.

3. You might not answer your question. That's OK. You might revise your question. That's OK, too. This is a chance to follow your own nose.

4. You do not need to create a final product. This independent study is about the process, not making a product.
5. I might ask you to share what this process is like with the rest of the class, in a relaxed way. No presentations.
6. Work hard, take chances, and have fun!

Some example fourth-grade independent studies:

- A student who was passionately interested in airplanes decided to approach the mathematics of flying. He wanted to know how engineers decided how big the wings needed to be.
- Two girls who loved soccer explored the geometry of kick angles. They told me, "In soccer, I learned that I'm supposed to kick the ball to where I think they're going, not where they are. How does my body figure out where that is?"
- One student who had loved our symmetry unit explored symmetry in art, both by studying artwork and creating it.
- A student who was interested in economics created a fictional portfolio in which he gave each student in the class $25 and invested it in different ways. "I learned it's a lot more complicated than I thought it would be!"

That stock market study was the one that made me realize I was doing independent studies wrong. My problem wasn't that he hit some roadblocks at compounding interest. That was fine. My problem was that I was only offering this kind of work to students who already loved math.

Matt was the student interested in the market. He loved working on his study and talked about it a lot. One day, I noticed Matt and his friend Rafe—who was on an IEP—stayed in from recess together. I stopped by to see what they were doing, and they were working on the stock market problem. Rafe was making sense of the graphs and helping Matt understand them. Over time, several more of Matt's friends joined in on the work, all on their own time. Their enthusiasm was contagious.

That's when I realized that *all* students need opportunities to pursue their interests in mathematics. *All* students need opportunities to ask questions, follow their thinking, and look at their world through a mathematical lens. *All* students need to know that math is one way (along with science, history, reading, etc.) to ask and answer your own questions. *All* students need to be empowered by math, not just engaged in it.

When I return to full-time teaching, I look forward to figuring out a way to give all students opportunities to engage in mathematical independent studies. I don't know how much time I'll be able to carve out, but I will carve out some. They deserve it.

> The having of wonderful ideas is what I consider the essence of intellectual develop-
> ment. And I consider it the essence of pedagogy to give [a student] the occasion to have

his wonderful ideas and to let him feel good about himself for having them. (Duckworth 1987, 1)

Deborah Nichols, first and second grades

When Students' Questions Drive Teaching and Learning: "Are shapes math?"

We've now looked at ways to increase questioning through a quick warm-up or transitional routine with *101questions* and in full lessons with *Notice and Wonder*. We've thought about how to incorporate problem posing, riffing off problems, and independent studies. Let's spend some time in Debbie's classroom to see what it looks like when students' questions drive our math teaching at the unit level.

Deb and her students were wrapping up their thinking about calendars—where calendars are found, what they're for, what they have—when this conversation happened:

Gregory: Calendars can be found in the zoo.

Debbie: Do you think you can find a calendar in a zoo?

Students: No!

Gregory: Time is in a calendar, and they have to know what time to open and they have to know what time to feed the animals.

Debbie: Do you think they have to have a schedule that says feed the animals at this time? Absolutely.

Andrew: That makes no sense.

Debbie: You're not convinced?

Andrew: The zoo has nothing of math.

Debbie: You think the zoo has nothing to do with any math?

(Andrew nodded.)

Lydia: Everything is math. Because, the giraffe has spots on them and those are patterns.

Eddie: That's not really kind of math, because a pattern technically isn't math.

Lydia: A pattern is math.

Eddie: It's not math. You just see spots on a giraffe. It's not like there's numbers in them.

Lydia: But shapes are math.

Edgar: There is math in the zoo because circles and spots are patterns. And shapes.

Eddie: (Emphatically.) But shapes aren't math.

(Long pause.)

Gregory: How are shapes not math? Shapes can be fractions and fractions are math.

(Think time.)

Debbie: Are shapes math?

Students: "Yes!" "No!"

Gloria: There are shapes. They're for math, and they're shapes. So you can learn about all the different kinds of shapes that you don't know.

Debbie: How many people say shapes are math?

(Some hands up.)

Debbie: How many people say shapes are not part of math?

(Some hands up.)

Debbie: How many people aren't sure and would like to explore it more?

(Some hands up.)

Debbie: We're going to check that out.

Debbie was planning to launch a geometry unit anyway, so she decided to take up Eddie's and Andrew's question and run with it. Her first step was to find out what else students wondered about shapes. Deb had students work independently and together to generate questions and then come together to share with the class. She made it clear that students' questions were central and important: "I would like to hear some of your questions so that we can figure out what we want to investigate!" Deb recorded as students shared their questions:

How big can a circle go?

Are shapes life? Nature? Water?

How many shapes are there?

How do shapes get their form?

What was the first shape made?

Are shapes even math?

What do shapes do?

Are shapes fractions?

What are the kinds of shapes?

How many shapes are in a house?

How round can a circle be?

Are shapes fragile?

How long can rectangles be?

How big can a square get?

Are numbers and letters shapes?

Where can you find shapes?

Are there shapes in other shapes?

What can you make with shapes?

How long does it take to learn to make them?

Can shapes be in the sky?

Are shapes time?

Are shapes permanent?

Are shapes the same all around the world?

Can circles change their form?

Can shapes be found in insects? Food? Planets? Animals? People?

Is a heart a shape?

I've sat with these questions for a long time. *Are shapes permanent? Are shapes fragile? Are shapes the same all around the world? Are shapes life?* These are incredible one-line poems, full of potential and daring. I wonder if older kids would be able to ask such powerful questions without worrying what questions the teacher *wanted* them to ask? What about adults? What would happen at a staff meeting if we asked teachers to share their questions about shapes? Could we wake up our dormant curiosity, stop worrying what others might think, and use our imaginations? Can we relearn questioning from these six- and seven-year-old students and their beautiful ideas?

I've Gathered Their Questions—Now What?

I've seen many elementary teachers use the KWL structure: *What do you* know? *What do you* want *to know? What did you* learn? I've never been a fan because, on implementation, what I usually see is the teacher asks kids what they want to know, gathers great questions, and then marches through the unit as originally planned without taking the students' questions into account. Taught that way, KWL becomes a whole-class oral assessment of prior knowledge, and that's it. Students can feel more than a little duped when they think they're going to have a chance to pursue their questions and then don't.

Debbie did something really different here. She kept students' questions central throughout—creating responsive learning experiences that would help students make some headway on their questions—while still managing the flow of the unit. That's not a simple proposition, especially with other subjects to teach, time constraints, and a multiage setting. Let's look at some specifics from the unit to get a sense of how Debbie balanced her need to teach first- and second-grade geometry with students' need to pursue their own questions. How can we teach math with students' questions at the center in any kind of practical way?

Digging Deeper into the Questions: "Which question is going to help you learn the most?"

Debbie's next step was to bring everyone back together and ask, "Which of these questions is most important? Which question is going to help you learn the most? What are you going to learn?"

Students discussed the different questions and decided to narrow down the list and focus on a few favorites. The highest vote getters were:

Are there shapes in other shapes?

Are shapes fractions?

How do shapes get their form?

Are shapes permanent?

Debbie said, admiringly, "Those are questions I never ever would have thought of! Those are questions I really have never taught when we've studied shapes before."

Students decided which questions they personally wanted to pursue and formed groups around them. Debbie asked groups to meet together and generate "more questions about that question." She encouraged students not to worry about answering the questions just yet, and instead dig into the questions more deeply. For example, the "Are shapes fractions?" group created this list of supporting or related questions (Figure 7.7):

Do fractions have something to do with measurement?

What are fractions?

What are shapes?

How can they be fractions?

Can shapes be fractions?

Can fractions be shapes?

Who made the first fraction?

Can fractions be math?

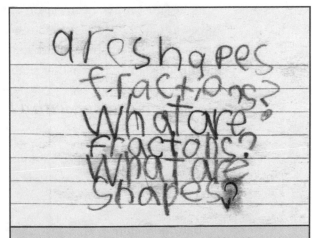

Figure 7.7 *One student's wonderings: "Are shapes fractions?"*

Now that students were thinking deeply about their questions, Debbie asked a series of questions she repeated throughout the unit: "What do I need to get ready for you tomorrow so you can start? How do I help you? What materials are you going to need?"

Students shared some ideas, and their ideas were all over the place! For example, the fractions group asked for fraction cards with fraction math problems on them. The "Are shapes permanent?" group asked for permanent markers to draw their shapes, with the plan to run their drawings under water and see whether the shapes stayed or not. Debbie listened carefully, and then said, "I'm trying to figure out how to help you. Let me do some thinking tonight. I'll talk with Ms. Zager, and we'll see if we can figure out how we can all learn something and start our investigation of shapes."

This is a critical moment. There are many directions Debbie could have taken with the kids at this point. For example, she could have:

1. Let the students implement their plans, knowing they weren't likely to get anywhere productive at first but have faith students would learn something in the process.
2. Think about what she knew students needed to answer their questions and develop learning experiences that would help them get there, even if the kids didn't know it yet.
3. Forget this whole rambling question thing and return to teaching a comfortable, familiar geometry unit.

Debbie opted for number two in this case. While there is certainly value in the first choice, and sometimes we need to make a time and a place for it, the academic year is finite, and Debbie decided she couldn't afford to head down dead ends that were clearly so long and possibly fruitless. She wanted to keep students' questions central but felt like the kids needed some guidance. This is such an important point: honoring students' questions doesn't mean the teacher hangs out in the staff room during math, leaving kids totally on their own. Students still need their teachers to facilitate, to guide, to support, and to probe. In other words, they still need us to teach! Deb knew that students did not yet have enough understanding of shapes to make substantive headway on their questions, and they needed some experience first. We talked after school and agreed it was time for students to explore shapes, develop intuition, and start to get a handle on attributes and language. As the fractions group had realized, it's awfully hard to know whether shapes are fractions if you don't know what shapes are.

Open Exploration with a Focus on Attributes: "What makes a shape a shape?"

The next day, Debbie pulled out tons of geometry materials (Power Blocks, tangrams, attribute blocks, pattern blocks, geometric solids, tiles, wooden blocks), and spread them out around the room.

Debbie: When you left yesterday, I realized you really haven't had enough time looking at shapes . . . We're going to be looking at the question, *What makes a shape a shape?* I would like you to go to as many places as you can today, and discover some of the properties of the shapes that are there. Another word you might use is *attributes*: some of the things that make them the shape they are. You don't need to know the name of the shape, but I want you to look at what makes that shape the shape that it is. I want you to look at shapes that might have similarities and might have differences. Maybe when you're looking at those shapes, maybe you want to compare, contrast. In the end, these are going to help us answer our questions.

Debbie has tremendous faith in her kids, doesn't she? She spent some additional time defining the important words *properties* and *attributes*, but she kept the learning experiences open ended because she trusted the kids would have wonderful ideas and make important discoveries on their own. These were the guidelines she gave her students:

Debbie: You're not just going to look at the shapes. You're going to play with them. Investigate them. Explore them. And see if they might tell you something about shapes you didn't know before. You can write down what you're noticing on paper, or you can keep your list in your head. You can go wherever you want, as long as a couple rules are followed:

1. What you use you pick up.
2. The person who builds something or makes something or explores something is the only one who gets to put that away unless they ask for help.
3. Nothing goes in your mouth.

Students eagerly fanned out around the room and began exploring. All students were engaged and focused, and there was a happy buzz about the room. After a good chunk of time, Debbie gathered students up for a classroom tour. We moved from group to group, listening in to what students had discovered. I found students' language and Deb's responsiveness as a teacher especially beautiful during this walk-around. I'm going to go into some detail and share several snippets to give you a feel for both the level of discourse and the level of mathematical thinking from these first- and second-grade students. Most of us fear what might happen if we give students this much control, so it's important to see how it actually panned out. Throughout, I found myself thinking about what Debbie did, said, and asked to encourage students as they had their wonderful ideas. How did she balance honoring students' ideas, fostering students' curiosity, gathering useful formative assessment for her, guiding students toward attributes, and providing mathematical language as it was needed?

Ceramic Tiles

Debbie: We're going to talk about what we're thinking about. Talk to us.

Karly: We made just a plain square like Sophie's, and we kept filling it in, and it got smaller and smaller and smaller (see Figure 7.8).

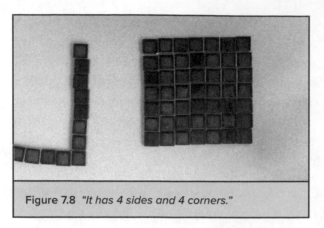

Figure 7.8 *"It has 4 sides and 4 corners."*

Edgar: And then it turned into one block.

Debbie: So can you tell us anything about what you noticed about those blue tiles?

Karly: We noticed that we can make a lot of triangles and squares and, like, frames.

Debbie: So if you were to say something that was a property or an attribute of those blue tiles, what would you say? A word? If I looked at just this (picked up one tile), what about this?

Jules: That they're not all light blue.

Debbie: They're not all light blue. So color! Color is a property.

Ricky: It's a square inside of another square.

Debbie: What else is a property of this?

Serena: It has four sides and four corners.

Debbie: It has four sides and four corners! Yay! Those are attributes and properties of these blue tiles.

Lydia: Nothing else can go inside it because it's already filled in.

Debbie: It is filled in. It's solid, isn't it? And that's going to be a property of this tile. It's solid. It's blue. Four sides and four corners. Somebody called these sides something else. Jules, was it you? You called them what? Somebody called them a word that starts with the letter *e*.

Serena: Edges?

Debbie: Edges! Yes.

Power Blocks

Debbie: What are you finding out about things here, in the power blocks?

Edgar: We builded the thing on the box! (Figure 7.9.)

Debbie: You built the thing on the box. And what shapes did you use to build it?

Edgar: We used, um, big triangles, medium triangles, diamonds, squares.

Figure 7.9 *"Big triangles, medium triangles, diamonds, squares"*

Debbie: Listen, hang on, he just used other properties, other attributes. He used the words *big* and *medium,* so size is a property.

Eddie: We made a rocket.

Debbie: So you can make things with those shapes.

Gregory: I noticed something about that: nothing is touching.

Debbie: So space or the amount of space in between something? Or how close things are?

Geometric Solids

Debbie: Gunther, you were doing something over here (Figure 7.10). What were you doing?

Gunther: It's sort of stretched out. (He was looking at the prolate spheroid, which is a three-dimensional, symmetric oval shape, like an egg but without a pointy end.)

Debbie: It's a stretched out circle. OK. What were you doing with it?

Gunther: I was trying to roll it this way (the long way). It just can't make it.

Figure 7.10 *"If one side is bigger than the other, it will roll in a circle."*

Debbie: Ah! So he was trying to see if it rolls.

Serena: So it's kind of like mine. I'm trying to make it roll down here and stop right here.

Debbie: Can all shapes roll?

Students: No!

Serena: Circles can and octagons.

Gunther: Mostly, ovals roll like that. Whoa, that's how a football goes.

Debbie: This one looks like an ice cream cone with a piece broken off, doesn't it? Can this roll?

Students: Yes. No.

Debbie: Can some of them roll better than others? Can a cube roll?

Students: No. Yes it can.

(Debbie tossed the cube.)

Gregory: It can move but not roll.

Jules: If one side is bigger than the other, it will roll in a circle. (Held up a cone.)

Debbie: Do you think an egg would do that?

Students: Yes.

Debbie: How about a cylinder? Will a cylinder roll?

Gloria: It needs to have a flat edge.

Debbie: It needs a flat edge to roll?

Serena: No, this one doesn't. (Held up a sphere.)

Debbie: Oh, what's that called? Do you know?

Serena: A circle.

Gregory: A sphere.

Same Power Blocks, Different Kids, Different Ideas

Debbie: What were you doing here?

Gregory: We were making mystery shapes and tracing them on paper (see Figure 7.11).

Debbie: Mystery shapes and tracing it on paper! And what were you doing, Nate?

Nate: I was looking at triangles. How triangles are different. These triangles are different because these triangles are flat, and other triangles are kind of flat at the top but this one doesn't look like a triangle because triangles are kind of bended.

Figure 7.11 *"We were making mystery shapes and tracing them on paper."*

Debbie: Triangles are kind of bended. (Deb held up a right isosceles triangle oriented like a pup tent.) So does this look like a triangle to you?

Nate: Yes, because triangles are supposed to have a long flat side.

Debbie: (Rotated it so the right angle pointed down, as seen in Figure 7.12.) What if it's this way, it is a triangle to you?

Nate: No. But it looks like an upside-down triangle.

Debbie: An upside-down triangle. (Rotated it so it's sitting on a base.) How about this way? Is that a triangle to you?

Figure 7.12 *"I was looking at triangles. How triangles are different."*

Nate: It looks like a sideways triangle.

Debbie: Do you think it's still a triangle?

Nate: Yeah, because if you switch it around . . . that looks like a slide.

Debbie: (To whole class.) What does this triangle have that those blue tiles had?

Karly: Corners and sides.

Debbie: (Excited.) What! Karly!

Serena: But those don't . . . (Pointing to geometric solids.)

Debbie: Go get it, and let's compare.

Serena: (Came back with sphere and ovoid shape.) But these two don't have corners and sides.

Debbie: Some shapes do have corners and sides; some shapes don't have corners and sides. Some shapes have (students choral counting) one, two, three sides and one, two, three corners. And some shapes have (kids choral counting) one, two, three, four sides and one, two, three, four corners.

Andrew: It can't be more than four sides.

Lydia: Yes it can be, because over here we found out that . . .

Debbie: Go get it.

Tracy: Gregory, is your mystery shape a shape that has sides?

Gregory: Yes.

Tracy: How many?

Gregory: (After counting.) Eight.

Lydia: I found out that there's shapes that have a lot of sides because this one has five. (Held up a hexagon.)

Debbie: Can you count them for me?

Lydia: One, two, three, four, wait, six!

Debbie: Oh, so some shapes can have six sides?

Eddie: And eight.

Debbie: And eight. Do you think a shape could have twelve sides?

Students: Yes!

Eddie: Or one hundred.

Debbie: Do you think a shape could have one hundred sides?

Students: No.

Debbie: Hmm. Let's walk over here.

Wooden Blocks

Kenlee: Well, first we decided to line up all the things of how they feel and how they look (Figure 7.13). We started doing how they feel. Like, this one is bumpy and this one is

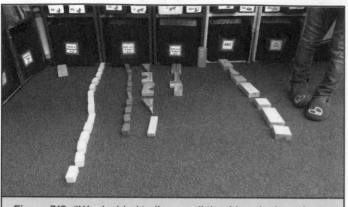

Figure 7.13 *"We decided to line up all the things by how they feel."*

smooth. Then we decided to see what shapes could make, like a castle.

After this tour in which so many wonderful ideas had bubbled up, Debbie asked kids to go somewhere different and keep exploring, which they did with purpose and focus. Toward the end of math time, Debbie gathered everyone together and continued to nudge students toward looking at attributes:

Debbie: What attributes did we talk about today? Did you hear us talk about sides and corners, and shape, and color, and round and flat, and big and small, and curved and straight?

Throughout this lesson, Debbie was encouraging students to shift from thinking about shapes by overall look (i.e., triangles are roofs or tents or look like witches' hats) to categorizing shapes by properties (i.e., triangles are closed shapes that have three straight sides and three angles). All students must go through this essential progression to make sense of geometry (Danielson 2016; Schifter 1999; Van Hiele 1984). Deb's careful listening helped her see which students were starting to analyze shapes' attributes and which students were still thinking visually about the overall appearance of the shape. Her students agreed they had lots left to learn, as evidenced by Nick's response to Deb's final question of the day:

> Debbie: How can I help you next?
>
> Nick: We need to learn more about different kinds of forms.
>
> Debbie: OK then!

Sorts: *"We need to learn more about different kinds of forms."*

Debbie decided Nick was right and kept going with a few more days of attribute and shape exploration. She pulled out her Venn circles, attribute blocks, and Power Blocks and asked

Figure 7.14 *How did this student decide to sort shapes?*

students to sort the shapes in some way that made sense to them, with the expectation that there were multiple solutions. In each case, the rest of the class watched the sort and then guessed the rule. Can you guess the rule in Figure 7.14?

The Need for Vocabulary: "We need to know the names of these shapes so we know what we're talking about."

The conversation about shapes during sorts were sometimes hard to follow. Students couldn't always communicate their ideas the way they wanted to because they lacked the vocabulary. Their *need* to communicate motivated them to learn the mathematical words (Harel 2013). Andrew was the first student to notice this issue:

> Andrew: We need to know the names of these shapes so we know what we're talking about.
>
> Debbie: How can I help you?
>
> Andrew: You could make a display. Like, with the shapes we've talked about. And their names. And words.
>
> Debbie: I would do it if you helped me make it, but I'm not going to make it myself. What you learn and make, I will gladly put up on that board, but it's not going to be teacher's pictures. It's going to be kids' work. Is that fair? (Andrew nodded.)
>
> Nate: I have a good idea. We could display the shape and what we learned about it.
>
> Debbie: How about if I give you time to research the language that you need so we can talk and know what we mean?

Over the next few classes, students gathered all the geometry words they could think of, sorted them, matched them to shapes, and eventually created a display using simple paper strips. Deb's students were much more engaged than students are in typical geometry vocabulary lessons because their work was meeting their real, felt need for communication. They made a beautiful display, shown in Figure 7.15. Also, by this point, students were convinced that shapes are math, so their first step was to change the

Figure 7.15 *"We need to know the names of these shapes so we know what we're talking about."*

title of this investigation from *Are Shapes Math?* to *Shapes Are Math.*

Regular and Irregular Shapes: "Is this a triangle?"

One of the classic issues in any geometry investigation is that students think only regular or equilateral shapes qualify. There were many student questions along the lines of "Is this a triangle?" Debbie opened the conversation by sharing this picture from Christopher

Figure 7.16 *"Hexagons have 6 sides and 6 angles and every one of them does!"*

Danielson's hexagon collection (2012), shown in Figure 7.16.

Debbie: Tell me what you see.

(She gathered observations for a while.)

Jules: They're all hexagons.

(Students argued this point.)

Jules: Well, hexagons have six sides and six angles and every one of them does!

Ricky: Some of them are the regular ones.

Kenlee: I never knew that there could be so many different ways!

Interestingly, students were able to think about hexagons more flexibly than triangles, probably because they have so much more experience with—and therefore misconceptions about—triangles. Debbie held several triangle discussions over the course of the unit, checking in on students' thinking as they gathered new ideas. Their misconceptions were persistent, which is normal (e.g., Schifter 1999, 364), but students were able to make progress, especially through example/nonexample work. For instance, Ricky was convinced that triangles had to have two or three equal sides:

Debbie: So, Ricky, do you ever have a triangle that has no equal sides?

Ricky: No, because it always has two equal sides.

Debbie: You think that there always has to be two equal sides?

Ricky: Two or three.

Debbie: So, can there be a triangle that has all equal sides?

Ricky: Yes.

Debbie: Can there be triangles that have no equal sides?

Ricky: No.

Most of the class agreed with him. Debbie got out a geoboard and some rubber bands and made a scalene triangle wherein the sides were fairly close in length but not congruent. Students agreed it was a triangle. Deb had Gregory come up with a ruler.

Debbie: You read to me the number that that reaches right there.

Gregory: Eighteen and a half.

Debbie: And this one is . . .

Gregory: Twelve and a half.

Debbie: OK, you read to me what this one says.

Gregory: Nineteen.

Debbie: So, now, is Ricky's assumption correct? Do triangles have at least two equal sides?

In this discussion, Debbie was using a tried-and-true method of pushing against students' working definitions to encourage students to refine and clarify them. Christopher Danielson described this process wonderfully (2014):

> This is how I teach critical thinking. Get the child to make a claim and to give a reason supporting it. Cook up a problematic example and ask for a new claim. Repeat. Quit before angering child.

In this triangle discussion, Debbie kept cooking up several scalene triangles that would test Ricky's claim. She knew 100 percent of her students wouldn't be convinced by the discussion, but she also knew she was nudging their thinking along. By the end, most students cautiously agreed that triangles had to have three sides, but the three sides might

Figure 7.17 *"Which of these shapes are triangles?"*

have different lengths. The development of their understanding will take more time and experience. (For further reading about the development of children's geometric thinking, I recommend Danielson's *Which One Doesn't Belong?* [2016].)

Students' ideas about triangles are particularly persistent because they've been raised on board books and pattern blocks that only include equilateral or isosceles triangles, oriented point up. I've been collecting problematic examples over the years, drawing from discussions with colleagues, conversations with kids, and the work of Schifter (1999), Clements and Sarama (2000), and the Developing Mathematical Ideas *Geometry: Examining Features of Shape Casebook* (Schifter et al. 2001). See Figure 7.17 for my current batch of favorites. I encourage you to ask kids, "Which of these shapes are triangles?" Their answers might surprise you!

Revisiting Students' Original Questions: "I still wonder, are shapes life?"

Now that students had some working ideas about shapes and their attributes and were getting a handle on the terminology, it was time to pick up students' questions again. For example, "What can you make with other shapes?" was a beautiful lead-in to composing

Figure 7.18 *"Create something that reminds you of something else."*

and decomposing shapes, so Debbie created opportunities for everyone to explore this idea. She cut colored paper in different shapes, including polygons and circles. She asked students to choose shapes they wanted to use and then to build something from those shapes. After everyone had looked, she asked students to "mess it up and make something different." They repeated this cycle several times. During one iteration, she asked students to "create something that reminds you of something else." Students built trains, robots, creatures, and so on. Students also spent a great deal of time putting manipulatives together and taking them apart, sometimes in open exploration, and other times to build specific shapes out of other shapes (Figure 7.18).

What was so striking to me about this geometry unit was that students' questions were driving both the overall investigation and the individual explorations. Periodically, Debbie and her kids looked back at their original questions and took stock, either through discussion or through open-ended writing assignments. Sometimes students found they had made headway. Sometimes they found they hadn't yet made progress on a question, but now they had the words and understanding to pursue it. And sometimes they just had delightful conversations about shapes, math, and the world.

Debbie also gave students opportunities to continue to ask questions. What a refreshing change from our typical classroom rhythm in which questions come only at the beginning and answers come only at the end. For example, halfway through the unit, Deb gave students a big piece of paper with plenty of room to write. She asked, "What do you still wonder about geometry? Are there any questions that you have thought about that you would like to explore or know more about? Please let me know and we will share them!"

Students pondered new and fascinating questions such as "How big can the number of sides go?" That question is worthy of some deep thought. And consider the wondering in Figure 7.19.

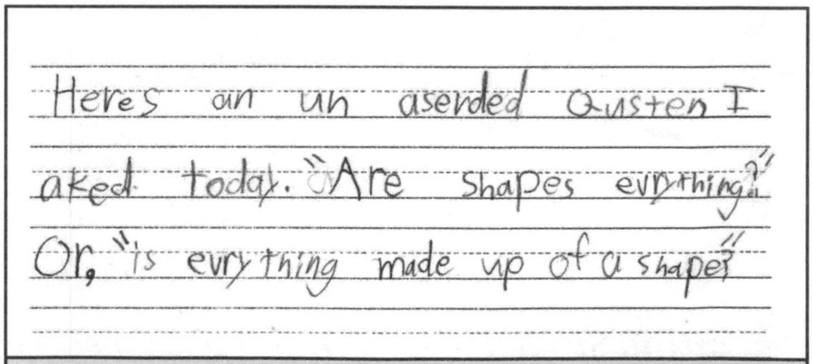

Several days later, the

> Heres an un aserded Qusten I aked today. "Are shapes evrything." Or, "Is evrything made up of a shape?"

Figure 7.19 *"What do you still wonder about geometry?"*

questioner said, "I think I have an answer to my question. I think shapes are not everything. Because what about a line? I don't think a line is a shape. Is a line a shape?" Talk about asking mathematical questions! Debbie carved out some time for students to explore lines, too (Figure 7.20).

Assessments for Learning and Teaching

Throughout the unit, Debbie built in ways to assess her students through observations, conversations, and written products. For example, Deb wanted to see how students were constructing shapes from attributes. She gave each student a geoboard and read several riddles she'd written. At first, all students' shapes were identical and regular. Then, Jules broke the possibilities open with her solution for this riddle:

> I am a polygon, but not a quadrilateral.
>
> I can have equal sides.
>
> I have an odd number of intersections or vertices.
>
> I have more than four intersections.

Every geoboard looked like the home-plate pentagon on the right of Figure 7.21, until Jules made the pentagon on the left. Now students realized they could make a range of polygons that would fit these criteria, including irregular pentagons, septagons, nonagons, and so forth. Jules caused a flurry of revision.

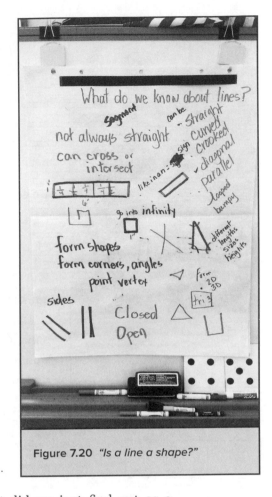

Figure 7.20 *"Is a line a shape?"*

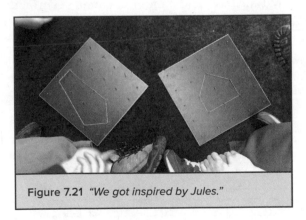

Figure 7.21 *"We got inspired by Jules."*

Debbie: What did we just find out as a group? How come when we first started almost everybody had an answer that looked like this? And then all of a sudden we started changing them, and we have different ways to look at things? How come?

Gregory: Because we got inspired by Jules.

Debbie: You got inspired by Jules? Tell me more.

Gregory: We thought that it would be cool to make a different shape.

For the rest of the lesson, students moved past thinking there was one right answer to the riddle and started experimenting with the range of solutions that met the criteria, including plenty of irregular shapes (Figure 7.22).

Debbie also used written assessments to see how students' ideas about geometry were

Figure 7.22 *"I am a polygon. I am a quadrilateral. One pair of my sides are parallel. One pair of my sides are not parallel."*

developing. These tasks tended to involve lots of student choice, such as the student work in Figures 7.23a and b. This student knows quite a bit about squares, doesn't she?

At the end of the unit, students had a long and delightful conversation about their original questions. Some were resolved, some remained open, and some had morphed into or sparked new questions. Debbie's students shared their thinking orally and then in writing individually so she could hear from each student. It was clear many kids had curves on their minds:

"Do curved sides count as sides?"

"Can shapes be curved?"

"I have a wonder. Can there ever be a perfect circle?"

This question about curves came to a head when we revisited the question, "Is a heart a shape?" Debate raged for almost half an hour!

Debbie could have kept going with her geometry unit, taking on polygons versus shapes with curved sides and going deeper into the wonderful geometry of hearts. But the reality was she had spent a long time on shapes, the end of the year was approaching, and she needed to draw this investigation to a close and come back to number studies. That's OK! An important idea to remember—and to convey to students—is that the end of a unit does not mean the questions are all answered and the understanding is complete. In fact, we want students to leave investigations generating new questions (Whitin and Cox 2003).

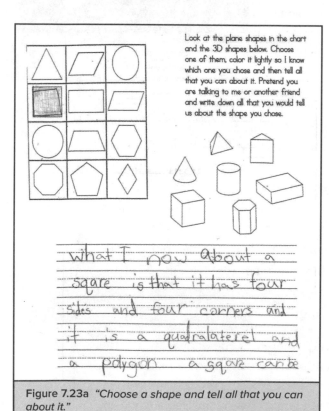

Figure 7.23a *"Choose a shape and tell all that you can about it."*

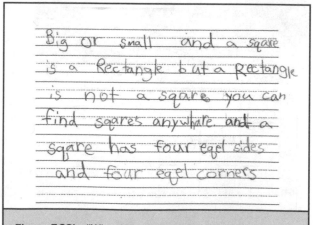

Figure 7.23b *"What I know about a square is . . ."*

What About the Standards in an Inquiry Unit?

One reason teachers might fear open-ended exploration and student questions is the pressure to get to all the standards. Debbie's unit is bursting with Standards for Mathematical Practice, but what about the content standards? Can she ensure she's teaching the standards even as she follows students' questions? Here are the relevant standards:

Reason with shapes and their attributes.

CCSS.MATH.CONTENT.1.G.A.1

Distinguish between defining attributes (e.g., triangles are closed and three-sided) versus non-defining attributes (e.g., color, orientation, overall size); build and draw shapes to possess defining attributes.

CCSS.MATH.CONTENT.1.G.A.2

Compose two-dimensional shapes (rectangles, squares, trapezoids, triangles, half-circles, and quarter-circles) or three-dimensional shapes (cubes, right rectangular prisms, right circular cones, and right circular cylinders) to create a composite shape, and compose new shapes from the composite shape.

CCSS.MATH.CONTENT.2.G.A.1

Recognize and draw shapes having specified attributes, such as a given number of angles or a given number of equal faces. Identify triangles, quadrilaterals, pentagons, hexagons, and cubes.

She got there anyway, didn't she? Reasoning with shapes and their attributes is central to the standards, and turned out to be central to students' questions, because shapes and their attributes are foundational. Any one of Debbie's students' questions would have led to shapes and attributes somehow. Egyptians were interested in them, modern-day geometers are interested in them, and kids are interested in them. Why? Because they're interesting! Perhaps knowing that students' inquisitiveness leads to the same ideas that mathematicians study and standard-writers emphasize can help us feel less pressure to tell and cover and explain. If we allow students to ask, we will likely end up in the same place but with much more engaged, empowered students.

Curious Math Teachers

I want to leave us with one more wonder: how do we model curiosity as math teachers? Modeling is a big part of teaching, and plays a role here, too. In my mind, there are two components: being curious about mathematics and being curious as teachers.

Almost none of us had our mathematical curiosity nurtured, encouraged, or developed when we were students ourselves. We were taught that doing math meant answering someone else's questions, and we did it. As math teachers, though, we have the opportunity to rediscover the curiosity we once had about numbers, shapes, and patterns. Every day, we have the chance to ask "What if?" and see what happens when we toy with a problem. We have the chance to wonder "Why didn't that work?" or "What's going on here?" We have the chance to be curious about mathematics and to show that curiosity to our students. What huge opportunities.

We have another opportunity to model curiosity every time one of our students shares his or her mathematical ideas. When I think about Jen, Shawn, Debbie, Heidi, and the other teachers you're meeting through the pages of this book, my mental images are never the classic ones of the teachers standing at the board, telling, or explaining, although they all explain on occasion. My images—based on many hours of observations—are of the teachers leaning forward, maybe with a head cocked or a hand on a chin, eyes focused on the speaker, giving the student his or her complete attention, doing what Jo Boaler called "communicating interest in student ideas" (Boaler and Humphreys 2005, 50–51). Figure 7.24 shows Heidi, listening.

She's not pretending to be interested to boost some child's self-esteem. She is sincerely interested because she values students and finds their mathematical ideas fascinating. Genuine curiosity is written all over her face, and her students are sure to notice.

Figure 7.24 *Heidi Fessenden, listening to a student*

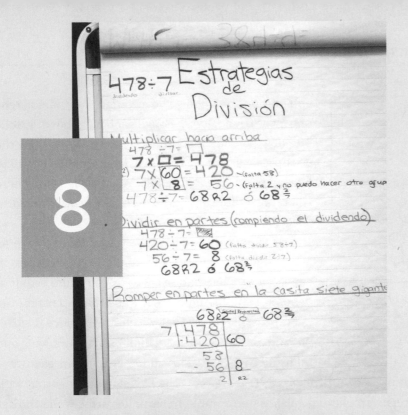

MATHEMATICIANS
CONNECT IDEAS

*I*n the fall of 1997, mathematician Dr. Daina Taimina was planning how to teach a geometry class at Cornell University and was "thinking about how to better explain hyperbolic geometry to [her] students" (Taimina 2009, 5). Hyperbolic geometry is the math of convoluted, crenulated, and ruffled shapes like curly lettuces, corals, holly leaves, Pringles potato chips, and even our own brains. Teaching it is challenging because the vocabulary is intimidating, the surfaces can be difficult to visualize, and the ideas are abstract, especially without concrete manipulatives to explore. Before 1997, despite hundreds of years of work on the mathematics of hyperbolic geometry, the best models mathematicians had were clumsy, fragile ones made of tiny strips of paper and tape, and computers were no help.

Dr. Taimina was an avid knitter and thought she might be able to stitch a model instead. She studied the patterns in knitted ruffles, counting how many extra stitches had to go in each row to create curvature, and noticed that stitches were added by the same ratio each time. "I was thinking of how to visualize that and remembered an old example of how fast gossip spread" (2009, 20). She thought of a version of telephone wherein one person starts with news

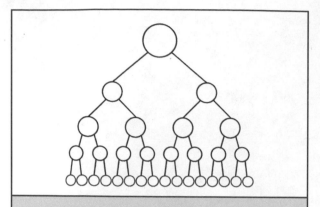

Figure 8.1 *Daina Taimina realized a sketch of how gossip spreads exponentially could be used as a crochet pattern for hyperbolic planes.*

and tells one neighbor. The next day, each person tells one more friend. Even though each neighbor only tells one new person, the number of people who know the gossip grows very big very fast, from 2 to 4 to 8 to 16 to 32, and so on (see Figure 8.1). What we're seeing here is a representation of *exponential growth*, which also describes hyperbolic geometry.

Dr. Taimina wrote, "First, I saw this picture as a mathematical graph. Suddenly, I saw this graph can be a crochet pattern where each line segment denotes a stitch. And there it was—the pattern for the hyperbolic plane. All that was left was to try it" (20). She did, first in knitting, which didn't work well, and then in crochet. As she added stitches in each row, her crochet frilled right up in beautiful curves (Figure 8.2). She began experimenting with different ratios and patterns, crocheting a class set of durable, hyperbolic surfaces she and her students could examine, investigate, and play with in a tactile way. Before long, her crocheted hyperbolic planes were featured in mathematical journals.

In 2005, Australian sisters Margaret and Christine Wertheim, cofounders of the Institute for Figuring, began crocheting a coral reef to draw attention to climate change. They extended Dr. Taimina's work, crocheting anemones, nudibranchs, sea slugs, and the many varieties of coral disappearing from their beloved Great Barrier Reef because of rising sea temperatures. More than 7,000 people have contributed pieces to the project so far, and the Wertheims have exhibited woolen seascapes at museums on every continent, including the Smithsonian. During her delightful (and highly recommended) *TED Talk*, Margaret Wertheim said the roots of this project "go into the fields of mathematics, marine biology, feminine handicraft, and environmental activism" (ted.com/talks/margaret_wertheim_crochets_the_coral_reef).

Indeed! Dr. Taimina and the Wertheims exemplify several different aspects of how thinking mathematically involves making connections:

- **We connect to what we already know.** It took a mathematician who was familiar with crochet to make the key connection here, because we build on our understandings and

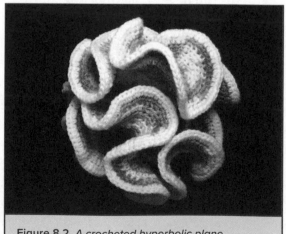

Figure 8.2 *A crocheted hyperbolic plane*

experiences. To borrow language from literacy instruction, when we learn, we activate and build on our prior knowledge or schemas. To continue the analogy, you could think about this type of connection as a math-to-self connection. (If linking math and literacy instruction appeals to you, Hyde [2006, 2014] and Siena [2009] are interesting reads.)

- **To build profound understanding, we connect one part of mathematics to another**. Dr. Taimina explored the relations between exponential functions and hyperbolic geometry to see the crochet pattern. We generally teach number and geometry as if they're unrelated, but powerful mathematics exists in the relationships between them. This is the math version of a text-to-text connection, or a math-to-math connection.

- **Mathematics exists in the world and can be a powerful force for social change**. Here is our math-to-world connection. The Wertheims' coral reef is a beautiful example that shows mathematics is all around us, and that we can use mathematics to understand and improve our world.

Three more ideas about connections are especially important to think about as math teachers:

- **New understanding often comes from trying to connect ideas**. Dr. Taimina's idea was to *try* stitching a hyperbolic surface. In this case, her first attempt failed, which gave her a new opportunity to learn. We absolutely want students to explore relationships among ideas by trying to make connections and generalizations and to look for similarities. When the connections don't hold, we must give students room to analyze missed connections and learn from them. There is rich mathematics to be discovered whether the connections hold or break.

- **Sometimes connections are made between ideas that don't seem at all connected at first**. As Wertheim said in her *TED Talk*, "Woolenness and wetness aren't exactly two concepts that go together!" Students often bring ideas to math class that seem out of left field. We need to take their ideas seriously because students are sense makers. They are trying to figure out where different mathematical ideas fit into their understanding of the world. And there might even be powerful math in the connection! In particular, we need to be mindful that students with different cultural knowledge and experiences than our own will make different math-to-self connections than we will. What a great opportunity to learn from (and about) our students and treat their ideas with respect. Dr. Taimina's story is powerful evidence that the field of mathematics is improved by participation of a diverse range of people who bring a wide array of experiences and knowledge. Hundreds of years of male mathematicians never thought of crochet!

- **Multiple representations and models are a big part of making mathematical connections**. Dr. Taimina's insight grew out of a need for a model that made sense. Drawing a representation of exponential functions was an essential part of her thought process, and it literally enabled her to *see* a new idea. Her diagrams and models deepened her own understanding: "Somewhere inside me confusion remained for many years—until I made a model and saw what is happening in the hyperbolic plane . . . it remained for me . . . . 'imaginary,' until I could experience straightness in the hyperbolic plane in a tactile way" (2009, 27). Drawing pictures and using manipulatives are not "little" or "young" strategies. This PhD-holding professor of mathematics is telling us she made sense by drawing a picture and using a manipulative. All mathematicians use these strategies, and we should teach them through all grade levels. As teachers, we can create especially fertile ground for making connections by asking students to analyze several different representations, strategies, or models of the same problem.

I'll be tugging at all six of these themes throughout the examples in this chapter.

Part 1: Connecting Math and the World

In this section, we'll look briefly at how to connect math and the world in two meaningful ways: (1) mathematics in daily life and (2) mathematics of social change.

Contextualized Math: "I sat through a whole year of geometry and nobody told me you could use it for anything!"

When I was a kid, my dad hired a local teenager and family friend, Patrick, to help him with the trim carpentry on a house. They were working in the prow of the home, which was shaped like the bow of a ship. The two walls came together at a 162° angle (Figure 8.3). Patrick was struggling to calculate the angles of the trim pieces right in the prow, until my dad told him to set the saw for 9°. Patrick cut the lumber, and the trim fit perfectly. He was stunned and asked my dad, "How did you know to do that?" My dad talked Patrick through how he used a pair of triangles to figure out the angle.

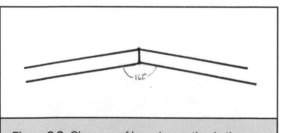

Figure 8.3 *Close-up of boards meeting in the prow of a home. How do you know what angle to cut the trim?*

Patrick asked, "But how did you know that? What do you call that? What's the name for that?"

My dad answered, "Well, Patrick, the name for that is geometry."

Patrick let loose a stream of expletives and started stomping all around the job site. After he stopped fuming, my dad asked, "What's wrong?"

Patrick shouted, "I sat through a whole year of geometry and nobody told me you could use it for anything!"

Geometry, in Patrick's mind, lived within the walls of the geometry classroom and the pages of the geometry textbook. It didn't connect to other areas of math, himself, or the world. When we compartmentalize mathematics into little boxes, we lose its power. What good is math if we can't transfer what we've learned to new situations, problems, or contexts?

One natural way to teach students how to apply and connect what they know to new situations is to let them practice with contextual math. To be clear, I am not arguing that we should tell kids they need to learn math in case they grow up to be carpenters. I am also not arguing our problems should all be real-world problems, especially not contrived, textbook, phony-sounding, real-world problems that don't fool anybody. Much of mathematics is done just for the fun and beauty of it, and our students should have plenty of time to explore pure mathematics. At the same time, math is all around us, and it is useful in life and in work. When connections to the world are natural and authentic, we should make our classroom walls porous. We don't want to create future Patricks, steaming mad that they sat through math classes without knowing anybody ever did anything with it.

One strategy I used in my classroom was to involve families and community members in my math class. At the beginning of the year, I told families that I loved when they came in and shared how they use math in their daily lives. I asked interested family members to let me know about their work and interests, and then I contacted them throughout the year when the content area was a good fit. A few examples I remember well:

- A mother who worked for the community arts center taught students how she visualized and used three-dimensional space.
- A mother who catered out of her home kitchen came in during our fractions unit. We cooked a recipe together, scaling it up to feed the whole class. Many of the ingredients were given in unit fractions: ½ teaspoon or ⅓ cup, so there was some good mathematical content. The parent told kids she did this kind of math on the fly, all day every day. She rarely used paper and pencil in the kitchen and shared some of her mental math and estimation strategies.
- A father who was an airline pilot came to class in uniform during our measurement and large-numbers unit. His challenge for the kids was to get him to London from Seattle. He did not have the fuel to take a circuitous route, so they had to find the best combination of paths along standard flight routes. He also introduced kids to spherical geometry— not a required standard but really fun—by showing them how he flies along the great circles, which are the shortest paths between two points on a spherical surface. Students worked in groups with aviation maps, calculating the number of miles, amount of fuel, and duration of each leg of the flight. It was so great I convinced him to come back every year, long after I no longer had his children in my class.

There is mathematics in almost every job or hobby. Whether they're plumbers or quilters, truck drivers or farm workers, our students' families and our local community members have a ton of collective expertise about using math in life and in work. Having a guest from students' families or the community share aspects of their mathematical lives can help defuse the myth that math is useless and random. As an added bonus, I found recognizing family members as experts was enormously helpful in building relationships. Family members got a sense of the kind of mathematical reasoning I was teaching and were much less wary, even though it looked different than the procedural math they grew up doing. These collaborations helped us build mutual trust and respect.

Community Involvement and Social Change

As the Wertheims showed, mathematics can be a powerful way to understand the world and a force for social change at a local, national, or global scale. Great lessons can start right on your school campus. For example, Jennifer Clerkin Muhammad's students gathered litter in the neighborhood around their school, analyzed the data they'd collected, and wrote persuasive letters to Dunkin' Donuts, asking them to decrease their use of Styrofoam coffee cups. Kassia Omohundro Wedekind's students explored the math of their school garden and then investigated community gardens and local food pantries.

In *Rethinking Mathematics: Teaching Social Justice by the Numbers*, Gutstein and Peterson (2013) have gathered essays, examples, and articles from a range of schools, grade levels, and issues. The websites www.rethinkingschools.org/ and www.radicalmath.org/ are both full of ideas for teaching the mathematics of wages, the gender pay gap, health care, predatory lending, climate change, immigration, military recruitment, smoking, income distribution, neighborhood displacement, racial profiling, wheelchair accessibility, HIV/AIDS, junk food advertising, representation in books, and any other current event or social justice issue you can think of.

If you consider any of those issues for a minute, mathematics and mathematical representations are central to the debates and discussion. To create mathematically literate citizens, we need to teach students powerful math connected to important contexts. "The stronger students' grasp of math, the better equipped they are to comprehend and change the world" (Gutstein and Peterson 2013, xii).

Part 2: Connecting Math to Math

When authors write textbooks and teachers plan lessons, they often isolate the different methods students need to know so that students can practice them in a focused way. But this can also strip mathematics of the connections that are at the heart of the subject. Students who work through long lists of isolated mathematical methods throughout their school careers do not know about drawing connections, and when they enter situations when they would benefit from making connections or extending what they know to a new situation, it does not occur to them that they can do so.

—Jo Boaler and Cathy Humphreys, *Connecting Mathematical Ideas*

In this section, we'll take an in-depth look at two powerful teaching strategies to encourage students to connect mathematical ideas—comparing multiple representations and focusing on relational understanding—and then we'll briefly look at what using multiple models can do for students.

The Power of Multiple Representations

A mathematical representation often highlights only one aspect of a mathematical concept. To restrict oneself to any one mathematical representation is to approach the concept blindfolded. A holistic picture of the concept begins to emerge only when one removes the blindfold and looks at the idea from different perspectives.

—Preety Tripathi, "Developing Mathematical
Understanding Through Multiple Representations"

Jennifer Clerkin Muhammad, fourth grade

Jake's House: "I want you to compare your representations, capisce?"

Every time I walk into Jen's fourth-grade classroom, I am struck by her brilliant use of mathematical representations to build students' understanding. Figures 8.4–8.6 show the sort of work typically posted on her walls.

In her language around representations, Jen often talks about how revealing they are, as in, mathematical representations can reveal the mathematics, including the relationships between mathematical ideas. Jen knows that comparing several different representations of the same idea or problem can help students build deep understanding and broad connections, as Tripathi described above.

In this particular lesson, Jennifer's class was beginning to work on multiplicative comparison problems, which can be much trickier for students than multiplication of groups. Jen started with representations so students could make sense out of the problem contexts first. She gave students the problem: *Darlene picked seven apples. Juan picked four times as many apples. How many apples did Juan pick?* Think about that problem for a minute. How could you draw it? Take a crack at it yourself first.

Jen asked students to draw a picture of what was happening in the problem on their mini-whiteboards. While students worked, she walked around, observing what they were doing. As Jen anticipated, representing the "four times as many" was challenging for most students. They were accustomed to four referring to four objects, but there weren't four

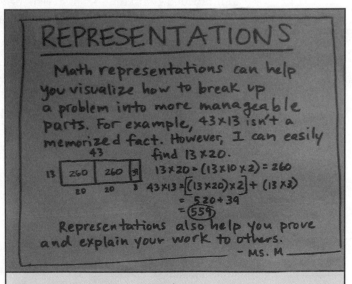

Figure 8.4 *"Representations also help you prove and explain your work to others."*

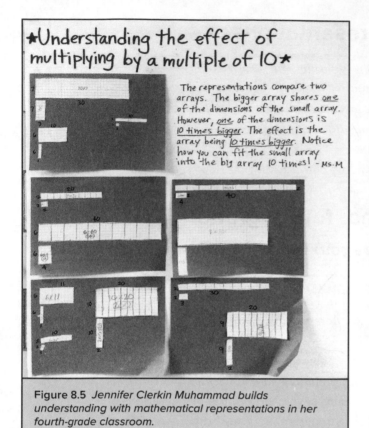

Figure 8.5 *Jennifer Clerkin Muhammad builds understanding with mathematical representations in her fourth-grade classroom.*

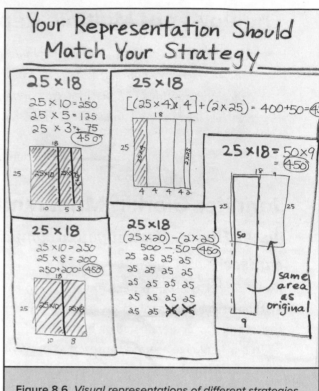

Figure 8.6 *Visual representations of different strategies can reveal the mathematics.*

objects in this story. The work in Figure 8.7 was representative.

Jen noticed that some students successfully represented the "four times as many" with both group and area models, as shown in Figures 8.8 and 8.9. She wanted those ideas to spread, so she told students to cap their markers:

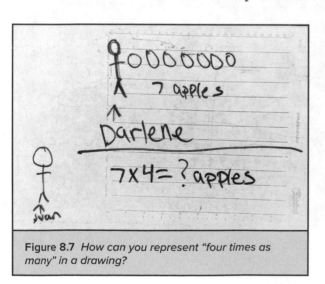

Figure 8.7 *How can you represent "four times as many" in a drawing?*

Jen: I'm going to give you guys about three or four minutes. What you're going to do is you're going to walk around the classroom with your board. Even if it's not quite done, that's OK. You're going to try and meet with three to four kids. You can meet with a couple more. That's OK. And I want you to compare your representations, capisce? And then when we share, I want you to tell me about a kid's representation that was different from yours, but that you agree with.

While students were circulating and talking, Jen listened in on conversations. She thoughtfully chose and sequenced a few representations to discuss in

Figure 8.8 *Can you see the "four times as many" in this representation?*

the large group. She gathered the class back together and projected these pieces of student work. Throughout the discussion, she asked questions that directed students to the mathematics: "Where do we see the four times as many in this representation?" "What would twenty-eight mean in the context of this story? What would this seven be? What would the four be? What do you think?"

Jen had students practice again with a measurement problem: *Franco's daughter is two feet tall. Franco is three times as tall as his daughter. How tall is he?* How might you draw this problem?

Jen asked students to make a picture of what was happening in this problem. This time, however, Jen's directions for discourse were a little different:

Jen: Here's what I'd like you to do this time when you share. I'm going to give you about three to four minutes. We'll see how it's going. I want you to try to find at least one person whose representation you agree with and that you think makes sense according to this problem, and at least one person whose representation you're not quite sure about. Maybe you think it doesn't accurately match what's happening here. And if you find that you disagree with someone, do you say it in a nasty way?

Class: No.

Jen: How would you say to someone that you disagree with their representation without making them feel bad? How might we do that? Andrew?

Andrew: Like you can say um, "I disagree with you"?

Jen: You could say, "I disagree with you" and say it in a nice, pleasant voice. Other ideas?

Janelly: You just say, "I have a different idea."

Jen: "Well, I actually have a different idea." Santiago?

Santiago: "I'm not really sure about that."

Jen: "I'm not really sure about that." And one last idea.

Alex: "Can you repeat what you said because I don't think it's right?"

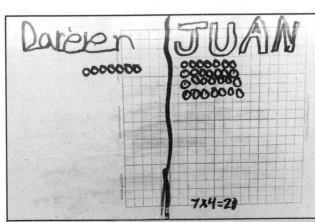

Figure 8.9 *What about here? Can you see the "four times as many"?*

Jen: Yeah, maybe, or maybe you just didn't quite understand what they did? And you can always say, "Nice try." Because I can tell you right now everyone did try their hardest. Capisce? So let's take three or four minutes. At least one you agree with, one you disagree with, and then we'll share.

Again, students had rich conversations walking around the room, and again, Jen directed students to the mathematics in the representations in the whole group. In this case, she guided students to make connections between the representations in Figures 8.10 and 8.11. Kazemi and Hintz call this a *Connect and Compare* discussion and describe how to facilitate them in detail in *Intentional Talk* (2014).

Figure 8.10 *Can you see the "three times as tall" in this representation?*

Figure 8.11 *What about here? Can you see the "three times as tall"?*

Jen: What do people notice that is similar, and what is different, about these two representations? And you don't have to tell me stuff like oh, this one has a smiley face and this one doesn't. Although that is true. What do you notice that's different?

After this second round of conversations, Jen felt like students were ready to get to work on a few multiplicative comparison problems. She released them to work with whomever they wanted and positioned herself on the rug for any students who would like support. Now and then, while those students worked, Jen circulated to see how the rest of the class was doing. She and I both noticed several students having trouble with one problem in particular. Make sure to draw it yourself so you can imagine where students might run into snags:

> Jake's grandmother lives 8 miles away from him. His aunt lives six times as far away from him as his grandmother. How far away does his aunt live?

Every student in the class was able to answer the question immediately: forty-eight miles. Many students struggled to represent the problem visually, however. Jen and I both wondered whether the language of this problem was tripping up students, especially because the majority of her students speak Spanish at home. We worked to clarify language with students in small groups and individually but saw students still struggling with their representations. In particular, Jamaica and Ella were stuck thinking linearly about this problem, as shown in Figure 8.12. They were not able to say where the 48 miles were in their representation or relate the "six times as far away" to their picture. They also did not understand that both distances were in relation to Jake's house.

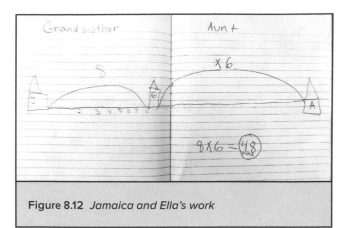

Figure 8.12 *Jamaica and Ella's work*

Given how many students struggled with it, Jen decided to use this problem as her closing discussion. There's great math in the problem, and Jen knew that giving students a chance to listen to other perspectives might help those who were stuck see the problem in a new way.

Jen: OK. So this one presented some challenge, huh?

Students: Ooh, a challenge, cool . . .

Jen: (Laughing.) So I want to share a few of the representations because people had lots of different ways of thinking about it. It's cool. So raise your hand if you'd like to have your representation up here for all of us to take a little peek at?

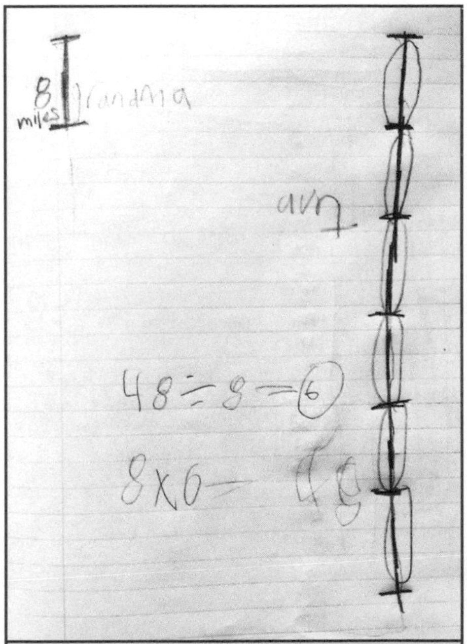

Almost every hand went up. Jen started with the representations shown in Figures 8.13 and 8.14. During the discussions, Jen pushed students to find the six, eight, and forty-eight in each representation, and compare the two.

After discussing these two diagrams, Jen asked Eden and Karla to bring up their representation. They had drawn a more concrete map of the problem, shown in Figure 8.15.

Figure 8.13 *Did Darien show the "six times as far" in his representation? What about the eight miles?*

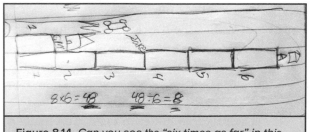

Figure 8.14 *Can you see the "six times as far" in this representation? How long must each rectangle be?*

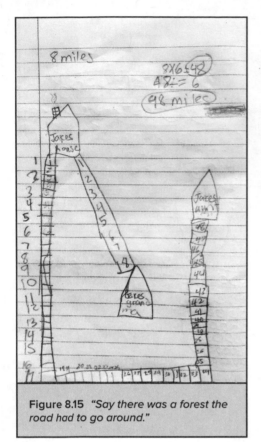

Figure 8.15 *"Say there was a forest the road had to go around."*

Karly: We did the grandma's house first. Um, and we made that eight miles.

Jen: So you started with Jake's house and then you made the grandma's house eight miles away?

Karly: Mm hmm. And then we wanted to do his aunt's house, which was forty-eight. So we did the same thing we did for eight. But we didn't have enough room to just go down forty-eight. So we kind of crossed it over and then went back up and around, like a road or something. It's like there wasn't, say there was a forest the road had to go around. There were no roads across from there.

Jen: So in other words, even though a bird, if it were flying, they could get there this way (showing a straight path from Jake's house to grandma's house), you're saying people cannot get there this way. You must travel around this way? That's the only way you could get there. OK. So what do we all think about this? It's kind of interesting, huh? What do people think?

Students discussed this representation, talking about how roads sometimes go around water or forests or other obstacles. At this point, Jamaica and Ella started whispering furiously, looking at their original solution and re-thinking where they'd put grandma's house.

Jen: Does this match the story problem?

Students: Yes.

Jen: Where do you see the six times as far? Who wants to come up and show it? Darien, do you see the six times there?

Darien: Well, I see it right, well, the first eight is, um, it's right here. That's one time . . . and then right here, sixteen is two times. So next is right here. And then here . . .

As Darien figured out each eight, Jen made a hash mark on the drawing, shown in Figure 8.16. Several students said, "Oh!" as she marked the

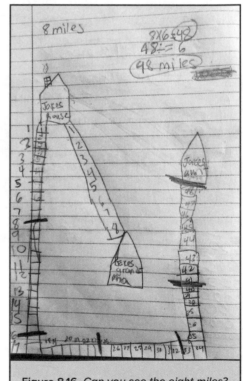

Figure 8.16 *Can you see the eight miles? Can you see the "six times as far"?*

six lengths of eight miles each. They were starting to be able to *see* the six times as far in the representation.

Ella, one of the students who was stuck on her representation before the whole-class discussion, raised her hand:

> Ella: I agree because it, it never said he had to pass by the grandma's house. And it was kind of better to do it this way. Now they can know how, like, how many miles they have to go to get to each house.

Jen facilitated a discussion of the possible ways students could have drawn this problem. Many students commented that they'd assumed the grandmother's house was on the way to the aunt's house. Eden and Karla's representation opened their eyes to a wider range of possible solutions. Afterward, Jen brought the discussion around to representations and problem solving:

> Jen: What did you figure out first? Did you already know forty-eight was going to be how many miles away it was before you started your representations?
>
> Karly: We knew it was going to be forty-eight first and then we represented it.
>
> Jen: Interesting. Did you do the groups of eight and then get your answer? Or did you already know the answer?
>
> Karly: We already knew the answer.
>
> Jen: You already knew the answer. That's kind of interesting. It's interesting because *sometimes the representation can help you get your answer. And sometimes it proves your answer.*
>
> Ella: Well, it kind of helped us know that we were wrong, because after we drew it, we were like, "Uh-oh." (Everyone laughed good-naturedly.)

Jo Boaler said, "Representing is part of both explanation (How can I make sense of this for myself?) and communication and justification (How can I explain/show/convince other people?)" (Boaler and Humphreys 2005, 102). When discussing the *Jake's House* problem, students used representations to make sense, to explain, to communicate, and to justify, as well as to discover what they didn't know. By having students compare their mathematical representations, Jen created favorable conditions for students to forge new understanding and connections. As Tripathi argued, "Using . . . different representations is like examining the concept through a variety of lenses, with each lens providing a different perspective that makes the picture (concept) richer and deeper. As the number of perspectives increases, we develop better insight into the concept" (2008, 439).

Finally, Jen's emphasis on multiple student representations is consistent with her commitment to equity in mathematics. Jen listens to each learner's thinking and values each person's perspective, which directly impacts her students' beliefs about who can and can't do math:

By relocating student-generated representations to the center of the instruction, the nature of how students experience mathematics changes dramatically. It reconsiders mathematics as a vibrant dialogue among different but equally valued thinkers. This deliberate approach to the teaching of mathematics . . . becomes vital if we are serious about creating greater equity for our students. (Imm, Stylianou, and Chae 2008, 459)

I have spent many hours in Jen's classroom, and the "vibrant dialogue" among her "different but equally valued thinkers" always bowls me over. It took me several visits to realize that Jen listens to students' representations as intently and respectfully as she listens to students' words. Every student is held in high regard as a serious mathematical thinker, capable of connecting ideas, having insights, and teaching others. Students take great care when creating their representations because they know their ideas are important, and they want to share their thinking with their mathematical community. The time Jen devotes to analyzing, comparing, and connecting students' representations is time incredibly well spent, every way I look at it.

Relational Thinking: Silos Full of Content Versus a Landscape of Ideas

Teachers feel incredible pressure to keep moving, to make it through the lesson, the unit, the curriculum. Continually adding new content, however, affords students few chances to step back and consider how ideas relate to one another. How might we find time for students to see that bigger picture?

Debbie Nichols, first and second grades

Gunther's Clock

In 1976, Richard Skemp wrote a seminal paper called "Relational Understanding and Instrumental Understanding" (2006). It's a wonderful and thought-provoking read that has been reprinted several times and is very much relevant today. In the essay, Skemp described two different meanings of "understanding" in math education, which he called "instrumental" or "relational." As an analogy, Skemp described how he learned to navigate a new town. At first, he learned "several particular routes" he needed to get around town: from where he was staying to where he was working, from where he was staying to the dining hall, from where he was working to his friend's office, and so on. This is instrumental understanding. He was able to get from point A to point B or point A to point C by learning "a limited number of fixed plans by which [he] could get from particular starting locations to particular goal locations" (94).

As soon as he had the chance, Skemp said, "I began to explore the town. Now I was not wanting to get anywhere specific, but to learn my way around, and in the process to see what I might come upon that was of interest. At this stage my goal was a different one: to construct in my mind a cognitive map of the town" (2006, 94). He was building relational understanding.

Skemp learned about the town through both approaches, but there are incredibly important differences:

> A person with a set of fixed plans can find his way from a certain set of starting points to a certain set of goals. The characteristic of a plan is that it tells him what to do at each choice point: turn right out of the door, go straight on past the church, and so on. But if at any stage he makes a mistake, he will be lost; and he will stay lost if he is not able to retrace his steps and get back on the right path.
>
> In contrast, a person with a mental map of the town has something from which he can produce, when needed, an almost infinite number of plans by which he can guide his steps from any starting point to any finishing point, provided only that both can be imagined on his mental map. And if he does take a wrong turn, he will still know where he is, and thereby be able to correct his mistake without getting lost; even perhaps to learn from it. (2006, 94)

This is one of my favorite quotations in all of mathematics education. A look through typical math textbooks reveals that we focus almost entirely on point-A-to-point-B instrumental understanding: *can students subtract two-digit numbers with regrouping, divide three-digit numbers by one-digit numbers, multiply fractions, find the least common denominator?* Each chapter is separate from the ones that come before and after. We're teaching that limited number of "fixed plans" to get from particular starts to particular goals. We can generate a lot of right answers and even high scores on standardized tests that way, but when our students get lost, they are lost, because they have no mental map of the terrain. If the problems look at all unfamiliar, learners have no idea where they are.

One day in Debbie's room, I watched her set aside time to develop relational understanding among her first- and second-grade students. They had been working with calendars, and their instrumental understanding was coming along fine, but it was specific to calendars and not connected to anything. Debbie wanted to push students to explore the terrain and build a mental map. She opened a conversation with the questions, "Why are we working with calendars during math? What do calendars have to do with math?" Deb played the skeptic as students suggested different ideas. For example:

Karly: You learn the days of the week.

Debbie: Yeah, but what do the days of the week have to do with math? I don't get it.

Students kept coming up with specific quantities in the calendar, and Debbie kept pushing them to go deeper. You can hear the difference between instrumental and relational understanding right in one of her responses: "Yes, we do a lot of *math skills* at calendar time. But what does the calendar *have to do with math?*" When students drew a blank, she gave a little guidance toward a connection with measurement.

Debbie: When we have to figure out how long something is what do we do?

Ricky: We could measure it.

Debbie: We measure it. We measure it, absolutely. When we have to figure out how much can fit in something what do we do?

Ricky: We measure it.

Debbie: We measure it. When we have to figure out how much time we have what do we do?

Ricky: Measure it.

Debbie: Why did you say *measure* again?

Ricky: You have to measure it to know exactly what time it is.

Debbie: So measuring. Using the calendar is a way that we measure things. We measure time. Not time on a clock but time that goes by in days and weeks and months and years.

Ricky: I always look at the clock to know what time it is.

Debbie: I always look at the calendar, because I need that calendar to help me tell the time. Serena, you're looking at me really funny, and I don't think you believe me. Serena, ask your question.

Serena: Well, how do you tell time when you look at the calendar?

Debbie: How do I tell time when I look at the calendar? What a great question! How do we tell time when we look at the calendar?

Jules: I don't know. Good question.

Debbie: All right. I'm going to split you in two groups. I'm going to give you each a calendar and you're going to put it in some kind of order.

(Debbie pulled out two large unbound calendars, with one poster for each month.)

Debbie: This is not this year. It's a different September, okay? Serena, you're going to take some people to the red rug and put these in some kind of way that will help you tell time. You're going to work together. You're going to go over there. And the people in this group, put these in some kind of way that help us to tell time.

The kids broke into two groups and began working. In Serena's group, the students quickly put the months in order in a linear way, starting with January. The rug wasn't big enough, so they ended up with two rows, each with six months, shown in Figure 8.17. Gregory, who is a natural leader, quickly took charge of the other group. He made a 3-by-4 array, with three months in each row, shown in Figure 8.18.

While Gregory was working, Gunther was quietly saying, "I have a different idea. I have a different idea." When he had a chance to work,

Figure 8.17 *"We put our calendar in order."*

Figure 8.18 *"I showed the seasons."*

Gunther arranged the months in a circle. His peers had no idea what he was doing and kept trying to straighten the months into rows. Debbie instructed them to wait and watch, and one-by-one, they realized he was making a clock, shown in Figure 8.19.

When he was finished, Gunther happily spun round on his knees in the middle. He said, "Do you see? Do you see? You told us to put it in a way that tells time. I looked at the clock. I know there are twelve months in a year and there are twelve numbers on the clock. The calendar is the clock of the year, and it goes around and around and around. The calendar is the clock of the year."

Debbie and I were thrilled with his connection, and we saw a few other students starting to understand. For example, Clint said, "This makes sense, because it still goes in order." Debbie brought over the teaching clock to help students make the connection concretely.

Debbie: Look, you have September right there. And you know what September is? (Debbie started to point to the 9 on the clock, but stopped herself.) Let's, let's count. If January's the first month, let's count. (Deb pointed to the numbers on the clock as the class chorally recited.) January, February, March, April, May, June, July, August, September. Look! September is the ninth month! That's for real, Gunther! (Deb pointed back and forth at the placement of 9 on the clock and September in Gunther's representation.) And October, November, December. December is the twelfth month, Gunther! Whoa! Bravo!

(The whole class clapped.) Do you know what this helps me know, Gunther? The calendar tells us time, doesn't it? It tells us the time in the year, Serena. The months have a certain order, and they happen over and over and over. It keeps going. When we finish one, we start the next. So your question was, "'How does the calendar help us tell time?" It helps us measure the passing of time in a year.

Figure 8.19 *"Do you see? The calendar is the clock of the year."*

Debbie and her students gathered around Serena's group's work to see how they'd organized time differently. They also looked at Gregory's way before heading out for recess. Afterward, Debbie and I sat down together to marvel. In all our years of using clocks and calendars, neither of us had made this connection before.

The following week, I was surprised to see Debbie ask Gunther to make his clock on the floor again. When I asked her why, she said, "I know they don't have it yet." I was struck, again, by Debbie's wisdom. The prior week, Debbie and I understood what Gunther was saying, but that didn't mean the rest of the class had followed his thinking. In fact, we could be sure most of them didn't understand, because learning takes time and repetition. My friend's nine-year-old son, Luke, explained learning math this way: "Sometimes you don't get things the first time. It's like you have to change the angle of your light on the prism until . . . BOOM! The rainbow." Hearing one explanation, once, wasn't nearly enough for students to see the rainbow. Teachers have to work hard to remember that an expressed idea is not an understood idea. Cathy Humphreys described it this way:

> One of the most seductive traps a teacher can fall into is to assume that once a correct answer has been publicly stated (either by a student or by the teacher), it has become common knowledge. (Boaler and Humphreys 2005, 109)

Debbie knew Gunther's connection was far from common knowledge, so she set aside time to revisit it. She had index cards ready with the twelve numbers on them, and Gunther was happy to place a number on its corresponding month: 1 with January, 2 with February, and on, as shown in Figure 8.20. That change in the representation alone caused a series of "Oh!" and "I get it!" comments from the students, as they started to see the connection between calendars and clocks. Debbie asked students what they noticed, and the class launched into an open-ended conversation in which they made connection after connection.

Figure 8.20 *"The month is kind of like the hour hand. And the days of the month are the minutes, like the minute hand."*

Seasons, Fractions, and Multiplication

Students thought about where the seasons were on this clock, and they could visually see that the year was divided into four equal parts. Students then figured out where the seasons started and ended, gesturing to show spring, summer, autumn, and winter.

Debbie: Each quadrant has a certain number of months that kind of fit into it? How many?

Gunther: Three.

Debbie: Three here and another three and three more.

Gunther: Yup.

Debbie: Let's add them up. Three, and three are . . .

Class: Six.

Debbie: Six and three . . .

Gunther: It just made me learn something about math.

Debbie: What did you learn?

Gunther: Three times four is twelve.

Debbie gave students a few minutes to make sense of that claim and count for themselves, exploring multiplication a bit.

Numeric Notation of Calendars

Eddie: Um, January's first so it has a one.

Debbie: It does. And you know what big people do when they write a date in January? They say, "one."

(Debbie had students practice a few written dates.)

Debbie: What if I said the tenth month of the year?

Students: October.

Debbie: Ta da!

Units and Scale

Clint: The month is kind of like the hour hand. And the days of the month are the minutes, like the minute hand.

Debbie: So you're thinking that these tick by, Clint? You're thinking the days tick by like the minutes tick by? Oh . . .

Gunther: The hours in a day would be the tiny things on the clock. The seconds.

Ricky: Oh, so those five dots between each hour would be between each month.

Gunther: Not five though. Those little lines are the days inside the month.

Debbie: So how many dots would you want in between, um, nine and ten?

Gunther: Thirty dots. Because there are thirty days in September.

Division, Odds, and Evens

Students noticed that some months had thirty days, some had thirty-one days, and February had twenty-eight days, and had been pondering why.

Gregory: Um, I think I know why there's not like the same numbers of days. It's because, I'm not sure about this, but I think 365 is not an even number.

Debbie: How do you know that?

Gregory: I don't.

Atticus: It's an odd number. Because, if you go back to the one digit numbers, five is an odd number. The last number's five. So then it would be an odd number.

Gregory: OK. So that's why the months have different amounts.

As is true for several of their connections, the students' thinking isn't quite complete here. That's OK. The kids were exploring the landscape, bouncing from one idea to the next, getting a first feel for how their ideas connected. There's no need to follow each idea all the way through to perfect clarity.

Cycles

Several of the conversations, gestures, and comments came back to this idea of going around and around and starting all over again when we finish December. We usually write calendars sequentially or linearly, so the relationship between December and January is obscured. Arranging the clock circularly allowed students to see the cycle. Greta, in particular, commented repeatedly about the end of one year and the beginning of the next. Debbie told me later, "Sometimes, simply the *arrangement* of things can help the lightbulb go on."

Debbie: Gunther, you really taught us something by organizing your thoughts. And we went back to learning about the calendar as a way to . . .

Students: Tell time.

Debbie: Tell time.

One distinction Skemp (1976) made between instrumental and relational learning is that instrumental learning involves a "multiplicity of rules" that each apply to specific conditions, whereas relational learning involves "fewer principles of more general application" (90). Skemp gave the instrumental example of memorizing separate rules to find the areas of triangles, rectangles, parallelograms, and trapeziums, versus the relational example of relating all those shapes to rectangles and using those relationships to find their areas.

In the case of Gunther's clock, the larger principles of units, measurement, and cycles came into play in a major way, as well as wonderful work exploring the relationships among numbers. These are powerful concepts that apply to many different content areas, both in and out of math. When Deb's students go on to learn about life cycles; scientific cycles like rock, weather, or water; economic cycles; or political cycles, they may connect back to Gunther's calendar and continue to add detail, color, and robustness to their mental maps.

A final point for this example: no matter what you read in the latest media story about education, there is never a need to choose between proficiency and understanding. Debbie's students spent plenty of time learning to read, to write, and to use calendars in addition to these few sessions in which they explored the cognitive terrain around calendars. Her six- and seven-year-old students know the days of the week and the months of the year and can move around the calendar as is developmentally appropriate. What Deb did differently, though, was intentionally give students opportunities to discover larger ideas and principles, explore connections and relations, and create powerful mental maps. She sent them for a walk around calendar town, so to speak, to see what they noticed without the narrowing focus of a specific learning objective. The payoff for the amount of time invested was huge and a reminder to me to carve out explicit opportunities for my students to connect. I've written Debbie's opening question as a sentence frame on a sticky note on my bulletin board:

What does_____ have to do with_____?

Good question. That's a keeper.

One Problem, Many Models

Most modern curriculum and standards encourage the use of multiple models, from ten-frames to number lines, area models to algebra tiles. The use of multiple models can be a terrific way to encourage relational thinking, but only if we give students opportunities to make connections among the models.

Becky Wright, Kindergarten, Rollinsford, New Hampshire

"I noticed that everybody found a way to make six that made sense."

Becky's kindergarteners were using rekenreks (sometimes called bead frames or arithmetic racks, shown in Figure 8.24) to build six, and Becky was writing the corresponding equations. Her students had found that $6 = 2 + 4$, $6 = 1 + 5$, $6 = 3 + 3$, and $6 = 6 + 0$, but they hadn't yet thought beyond that. She decided they needed to switch models and see what happened.

She took them out into the hallway where there was a long number line taped to the floor. There were stickers placed at 0, 1, 2, 3, 4, 5, and 6. Becky's students started at 0, and asked, "How can you get to 6?" The first several students stepped on each number, walking 1, 2, 3, 4, 5, 6. Becky asked, "Are there any different ways?" and then Ella stepped up to 0. She jumped from 0 to 3, and 3 to 6. The other kids were amazed. "You can do that?"

Now students were ready to try ideas! They jumped from 0 to 2, then 4, and then 6. They jumped a big jump from 0 to 4, and then a smaller jump from 4 to 6. Becky had brought chart paper into the hallway, and she represented their jumps on written number lines as they went. For example, if a student jumped from 0 to 1, then from 1 to 3, then from 3 to 6, she recorded their movement as shown in Figure 8.21.

After they found several combinations, they went back in the classroom and compared their bumps on the number lines (Figure 8.22) with the equations they'd generated (Figure 8.23). They added some equations they had jumped, and they labeled their jumps with equations.

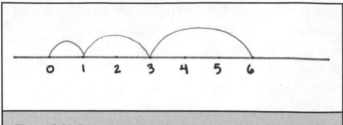

Figure 8.21 *Representation of a student jumping from 0 to 1, then to 3, then all the way to 6*

Figure 8.21 could now be represented as 1 + 2 + 3 = 6.

The following day, Becky posted the chart in Figure 8.22 again and asked students to build the equations with their rekenreks. Figures 8.24 and 8.25 show solutions for 6 + 0 and 2 + 2 + 2, respectively. Students had plenty of rich discussion with partners and in the large group and then headed off to play math games that would deepen their understanding of 6.

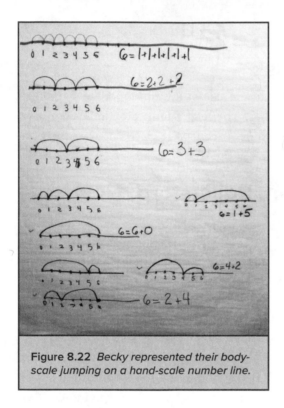

Figure 8.22 *Becky represented their body-scale jumping on a hand-scale number line.*

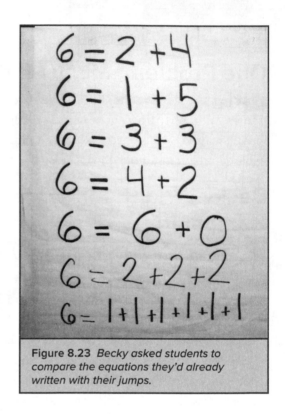

Figure 8.23 *Becky asked students to compare the equations they'd already written with their jumps.*

All students have preferences—models they tend to use and models they tend to avoid. In this lesson, Becky enabled students to build bridges from their preferred models to ones that were not yet comfortable. Some well-intentioned curricula attempt to give students this variety of experiences with models. In practice, however, I see students with math-class whiplash, caused by lurching from one topic to the next or one method to the next, seemingly without rhyme or reason. What made this investigation feel intentional and coherent was that Becky built it around her students' thinking. She encouraged her kids to look deeply at the mathematics from multiple perspectives and to switch from one perspective to another fluently. Becky asked her students:

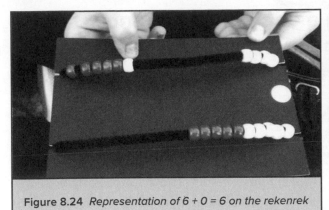

Figure 8.24 *Representation of 6 + 0 = 6 on the rekenrek*

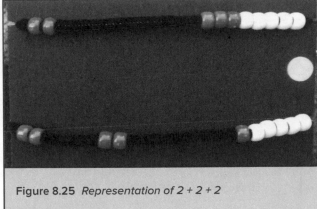

Figure 8.25 *Representation of 2 + 2 + 2*

"Can we use our rekenreks to build what we jumped?"

"Are there any equations we can write in numbers but can't build with the rekenreks?"

"How could we write the way you walked on the line?"

"Are there any number lines up here we haven't built yet?"

"Are there any equations we didn't jump on the number line?"

These are all linking questions. Becky was encouraging kids to connect the way they saw six in one model with the way they saw six in another (Figure 8.26). As Arcavi said, "Flexible and competent translation back and forth between visual and analytic representations of the same situation . . . is at the core of understanding much of mathematics" (2003, 235). What a robust understanding Becky's students are building!

Part 3: Connecting Math to Self

In this section, we'll look at three possible relationships between students and new mathematical ideas: disconnections, successful connections, and attempted connections.

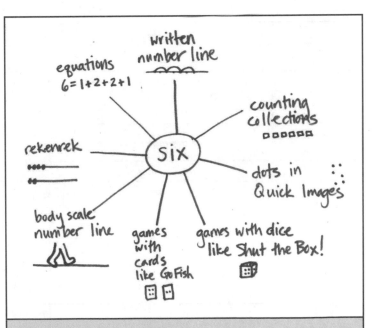

Figure 8.26 *Multiple models lead to a robust understanding of mathematics.*

Disconnection: When a Lack of Proficiency Is Really a Lack of Connection

Emily: "Because it has a story"

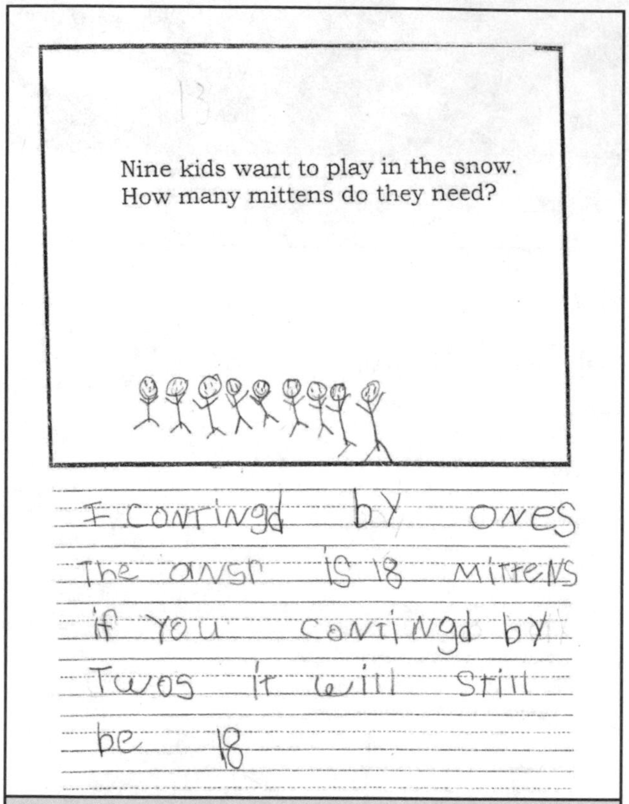

Figure 8.27 *Emily's solution to the mittens problem*

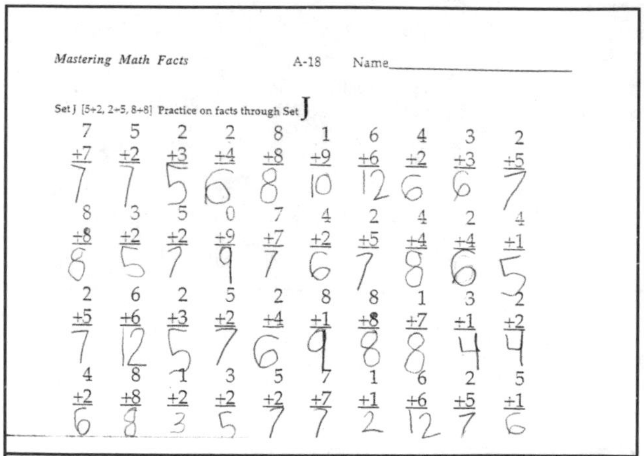

Nine kids want to play in the snow. How many mittens do they need?

I contingd by ones The ansr is 18 mittens if you contingd by twos it will still be 18

Figure 8.28 *Emily's drill worksheet*

Emily is a first-grade student in Debbie's room. She is a student Debbie and I worry about because she doesn't yet ask questions or advocate for herself, and she often tries to hide her confusion. She is soft-spoken and takes a lot of time to process ideas, and we think she misses a lot in whole-class conversations. I noticed two pieces of her work, shown in Figures 8.27 and 8.28, completed in the same week.

I was fascinated by this juxtaposition! Emily was able to solve a multiplication story problem correctly, but wrote nonsensical answers for sums with addends greater than 6 on a drill worksheet. She can clearly memorize and recall 6 plus 6 equals 12 but does she *understand* it? Not if she thinks 7 + 7 = 7 and 8 + 8 = 8. Meanwhile, given no guidance, Emily thought through the mittens problem, drew an accurate representation, and found the correct answer. So what exactly is going on with her number sense? I interviewed Emily so Debbie and I could figure out what she understood and what she needed. I started with the mittens problem.

Tracy: I have a question for you. How did you do this mittens problem?

Emily: Counting by ones and counting by twos.

Tracy: What did you count by ones and what did you count by twos?

Emily: I counted the kids by ones and the arms by twos.

Tracy: Can you show me that?

Emily counted the nine children successfully: 1, 2, 3, 4, 5, 6, 7, 8, 9. Then she counted the mittens by twos successfully: 2, 4, 6, 8, 10, 12, 14, 16, 18.

Tracy: I see. So now I have a different question for

you. I'm going to write it here. What is 9 plus 9? (I wrote *9 + 9.*)

Emily: 18.

Tracy: How do you know that it's 18?

(Emily pointed to the mittens problem, which was off to the side.)

Tracy: Because of your mittens problem?

Emily: Yes.

Tracy: OK. Now, I have a new question for you. 7 plus 7. What's that? (I wrote *7 + 7.*)

Emily: Seven?

Tracy: How come?

(Long pause, and then Emily shrugged.)

Tracy: Can you draw me a picture of 7 + 7?

(Emily drew seven hearts and stopped.)

Tracy: How many hearts are there?

Emily: Seven.

Tracy: Now we have seven hearts. What happens if we're going to do 7 plus 7? What does that look like?

(Emily shrugged.)

Tracy: What does it mean to plus or to add?

Emily: Add one?

Tracy: Add one. Where'd one come from?

Emily: One whole?

Emily looked confused. I got the feeling she was guessing, tossing vocabulary my way. I decided to see whether contextualizing the problem might help her make sense.

Tracy: Would it help if there were a story?

(Emily nodded and smiled.)

Tracy: OK. Emily had seven hearts. Ms. Nichols gave her seven more hearts. How many hearts does Emily have altogether?

(Emily thought quietly for a few moments.)

Emily: Thirteen?

Tracy: How did you figure that out?

Emily: Counted.

Tracy: Show me how you counted, OK? You counted all in your mind. What did you do?

Emily: Counted by ones.

Tracy: Did you start with the number 7?

(Emily nodded.)

Tracy: And then what did you think in your mind?

Emily: Counted seven.

Tracy: Can you show me on your fingers or on paper how you counted seven?

Emily: (Counted on her fingers.) 7, 8, 9, 10, 11, 12, 13.

Tracy: Oh, so you're counting seven more. Can you draw the second set of seven hearts? These were the hearts you already had, and now you are going to get seven more.

(Emily drew them all.)

Tracy: And now how many hearts do you have altogether?

Emily: Thirteen.

Tracy: Show me the counting.

Emily started at the first heart and quickly counted them all, but didn't synchronize her pointing with her counting.

Emily: Fourteen?

Tracy: Make sure, when you touch, you say that number. So go ahead and slow down and count them one more time for me. (Emily counted them all again, this time correctly, arriving at fourteen.)

Tracy: So, I have another question for you. If there are seven kids and they want to go play in the snow, how many mittens do they need?

Emily: Fourteen.

Tracy: How come?

Emily: Because there are seven kids and you need seven more.

Tracy: Because each kid has how many mittens?

Emily: Two.

When I listened to my recording, I kicked myself here. I am not sure exactly what Emily meant by "There are seven kids and you need seven more." I wish I had asked more questions, instead of putting words in her mouth. Old habits die hard. I am sure she was trying to connect the story problems with the naked numbers, but I am not sure quite what she understood.

Tracy: So, I was looking at this piece of paper (picked up the facts page), and you know a lot of your math facts! But I noticed a lot of times when it's a double, like 7 + 7, you wrote 7. That made me wonder—that's why I wanted to talk to you, because it made me wonder about addition. So which kind of problem is easier for you? This kind of problem or this kind of problem? (Holding up the naked numbers page and the mittens problem page.)

Emily: The mittens problem.

Tracy: Why?

Emily: Because it has a story.

Tracy: Does it help you to have a story?

(Emily nodded.)

What does Emily know?

- She can make sense of a story that involves numbers.
- She can figure out both a joining (result unknown) addition problem and a multiplication problem if she has a story context that she can visualize.
- She can draw a representation and use it as a direct model of the story.
- She is eager to try more sophisticated counting strategies like skip-counting and counting on, but she doesn't quite use them correctly yet. They're on her horizon.

What became clear to me during this conversation was that Emily knows a lot about mathematics but hasn't yet connected what she knows about math to either symbolic representations (7, +, =) or to the vocabulary (plus, add, etc.) we use in mathematics. This disconnect is not at all surprising and has been researched quite a bit. We can gain insight from the work of three different, important researchers in this area.

Cognitively Guided Instruction

Tom Carpenter, Elizabeth Fennema, and the rest of the Cognitively Guided Instruction group have been studying how young children learn mathematics for decades. What they've discovered is that students enter school with quite a bit of conceptual understanding and insight about mathematics:

> Until recently, we have not clearly recognized how much young children understand about basic number ideas, and instruction in early mathematics too often has not capitalized on their rich store of informal knowledge. As a consequence, the mathematics we have tried to teach in school often has been disconnected from the ways that children think about and solve problems in their daily lives. (Carpenter et al. 1999, xiv)

In their daily lives, students "think in terms of the *actions or relationships* portrayed in the problems" (Carpenter et al. 1999, 2). Emily was able to make sense of the story problems because she was able to think about the *joining action* of having hearts and getting more hearts or the *multiplying action* of children wearing pairs of mittens. In both cases, Emily was successful when she directly modeled the action in the problem. She does not yet see relationships or actions in naked number problems, so she has no strategies to think them through. Emily knows this about herself and told me she prefers problems with stories.

Kathy Richardson

Kathy Richardson has insight about Emily's lack of connection between quantities and symbols:

> Children who deal almost exclusively with symbols begin to feel that the symbols exist in and of themselves, rather than as representations for something else. They do not connect what they know from experience to the symbols they are working with.

> The number combinations and relationships children need to understand can only be learned through counting, comparing, composing, and decomposing actual groups of objects. The fact that three and four add up to seven needs to be experienced until the child knows that particular relationship. Just learning to say "3 + 4 = 7" does not guarantee the child really knows the underlying relationships implied in those words . . . The connection in the child's mind between the experience and the symbol is critical, and is the key to developing facility with basic math facts. (2012, 46–47)

In Emily's case, we can see clearly that she does not yet have a connection between her experience and mathematical symbols. Richardson advocates for ample experience counting and working with objects so students can develop those connections:

> All children progress through certain levels of understanding, albeit at different times, and often without adults' awareness. For example, when children first learn to add numbers like 3 and 4, they think of this as "1 and 1 and 1," and another group of "1 and 1 and 1 and 1." The only way they know to determine the answer is to count all the objects. Later, they will recognize three objects without needing to count them, and will be able to start with 3 and count on to 7. Subsequently, they will more often see that 4 is composed of 3 and 1, and will be able to use the idea that 3 and 3 are 6, so 3 and 4 must be 7. Eventually, they will know that 3 and 4 are 7 without having to think about it. If teachers ignore these stages and just ask the children to memorize the words "three plus four equals seven," they are, in effect, asking them to learn a 'song,' rather than learn the important relationships these words describe. (xiv)

Street Math and School Math

Terezinha Nunes Carraher, David William Carraher, and Analúcia Dias Schliemann conducted a seminal ten-year study looking at the relationships between "street mathematics" and "school mathematics" among children of street vendors in Recife, Brazil (1985, 1993). These children helped their parents, enacting transactions when their parents were busy. The researchers posed as customers and asked the children to perform calculations on possible purchases. Within a week, the researchers gave the children a paper-and-pencil test using the same numbers they'd used in the street calculations. The tests were a mix of story problems and naked number problems. The results were stunning:

- The children solved 98.2% of the street math problems correctly, using mental math exclusively.
- The children solved 73.7% of the contextualized word problems on the formal test correctly.
- The children solved 36.8% of the naked number problems on the formal test correctly. (1993, 21)

For example, compare the work of this nine-year-old child in the two settings:

Street Math

Customer: OK, I'll take the three coconuts (at the price of Cr$ 40.00 each). How much is that?

Child: (Without gestures, calculates out loud) 40, 80, 120.

School Math

Child solves the item 40 × 3 and obtains 70. She then explains the procedure, "Lower the zero; 4 and 3 is 7'." (Nunes, Schliemann, and Carraher 1993, 24)

The researchers observed that students tried to apply school-prescribed routines and algorithms, generally without success, as soon as they were put in a more formal situation. They no longer assessed their answers for reasonableness and did not rely on the "human daily sense" that had served them so well in their street math calculations (1985, 29).

Next Steps for Emily

This body of research makes the way forward quite clear. Meaningful work for Emily would include:

- Lots of simple story problems in which she would be able to think about the *actions* and *relationships* in the story. These problems should include joining, separating, comparing, multiplying, dividing, and looking at parts and wholes of sets. Connecting the mathematics to a story or context gives Emily a way to make sense. In addition to the essential Cognitively Guided Instruction book *Children's Mathematics* by Carpenter et al. (2014), Chapters 4 and 5 of *Math Exchanges* by Kassia Omohundro Wedekind (2011) are particularly helpful here.
- Work with objects and pictures so Emily can connect numbers to quantities. Emily needs to understand what *seven* means. Working with seven cubes, pompoms, blocks, dots, hearts, horses, seconds, inches, stars, tiles, and beans will help her develop a meaningful understanding of *seven* and start her thinking about how much two sevens are.
- Explicit work connecting her "human daily sense" with the vocabulary and symbolic representations of mathematics: "When you combined 5 blocks and 8 blocks by pushing them together to make one pile of 13 blocks, you added them together. That combining or joining is what we mean by the word *adding*. Here's how we can write what you did: 5 + 8 = 13. Let's look at your blocks. Where in your blocks do you see the 5 . . ."
- In addition to all this explicit work with connections and operations, Debbie and I talked about how much counting practice Emily needs. While she was eager to count mentally, count by twos, and count on, I noticed she did not quite have one-to-one correspondence

in her counting, and doesn't notice if she double-counts or skips objects. She also didn't know where to begin counting on. Debbie planned to incorporate *Counting Collections* (www.teachingchannel.org/videos/skip-counting-with-kindergarteners and www. teachingchannel.org/videos/counting-collections-lesson are great examples), as well as other counting and subitizing routines such as *Choral Counting* and *Quick Images*. She'll use ideas from *Number Sense Routines* by Jessica Shumway (2011) to incorporate daily practice.

Notice I am not recommending more naked number drill worksheets. As Kathy Richardson said, that kind of practice, at this point, is only teaching Emily songs. She needs to build deep connections between and among numbers, quantities, contexts, representations, symbols, and actions. The fact fluency will come, along with wonderful number sense and a student who understands mathematical relationships. We want no gap between street math and school math. If we build on Emily's mathematical thinking in her daily life and help her connect math problems to stories, actions, objects, and representations, Emily will someday be able to explore numbers in their own context. First, she needs to understand what numbers are.

Successful Connections: Making Sense by Building on What You Know

When students grapple with something new, they often try to use concepts they've figured out in other contexts to see whether they'll work under the new conditions. They might extend mathematics they've learned in school or connect to experiences they've had in their daily lives. Over the years, I've jotted down many examples of students gaining insight about a new area of math from these sorts of bridging connections:

"I've noticed that you can switch the numbers around when you multiply, and it doesn't make a difference, just like when you add. If you add 6 plus 4, you get 10. If you add 4 plus 6, you get 10. Same thing when you multiply: 6 times 4 is 24; 4 times 6 is 24. It doesn't work in subtraction, but it definitely works in addition, and I think it works in multiplication."

"I was thinking about how a quarter of an hour is 15 minutes, but a quarter of a dollar is 25 cents. At first I thought, that doesn't make any sense! A quarter is a quarter, right? But then I realized they're quarters of *different things*. An hour is 60 minutes, but a dollar is 100 cents. So a quarter of an hour is different than a quarter of a dollar. I think we have to say what we're taking the fraction *of* for the fraction to make any sense. Just saying one-quarter, or one-eighth, or one-whatever doesn't make any sense unless we say one-whatever *of* something."

"Why is a triangle with three equal sides and three equal angles called an equilateral triangle, but a rectangle with four equal sides and four equal angles is called a square?

Why isn't it called an equilateral rectangle? Isn't it the same thing?"

"Maybe this is one of those problems where we have to figure out all the possible ways we can arrange it. I did a problem like this last year, with shirts and pants and how many outfits can you make. I think it's going to be something like that."

"I think one-fourth is smaller than one-third because, when we use measuring cups to make brownies and stuff, I noticed the one-fourth one fits inside the one-third one. So it's gotta be smaller. Even though four is bigger than three, one-fourth is smaller than one-third. Something different is going on here."

"When I made the table, the numbers were getting bigger and bigger. And now, I'm looking at the graph, and the line is going up and up. Wait a minute . . ."

This kind of thinking is beautiful and something we want to encourage. These students are all generalizing, searching for meaning, and looking for structure. They're connecting one part of math to another or connecting mathematics to the world around them. We want students actively making sense like this.

Attempted Connections: Powerful Learning When the Relationship Doesn't Hold

Sometimes learners attempt to connect ideas that don't actually connect, and the math doesn't hold. For example, if a student conjectures that $\frac{1}{3} > \frac{1}{2}$ because "3 is bigger than 2," he is incorrectly trying to apply what he knows about whole numbers to fractions. Researchers typically call this type of mistake an *overgeneralization*, meaning the student is applying a rule too broadly.

I have found it helpful to reframe overgeneralizations as *attempted connections*. The student is using a habit of mind we want to encourage—he is drawing on mathematics he's learned in one domain and applying it to another domain to see what will happen. If the math holds, he has made a connection. If the math breaks, he has attempted a connection. Both results are mathematically productive.

Jennifer Clerkin Muhammad, fourth grade

38 × 12 = 40 × 10

Jen was using the *I think _____ is unreasonable because _____* structure we saw in Chapter 5, "Mathematicians Are Precise." In this case, her focus was double-digit multiplication. For each problem, Jen gave students some time to estimate mentally and then asked students to write their estimates on their whiteboards so they could discuss their reasonableness. After discussing 21 × 33 as a whole class, she asked students to estimate 38 × 12, and then walk around with their whiteboards and discuss strategies with one another.

During the discussions, a heated argument broke out in the back corner. Jasmine said she could "take 2 from the 12 and give it to the 38" to turn 38 × 12 into 40 × 10, and the answer would be *exactly* the same. Leo said that was a good estimation strategy but it wouldn't give the exact answer. Jonah agreed with Jasmine and argued the two problems were exactly the same. Jasmine wrote her conjecture as shown in Figure 8.29.

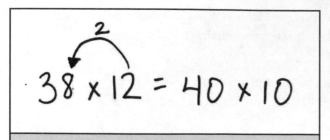

Figure 8.29 *Jasmine's conjecture*

Jen gathered everyone together and listened to students' arguments for several minutes. It became clear that Jasmine, Jonah, and their peers were trying to make a connection between multiplication and addition. Over the past several years, these fourth-grade students have learned to decompose and compose numbers when adding by making tens, using landmark or "friendly" numbers, and moving numbers around to make them easier to work with, all while maintaining equivalence. For example, if this were an addition problem where the ones added to 10, like 59 + 21, we'd expect many students to compose a 10 by "taking 1 from the 21 and giving it to the 59" to make 60 + 20.

Jasmine and the rest of the kids who tried 38 × 12 = 40 × 10 were trying to use the same approach in multiplication. Their attempted connection is totally logical, especially if they are thinking of multiplication as repeated addition, or adding in groups. The question is, Does it work? Why or why not?

Rather than tell the kids whether Jasmine was right or wrong, Jen knew she wanted students to make sense of the mathematics. She opened the question to the whole class and found her students were evenly split about whether Jasmine's conjecture was true or false. Jen asked students to reason through what it did to the values in the problem to increase 38 to 40 and decrease 12 to 10. Students decided that:

> going from 38 × 12 to 40 × 12 would make the problem *larger* by two 12s, or 24.

> going from 38 × 12 to 38 × 10 would make the problem *smaller* by two 38s, or 76.

By that point, many students were saying "It doesn't work!" even though they hadn't quite taken that reasoning all the way through to 40 × 10. Other students looked lost. Jen studied her class for a moment and decided she needed time to plan her next steps. Even though Jen and I are both experienced fourth-grade teachers, neither of us had anticipated this particular attempted connection, so we hadn't done enough thinking about how to capitalize on the opportunity it provided. Jen told the class she wanted to table Jasmine's conjecture until the following day so she could talk with colleagues, generate teaching ideas, and make thoughtful decisions.

When we talked on the phone later that night, Jen and I found we'd both spent quite a while playing with the problems 38 × 12 and 40 × 10 to make sense of the mathematics ourselves. I can't emphasize this step enough; it simply can't be skipped over. If you haven't yet pulled out a pencil and tried Jasmine's way to see what happens, now is the time.

We traded ideas in the days after the lesson, and I'll fill you in on what happened with Jen's class shortly. It was so interesting to talk about it together that I found myself bouncing this problem off many colleagues to see what good ideas I could gather. Over a few weeks, I showed Jasmine's conjecture to every math teacher I saw, and asked, "Can you help me think about this cool thing a student said? What would you do with it? Where would you go next?" I got some great advice, including several ideas that hadn't occurred to me.

One suggestion was to go to small numbers the students knew well, such as the problem in Figure 8.30, and ask, "Does it work?"

Another thought was to go to numbers that are far apart, to magnify the effects of what look like small adjustments, as shown in Figure 8.31.

Several teachers suggested that students should create arrays so they could see that the two rectangles are not equivalent, and 40 × 10 < 38 × 12, as shown in Figure 8.32.

Several teachers thought about using a context. I live in New England, where we do a lot of apple picking, so that was a common suggestion. We wrote the story problem shown in Figure 8.33.

With a context, we can ask students, *What does that 38 mean? What does that 12 represent?* And, most important for this claim, *What does take 2 from the 12 and give it to the 38 mean?* Pause for a moment and try putting words to this action. What does it mean in the apples story?

Eventually, after some muddling around, students will figure out that *taking 2 from the 12* means *taking 2 apples out of each of the 38 baskets,* leaving each basket with 10 apples inside (Figure 8.34). Then, *What does it mean to give 2 to the 38*

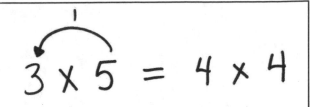

Figure 8.30 *Does it work with smaller numbers?*

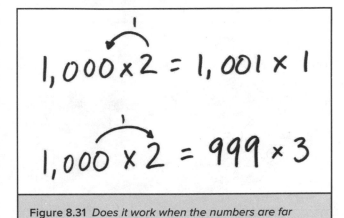

Figure 8.31 *Does it work when the numbers are far apart?*

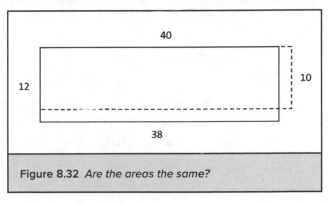

Figure 8.32 *Are the areas the same?*

Figure 8.33 *Does contextualizing Jasmine's conjecture help clarify things?*

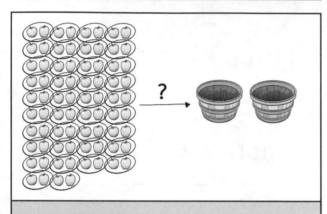

Figure 8.34 *What does take 2 and give it to the 38 mean?*

Figure 8.35 *What does take 2 and give it to the 38 mean?*

to make 40? Can we weave those pairs of apples into baskets? Can we turn one unit into another, as shown in Figure 8.35?

There are many strategies we can use to multiply, but what we can't do is take apples and turn them into baskets. I'm not invoking a rule here. I'm invoking the "human daily sense" we talked about with the street math and school math study. Unless your students are alchemists, once they've assigned units by deciding which are baskets and which are apples, they need to stay consistent throughout the problem. Apples stay apples and baskets stay baskets.

Jen decided to use this last approach, to contextualize the problem and ground it in stories, because at least some of her students weren't thinking about what the different numbers meant when the problem was abstract. Students were hearing from their classmates that Jasmine's conjecture doesn't work, but Jen wanted her students to grapple with why.

Jen: What I want everybody to do is erase your whiteboard, and write a story problem about 38 × 12.

Students worked individually, then together, before Jen asked them to share out. She told the class, "Make sure that we're listening to see if we think these stories are in fact representations of 38 × 12." After listening carefully to each story, Jen pushed against the context, encouraging students to engage with the problem, visualize the action or relationship, and think about whether it was multiplication:

Danny: Chris has 38 packages of markers. There are 12 markers in each package. How many markers does he have?

Jen: What do we think about that one? Is that multiplication? What do you *see*?

Rosa: Ms. Muhammad had $38. Rosa had 12 times as much money. How much money did Rosa have?

Jen: Wait. Who has more money, me or you?

Rosa: Me.

Jen: I like how you wrote the story to give yourself more money. (Laughing.) Hey, what kind of problem is that?

Rosa: Multiplicative comparison.

Leo: I was bragging to my friend Jasmine that I had 38 pencils. Lucas said he had 12 times as many pencils as I had. How many pencils did Lucas have?

Jen: Whoa. That's a lot of pencils. Why does Lucas need so many pencils?

Maria: I had 38 cookies. I needed 12 times as many cookies to take to the party. How many cookies did I need?

Jen: You need 12 times *more* cookies than 38? What kind of party are you going to? How many people are coming that you need that many cookies?

Yasmani: I made 38 cupcakes. On each cupcake, there are 12 cherries. How many cherries in all?

Jen: Are these jumbo cupcakes? How do you fit 12 cherries on each one?

Over the next several days, Jen gave students time to create problems, to solve problems, and to represent their problems. Students were starting to build conceptual understanding of multiplication, including how it is similar to addition, and how it is different. The context problems, in particular, pushed students to think about units, which helped Jasmine and her peers start to see a key difference between multiplication and addition:

When we add, we add *like* units.

    flowers + flowers = flowers

    chairs + chairs = chairs

    hours + hours = hours

    centimeters + centimeters = centimeters

When we multiply, though, we're dealing with *different* units.

    the number of bunches × the number of flowers in each bunch = the number of flowers

    the number of rows × the number of chairs in each row = the number of chairs the number of hours × miles per hour = the number of miles

length (centimeters) × width (centimeters) = area (square centimeters)

In addition and subtraction problems, we sometimes think of:

part + part = whole *or*

start + change = result

If we know any two values, we can figure out the third because addition and subtraction are inverse operations.

In multiplication and division, we can think of:

number of groups × number of things in each group = number of things *or*

unit A × unit rate (A per B) = unit B

Again, if we know any two of those values, we can figure out the third because multiplication and division are inverse operations. We can use what we know to figure out the quantity we don't know.

Returning to Jasmine's 38 × 12 conjecture, we can see that, in her attempt to build on the *similarities* between addition and multiplication, she overgeneralized because she didn't yet understand the *differences* between addition and multiplication. Learning multiplication requires knowing both *what it is* and *what it isn't*. Jasmine's attempted connection helped her class explore the boundaries between the operations and identify how the operations are related but distinct.

Questions worth exploring, either with your students, with your colleagues, or on your own:

How is multiplication like addition?

How is multiplication different from addition?

How is multiplication like division?

How is multiplication different from division?

Generalizing About Overgeneralizations

I often see students overgeneralize, and I usually see teachers appeal to rules in response:

"No, you can't do that with fractions."

"That only works for adding."

"You're not allowed to do that when you subtract."

"You can't . . ."

"You have to . . ."

"No. The rule is . . ."

When students are told they can't do something mathematical because there's a rule against it, they develop myths about mathematics: that it's full of rules, that authority figures tell you what you can and can't do, that you have to follow directions instead of figure it out.

What's a better response when a student attempts a connection that doesn't hold mathematically? Rather than appeal to rules, appeal to the math:

"Let's try it out and see!"

"Does it work? Always? Sometimes? Never? Why?"

"Can anyone think of an example where Akira's claim doesn't work?"

"This is an interesting idea! Let's see if it holds up to scrutiny."

"Huh. That connection seemed like it made sense. Why didn't it work?"

With some exploration over time, your students and you will be able to figure out whether the attempted connection is valid or an overgeneralization. There's no need for you to render a verdict or immediately tell students what's right:

> In traditional systems of instruction, teachers are asked to provide feedback on students' responses, to tell them whether they are right . . . this is almost always unnecessary and usually inappropriate. Mathematics is a unique subject because . . . correctness is not a matter of opinion; it is built into the logic and structure of the subject . . . There is no need for the teacher to have the final word on correctness. The final word is provided by the logic of the subject and the students' explanations and justifications that are built on this logic. (Hiebert et al. 1997, 40)

New Connections: "I'd never thought about it that way before!"

I've been thinking about 38 × 12 for a long time, ever since I observed the lesson. I have learned so much about multiplication from exploring Jasmine's attempted connection, both on my own and with colleagues. I've noticed that teachers who enjoy teaching math are as excited about her conjecture as I am. Several teachers said, with pleasure, "Whoa! I never thought about it that way before!" In my experience, teachers who have strong content backgrounds in math get excited when they have a chance to learn something new. Teachers who are less secure about math have a different narrative running through their minds. Some teachers have told me they think, *What am I doing here? I don't even know how to multiply? I was supposed to learn that in fourth grade. And I'm supposed to be the expert!*

I was talking these ideas through with Rebeka Eston Salemi, coauthor of *Math for All: Differentiating Instruction, Grades K–2,* with Linda Dacey (2007) and classroom teacher for more than thirty years. She compared our reaction to learning something new in math with learning something new in literacy. She shared that her granddaughter was in eighth grade and about to read *To Kill a Mockingbird*. Becky told her, "Tell me when you're reading it and I'll read it with you because I learn something new every time I read it!" Similarly, when we read aloud a book we've read twenty times and a student points out something we have never seen before or makes a new connection, we get excited. We say, "I never noticed that before! Wow! Thank you for sharing that!" Becky wondered, "Why don't we talk like that in math?" Good question.

We need to give ourselves permission to say, publicly, and with delight, "I never thought about it that way before!" whether *it* refers to addition, fractions, or place value. It is long past time for us to respect the beauty, power, and importance of elementary mathematics, instead of having contempt for "the basics." Researcher Liping Ma wrote about the need for teachers to have "profound understanding of elementary mathematics":

> Elementary mathematics is not a simple collection of disconnected number facts and calculational algorithms. Rather, it is an intellectually demanding, challenging, and exciting field—a foundation on which much can be built. (1999, 116)

The difference between seeing elementary math as a "collection of disconnected" facts, procedures, rules, and algorithms and seeing it as an important, fundamental, and interesting field of study in its own right lies in studying the big ideas, and seeing the connections among them. These conceptual bridges form a "deep, broad, and thorough" network of powerful ideas (Ma 1999, 120).

I want our students to have that network. And I want us to have it, too.

Because most of us were taught to memorize the rules and follow the steps as kids, we see mathematics as silos full of isolated content, each with their own codes, rather than an open landscape of interconnected ideas. As we grow as math teachers, we need to take down those walls and explore connections and relations. Right alongside our students, we can figure out what's really going on with the mathematics so we finally understand, and then understand deeper, and then understand deeper again.

> Conceptual understanding is not like an on-off light switch: you don't *understand* a concept in an all-or-nothing fashion. Initially we grasp some aspect of the concept and build upon it, adding and elaborating our understanding . . . In general, the more connections of the right kind, the more examples in different but relevant contexts, the more elaborate the networks of ideas and relationships—the deeper, richer, more generalized, and more abstract is our understanding of a concept. (Hyde 2006, 41)

I'd been multiplying successfully for thirty-seven years before Jasmine made her conjecture. Thanks to a ten-year-old, I now have a much "deeper, richer, more generalized, and more abstract" understanding of multiplication. I wonder what problem, question, mistake, or example will help me build connections about multiplication next?

MATHEMATICIANS USE INTUITION

When people talk about mathematics, they often use words like *logical, certain, objective, absolute, black and white*. Sometimes I even hear the words *cold, calculating,* or *unfeeling,* as if mathematicians are giant, bipedal brains, devoid of human emotion, struggle, creativity, or imagination. If you'll remember Reuben Hersh's "front and back" structure from Chapter 1, "Breaking the Cycle," this societal image of the detached, walking brain is the front. A peek behind the curtain reveals that mathematicians experience the full range of feelings and use all their intellectual and creative faculties when they work.

I have come to see mathematics as a creative art that operates within a logical structure. If that statement sounds paradoxical or contradictory, think about it as a yin and yang relationship. Contrasting pairs of ideas—logic and art, creativity and structure, truth and beauty, instinct and reason, passion and discipline—are the left and right hands of mathematicians. In media portrayals, we usually see one but not the other. I have learned that these dualities are what make understanding and doing mathematics possible, and mathematicians often write and speak about them. For example, David Hilbert wrote in 1932:

In mathematics, as in any scientific research, we find two tendencies present. On the one hand, the tendency toward *abstraction* seeks to crystallize the *logical* relations inherent in the maze of material that is being studied, and to correlate the material in a systematic and orderly manner. On the other hand, the tendency toward *intuitive understanding* fosters a more immediate grasp of the objects one studies, a live *rapport* with them, so to speak, which stresses the concrete meaning of their relations. (iii)

All too often in math education, we focus on the "systematic and orderly" but leave out the "intuitive understanding" and "live rapport." In her article "Why Is Intuition So Important to Mathematicians but Missing from Mathematics Education?" Leone Burton reported that the overwhelming majority of the working mathematicians she interviewed "recognized something important which might be called intuition, insight, or less frequently, instinct at play when they were coming to know mathematics" (1999, 28). In Burton's interviews and elsewhere, mathematicians talk about having a *feel* for the problem, a *hunch* about how it's going to work out, a *gut instinct* for where a path might lead. Almost as soon as phrases like these leave mathematicians' mouths, words such as *check, prove, justify*, or *verify* follow.

These essential ideas—intuition and proof—complement each other beautifully, and neither is sufficient alone. Intuition might get a mathematician started on a problem or even guide her all the way through a solution, but she is not satisfied until she has verified her work by understanding *why*, especially because intuition can feel tantalizingly right but end up totally wrong. That's why a disciplined mathematician subjects her intuition to the skepticism and scrutiny of mathematical reasoning and proof.

The more I learn, the more I realize how off the mark my own math education was. We spent so much time focused on steps and sequences; yet, the process of doing math is neither linear nor sequential. Mathematicians zigzag between intuition and verification, grabbing tools and adopting perspectives from both, sometimes immersing themselves in one approach more than the other as they imagine, conjecture, generate counterexamples, refute their own ideas, refine their thinking, and dream up new hunches to pursue (Lampert 1990). The gut leads the mind, and the mind checks the gut. Yin and yang in balance. What's extra lovely about this relationship is that each side strengthens and supports the other.

When we build true, deep understanding of mathematics and why it works, our intuition gains wisdom. We learn from the dead ends and attempted connections, the patterns that held and the solutions we found. Equipped with sharper, more experienced intuition, we are better able to sense the path toward the next mathematical truths. Similarly, each time we construct a convincing, sound argument, we build rigorous thinking we can use to hone our intuition. Fields Medalist Terry Tao wrote about this powerful, synergistic relationship:

The point of rigour is *not* to destroy all intuition; instead, it should be used to destroy *bad* intuition while clarifying and elevating *good* intuition. It is only with a combination of both rigorous formalism and good intuition that one can tackle complex mathematical problems; one needs the former to correctly deal with the fine details, and the latter to correctly deal with the big picture. Without one or the other, you will spend a lot of time blundering around in the dark (which can be instructive, but is highly inefficient). So once you are fully comfortable with rigorous mathematical thinking, you should revisit your intuitions on the subject and use your new thinking skills to test and refine these intuitions. (2007)

In this chapter and the following two, we'll explore these ideas of intuition, reasoning, and proof—and the relationships among them—in the classroom. What is the younger student's version of what Terry Tao described? And what role do intuition, reasoning, and proof play in effective mathematics teaching? Let's take them in turn, starting with intuition.

An Essential Idea: Intuition Is Developed

People have amazing facilities for sensing something without knowing where it comes from (intuition); for sensing that some phenomenon or situation or object is like something else (association); and for building and testing connections and comparisons, holding two things in the mind at the same time (metaphor). These facilities are quite important for mathematics. Personally, I put a lot of effort into "listening" to my intuitions and associations, and building them into metaphors and connections.
                    —William P. Thurston, "On Proof and Progress in Mathematics"

Many people believe that most of us are born with a "bad math gene," and some lucky few are born with a "good math gene." They think people who do well in math have a natural, innate, instinctive "feel for math." What mathematicians have taught me, however, is that this feel for math—mathematical intuition—comes from experience and practice:

My intuitions are based on my knowledge and my experience. The more I have, the more robust my intuitions are likely to be. (Burton 1999, 29)

The more we use, check, examine, and refine our intuition, the savvier it gets. As a teacher, this idea makes me sit up and take notice: *mathematical intuition is developed*. What fantastic news: if it's something that is developed, we can structure our teaching so all our students develop it!

That said, teaching intuition is a nuanced, complex idea and one we have not historically valued or emphasized in professional development for math education. I understand we're in new territory here. I'm hoping, by the end of this chapter, you'll feel excited and equipped to teach students how to use and improve their mathematical intuitions. We're going to focus on three key ideas:

- **Building Intuition Around New Concepts**—structuring exploration and experiences that build students' mathematical feel for new ideas

- **Listening to Intuition During Problem Solving**—teaching students to engage in Hilbert's "live rapport" with their mathematics, continuously, even during calculations
- **Strengthening Intuition with Practice**—developing and refining students' mathematical instincts by emphasizing thoughtful estimation

Part 1: Building Mathematical Intuition Around New Concepts

Intuitive experiences must be acquired by the student through his/her own activities—they cannot be learned through verbal instruction.

—Erich Wittmann, "The Complementary Roles of Intuitive and
Reflective Thinking in Mathematics Teaching"

That's a quote to read a couple of times. To build intuition, students must do the thinking, reasoning, and experiencing themselves. Top-down teaching techniques such as memorization, lecture, and recitation may teach students procedures or vocabulary, but they *do not* foster students' intuition. No wonder many of us feel uneasy with mathematics as adults, right? We're uncomfortable because the form of math instruction most of us experienced—I do, we do, you do—is not one that cultivates intuition.

So what does?

Mathematician Reuben Hersh argued that our experience manipulating objects, symbols, representations, and mental images is how we develop mathematical intuition:

> Intuition ... is the effect in the mind/brain of manipulating concrete objects—at a later stage, of making marks on paper, and still later, manipulating mental images. This experience leaves a trace, an effect, in the mind/brain. That trace of manipulative experience is your representation of the natural numbers ... We have intuition because we have mental representations of mathematical objects. We acquire those representations, not mainly by memorizing formulas, but by repeated experiences. (Hersh 1997, 65)

"This experience leaves a trace, an effect, in the mind." I love that image. If our intuition is the trace left by our experiences, then we need to think carefully about what sorts of experiences we create for our students. What traces do we want to leave now, so students can create meaningful mental images and representations later?

I agree with Hersh that ample experience manipulating physical objects helps students create associations, relationships, and mental representations they can later imagine and describe symbolically. Students use their hands, bodies, everyday objects, and classroom math tools to make sense. As Deborah Loewenberg Ball argued, however, bins of manipulatives alone will not cure what ails us: "Although concrete materials can offer students contexts and tools for making sense of the content, mathematical ideas really do not reside in cardboard and plastic materials" (1992, 47). We only teach with math tools effectively if they are part of a larger teaching and learning context:

> Creating effective vehicles for learning mathematics requires more than just a catalog of promising manipulatives. The context in which any vehicle—concrete or pictorial —is used is as important as the material itself. By context, I mean the ways in which students work with the material, toward what purposes, with which kind of talk and interaction. The creation of a shared learning context is a joint enterprise between teacher and students and evolves during the course of instruction. Developing this broader context is a crucial part of working with any manipulative. The manipulative itself cannot on its own carry the intended meanings and uses. (Ball 1992, 18)

In the following classroom example, we'll see this shared learning context in action. Students developed beautiful intuition about a new concept through hands-on work because that work was embedded in purposeful teaching and a safe learning environment. Jen Clerkin Muhammad combined open and guided exploration with manipulatives, written student representations, lots of student talk and reflection, and a focus on estimation to build students' intuition and understanding about angles.

Jennifer Clerkin Muhammad, fourth grade

Estimating Angles: "The more you do this, the more comfortable you'll be, and the better you'll be able to eyeball."

Angles are a tricky concept to teach and an important component of fourth-grade mathematics. Students generally hold misconceptions about what an angle is. Is it the distance between the lines? Or the length of the lines? Lots of students would say that angle B is greater than angle A in Figure 9.1.

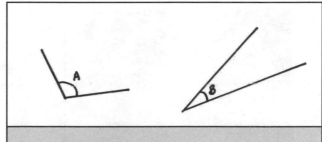

Figure 9.1 *Which angle is bigger?*

Students also confuse angles with the area of the space inside the lines and sometimes focus on "filling" up the space. Many students think about angles as pointy corners, and it takes quite a bit of work to get them thinking about angles as quantities or an amount of *turn*. Even the unit, *degrees*, is confusing for students because they understand degrees only as a measurement for temperature.

For students to understand angles in the connected, relational way we talked about in Chapter 8, "Mathematicians Connect Ideas," they need opportunities to use multiple representations and different approaches. For example, many teachers I know use body-scale mathematics to help students feel the movement of angles at their elbows or knees, shoulders or hips. We have students stand and rotate their bodies by certain angles as well, to get at that idea of turn. We build, flex, and rotate angles with straws and twist ties, oak tag and brads, door hinges, clock hands, and so on, as well as with math tools such as pattern blocks and protractors.

Because Jen emphasizes estimation, reasonableness, active sense making, and intuition in her math teaching every day, I made a point of seeing her introduce angles. As always, I came away with loads of new ideas. Throughout the unit, Jen was guided by TERC's *Investigations in Number, Data, and Space* curriculum, which includes quite a bit of time for students to explore and build deep understanding (2008). Even with such a conceptually strong curriculum, however, Jen has noticed that:

> *Once students have a worksheet, it all becomes about the worksheet. The kids have these questions they need to find the answer to, and, even if they're good questions, it becomes about those questions instead of, "What are you noticing?" I wanted to give them time to explore and just see what they noticed. As they explored, they would end up discovering a lot of what was being asked anyways, but without that pressure of, "Here's the question, and I have to find the answer to it."*

Because of this astute observation, Jen has learned to hold the worksheets back for a bit in key lessons and to insert extra discovery-based, intuition-building experiences. After students have constructed some understanding and gotten a feel for the mathematics, she usually gives them the assignment so they can practice, build skills, apply their understanding, and communicate

Figure 9.2 *How can you use one angle to figure out the others?*

their thinking. By the time students are answering questions, they feel confident and move along fairly quickly. Using this method, Jen finds she stays within range of the district pacing guide, even though she's adding time for discovery.

In the days before I observed Jen teach angles, students had been working with Power Polygons (transparent geometric manipulatives). At the beginning of the first day, Jen gave students a little time to play with the manipulatives so they could build and discover. Like many teachers, Jen introduces every new tool or manipulative this way. Management is much easier once students have had a few minutes of free time with the tools, and they often make great discoveries on their own.

Once students explored a bit, Jen guided them toward investigating angles. As per *Investigations*, Jen started with right angles, including composing right angles with two or three smaller angles (Figure 9.2). The day I visited, Jen's students were ready to derive the measurements of those smaller angles, compose new shapes with them, and explore angles greater than ninety degrees. Jen opened by reviewing what they'd done so far:

Jen: What did we talk about yesterday?

Sonya: Yesterday, we were using polygons to make right angles.

Jen: To make right angles. Would anyone like to say that differently? Camden?

Camden: We were using shapes to make ninety-degree angles.

Jen: Ninety degrees. Excellent.

Maribel: For example, you use these two little triangles and they were both forty-five-degree angles, and then you put them together to make a ninety-degree angle.

Jen: Thank you for that segue. That's exactly what I was going to say! So the example that I had given is I had put these two triangles. (Held up 45-45-90 right triangles.) Raise your hand if you can remember one of the names of that kind of triangle. (Hands up.) Talk at your tables.

(Jen gave students a few minutes to talk. She moved around, eavesdropping.)

Jen: I heard a couple of things. Santiago, what was one thing that you mentioned?

Santiago: It's a right triangle.

Jen: He says it's a right triangle. And what makes it a right triangle? Santos?

Santos: It has a ninety-degree angle.

Jen: It has a ninety-degree angle. Excellent. I heard some people call it a right angle. So then Maribel said something really interesting about the size of those two small angles. Can you talk at your tables about what she said?

(Again, Jen walked around, listening intently to small-group talk.)

Jen: I heard a lot of kids say the size of this little angle right here was forty-five degrees. Can you prove that somehow with maybe an equation on your whiteboard? If you do one equation, can you come up with a second equation or maybe even a third one? How did you know it would be forty-five degrees?

(Students worked in groups.)

Jen's students shared and discussed the equations they used to derive the angle's measurement:

$$90° \div 2 = 45°$$
$$45° \times 2 = 90°$$
$$45° + 45° = 90°$$
$$90° - 45° = 45°$$

Jen: OK. So, I'm not sure if you guys realize this, but you now have a measuring tool—an angle-measuring tool. What am I talking about? What do you mean I have an angle-measuring tool with this? How is this a tool? Talk to people at your table.

(Students talked with animation.)

Jen: OK, I want to hear from a couple of people. I haven't heard from this table. How would

I use this as an angle-measuring tool? It's just a little right triangle. What do you think, Annie?

Annie: Because if you find a shape that you think has a forty-five-degree angle or a ninety-degree angle, you can use that to make sure it does.

Jen: Oh, interesting. Does anyone have something different than what Annie said?

David: You can also predict what the angle is by using a right triangle, because if you predict, like—these are friendly angles. You can use a right triangle with ninety and forty-five degrees to see if it's close to your estimates.

Jen: That is so interesting and something we're going to be using. I love that you called them friendly angles! It kind of reminds me of landmark numbers, but, landmark *angles*, right?

(David nodded.)

Jen: And I would definitely say a ninety-degree angle is the most famous angle, wouldn't you say?

David's connection to *friendly numbers* or *landmark numbers* is powerful! Jen wants her students to have a feel for the size of angles, to be able to estimate them, to have intuition about them. The landmark or benchmark angles of 15°, 30°, 45°, 60°, and 90° are the most important references for estimating angles of any size. If students have a strong sense of the size of these angles, they will be able to create mental representations much more easily.

Notice also that David used the words *predict* and *estimates*. Jen has worked hard to build this habit of mind among her students, and it's paying off. David was able to transfer the technique of making and checking estimates from numbers to geometry. This connection was especially notable to me because I often see students think of geometry as a completely separate world from the rest of math.

Up to this point, Jen was tracking her curriculum closely. Here is where she deviated by adding a structured, intuition-building experience:

Jen: So here's what I want you to do. And this is going to take some perseverance. Yesterday, you came up with some really cool ways of making ninety-degree angles, like this way. (Showed a 60° plus 30° solution). Some kids even came up with three different angles to make ninety degrees. Do you remember that? Here's your job. You just told me that these small, acute angles are forty-five degrees each. I want to see, can you try and discover the size of some of these other angles? (Held up the bag of Power Polygons.) And I'm not even going to tell you how to start. You're just going to experiment with it.

There was a lively buzz in the room as kids shared strategies and worked together. Students naturally connected one discovery to another as they compared the sizes of the different angles. I heard Phoebe say, "It's like one of the angles is the key that unlocks the other angles!" Of course, different students found different keys. Some students stayed with right

Figure 9.3 *This student used right angles as a benchmark.*

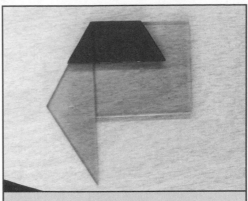

Figure 9.4 *Students used what they knew to figure out what they didn't know.*

angles as their landmark angles and figured everything out in relation to them (Figure 9.3). Other students composed unfamiliar angles and then tried to derive their measurements using known angles (Figure 9.4). Several students decide to compare and categorize the angles without any prompting, marking their findings right on their Power Polygons (Figure 9.5).

There were no barriers to entry, caps to learning, or "right ways" to work in this lesson. While some students were figuring out combinations to make right angles, others were wondering how many degrees there are in all the interior angles of a hexagon, and whether that number stays constant with different-shaped hexagons. This task was inherently differentiated and accessible to all of Jen's students.

Thinking more broadly about intuition and proof, I was struck by how naturally students moved through *cycles of estimating and verifying.* I placed cameras in different areas of the room and recorded several student conversations. This discussion is representative:

> **Karni:** This one is definitely bigger than 90 degrees. I think it's more like 110 degrees, or 120 degrees.
>
> **Magda:** Yeah. Actually, I think it's bigger than that. Maybe 120 degrees or 130 degrees. Let's check it and see.
>
> **Karni:** This one is 60 degrees, I think. Do you agree? (Picking up the blue rhombus and pointing to the

Figure 9.5 *"One of the angles is the key that unlocks the other angles!"*

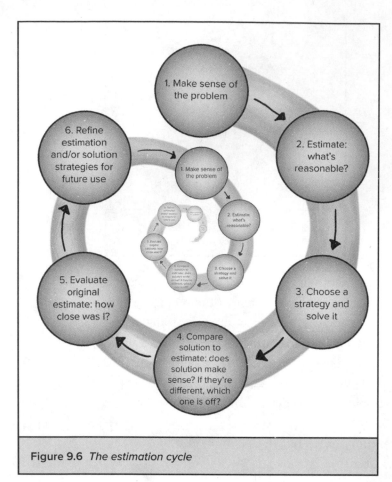

Figure 9.6 *The estimation cycle*

60-degree angle.)

Magda: Yeah, that's what I got, too.

Karni: OK. Let's see how many sixties fit in there.

(Students composed the angle with two 60-degree angles.)

Magda: Sixty plus 60 is 120. It is 120 degrees!

(The girls high-fived.)

Karni: We were close!

Karni and Magda have internalized the thinking process Jen has been promoting all school year: they routinely estimate, verify, and reflect as needed. I visualize their process cyclically, as shown in Figure 9.6.

I see Steps 1 through 4 taught in many classrooms in some form of estimate–solve–check. The thinking involved in Steps 5 and 6—evaluate the estimate and refine strategies—is rarely taught but absolutely essential (Wittmann 1981). Without scrutiny or reflection, our intuition doesn't get wiser.

In this case, Karni and Magda evaluated their estimates and found they were close to the exact measurement, so they didn't spend time refining their strategies. In another group, however, Alejandro estimated an angle to be 180 degrees and it turned out to be 120 degrees, so I had a chance to watch him work through the refinement process beautifully. He stopped and looked at all the angles with a furrowed brow. After a long time, his eyebrows shot up and he said: "Oh! I see what I did! I thought these" (picked up brown rhombuses) "were forty-five degrees. I pictured four of them. It was four of them, but they're not forty-five degrees! They're thirty degrees. That makes sense now." He resumed thinking quietly for another minute, then said, "Huh. They're smaller than I thought. Which one was forty-five degrees then?"

Alejandro and Leon found an angle they knew to be forty-five degrees and compared it to the thirty-degree angle. They stacked them on top of each other and carefully looked at the difference. This kind of thinking is exactly what I mean by evaluating and refining intuition. Going forward, Alejandro's and Leon's intuitions will be wiser and more accurate because they took the time to recalibrate their mental angles, rather than rushing ahead to the next problem. This is classroom time well spent!

All four of these students—Karni, Magda, Alejandro, and Leon—demonstrated the "live rapport" Hilbert talked about in 1932: "*Intuitive understanding* fosters a more immediate grasp of the objects one studies, a live *rapport* with them." These students engaged in active conversations with one another, themselves, and the mathematics. Jen has modeled and taught this lively dialogue all year, and students have internalized it: "Huh. They're smaller than I thought." Jen's students develop and refine their intuition as a habit, especially when they make mistakes, whether she's watching or not.

After ten or fifteen minutes of productive work time, Jen asked students to pull out their blank math notebooks (1) to trace and label their angles and (2) to use equations to record the angles they'd derived, for example, 90° + 45° = 135°. It was an additional challenge to represent their thinking in diagrams and numbers, which pushed students to clarify each measurement. Several students had to stop and think through their solutions again in order to write them, which reinforced and deepened their new understanding.

After a little time, Jen brought everyone together on the rug to focus explicitly on estimation:

> Jen: So, I'm going to show you an angle right now. And I know some of you actually already know the measurement because you figured it out before. So, if you know, I'm going to ask you to just keep it on the down low, OK? What I want you to tell me is how you would *estimate* the size of this angle. What could you *use* to help you estimate? What if you stumbled upon this angle right here, and you had to make your best guess about the size of it, and you didn't have a protractor, which is a really special tool to measure angles, and you didn't have your Power Polygons. What would you use to help you, or help you estimate the size? Talk to the people near you.

Jen projected an equilateral triangle. After students talked to one another, she had them share out.

> Kimberly: I know that the point of the rhombus is thirty degrees. So, I think two of them would fit and that would be sixty degrees.
>
> Jen: So, you're kind of imagining that skinny rhombus, that brown one?
>
> Kimberly: Yeah.
>
> Jen: She's picturing two of those together would make that angle, so she's thinking it's about sixty degrees. That's one way to estimate it. What are you thinking, Saul?
>
> Saul: I'm thinking of a right angle, and thinking is it more or less than a right angle?
>
> Jen: I love that, because the right angle is an angle we all know, right? Is this angle bigger than a right angle or smaller?
>
> Students: Smaller.
>
> Jen: Smaller. So what we're going to do now is we're going to use those tools that you guys just discovered. And before that you're going to use your estimation skills.

Jen assigned the worksheets from her curriculum but made an important modification. She asked students to estimate the angles given on their worksheets and to talk about their estimates with one another first. Once they'd discussed, adjusted, and recorded their estimates, they used their Power Polygons to determine each angle's measurement. As always in Jen's room, there was a serious, active buzz among her students. Several times, I heard kids say, "Oh, I figured that one out on my own before!" They finished the assigned problems successfully and seemed pleased and proud to have discovered the mathematics independently.

Jen closed the lesson by reiterating the importance of estimation:

> Jen: We always want to make estimates no matter what we're doing. You don't want to do any sort of math blindly; you want to have an idea about the problem so that, when you do get an answer, you know if it makes sense. Estimating is that conceptual part. To be able to eyeball it, you can't just rely on this tool or that strategy. You have to think!

She also emphasized the importance of experience in developing a feel for the mathematics:

> Jen: The more you practice and use these tools, the more you can eyeball things. You'll get more comfortable. The more time you can manipulate these tools, the more you'll make these discoveries, and the more you'll be able to trust your estimates over time. The more you estimate, and then check it, the better you'll estimate.

Intuition can be developed and refined, right? Talk about building a growth mindset!

Why Did This Lesson Work?

Jen modeled one practical way teachers can structure opportunities for students to build intuition. By shuffling her lesson components a bit, Jen was able to carve out instructional time for students to build mathematical intuition and then use the curricular materials to reinforce their new learning. In this way, Jen gave explicit attention and dedicated class time to building students' intuitions about angles without adding to the total amount of time the lesson took.

Also, this exploration was so successful because Jen has created a safe, social learning environment. Students feel comfortable sharing partially formed ideas, incomplete thoughts, and revisions to their thinking. Students see themselves as sense makers, capable of exploring content rich with mathematical ideas. Jen's emphasis on teacher-student and student-student communication was central to the effectiveness of this lesson: students engaged in academically productive talk throughout their work, which pushed them to verbalize and clarify their fledgling ideas. Likewise, creating written representations and numeric expressions challenged students to build new understanding.

Finally, Jen's students were completely engaged, curious, and productive without any prompt or contrived need for angle measurements. While an enticing question, challenge, or problem can motivate a student investigation, one is not always necessary. Angles are interesting all by themselves. There was no need to dress them up in a gimmick or embed them in a cute worksheet with cartoon characters to capture students' attention. Students were plenty perplexed by the ideas alone.

So where did the manipulatives fit in? They were an essential part of this lesson, for sure. It's awfully hard to build intuition about angles without angles to manipulate, and pictures of angles in a workbook would have been a terrible substitute. But it's important to remember that it was Jen's intentional and purposeful use of the tools, situated in a complex learning context, that created opportunities for students to build new mathematical intuition and conceptual understanding, as shown in Figure 9.7.

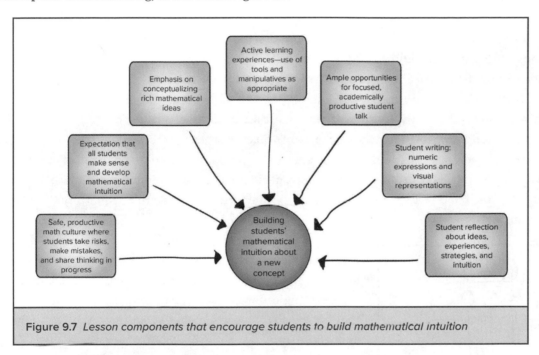

Figure 9.7 *Lesson components that encourage students to build mathematical intuition*

Part 2: Listening to Intuition During Problem Solving

Jen's angles lesson demonstrates the power of investing time in building students' intuition around new concepts, but that's not enough. We can't just emphasize intuition at the beginning and end of a unit or the beginning and end of a problem, which is the estimate-first, solve, and-check-your-answer-at-the-end model. To engage in Hilbert's "live rapport," students need to *keep the conversation going all the way through the problem*. Just like students need to monitor their comprehension when reading and recognize when they're no longer understanding, students need to monitor their thinking in math and realize when they are no longer making sense. Jen and I have talked many times about how students will show good understanding and intuition during discussion but shift to procedural answer-getting as soon as there is a "real" problem in front of them. As I quoted Jen in Chapter 5, "Mathematicians Are Precise": "As soon as paper and pencil get involved, it's all about getting that answer, and they stop thinking."

Exactly. And it doesn't just happen with students. Recently, I was working with a group of elementary teachers who did not have much personal experience arguing and debating math. I wanted a morning warm-up that would get them staking out positions, so I chose one of my favorite questions from John Stevens's outstanding website *Would You Rather?* at wouldyourathermath.com:

> Would you rather have a stack of quarters from the floor to the top of your head, or
> $225?

As always, this example will make a lot more sense to you if you take a stab at the math first, yourself. So, which would you rather have, a stack of quarters from the floor to the top of your head, or $225? Take a couple of minutes to play around with it.

Just as I'd hoped, within a few minutes, all the table groups were engaged in animated discussions. Part of the beauty of this question is that solvers have to figure out what information they need. I had the thickness of a quarter ready for them, should they want it, but nobody asked. Instead, each group had someone who remembered that one roll of quarters is worth $10, and all the groups independently decided to use that referent to estimate the value of their stack of quarters. The big question became, How long is a roll of quarters? The table groups' estimates were all in the 3.5- to 5-inch range.

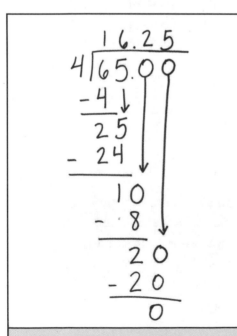

Figure 9.8 *"And then I brought down a 0 so it was a 10."*

After the groups worked out their answers, I asked a primary teacher, Sheila, to come to the chart paper and lead the discussion so she could practice recording and representing different strategies. One group explained that they had decided to use 4 inches to estimate a roll of quarters and chose one teacher's height—5'5", or 65 inches. They divided 65 inches by 4 inches to see how many rolls of quarters it would take to reach the top of her head. I sat quietly while Sheila painstakingly recorded each step of the long-division algorithm they'd used (Figure 9.8): "And then I brought down a 0 so it was a 10, and 4 goes into 10 two times, so I wrote 2 above and 8 below . . ."

Several minutes had passed by the time Sheila had written 16.25 above the long division symbol, and nobody seemed able to remember what was going on. What was that 16.25? What did it mean? Sheila turned to me and said, "Time out. I'm lost."

I loved this moment.

Sometimes, when solving a math problem, we get lost in the details, especially if we take a long trip through some procedural math. In this case, the room had lost track of the problem. They got caught up in the weeds of the long-division algorithm and weren't using intuition anymore. Sheila did a great job recognizing that she had lost the problem, which is just what we want students to do when they get lost. I was proud of her for being confused, publicly!

I put Sheila's question to the whole group and gave everyone some time to reconstruct why the teachers had been dividing and what those numbers meant. Eventually, people realized that 16.25 meant they thought it would take 16.25 rolls of quarters to create Laura's height. If each roll of quarters was worth $10, then their estimate was her height was worth $162.50, so $225 was a better deal. They seemed content. I wasn't.

I asked, "Is it reasonable to calculate the number of rolls of quarters to the hundredths place? How sure are you about that five-hundredths of a roll?" It took some time and discussion for the teachers to zoom back out of the problem, think about what they had done, and decide whether it made sense. As they reflected on it, the teachers expressed feeling "more mathematical" or "more correct" to calculate the division problem to the last possible place. This feeling makes sense in light of how they were taught math themselves, where "exact" answers were the ultimate goal:

> Obsessions with exact answers often force unnecessary calculations and keep peo-
> ple from gaining experience and confidence in estimation judgments. They can kill
> intuition with detail . . . and reinforce the false notion that exactness is always to be
> preferred to estimation. (Usiskin 1986, 15)

Most of these teachers were so tempted by the appeal of precision and completeness that they forgot their calculation was based on a ballpark estimate of 4 inches. What kind of sense did it make to calculate the number of rolls to the hundredths place when they started with an educated guess? And, even if they could calculate to the hundredths place, did they need to? Compared to $225, anything in the $160s was clearly inferior. If they'd stayed in touch with the question and kept thinking actively about 65 divided by 4, they would have been happy with a quotient of "16 and a little bit," which translates to "a little more than $160." All this calculating could have been mental math and intuition, rather than being "killed by detail." (By the way, imagine their surprise when they later learned that a roll of quarters is actually about 2¾" long? Forget about those five-hundredths of a roll; the teachers were off by more than seven rolls and $70 because of their initial estimate!)

As a coach, I was thrilled these teachers had a chance to experience what their students experience regularly, hoping it would inform their teaching. They felt what it was like to start out thinking about the problem deeply, switch off their intuitions when they started calculating, lose confidence, and have trouble making sense again. This is just what kids tend to do, especially if they have been taught procedural math and algorithms. The essential question becomes, how can we teach students to keep making sense throughout a complete mathematical venture, to stay in touch with their reasoning and intuition?

The answer to this question is not easy. What I have learned over three years of focused observations is that the best solution is a relentless, many-times-per-day, dominant emphasis on *making sense*, so students develop the habit of examining their reasoning and intuition. Highly skilled math teachers ask a steady drumbeat of questions that students eventually internalize, like we've repeatedly seen Jen Clerkin Muhammad's students do. They ask students to wrestle with these questions in individual conferences, in small-group discussions, in turn-and-talks, in large-group conversations, and in written reflection. They wait patiently for students to think deeply before answering. And they ask these probing questions *whether students' answers are right or wrong.*

I've gone back through my observation recordings from every teacher featured in this book and have synthesized their live-rapport questions. I hope you'll try asking these questions in your teaching. As you practice asking them—and listening carefully to students' oral and written responses—the language will become natural, and you'll make them your own.

Questions to focus on sense making at the beginning of the problem:

- What's going on here?
- What are you noticing?
- What do you wonder?
- Tell me something about this problem.
- Forget about the question for a second. What's going on in this situation?
- What do you estimate the answer might be?
- What do you predict the solution might look like?

Questions to redirect students to the problem while solving:

- Can you read the problem aloud again?
- Let's go back to the question for a second. Is everything still making sense?
- Let's refresh our memories about what each of these numbers represents. What's the _____ mean?
- Let's put numbers aside for a second and think about the units. Do they check out?
- Wait a minute. I'm trying to visualize what's going on in this problem. Does that seem possible?
- Did you have a picture in your mind when you read the problem? Can you share it with us so we can see what you saw?

Questions to teach students to expose and analyze their decision making throughout:

- Stop there for a second. We're in the details, but can you remind us why you were figuring that out in the first place?

- Before you calculate that, can you tell us why you'd want to?
- What are you planning to do with that information, once you find it out?
- What's that going to do for you?
- Why do you need to know that?
- Tell us why that matters.
- What made that an appealing way to start?
- How did you decide what to do next? What was your rationale?
- What were you hoping for when you made that decision?
- Did you have a plan, or were you trying things out?
- Were you going on a gut feeling here, or did you have a plan?
- Were you working off a hunch? Did it work? Why or why not?
- Where'd you get the idea to do it that way?
- Slow down. We want to follow your thinking. Can you tell us your reasons for approaching it that way?

Questions to encourage relational thinking to make sense:

- Oh, so you were remembering another problem? Can you tell us about that?
- Oh, so you thought about [a connected concept]? Can you tell us how that relates?
- How did thinking about your experience with _____ help you here?

Questions to teach students to check in with their intuitions during problem solving to develop a feel for mistakes and inconsistencies:

- What was going through your head when you noticed that?
- Was everything fitting together at that point?
- Did you feel satisfied, like everything made sense?
- What tipped you off that something wasn't right?
- Did anything jump out at you?
- Oh, so that raised some red flags for you?
- What caught your eye and made you think something might have been off?
- How did you know you were wrong?
- Does anything strike you as unreasonable here, or does it hold together?
- Is anything about this work troubling anyone?
- Does her approach seem reasonable or unreasonable to you? Why?
- When did the bells start going off, like maybe this approach had a problem?

Questions to teach students to apply intuition to their solutions:

- How do you feel about that answer?
- How confident are you?
- Does that sit right with you?
- Do you believe that?
- Do you believe yourself?
- What's making you doubt?
- What would convince you?
- You seem unsettled. Talk to us about why.
- When your estimate and your answer didn't match, what did you think?
- Does that seem reasonable?
- Did that match what you expected?
- That was a surprising result! Do you think it's true?
- Was it about what you thought it would be or not?
- Does it make sense that _____ is bigger/smaller than _____?
- Does that pass the commonsense test?
- Is anything nagging at you, or are you completely satisfied?
- How close was your estimate?
- It feels counterintuitive, doesn't it? Say more about that.

Questions to encourage students to refine their intuitions going forward:

- Did anything surprise you here, or did it work out like you expected?
- So you think the math is right, but the result doesn't make sense? Interesting! Let's talk about that.
- How did you reconcile those two thoughts/answers/ideas?
- What are you thinking now?
- Where do things stand?
- What are you reasoning through now?
- Did you end up reexamining anything you'd thought you knew?
- What would help you settle your remaining questions?
- What's next? Where will you go from here?
- Did anyone change your mind today? How?
- What new questions are you asking now?
- What new understandings did you come to?
- What do you think you'll remember for next time?

When teachers use this sort of language—*daily*—it sinks in. Students come to expect that making sense is part of doing math. Students value intuition while recognizing its limitations. Most important, by externalizing the interior dialogue we want running through students' minds, we make mathematical thinking transparent in the classroom. When we ask live-rapport questions, we create opportunities to highlight, examine, and model active sense making. Let's look at a brief classroom example to see how this works.

Julie Clark, fifth grade

"We were pondering and pondering and pondering the problem."

Julie's students had worked in pairs on an excellent problem adapted from the *Connected Mathematics Project 2* (Lappan et al. 2009):

> Jane and Don's mathematics classes are selling sub sandwiches as a fund-raiser.
> Jane's class has reached ⅔ of their goal and Don's class has reached ¾ of their goal.
> Jane says her class has collected more money than Don's class.

Students were asked to show and explain both how Jane could be *right*, and how Jane could be *wrong*, so they had to do quite a bit of reasoning. Take a second to think about the problem yourself. How could Jane be right? How could Jane be wrong?

Julie jumped on the opportunity for students to think aloud here, to externalize their thought processes for the benefit of their classmates:

Julie: I want to look at this problem, because a lot of you kind of stumbled when you got there. You thought, wait, she *can't* be right. So let's talk about what's going on in that problem. Right off the bat, you're thinking, "No can do. That doesn't work . . . Um, yeah. She's just wrong." So, then, you had to really look at it and prove her right. So, how could she be right? How can two-thirds be more than three-fourths? Go ahead and talk at your table. How did that make sense? How can that happen?

Students shared different solutions, proving that Jane could have raised more money by meeting two-thirds of her goal if her goal was larger than Don's. For example, if their goals were both $300, then Don's class raised more than Jane's. But, if his goal was $300 and her goal was $450, Jane's class raised more money than Don's. At that point in the class discussion, the math was settled, but Julie kept asking about students' thought processes. Austen shared her story:

Austen: At first, Rita and I were like, "OK, she's wrong. This is going to be very easy. But we've got to prove her *right*." So then we were just pondering and pondering and pondering the problem, until finally I remembered something from last year when we were studying fractions, and the question was how could they have ate the same amount of the milkshake or whatever if they had different fractions. I looked up there (pointed to the question) and it said *nothing* about the goals being the same. And Rita said, "No, they *have* to be the same." But then it's impossible to prove her right!

Julie: Then it's impossible! A lot of you thought this is impossible; it can't be done. You had to think outside the box a little bit. You had to let go of that consistent goal.

Eddie: For me and Brenda, we looked at it and thought, "That doesn't seem right." But then we read it again noticed it said "their goal" and realized that their goals don't have to be the same. But if you didn't realize that, it would be really hard.

Julie: Yes, if you don't let go of that consistent goal thing . . . And so often we have that mindset that it's going to be the same. Like you said, you pondered and pondered and pondered and thought, "How can this be?"

Austen: I was so happy when I figured it out!

Julie is obviously teaching perseverance here, but she's also teaching students to—in Austen's word—ponder. To question mindsets and assumptions. To think through the math. To engage with problems, vigorously. To work together. To consider their intuitions. To think about whether things seem reasonable or not. To change their minds. To value the process. To make sense.

Part 3: Strengthening Intuition with Regular Practice

Visual Estimation and Number Sense: Much More Than Rounding

As I've been hinting at throughout this chapter, number sense, estimation, and mathematical intuition are very much intertwined. There are several other layers of meaning to the phrase *mathematical intuition* (e.g., see Hersh 1997, 61-66), but I would argue that developing an intuitive feel for numbers, shapes, quantities, operations, and functions and how they relate to one another is the most important element of intuition we teach in school.

When I visit classrooms, I see an increasing emphasis on developing computational number sense, with more teachers using number talks and ideas like those in *Number Sense Routines* (Shumway 2011). These are excellent developments, and I highly encourage educators to incorporate these practices into their math teaching. One trend I notice, however, is we're still not doing enough estimating, even though there's quite a large body of research showing that "the ability to estimate is associated with the acquisition of number sense" (Montague and van Garderen 2003, 437).

To clarify, when I use the word *estimate*, I mean a much bigger set of ideas than rounding. When I was a kid, "Estimating" was a unit in my textbook. All year, we'd calculate problems exactly, using the prescribed methods. During the "Estimating" unit, we rounded numbers following the 1–4 or 5–9 rule, computed with those rounded numbers, and called the answer an estimate (Schoen, Blume, and Hart 1987). When the unit was over, we returned to calculating exactly. That's not the idea I'm promoting here!

Estimation is a vital component of quantitative reasoning, problem solving, mathematical modeling, and sense making, as well as a life skill. We estimate magnitudes, quantities, measurements, and calculations. Students need a variety of estimation strategies they can use in different situations, depending on their reason for estimating, how good of an estimate they need, or how good of an estimate they can get. Estimating is a complex, conceptual skill: "There appears to be an inextricable link between estimation in a number domain and understanding mathematical concepts in that domain" (Schoen, Blume, and Hart 1987, 2). Nevertheless, "textbooks do not present estimation as a higher order skill: instead, an algorithm for 'rounding-then-computing' and estimation as a 'close guess' are briefly taught and then rarely revisited" (Seethaler and Fuchs 2006, 240). Rounding rules are "taught and learned as essentially a rote skill with no connection to understanding of any sort" (Schoen, Blume, and Hart 1987, 4).

For the past several years, researchers have been studying the relationship between our approximate number system, which is how we size up quantities without counting or symbols, and whether students succeed in math class. While there is still more to learn, this research has yielded powerful results that relate to our classrooms:

- Differences in approximate number system acuity correlate with a wide variety of math achievement measures. The better the student's number sense—and it's been measured in very young children—the better students do in math class all the way through school, right through their college-entrance exams (Chen and Li 2014; Halberda, Mazzocco, and Feigenson 2008; Libertus, Feigenson, and Halberda 2011, 2013; Libertus, Odic, and Halberda 2012; Mazzocco, Feigenson, and Halberda 2011).
- The approximate number system is trainable and developing it correlates with improvements in computation as well. For example, over the course of several sessions, adults improved their visual approximations with practice. Even though the trainings were only focused on visual approximations, study participants also made significant improvements in their numeric computation (Park and Brannon 2013).
- Practice with approximate number tasks (e.g., adding or comparing large numbers of dots) improved both the speed with which children solved easier paper-and-pencil arithmetic problems, and the accuracy with which they solved harder arithmetic problems. This well-designed, rigorous study demonstrated there is a direct, causal relationship between developing our approximate number system and success with exact computation (Hyde, Khanum, and Spelke 2014).

In short, developing students' number sense and visual estimation helps them (1) improve their estimation skills and (2) improve their computation. Win-win!

Unfortunately, research has also shown that we are doing a poor job of teaching any type of estimation. For example, in one study, 78 percent of third-grade students scored 37 percent or less on a computational estimation assessment, and the highest-performing students barely topped 50 percent (Seethaler and Fuchs 2006, 240). In another study, the researchers assessed fourth-, sixth-, and eighth-grade students' visual estimation and reasoning with discrete quantities and measurements. Example questions:

- About how many M&Ms would it take to make a line that is 1-inch long? (Students were shown an M&M.)
- About how many days have you been alive?
- About how tall is the average two-story house? (Multiple choice: 10 feet, 30 feet, 90 feet, 270 feet)

Students' estimates were considered correct if they answered within a wildly generous 50 percent of the exact answer; yet, *almost all students failed* (Montague and van Garderen 2003, 443).

Throughout the classroom examples I've shared in this book, you've seen a lot of high-quality instruction of computational estimation strategies, especially from Jennifer Clerkin Muhammad. Jen teaches students to think about reasonableness for every problem, and her kids develop estimation as a powerful habit of mind. She teaches students to have active internal and external dialogues with the mathematics and with one another, so they are always engaged and thinking about whether their work makes sense. Rather than add a new classroom example of computational estimation here, I highly recommend you reread "Estimation to the Rescue!" from Chapter 5, "Mathematicians Are Precise," in which she taught the sentence frame, "I think _____ is unreasonable because _____," and consider how you could use this teaching strategy to build students' numeracy and mathematical intuition. It's such a rich example that it's worth reading more than once.

I want to use this space to share instructional strategies for teaching visual estimation because it's so important, and we haven't discussed it yet. The best resource I know to give students a range of valuable estimation experiences that build number sense, intuition, and a sense of reasonableness is *Estimation 180*.

Andrew Stadel's Estimation 180 (estimation180.com)

"Building number sense one day at a time"

Andrew Stadel is a middle school math teacher in California who blogs at mr-stadel.blogspot. com. Andrew has assembled a wonderful collection of visual estimation challenges to last all year, www.estimation180.com, which he has made free and public. By all means, go click around the site for a few minutes and get a sense of the images and short videos Andrew has posted! Some of my favorite aspects:

- Andrew has chosen a thoughtful mix of quantities, measurements, and units. Over time, students estimate height, capacity, time, distance, amount, weight, proportions, values, and area. They also regularly compute with whole numbers, fractions, and decimals, and there are plenty of opportunities to think about ratios and percents if your students are ready for them. Whatever content standards you teach, *Estimation 180* is chock-full of them.

- There is an element of fun in the collection. Students estimate how much bacon shrinks when it's cooked, how many sheets are left on a roll of toilet paper, and the length of songs like "We Will Rock You!"

- The challenges are inherently engaging and motivating. Every time I've seen or taught an *Estimation 180* lesson, students are animated and deeply invested in the challenge. After students have had time to wrestle with the problem, when teachers are about to reveal the count or measurement, the dramatic tension is palpable! Once it's revealed, there are gasps, groans, and cheers as students assess their estimates. Moments later, there's a buzz of great thinking like, "Wait, how could that be?" and "Oh, I think I was too low because . . ."

- Andrew created short sets of interrelated challenges, which provide outstanding opportunities for students to make connections from one problem to another. For example, the Day 1 challenge is to estimate Andrew's height. In a later challenge, shown in Figure 9.9, Andrew is standing next to his son. In Figure 9.10, Andrew's son is standing next to Andrew's daughter. In sets like these, students apply what they've learned one day to new situations the next day, so they have to make connections.

Figure 9.9 *Andrew is 6'4". What is Andrew's son's height?*

Students often have to draw from several content areas to estimate. For example, when students estimate the length of Santana's "Oye Como Va," they have a picture of the elapsed time status bar, stopped 1:26 into the song. Students need to use proportional reasoning to estimate how long the entire song is as well as measurement skills and unit conversions when dealing with seconds and minutes.

Estimation 180 gives us a valuable chance to introduce issues inherent in mathematical modeling, which is a huge component of secondary mathematics. For example, students estimate how many people can fit in a hospital elevator. To answer, students will need to think about variation and sources of error. How big are the people? What about stretchers or wheelchairs (a likely situation in a hospital elevator)? Is the limit of the elevator's capacity really the number of people or the weight? What's the

Figure 9.10 *What is Andrew's daughter's height?*

relationship between the two, and how would an engineer use them to set the limit?

For each challenge, students are asked to give an estimate they know is too low and another that is too high. These bounding estimates are so important. We're working toward the idea of a reasonable range of estimates, which is one of the most common ways we estimate in daily lives. (Think about how often we say something will take fifteen to twenty minutes, cost $5 or $6, or is around 8–10 blocks/miles away.) If students give silly lows and highs such as 1 or 1,000,000, you can encourage them to choose the lowest and highest values they think are just on the edge of *reasonable*. Over time, they'll be able to give a narrow interval of possible answers. Also, students who are worried about estimating "right" often feel much less nervous when asked for an answer they know is wrong because it's too low or too high. The bounding estimates are a great way to help tentative and struggling students enter a meaningful math discussion.

Estimation Strategies

Estimation 180 is an open-ended resource that can be used in many different ways, in different grade levels. Whether you use it daily or choose specific lessons to complement your curriculum, the most important thing you can do is focus on students' *reasoning* and *arguments*. Students need to learn that estimating involves strategy and is not the same as guessing. Class discussions around strategies, including reflecting on our estimates and refining our strategies, are powerful opportunities for students to build number sense and mathematical intuition in a variety of contexts.

In these discussions, we can analyze the most common estimation strategies, described next. I've found different people use different names to describe them, so I'll include all the names I've heard. At least within your school, it would be great to agree on a term for each strategy.

To give you a sense of responses you might expect from students, I'm including examples of students' explanations from Kristin Gray, who has generously shared her students' *Estimation 180* work with me. Kristin teaches fifth grade in Lewes, Delaware, and writes a terrific blog at mathmindsblog.wordpress.com.

Guessing

At first, many of your students will guess without support or reasons:

- "I've never weighed a turkey before so I just guessed."
- "I think it's logical to me that there would be 1,000 because 100 would be too little and 1 million would be too much."
- "I said 138 because that seems like that would be great."

I wouldn't call guessing a strategy, but it is a starting place. As you continue with *Estimation 180*, students will develop more sophisticated approaches and arguments.

Context Clues/Prior Experience

Intuition is the trace left by our experiences, remember? *Estimation 180* is a great place for students to bring their common sense and experience into math class. Most of our students have listened to music, eaten chocolate, filled containers, seen partially eaten pies, and looked at how many pages are in books. If some of the pictures are culturally unfamiliar, you can encourage students to relate the image to a corollary they understand. It's important for students to see mathematics as part of their lives, and their lives as part of mathematics. Their experience and common sense are valuable in the math classroom:

- "It looks like a cough drop bag, which I have quite a bit of experience for."
- "In the toilet paper commercials they usually compare their brand [with another] brand for how many sheets they have and that's 200 sheets."
- "I have a box of tissues like that and it says ten."

Referents/Benchmarks/Standard Comparisons/Scale

In our daily lives, we all use informal yardsticks. For example, I know a staple is about a centimeter wide; the distance from the tip of my thumb to the tip of my outstretched pinky is about 8 inches, a box of butter weighs 1 pound, a bottle of wine is 750 milliliters, and so on. When I estimate, I regularly use these referents. Part of our estimation work is to encourage students to develop their own set of referents and use them in their estimates.

Joe Schwartz, a math specialist in East Brunswick, New Jersey, has found *Estimation 180* to be a terrific context for developing these referents. For example, during the series of challenges in which students estimate the distance (in miles) between cities, Joe and his colleague, fourth-grade teacher Jeff Bressler, realized their students didn't have a good feel for how long one mile was. Joe and Jeff put the big miles on temporary hold and asked students, "How many times do you think you'd have to walk around our school to walk a mile?" Students used an aerial photograph to estimate and then calculate the number of laps they'd need to take. Joe and Jeff recognized that they had a great opportunity to give students a feel for elapsed time, rate, and distance, so they asked them to time themselves walking the mile. By the end of the mini-unit, students had gained several referents: they knew they could walk a mile in about twenty minutes; they could relate a mile to the distance around a building they knew intimately; and they had the physical memory of walking the mile in their legs. Treat yourself and read about the complete investigation at Joe's blog: exit10a.blogspot. com/2014/04/our-first-real-3-act.html.

Joe regularly uses this strategy of helping students develop personal referents. For example, he taped four boxes of soap together so students could feel the weight of one pound. Similarly, Jen Clerkin Muhammad has a bin of empty jugs and containers: a pint, a quart, a gallon, one liter, two liters, etc. They're available for students so they can visualize sixteen ounces or one-third of a two-liter bottle, or compare different volumes to see which units are bigger. This firsthand experience with both standard and informal units of measure helps students develop intuition about their magnitudes and a sense of what's reasonable.

Using *Estimation 180* regularly helps students gain familiarity with a wide variety of units and can spark great conversations about them. Also, Andrew usually includes something in the picture for scale—a pencil, an adult, a measuring cup, a doorway—that students can use as benchmarks. In the sets of related problems, one day's estimate becomes the next day's referent, which encourages students to compare items to one another. You can hear Kristin's students making these sorts of connections:

- "The soda can is 12.5 (ounces), and it is double and a little more. I then think it is 27."
- "I think that 3 sheets of toilet paper is 1 foot so I divided 425 by 3, and I got 141, but I rounded it up to 150 (feet)."
- "The lamppost looks a little taller than three times Mr. Stadel's height."
- "We did almonds and they are bigger than cheese balls and they look like the same size jar. The almonds were about 1,120 almonds, so I guess one jar is about 2,000 (cheese balls)."

These students are using what they know to estimate something they don't know. That's a powerful problem-solving approach, across the board.

Sampling/Disaggregating/Layering/Chunking/Grouping/Scaling/ Decomposition-Recomposition

In this strategy, students count or estimate a piece of the overall picture and then use multiplication to scale their estimate up. This is a sophisticated statistical strategy used by adults both in their work and in their daily lives. For example, if you were going to estimate the global population of oak trees, the percentage of teenagers who started smoking this year, the number of nails you'd need to build a 2,000-square-foot house, or how many string beans you should buy to serve twelve people at Thanksgiving, you're almost certainly going to count or measure out a subset and multiply in some form or another.

To estimate those beans, you might use weight. You might read online that you should figure a quarter pound of green beans per person, and then multiply to find that you need to buy three pounds. Or, you might use volume. You could use a standard unit, and decide each person should have three-fourths of a cup of beans, so you need to buy nine cups total. Or, you could use an informal unit to estimate. I'm sure I'm not the only one who can be found standing in the produce aisle, staring at a handful of green beans. I'm imagining the plate and visualizing a reasonable serving. Once I've settled on the approximate volume of one portion, I toss twelve of those handfuls, plus a few extra, in my bag.

These string-bean methods are a few of the possible variations on this idea of using a sample size. What all the variations have in common is they are useful for *estimating a total population without counting every individual member*. The particulars of the strategy in a given situation depend on how good of a final estimate we need—or can realistically get—and how the individuals are presented. Are they distributed in regular layers, slices, or arrays like cases of beer, cartons of eggs, or windows on a skyscraper? Are they liquids or items piled in a disorganized heap like almonds in a bowl, where scoops, ounces, or cups might be better? Are they scattered irregularly, like seashells on a beach, so we need to superimpose some kind of organization? There is a lot of flexible thinking to be done with this strategy, so we need to give students many opportunities to use it, examine their results, and refine their techniques.

Fundamentally, sampling helps students think about groups, arrays, volume, and scale and get comfortable with the structure of multiplication. As an added bonus, you'll find the need for mathematical vocabulary such as *row, column, group, slice, layer, base, length, width, height, weight, volume*, and *array*. These terms may emerge naturally in discussions about sampling strategies, because students need them to communicate their thinking to one another:

- "I think that there are 100 sheets of paper in one notebook and there are 12 notebooks so I guessed 1,200."
- "24 strips. 210 staples in each strip. 24 × 200 = 4,800. 10 × 24 = 240. 5,040."
- "I counted in my head an imaginary line of scoops."
- "I think 700 because I think 200 fills one row, and I counted up to 600 and there was sort of like a half row so I got to 700."
- "I think that 5 cups will fill the bottom and it's 2 cups high, so I guessed 10."
- "One row is 4 and there is 10 rows it looks like so 4 × 10 = 40."

Now that we have a sense of the estimation strategies we can expect to see, I want to give you one more idea about using *Estimation 180* in your classroom.

Joe Schwartz, East Brunswick, New Jersey

Estimation 180 *on the Number Line*

Joe, as noted above, is an experienced math specialist and has done quite a bit of experimenting with *Estimation 180* from grades two through five. One innovation he and his Chittick Elementary School colleagues made was to have students record and refine their estimates on an open number line. Joe has shared students' work both on his excellent blog, exit10a. blogspot.com, and with me directly, and I would shout his use of the open number line from the rooftops if I could. It's brilliant.

In recent years, there has been an increased focus on representing numbers, especially fractions, on the number line because it is a powerful mathematical tool that helps us solve problems, model strategies, and represent our thinking. In my observations of different curricula, however, I have noticed that publishers often provide premade number lines for students, which scaffolds the power and thinking right out of the tool.

Joe and his colleagues decided their students should create their own number lines to use with *Estimation 180*. Students choose where the number line starts and stops, what the scale should be, and how to show the range of reasonable numbers. For each challenge, students place their too high, too low, and just right estimates on an open number line. When the teacher reveals Andrew Stadel's measurement, students record that as well.

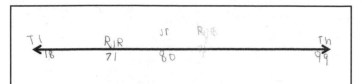

Figure 9.11 *What do you notice about the student's number placement here?*

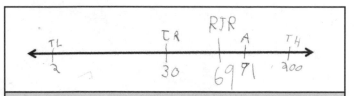

Figure 9.12 *What do you notice about the size of the intervals on this number line?*

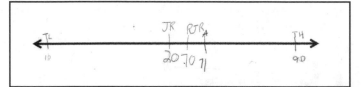

Figure 9.13 *What do you notice about where this student put her numbers?*

These student-created number lines turned out to be fantastic formative assessments: Joe and his colleagues could literally "see" students' mental number lines, which informed their instruction. For example, teachers noticed that students usually sequence the numbers correctly, which is great, but they often place their "just right" (JR) estimates right in the middle between their "too low" (TL) and "too high" (TH) estimates, regardless of the numbers, as you can see in work samples from Kristin Loux and Maggie Anderson's second-grade students.

In Figure 9.11, you can see a student placing 80 halfway between 18 and 99. As students added more numbers to their number lines—either "revised just right" (RJR) estimates or the "actual" (A) measurement as measured by Andrew—teachers could see that many students had no real sense of how big the intervals between numbers should be, as shown in Figures 9.12 and 9.13.

Joe described the conversation among the teachers about this finding:

We really noticed the problem with the intervals. Let's say a student's too low was 5, their too high was 100, and their just right was 10. The 10 would always go right in between their too low and their too high, regardless of where it actually fit. And so we—meaning the teachers and myself—sat down and thought, What was appropriate to expect from elementary school students about that kind of number sense? Was it realistic to expect them to be able to place it correctly? Or should we just be happy that they know that 10 is in between 5 and 100 and leave it at that?

We decided that we could start to get a little bit pickier about how they were putting the intervals on their number line. We began teaching students to find a midpoint between their too high and their too low, and then use that as a basis for judging where their just right should go. As the year progressed and we were a little bit pickier about having those number lines be correct, we did see an improvement in where they were placing their estimates.

During *Estimation 180* work with younger students, Joe discovered that using a body-scale number line helped students think about the placement of numbers on the number line:

I made an estimation challenge with strawberries: How many strawberries were in a container? I modeled it with the class first. Our too low was 2, our too high was 50, and the just right was 15. They wanted to put the 15 right in the middle. The teacher had a big class number line, so I had one kid stand at 2, one kid stand at 50, and one kid stand at 15. They could see that the kid who was standing at 15 was standing pretty much right next to the kid at 2 and pretty far away from the kid who was at 50. So they were like, "Oh, 15's not right in between 2 and 50!"

None of this great work would have happened if students worked on premarked number lines!

Joe's approach has a second major benefit: he gives students explicit opportunities to revise their mathematical thinking in an authentic way. When we estimate, we often start with a ballpark range, do a little bit of figuring, and then recalibrate. If we are way off, we might abandon the first estimate and start over in a new range. If our first estimate was reasonable, we fine-tune it as we work, zooming in on tighter and tighter intervals. To teach this process, Joe pauses periodically and asks students to revise their estimates:

The students have a too low, a too high, and a just right. We start to play the video, and then we stop it. Students reevaluate and can put another guess down somewhere. We keep playing it and stop it again. By the time we get to the end, students have five or six numbers placed along this number line. We really like that. We like the idea that the kids have to figure out where to place the numbers, especially when they see the reveal at the end. Where does this new number go in terms of the number line that I've constructed?

For example, Joe created his own *Estimation 180*–style challenge where he asked second-grade students how many cherry tomatoes were in the box shown in Figure 9.14.

Students created their number lines and placed their bounding and just right estimates, along with explanations. In each class, Joe played the video of him counting the tomatoes and paused when he'd counted about fifty tomatoes. He gave students time to evaluate and revise

Figure 9.14 *How many cherry tomatoes do you think are in this container?*

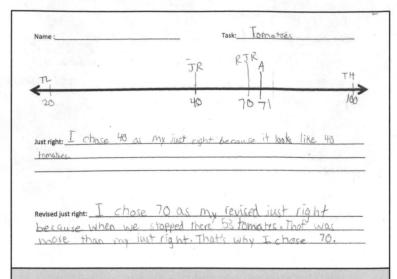

Figure 9.15 *This student explained how he reconsidered his estimate when Joe stopped at 53 tomatoes.*

their estimates based on what they'd seen, and add revised just right estimates to their number lines (Figures 9.15 and 9.16). Joe is careful to use the word *revise*, not *correct*. There is a big difference. Their original estimates are not wrong, and he has students keep them on the number lines to show their thought process—no crossing out or erasing!

This iterative process of revising estimates is a great way to teach students to scrutinize, to reflect on, and to refine their estimation strategies. With practice, students become quite skilled at identifying reasonable boundaries for estimates, exploring different sections of the number line, understanding magnitude, and thinking flexibly about numbers.

To see more examples of Joe's work with *Estimation 180*, take a look at his wonderful blog. I've gathered several posts at stenhouse.com/becomingmathteacher. Throughout, you'll see Joe's goal is to help students connect their thinking in *Estimation 180* with the rest of mathematics, and intuition is the tie that binds:

> *Ultimately, what we really want them to do is to take this habit of mind and transfer it into their problem solving. Ultimately, it doesn't really matter how many strawberries are in the box. It's the procedure of how you move through the thought process. And when you come up with your answer, does it fit with what your intuition was? That's a thread that runs through a lot of what I do: getting you to use your intuition.*

Developing Intuition in Students Who Need It Most

I was chatting with a middle school special education teacher about intuition and proof. Our conversation went something like this:

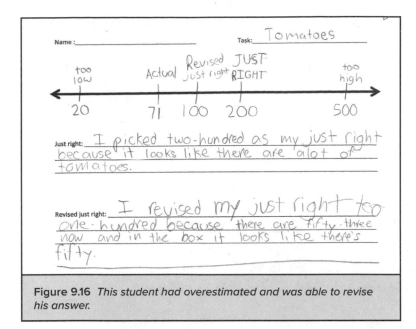

Figure 9.16 *This student had overestimated and was able to revise his answer.*

Tracy: Every time we prove something, our intuition gets a little wiser, because we've had the chance to make sense of the math ourselves—to be sure it's true—so we really *believe* and *understand* what we're doing. The cool thing is we get to take that experience with us into the next problem.

Teacher: That makes perfect sense. And that's why my students have so little intuition. They've never been allowed to prove anything to themselves: they've just been told.

I was dually certified in both general and special education, and my experience matches hers. Rules, procedures, algorithms, vocabulary words, and methods are delivered to students with disabilities, and they are expected to use them whether or not they believe them or intuitively understand them. The rationale I usually hear for this teaching emphasis is time. The thinking goes: These students are already behind, and they need extra repetitions to learn something new. We've got to get them procedurally fluent at least, so we need to spend extra time practicing computation, basic facts, and vocabulary until they know them automatically and can be proficient with those skills.

Skills certainly matter, and I believe in distributed computation practice. But if we follow this logic to its natural conclusion, we end up with what we often have: students who can carry out procedures accurately but only if we tell them what operation to use and supply them with graphic organizers, cues, hints, and tricks. We also have students who don't think about whether their answers are reasonable, don't see math in the world around them, don't connect one problem or concept to another, and don't transfer the skills they have to new contexts. Oh, and they don't like math either.

Time *is* tight, but it's really worth it to step back and think about alternatives to this instructional approach. It's true some special education students need more repetition, so what if we gave them *extra opportunities to make sense*?

Mathematics educators have long argued that students with a deep understanding of a mathematical topic are much more likely to retain and apply mathematical ideas flexibly. Most students need many opportunities to deeply understand a topic. For MD students [students with mathematics learning difficulties], who often exhibit difficulties retaining and applying their mathematical ideas flexibly, furnishing more conceptual experiences than usual is even more crucial. These conceptual experiences are the very ones that let children develop number sense and flexibility, and instruction should focus on those goals. Therefore, an important step in proficiency in number and operations is to organize the curriculum to give children many more opportunities to make sense of these mathematical ideas—not just to practice skills but to conceptually understand. (Rathmell and Gabriele 2011, 115)

Andrew Gael is a special education math teacher at the Cooke Center for Learning and Development, a nonprofit, private provider of special education services in New York City. Andrew blogs at thelearningkaleidoscope.wordpress.com and has generously spent quite a bit of time sharing his experiences and thinking with me. I find the way he thinks about sense making in special education extremely helpful. For example, he told me:

> *A lot of professionals are very good at scaffolding and creating the step-by-step processes that lead to success for special education students. Something that I've been advocating for is that* we don't scaffold out the mathematical thinking that goes into solving a math problem.

"I refuse to scaffold out the sense making" is a mantra for Andrew, and it's a worthy one! The question then becomes, What should we scaffold? Special education students need modifications, accommodations, scaffolds, and supports, so what should they be?

> *The main modification that we're able to provide is time. One of the main things that our students need is the time to sit with the problem and make sense of it.*

This might be the simplest—and most difficult, in our current educational climate—adjustment we can make. As we advocate for our students, we need to argue for the time they need to learn.

Andrew also supports his students by teaching in a highly focused way:

> *One of my units is about equivalence. Wherever the kids are in their computation levels, we can study what's on either side of the equals sign. Whether they're using variables or not, they can use algebraic thinking . . . So, in one of my lessons, I gave them all calculators because computation wasn't the point of the lesson. That's an*

essential thing in special education that people don't focus on: finding out the key to your lesson and then ignoring everything else. If the key to my lesson was equivalence, I don't need them to spend all period multiplying!

In special education classes, you need to pinpoint the purpose of your day and then ignore everything else. I think people get too bogged down in math classes, specifically, because they think they need to use every opportunity for practice. They think, "If multiplying is part of the day, we might as well spend the time multiplying." But, no! Forget that. I'll give them a calculator and we'll spend some time enjoying math and having fun with it and figure things out.

I love this thinking! I often see educators break components of complex problems down for students and then expect students to compute each part fully. By the time students finish the problem, they have forgotten what the question was, and they certainly don't care. Meanwhile, the students still didn't complete the whole problem because the educator was the one who made sense of it. At least some of the time, could we switch that around? How about having the students make sense of the problem and tell the educators what to calculate? Or, as Andrew suggests, how about having the student make sense and then use a calculator for the computation? In this way, students get to try their ideas out and check them—to go through cycles of making sense and verifying—and own the thinking. As Andrew said, "Math is only enjoyable if you're in charge of it—if you're making sense of it."

Andrew draws from several rich curricula with his students, choosing problems from the Math Forum; *Estimation 180*; *Investigations in Number, Data, and Space*; Fosnot and Dolk's Young Mathematicians at Work series, Math in the City, Cognitively Guided Instruction, and high-quality tasks from the Math-Twitter-Blog-o-Sphere (#MTBoS). To make this work accessible for his students, he chooses from a variety of accommodations and modifications, depending on the level of need. He might use simple graphic organizers that help students *Notice and Wonder* (described in Chapter 7, "Mathematicians Ask Questions"). He often has students draw visual representations of the problem scenario before starting to solve. He might remove extraneous information or make the language more accessible. But he refuses to scaffold out the mathematical thinking.

Way back when, during my special education master's program, University of Washington professor Ilene Schwartz talked about this word, *scaffold*, and I've never forgotten it. She had us imagine a building under construction with scaffolding all over it. She said something like, "The whole idea is, at some point, *you take the scaffolding down, and there should be a building there that can stand on its own.*" If what we're doing with students is to tell them to do this, and then do this, and then do that, is that really scaffolding? Are we doing something temporary that builds something structurally sound? Can we eventually take down that prompting?

If we're the ones always saying, "Wait a minute, does that answer make sense?" and directing students to go back and check because they're oblivious to reasonableness, we've probably built permanent scaffolding. We need to be able to remove that cue. If we focus our math teaching so all our students develop, refine, and trust their mathematical intuition, we'll hear *them* saying:

- "Oh, I think I know what might happen here . . ."
- "I'm thinking this is going to be . . ."
- "Wait. I'm lost. I have to back up and think it through again."
- "Yeah, that sounds about right."
- "Huh. That's not what I expected. Either my estimate was off or my solution was. Or both."
- "That sounds reasonable because . . ."
- "That makes sense to me."

That's when we know our instruction is working.

10

MATHEMATICIANS REASON

*I*n Chapter 9, we explored ways to teach students to develop their intuitions—to listen to their inner voices and gut instincts, follow their noses, and gain a feel for mathematics. In this chapter and the next, we'll flip the coin over and look at the powerhouses on the other side: mathematical reasoning and proof.

Successful mathematicians both *trust* and *doubt* their intuitions. Knowing when to trust and when to doubt is part of the art of mathematics, which we need to teach students from the outset. The main reason to doubt our own intuition is that sometimes it's way off! We'll be certain a hunch is true—we'll *feel* its rightness in our bones with certainty—and we'll be wrong because we missed something. That's why we need to train ourselves to be skeptical, to question our assumptions, and to subject our instincts to cross-examination. As Stewart said, "Mathematicians need proofs to keep them honest. All technical areas of human activity need reality checks" (2006, 79).

Sometimes our intuition is wrong because of a misconception in our thinking or a gap in our content knowledge: we have a conflict between what we've thought was true in the past and what we're seeing now. This cognitive dissonance can be a powerful motivator if we handle it right. Students who are perplexed can be amenable to learning something new that will resolve their clashing ideas, adding wisdom to their intuition and knowledge to their analytical reasoning.

Other times our intuition is wrong because, while most mathematics makes great sense, some concepts are nonintuitive or counterintuitive. Think about negative numbers. For most of us, they feel all wrong; they're unlikely, surprising, even a little disturbing. Historically, we've told students to ignore that uneasy feeling and just follow rules around concepts they can't intuit, arguing the rules are true because authority figures say they are true. They're in the book! This approach has turned many students away from math, including my mother, who told me, "They lost me at negative numbers. I think they just made them up." She dropped her voice to a hush, leaned close, and said, "I still don't believe they're real."

My mother remains in a place of doubt because she has never *proved* negative numbers exist in any kind of satisfying way. The persistence of her doubt shows how powerful intuition is! Teachers have been arrogant to think we can just override that internal voice, that unsettled feeling, that desire for math to make sense. Rather than teach students to suppress and ignore that feeling of unease, we need to teach students to honor it. Nobody should accept the validity of any mathematical statement that rubs up against intuition without compelling proof. My mother is thinking like a mathematician when she remains unconvinced in the absence of really good reasons, and I told her so.

Elementary and middle school math teachers are there when students first experience conflict between what they intuit mathematically and what their analytical thinking demands. Lockhart framed this conflict as the driving need for proof: "Rigorous formal proof only becomes important when there is a crisis—when you discover that your imaginary objects behave in a counterintuitive way; when there is a paradox of some kind" (2009, 72). When we view elementary and middle school content through this lens, we see several concepts that cause crises for students. My professional learning community on Twitter brainstormed these counterintuitive concepts:

- **Zero.** How can a number be neither negative nor positive? How can zero be a number? What *really* happens when you try to divide by zero? Why?
- **Equality and Equivalence.** What do you mean 7 + 5 *is the same as* 8 + 4?
- **Negative numbers.** Do they exist or are they imaginary? What about operations with negative numbers? What exactly *is* a negative times a negative, and why does it equal something positive?
- **Fractions and Decimals.** How can anything be *between* the counting numbers? Fractions look like they're made up of other numbers, but they are numbers themselves, so which is it? What is going on when we multiply by fractions and decimals and products get smaller? What does dividing by a fraction even mean? How come more digits in a decimal don't necessarily mean the number is bigger? Why is 2.9 > 2.10? Why

is ¾ the same as 0.75? What happened to the 3 and the 4?

- **Exponents, powers, and roots**. Especially when they're fractional or negative. And what about raising a number to the zeroth power?
- **Irrational numbers**. What do you mean they never end? *Ever?*
- **Infinity and Rational Numbers**. How can there be an infinite number of numbers between 1 and 2, or between 0.1 and 0.2? I thought infinity was big?
- **Area, perimeter, surface area, and volume**. It feels like there should be clear relationships among them, but they act in all kinds of surprising ways.
- **Probability**. If a family has 7 girls in a row, how can their odds of having a boy next still be 50/50?
- **Properties of operations**. How come $9 + 7 = 7 + 9$, but $9 - 7 \neq 7 - 9$? How come $120 \times 12 = (120 \times 10) + (120 \times 2)$, but $120 \div 12 \neq (120 \div 10) + (120 \div 2)$?

These counterintuitive concepts are natural motivators for rich, wonderful mathematical investigations. By digging into them enough to resolve doubt, students will see that mathematics makes sense, even when it's initially surprising.

One of the ways we've historically destroyed students' natural mathematical reasoning is by asking them to take these rich, counterintuitive concepts on faith or authority in elementary and middle school but spend geometry class "proving" math that's obvious, established, or trivial (Lockhart 2009). No student is going to fall in love with mathematics by writing a two-column, alphabet-soup proof of something they don't care about and can see is true before they start. Who wants to go through the motions of a proof that's already written in the textbook, old hat to the teacher, and all over the Internet?

Instead, students should be proving when they feel genuine doubt and skepticism. By listening to that powerful, intuitive voice, they'll know when there is a mystery that needs to be solved. When they've learned how to use mathematical reasoning to prove what's true, they will be able to understand and accept concepts with wiser, honed intuition. Our goal is to teach students how to use proof, reasoning, and intuition to make deep sense of mathematical concepts—to have logical proof and intuitive acceptance "blend in an unique synthetical form of mathematical understanding" (Fischbein 1982, 15). In other words, to have the heavens align and leave us completely satisfied—heart, gut, and mind.

Laying the Groundwork for Proof: Mathematical Reasoning

There are many thinking skills mathematicians need *before* learning how to prove mathematical claims. In elementary and middle school, in particular, we need to focus on this kind of prerequisite thinking, or *mathematical reasoning*: "Mathematical reasoning is an evolving process of conjecturing, generalizing, investigating *why,* and developing and evaluating arguments" (Lannin, Ellis, and Elliott 2011, 12). Mathematical reasoning is how we take an idea from, "Huh, I noticed something," through play and testing, to nailing down a specific claim, and into a focused effort to justify, revise, or refute. All of that work precedes proof.

The process of mathematical reasoning and proving holds some similarity to the process of writing. We can describe an idealized writing process—plan, draft, revise, edit, publish—that writers use to move from idea to finished product. Yet, while there is a general progression from beginning to end, the writing process is not linear. It's sometimes circular, recursive, disjointed, or simultaneous. Writers spend a great deal of time flowing—or lurching, or stumbling—back and forth among planning, drafting, revising, and editing until we are satisfied. Only then, and only sometimes, do writers begin to erase the tracks of that work and create a polished product: published writing.

The math analogue—idealized mathematical reasoning—also has steps. But, like writing, the process of making mathematics is not linear. It's sometimes circular, recursive, disjointed, or simultaneous, and mathematicians flow (and lurch and stumble) among the parts until they are satisfied. Only then, do they begin erasing the tracks of their work and create a polished product: a published proof.

During the course of their educations, students need to learn all the parts of these processes well. They are foundational skills. But just like we don't publish every piece of student writing, we won't ask students to prove every piece of mathematical work. Just like marching students through the steps of the writing process every week is a sure way to teach students to hate, misunderstand, and resent writing, marching students through the steps of mathematical reasoning each unit would make students hate, misunderstand, and resent math. Just like we sometimes focus on one element of writing to teach it (e.g., voice or sentence fluency), we will sometimes focus on one element of mathematical reasoning in order to teach it (e.g., sniffing out patterns or looking for counterexamples). And just like we should use the many years of schooling to build competent, flexible, thoughtful writers, we should use the many years of schooling to build competent, flexible, thoughtful mathematical thinkers. Therefore, while I will share classroom strategies and ideas for the various components of mathematical reasoning in a general progression, I hope you'll resist the urge to turn them into a project or checklist.

I also hope you won't feel overwhelmed or worried about teaching all this new content, because it's mostly not extra content. Mathematical reasoning is the stuff of the National Council of Teachers of Mathematics' Process Standards and the Common Core Standards for Mathematical Practice. These are the thinking skills and habits of mind you and your students can use while engaging in deep study of any mathematical content. They are, in fact, outstanding ways to teach the content you're already planning to teach. I hope you'll tinker with an element here and try out a strategy there, making it work for you and your kids, in your context.

Elements of Mathematical Reasoning

We are teaching in an exciting time: there is quite a bit of new thinking about how even the very youngest students can engage in mathematical reasoning and, eventually, proving. Four excellent books have been published about mathematical reasoning, and each has deepened my thinking and teaching considerably. I highly recommend:

- *Thinking Mathematically: Integrating Arithmetic & Algebra in Elementary School*, by Thomas P. Carpenter, Megan Loef Franke, and Linda Levi (2003)
- *Connecting Arithmetic to Algebra: Strategies for Building Algebraic Thinking in the Elementary Grades*, by Susan Jo Russell, Deborah Schifter, and Virginia Bastable (2011)
- *Developing Essential Understanding of Mathematical Reasoning, Pre-K–Grade 8*, by John Lannin, Amy B. Ellis, and Rebekah Elliott (2011)
- *Thinking Mathematically*, by John Mason, Leone Burton, and Kaye Stacey (2010)

I can't possibly go into the same depth in two chapters as these authors have done in their books, but I hope I can provide a useful synthesis of their arguments and add to the conversation with new examples, teaching strategies, and connections. In that spirit, I've drawn heavily from these four works to describe key elements of mathematical reasoning: *noticing patterns, conjecturing and generalizing, crafting claims,* and *exploring why*. I've also added a hypothetical classroom scenario to help ground these ideas. Once we have shared language for the different types of mathematical thinking we want students to learn, we'll get right to high-yield strategies for teaching them.

Noticing Patterns

Mathematics is often described as the science or study of patterns. The first step in mathematical reasoning is to sniff out interesting patterns in numbers, shapes, operations, relationships, and so on. Once we've noticed and identified the patterns, we can play with them, test them out in different conditions, see when they hold and when they break, and figure out what structures they reveal.

Because children are natural mathematical thinkers, they notice, explore, test, and extend patterns all the time as they make sense of their world. For example, my daughter Daphne was six years old when she brought her hairbrush over to me and said, "I found math, Mommy! No matter how you put an elastic on, it has to cross somewhere" (Figure 10.1). She made this beautiful conjecture about topology because she observed and investigated a pattern in ponytail holders. I was overjoyed that she rightfully recognized this type of thinking as mathematics.

As teachers, our work is to create conditions in which students are actively making sense of mathematics and thereby

Figure 10.1 *"I found math! No matter how you put an elastic on, it has to cross."*

noticing patterns. We need to nurture safe learning environments so students will share out and be heard with respect. And we need to work with the patterns ourselves so we can think about which ones are most likely to yield fruitful learning for our students. Which patterns might lead to deep understanding?

> Sheila: (Leaning over to her classmate, Janae.) Wait, what is going on here? Look at this! I started putting these in my calculator, and look what I found!

(She points to her notebook, where she's written the following.)

$$6 \div 6 = 1$$
$$7 \div 7 = 1$$
$$12 \div 12 = 1$$
$$1{,}254 \div 1{,}254 = 1$$

Janae: Whaaaat?

Conjecturing and Generalizing

Once mathematicians notice patterns, they can explore, test, and play with them. A major part of their thinking process is developing hypotheses and testing them to see whether they're true. In mathematics, these hypotheses are called *conjectures*, and we can think of them as working theories or tentative ideas about what is going on. Conjecturing is powerful, playful, and active. It's also brave. "From the standpoint of the person doing mathematics, making a conjecture . . . is taking a risk; it requires the admission that one's assumptions are open to revision, that one's insights may have been limited, that one's conclusions may have been inappropriate" (Lampert 1990, 31). Once again, we see the importance of creating classroom environments where students feel comfortable taking risks, revising their thinking, and changing their minds.

Very often (but not always), conjecturing involves *generalizing*, which involves going beyond a specific example and looking for an underlying relationship that holds universally. When generalizing, mathematicians might look for common ground among different cases, or they might extend reasoning by testing a conjecture in a new scenario (Lannin, Ellis, and Elliot 2011). In either case, mathematicians use specific examples as entry points into larger truths. We move from "Is it true in this case?" to wondering about the general case: "Will that always be true? What's the relationship here? What is going on?"

> Sheila: I think anything over itself is gonna be one. Wait. What if it's a decimal? I'm going to try 2.3.
>
> (Sheila types in 2.3 ÷ 2.3 and finds it equals 1.)
>
> Janae: Whoa! It still works. I wonder if it works for *every* number?
>
> Sheila: Let's keep trying! What about negative numbers? Let's try -12 ÷ -12.

Crafting Claims

As students test their conjectures, they eventually become convinced that their conjectures are valid, valid only in certain cases, or invalid. If a mathematician is sure her conjecture is valid but she hasn't yet proved it, she has made a *claim*. Claims are more specific and certain than conjectures: "Students move from I think/don't think to I know/It is/It has to be" (Lampert 1990, 54).

The process of crafting claims has several parts, and we need to teach them all:

- Students need to learn how to articulate claims so that everybody in their mathematical community is talking about the same thing. Students need to nail down the vague language they used to describe the pattern, replacing *it* and *that* with specific, precise language everybody understands.
- Students need to *specify the conditions* of the claim. When is the claim true? With what sets of numbers or shapes and under what circumstances? What constraints do we need?
- Students need to learn how to *doubt the claim*. One of the most important mental disciplines of mathematics is learning to ask, "How could I prove myself wrong?" or "How could I break it?"
- As students test, extend, and clarify, they'll often need to *revise the claim* in light of their findings. It may fall apart all together; it may need to be restricted to a smaller set of numbers; or the language might need to be changed.

Sheila: (To class.) Janae and I figured out that anything over itself is one.

Marcus: What do you mean anything? What are you talking about?

Sheila: Any number. If you divide it by itself it's one.

Ms. Davis: I heard you say if you divide *it* by *itself*, *it* is one. What are those *its*? I'm confused.

Sheila: OK, OK. Um. When you divide a number by itself, the answer . . . the um, quotient . . . is one. I've tried it with decimals, and it's still true!

(Sheila comes up to the projector and shares the work in her notebook.)

Terri: Ooh, I want to try!

Ms. Davis: Let's write Sheila's claim up here. (She writes, *When you divide a number by itself the quotient is one.*) Is that what you're claiming, Sheila?

Sheila: Mm hmm.

Ms. Davis: OK. Take some time to work together and explore this claim. Do you agree or disagree with this claim, or do you have a revision to suggest?

(Students work in pairs and threes, trying different cases and tinkering with Sheila's claim. Ms. Davis listens in on Martin and Davon as they work.)

Martin: Let's try it with fractions. I wonder if we can disprove it that way.

Davon: Yeah! Wait. How do I write a fraction divided by a fraction? What does that mean?

(At that moment, there was a cry of "Whoa!" from the back of the room.)

Tanya: Try it with zero, everybody! It breaks the calculator!

Explore Why

As students start to feel more convinced about the validity or invalidity of a claim, they will press for reasons. *Why*? How come it's true or false? What is really going on here? Now we have an opportunity to dig into important concepts while we teach students how to justify or refute claims with mathematical arguments. Certainly, a big part of the learning here is what makes for a compelling mathematical argument. What counts as justification in mathematics?

During this work, students build on ideas they already understand and agree on, connecting one idea to another and referring to prior problems and conceptualizations until they are satisfied. They'll need to continue to doubt, critique, and question as they seek connections and generate representations. This is hard stuff, and it takes time, but the payoffs are huge. As you can see in the following excerpt, it's not a smooth, straight path from a well-articulated claim to a convincing mathematical argument. Here's one small snippet of a larger investigation into *why*.

Ms. Davis: Davon, what was your question? What does a fraction divided by a fraction mean?

Davon: Yeah. I'm not sure. But I was thinking that I could write the fractions as decimals and it works that way. Like, ½ ÷ ½ is the same thing as 0.5 ÷ 0.5, and that equals 1.

Kaylee: Yeah, that's how I did it. I switched them to decimals, and all the fractions I tried worked.

Ms. Davis: So are you convinced?

Kaylee: Um, not really. I mean, I see *that* it works, or at least it has so far with everything but zero, but I don't get *why*.

Ms. Davis: Terrific. So you're not satisfied because we don't have complete mathematical arguments yet. What questions are you still thinking about?

Kaylee: I'm thinking about Davon's question. I'm not sure what it *means* to have one-half divided by one-half.

Ms. Davis: Here's a question that might help us. What's a story that goes with the problem one-half divided by one-half? Think for a minute or two, and then let's hear some ideas.

Lawrence: Maybe, if you have half a recipe and then you decide to make half of that?

Janae: But isn't halving a recipe dividing by 2, not by one-half?

Ms. Davis: I am loving this conversation. We're getting into the good stuff now!

Martin: Well, I was thinking that, if you have half a cookie, and you want to make pieces that are half a cookie, you have just enough cookie for one piece. Is that ½ ÷ ½? Or am I wrong?

Ms. Davis: I don't know. Take some time to talk about that with your partner. What do you think about Martin's idea?

As students work, Ms. Davis circulates, listening in on conversations. She notices Diego and Constance having a productive conversation, and asks them, "When we come back together, will you share your thinking with the class?" Diego and Constance agree and take a few minutes to prepare. Ms. Davis pulls everyone together and directs attention to Diego and Constance.

Constance: We were thinking about Martin's question, but with whole numbers because that's easier for us. Diego had the idea to draw some pictures to help us.

Diego projects work similar to Figure 10.2 so everyone can see and begins explaining.

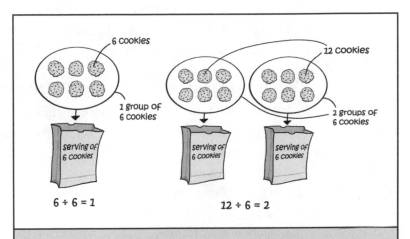

Diego: If you have six cookies and you want to make groups that have six cookies in them, you have just enough for one group. If you had twelve cookies and you want to make groups that have six cookies, you'd have enough for two groups, right? It's the same thing. It just sounds funny when it works out to be one group.

Figure 10.2 *"If you have six cookies and you want to make groups that have six cookies in them, you have just enough for one group."*

Constance: So, if you have eight cookies and you want to make groups that have eight cookies, you have enough for one group. If you have four cookies and you want to make groups that have four cookies, you have enough for one group. Isn't it the same for any number? I'm not gonna draw it, but if you have two million cookies and you want to make groups that have two million cookies, you have enough for exactly one group. Two million divided by two million makes one. We're pretty sure this is why Sheila's claim works.

Monique: I get what you're saying, but I thought about it in a totally different way. I was thinking about multiplication.

Ms. Davis: Tell us more.

Monique: Well, you know how 2 × 3 = 6 and then 6 ÷ 2 = 3? Well, isn't it the same thing? 2,000,000 × 1 = 2,000,000, so 2,000,000 ÷ 2,000,000 = 1. You just turn it around.

Janae: Oh! I get it! Wait . . . No, I don't. But, I did for a second . . .

Ms. Davis: (Laughing and smiling.) We're definitely on the edge of something here. We have Martin's story, we have Diego's and Constance's representation and thinking, and we have Monique's connection to inverse operations. We still have some questions about fractions, and we haven't dealt with what happened with zero yet. Let's keep going until we can put some of these pieces together into an argument.

Teaching Strategies for the Elements of Mathematical Reasoning

Obviously, mathematical reasoning and proof is complex, meaningful, and sophisticated, which is why we need to teach the different elements in many ways over several years. Let's turn our attention to classroom strategies that will help us teach students how to notice patterns, conjecture and generalize, and craft claims. We'll tackle *explore why* in Chapter 11, "Mathematicians Prove." I've grouped the instructional activities and teaching strategies to highlight the dominant elements of mathematical reasoning in each one, but there's plenty of overlap. If a teaching strategy works on a few big ideas at once, so much the better!

Teaching Students to Notice Patterns

I once visited a botanical garden with my mother and fell in love with a particular tree with heart-shaped leaves, a sweet fragrance, and gorgeous fall color called a katsura tree. I was sure I'd never seen it before. When I returned home, though, I saw katsura trees everywhere: in the front yard of a house two blocks away, on the edge of the pond in our city park, on campus at a school I visit. Now that I knew what to look for, I was able to see.

So it is with students noticing patterns in math. Noticing patterns is not one of those skills we need to teach in a heavy-handed way; rather, what we need to do is learn how to recognize, honor, and build on the noticing our students are already doing. When I am in classrooms, I hear students notice patterns with incredible frequency. Usually, they state what they see in a parenthetical way and then return to calculating, as if noticing mathematical patterns is somehow a distraction from the "real" work of computation.

We need to make it clear to students that noticing patterns, wondering about them, and investigating them *is* doing math. A great first step for you is to tune your ears to hear your students' patterns like I trained myself to recognize the katsura tree. You might want to carry a notebook with you and jot down the different patterns you hear. What sorts of classroom routines lead to students noticing patterns in your class? Which of the students' patterns might lead to powerful investigations of the structure of mathematics? Which might be good candidates to pick up and explore?

While students notice patterns during a wide variety of mathematical activities, some instructional routines are particularly effective for generating ripe patterns to explore. Russell, Schifter, and Bastable recommend three different routines: *What Do You Know About _____?*, *Number of the Day*, and *Is the Number Sentence True?* (2011, 16–19). These are excellent suggestions. I'm going to offer two additional instructional routines to add to your list: *Choral Counting* and *Visual Patterns*.

Choral Counting

Over the past several years, I have grown increasingly convinced that we need to count with kids, often, over time, and much later than we currently do. I've been especially influenced by Jessica Shumway's *Number Sense Routines* (2011) and the counting work and ambitious teaching practices coming out of the Learning In, From, and For Teaching Practice (LTP) collaboration (Magdalene Lampert, Elham Kazemi, Megan Franke, Angela Turrou, Hala Ghousseini, and Heather Beasley). There are several effective counting routines, but for pattern work, *Choral Counting* tops my list.

The idea behind *Choral Counting* is simple. The teacher, thinking about what mathematical concepts and skills are appropriate for her students, chooses a starting number, an ending number, an interval, and whether to count forward or backward. For example:

- Starting at 8, count up by tens to 168: 8, 18, 28, 38, 48, …
- Starting at 0, count up by three-fourths to 12: ¾, 1½, 2¼, 3, 3¾, 4½, 5¼, 6, …
- Starting at 12:00, count up by 20 minutes to 4:00: 12:00, 12:20, 12:40, 1:00, 1:20, …
- Starting at 4,125, count up by two hundreds to 7,125: 4,125, 4,325, 4,525, 4,725, 4,925, 5,125,…
- Starting at 20, count down by threes to -25: 20, 17, 14, 11, 8, 5, 2, -1, -4, -7, -10, …
- Starting at 0.15, count up by 0.01 to 0.45: 0.15, 0.16, 0.17, 0.18, 0.19, 0.20, 0.21, …

As students count aloud together, the teacher records their count publicly so students can see patterns emerge and refer to the representation during discussions (Figure 10.3).

The teacher might record the count in a number grid, in a vertical or horizontal list, or along a number line, depending on the count and what patterns she hopes to highlight. For example, in this count from

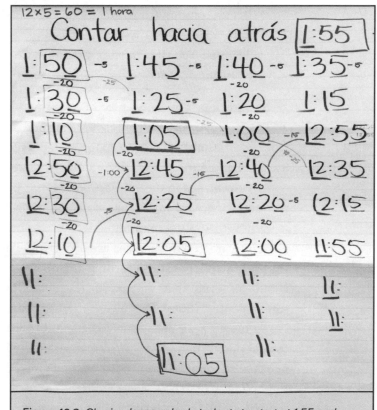

Figure 10.3 *Cherise Jones asked students to start at 1:55 and count down by five-minute intervals. What do you notice?*

Angela Turrou, students counted by fives, starting at 21 and ending at 136. In this case, the teacher chose to use a grid and record numbers vertically:

21	41	61	81	101	121
26	46	66	86	106	126
31	51	71	91	111	131
36	56	76	96	116	136

What patterns do you notice? Can you describe them in words?

I urge you to pause here and watch a couple of classroom choral counts to get a feel for how they flow and see how they burst with opportunities for any grade level. In some of these Teaching Channel videos, the counts stand alone as warm-ups. In others, they are integrated with the rest of the lesson and assessment. They're all great, and they're all linked at stenhouse. com/becomingmathteacher:

- Laretha Todd (third grade): Discover Number Patterns with Skip Counting, teachingchannel.org/videos/teaching-number-patterns
- Drew Crandall (third grade): Reasoning About Multiplication and Division, teachingchannel.org/videos/multiplication-division-in-the-core
- Drew Crandall (third grade): Assess and Plan with Exit Tickets, teachingchannel.org/ videos/teacher-assessment-strategy
- Theresa Tse (first grade): Counting Collections to 100, teachingchannel.org/videos/ counting-by-ten-lesson

In addition, the University of Washington's Teacher Education by Design project, or TEDD, hosts an incredible resource at tedd.org. They have several videos of choral counts from additional grade levels, along with detailed descriptions, planning templates, counting ideas, example recordings, and guides for professional development facilitators.

As you can see in the videos, *Choral Counting* is much more purposeful and powerful than rote counting. Kazemi, Franke, and Lampert wrote, "This activity is targeted to help children learn how to apply computational strategies, notice and use patterns to make predictions, and reason through why patterns are occurring. This activity is not simply about rote counting. Instead the purposeful recording and choice of the counting task coupled with discussions about patterns that emerge as the count proceeds engages students in mathematical sensemaking" (2009, 14).

To meet these pedagogical goals and to facilitate *Choral Counting* effectively, we need to practice. When I work with teachers, we plan and teach several choral counts with one another so we all experience counts as learners and teachers. We've found it's especially important to plan how we'll record the count, a process Shumway described in *Number Sense Routines* (2011). Try writing the numbers in different orientations to see what patterns pop out and anticipate what discussions might emerge. How would the numbers look in a vertical

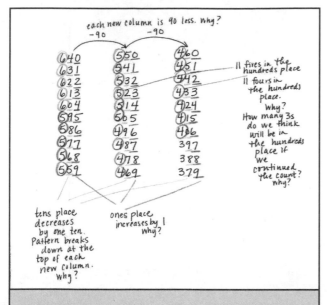

Figure 10.4a *How Allison Hintz plans a choral count. Notice that she explores the mathematics first.*

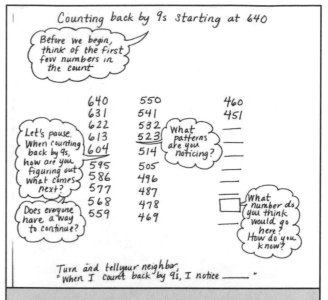

Figure 10.4b *Once she's played with the math, Allison plans her recording and questioning.*

or horizontal list? Perhaps a number line would work better? What about grids? Do you want to count down or across? Where will you break and create a new column? Would making columns five or ten numbers long help place value concepts emerge? How might you use different colors to highlight what you see? Figure 10.4 shows two pages from Allison Hintz's planning notebook. This is the thinking process.

As you plan how to record the count, think about productive places to pause and ask students about their thinking and the patterns they see developing. Open-ended questions such as "What do you notice?" are wonderful conversation openers. In addition, Kassia Omohundro Wedekind and I have found it helpful to choose a few questions from the following list for each choral count:

What is the next number going to be?

How did you know what number would be next?

Did someone figure out what number is next in a different way?

If we count _____ numbers, what do you estimate our last number will be? Why?

Now that we've counted some, does anyone want to revise your thinking/ change your estimate?

Why didn't anyone choose _____ as an estimate?

What patterns do you see?

What do you notice?

Is the number _____ going to be in this count?

What's a number that won't be in this count?

If we kept going, would we land on _____? Why or why not?

How much are we adding/subtracting as we go down the columns?

How much are we adding/subtracting as we go across columns?

Does this count remind you of any other counts we've done?

How does this pattern connect to _____?

If we kept going, what number would go here? (Indicate a space, e.g., the box in Figure 10.5, placed so students might use a pattern to answer, rather than fill in all the missing numbers.)

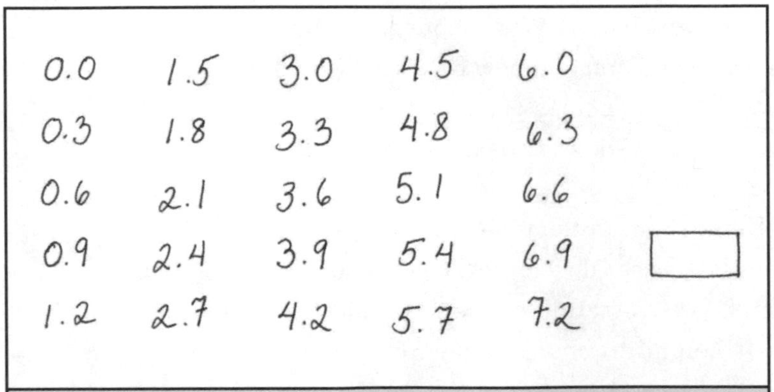

0.0	1.5	3.0	4.5	6.0
0.3	1.8	3.3	4.8	6.3
0.6	2.1	3.6	5.1	6.6
0.9	2.4	3.9	5.4	6.9
1.2	2.7	4.2	5.7	7.2

Figure 10.5 *What number would go in this box? How do you know?*

While every choral count is about patterns, I asked Elham Kazemi, Allison Hintz, and Angela Torrou about designing choral counts that would be especially likely to lead to generalizable patterns. They shared some outstanding ideas:

• Plan a series of counts related by factors. For example, count by fours one day and eights the next, and then compare the two counts. What numbers are on one count but not the other? What numbers would come up if we counted by twos? Twelves? Sixteens?

• Count by the same number two days in a row, but start with different numbers. For example, count by fours one day, starting at 4. Count by fours the following day but start at 7. Compare the counts and notice patterns.

• Plan a series of counts that will emphasize patterns in place value. For example, over a few days, count by 3s, 13s, 23s, 30s, and 300s, as shown in Figure 10.6. What's similar or different in the counts?

• Push students to think about when patterns will break or change, often over a decade or century. For example, Figure 10.7 shows two counts by elevens. Students will mostly cruise down those columns, but struggle after each set of 10. Also, compare the two recordings for a moment: What difference does including zero make?

- Do the same count a few times but record it differently. Give students time to discuss what they notice when they compare the representations. For example, consider the counts from Wendy Moulton and her kindergarteners and first-grade students in Figures 10.8, 10.9, and 10.10. What did the students notice when the numbers were recorded vertically? Horizontally? With different starting numbers?

The more I explore *Choral Counting*, the more possibilities I see. Playing with patterns, generalizing, predicting, and reasoning are built right into their structure. Whether you're counting by ones with kindergarteners, by decimals with fifth graders, or around the unit circle with high schoolers, *Choral Counting* can help you build tremendous number sense while teaching students quite a bit of mathematical thinking.

One last thought about *Choral Counting* in elementary school. We already do quite a bit of work with hundreds charts, multiplication charts, and calendars. How could we make our discussions around these useful tools rich and more like the discussions we have with *Choral Counting*? How could we use these routines as opportunities to look for and discuss mathematical patterns? What are we already doing that could be mathematized?

Growing Patterns and Algebraic Reasoning (visualpatterns.org)

When teaching students to notice patterns, it's important that we talk about different types of patterns. In primary school, we have historically emphasized *repeating patterns* like ABAB or square–circle–triangle, square–circle–triangle, or stomp–snap–clap–clap,

3s	13s	23s	30s	300s
3	13	23	30	300
6	26	46	60	600
9	39	69	90	900
12	52	92	120	1200
15	65	115	150	1500
18	78	138	180	1800
21	91	161	210	2100
24	104	184	240	2400
27	117	207	270	2700
30	130	230	300	3000
33	143	253	330	3300
36	156	276	360	3600
39	169	299	390	3900
42	182	322	420	4200
45	195	345	450	4500

Figure 10.6 *What do you notice when you see these counts side by side?*

11	110	209	0	110	220
22	121	220	11	121	231
33	132	231	22	132	242
44	143	242	33	143	253
55	154	253	44	154	264
66	165	264	55	165	275
77	176	275	66	176	286
88	187	286	77	187	297
99	198	297	88	198	308
			99	209	319

Figure 10.7 *Do any patterns break? Where? Why? What patterns jump out in the two different recordings?*

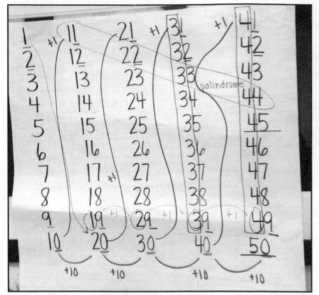

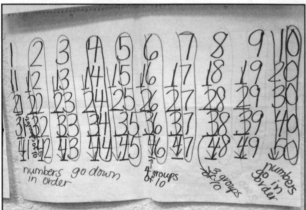

Figures 10.8 (Top), 10.9 (Middle), 10.10 (Bottom)
How does orientation affect what patterns you see?
How does starting at zero change things?

stomp–snap–clap–clap. During *Choral Counting,* students are often drawn to repeating patterns in numbers, such as "the numbers end in 0, 5, 0, 5, 0, 5, 0, 5 when I'm counting by fives." Repeating patterns are certainly one type of pattern, but it's essential that we don't limit students' concept of patterns to the small set of patterns that repeat (Liljedahl 2004). For example, consider Figure 10.11 (pattern 2 from visualpatterns.org). If this pattern continues, what will come next in the series? What will come tenth? One-hundredth? How do you know?

Figure 10.11 shows a *growing pattern,* as distinguished from a *repeating pattern.* In algebra, students will spend quite a bit of time investigating different types of growth patterns, which are described by different types of functions (e.g., linear, exponential, quadratic). Even though growing patterns do not repeat (like AABBAABB), they are still orderly, regular, and reliable. For any input, we can predict exactly one output. Functions have this predictability because there are *patterns in the relationships among the quantities*—patterns are built right into their structure.

Students often "hit a wall" at functions. I, for one, remember functions as a scary-sounding topic that mystified most of the class, including me. Researchers Warren and Cooper (2008) argued that we lose so many students at functions because we give them so little experience with growing patterns in elementary school. Students are familiar with the *static* calculations and patterns of arithmetic, but don't know how to recognize, describe, or analyze the *dynamic* patterns of algebra. Warren and Cooper's study showed there are significant benefits to exposing young children to patterns that move and vary through time, and that young students are quite capable of working with these growing patterns. We need to carve out a little of our precious classroom time to give students a solid foundation in growing patterns (Beatty 2014).

When students first attempt to describe visual, growing patterns, they will almost certainly focus on what comes next. If there are three cases shown, they'll try to build the fourth, then the fifth, then the sixth, and so on. This type of step-by-step thinking is called *recursive* thinking, and it relies on the repeated application of a rule or procedure. It's natural to try extending growing patterns with recursive thinking if we are most comfortable with addition and repeating patterns. For example, consider Figure 10.12.

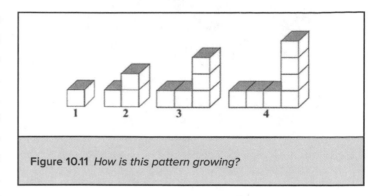

Figure 10.11 *How is this pattern growing?*

Many of us start by describing the pattern: It goes up by two each time (Figure 10.13).

It's true, there are two more dots at each step, and we can use that pattern to figure out what comes next. If we're thinking recursively and we're asked, "What will be the tenth term?" we will draw, build, or account for cases 6, 7, 8, and 9 first, because we are figuring out each case by comparing it to the one that came before. If we try to figure out "How many dots will there be at the fiftieth term? The one-hundredth term? Any term?" though, we suddenly realize the limits of additive, recursive thinking. It can't tell us much about cases that are farther away without some tedious work.

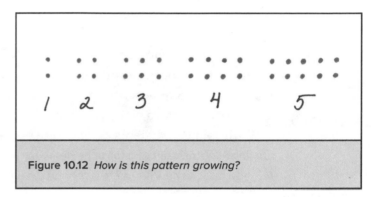

Figure 10.12 *How is this pattern growing?*

The insight we need to have is that there are two data sets here: the position in the pattern (interchangeably called position, case, term, or step) and the number of tiles (or dots, teddy bears, cubes, etc.) at each position. As the position in the pattern varies, the number of tiles

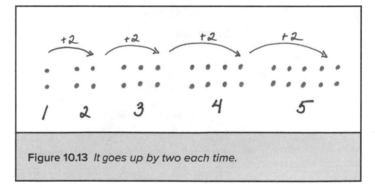

Figure 10.13 *It goes up by two each time.*

varies in a predictable way because there is a consistent relationship—a pattern—between the sets. When we're thinking recursively, we don't think much about the position number and only look for changes within one set—the tiles. When we start comparing the tiles to their corresponding step numbers, though, we begin thinking relationally. We can predict what the pattern will look like at *any* term because we have figured out the generalized, consistent relationship between inputs and outputs—the function.

In this example, once we recognize that this function doubles the position number, as shown in Figure 10.14, we know there will be 20 dots in the tenth case, 100 dots in the fiftieth

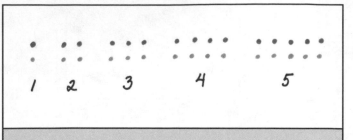

Figure 10.14 *How do the number of dots at each position relate to the position number?*

case, and 500,000 dots in the two-hundred-fifty-thousandth case, all without calculating the cases in between. We have cracked the function, regardless of whether we built it with cubes, described it with words or gestures, or wrote it algebraically as $f(n) = 2n$.

Growing Patterns in the Classroom

The best resource I know for teaching and learning *Visual Patterns* is Fawn Nguyen's collection at visualpatterns.org and her accompanying transcripts of student thinking at mathtalks.net. Fawn has gathered a year's worth of beautiful patterns and organized them in an accessible format. Older students will use symbolic notation and the language of functions to describe how the patterns grow. Younger students will use concrete objects or representations to describe the patterns. All students will learn to think algebraically and develop their pattern detection skills.

With younger students, focus on the process and have fun with it! Don't worry about the algebraic notation. Perhaps once per week, give students time to use cubes, tiles, or counters to build one of the *Visual Patterns* and then talk about how they see it growing. A few tips:

1. It's important that younger students physically grow the pattern to build their intuition and experience. They can use any manipulatives you have handy.
2. Make sure to ask students about cases farther down the sequence, rather than only asking, "What comes next?" because "What comes next?" encourages recursive thinking. If the students are looking at the first three cases, ask, "What will the fifth case look like?" or "How can you use the fifth case to see what happens in the tenth?" or "What stays the same? What changes?" The most important question to ask is, "How do you see the pattern growing?"
3. Similarly, give students patterns out of sequence sometimes. Playing the classic games *Guess My Rule* or *Function Machine* can be helpful here, because students will ask numbers at random as they try to figure out the rule. This kind of work interrupts students' tendency to think recursively.
4. Multicolored tools and writing implements can help students see patterns and share how they visualize their growth (Warren and Cooper 2008).

For example, let's think about ways to represent the growth of the first visual pattern we saw in Figure 10.11:

"It goes up by two each time, so there will be 9 in the fifth case because there are 7 in the fourth case. For the tenth case . . . um . . . I haven't gone that far yet. Um, 6, 7, 8, 9, 10, so 5 more twos is 10, so 19."

The student in Figure 10.15 is thinking recursively and is focused on adding two tiles with each step. Compare his work to these three solutions from Fawn Nguyen's middle school students, who are all thinking functionally. (While we can use any letter to describe the position in the pattern, it's conventional to use n.)

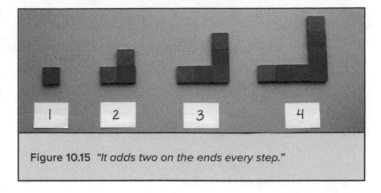

Figure 10.15 *"It adds two on the ends every step."*

"I saw n blocks horizontally, and $n - 1$ blocks vertically on top. My equation is $B = n + (n - 1)$" (Figure 10.16).

"I saw the number of blocks on the bottom is the same as the step number. And I also see the same vertically, but they share the corner block, so it's $2n - 1$" (Figure 10.17).

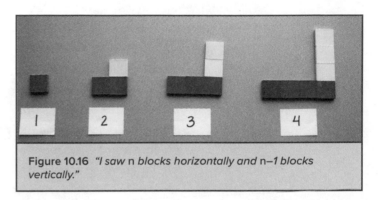

Figure 10.16 *"I saw* n *blocks horizontally and* n–1 *blocks vertically."*

"I ignored the corner block and saw that the horizontal blocks are always one less than the step number. Same thing vertically. Then I added the corner block. My equation is $B = 2(n - 1) + 1$." (Also see Figure 10.17). Isn't it interesting that the same representation applies to both these strategies?)

All three of these students have correctly described and generalized this pattern. Students will often see the patterns in several different ways, and proving that their assorted solutions are both true and equivalent is

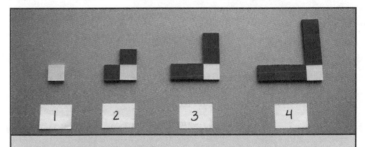

Figure 10.17 *These two students saw symmetry in the pattern once they addressed the corner block.*

a lovely challenge for a class. Fawn's *Visual Patterns* is a superb resource for teaching students algebraic thinking, noticing patterns, conjecturing, and generalizing, all in the context of working with patterns. The openness in these problems leads to rich, powerful discussions. For more ideas about using visualpatterns.org in your classroom, poke around the website. Fawn has shared several other teachers' blogs and examples of student work under the "Gallery" tab, and she transcribed students' descriptions of the patterns for the first twenty-eight days at mathtalks.net. The transcripts are a gift to teachers because they help us anticipate what our students might see and say.

Teaching Students to Conjecture and Generalize

> *Trying to articulate a sense of some underlying pattern is called generalizing. It means noticing certain features common to several particular examples and ignoring other features. Once articulated, the generalization turns into a conjecture which must then be investigated to see if it is accurate. This whole process is the essence of mathematical thinking.*
>
> —John Mason, Leone Burton, and Kaye Stacey, *Thinking Mathematically*

When students conjecture, they move past observing the pattern that is right in front of them to exploring what they can't yet see clearly. Conjectures are early hypotheses and partially formed ideas, not wild guesses. The language of conjectures is *I wonder if*, or *It could be*, or *I'm starting to think that*. It's important that we explicitly teach students to expect to revise their conjectures. If a student tests his or her conjecture and finds it has holes in it, it is untrue, or it needs to be reworked, he or she has made mathematics, *not* made a mistake. Revising and disproving conjectures is the stuff of math.

As students generalize, they expand their thinking from *specific* cases to *any* case or *any* class of cases, which we just saw in the context of *Visual Patterns*. You can listen for this transition in their language: students start using words like *any number, always, for any whole numbers*, or *it doesn't matter what you start with*. Magdalene Lampert observed this evolution in her students' thinking: "Students shifted around from talking about 'What *I* did' to figure out the problem to 'What *you* do.' They were referring to 'what *one* does,' distancing themselves from the procedures they were evaluating and making their assertions more general" (1990, 49). These bread-and-butter questions can help you encourage students to think generally:

> **Questions to Encourage General Thinking**
>
> Do you think this will always be true?
>
> Will that always work?
>
> Will that work with all numbers?
>
> What is the relationship between _____ and _____?
>
> What kinds of problems would this kind of thinking help you with?
>
> What's similar about these problems?
>
> What's different about these problems?
>
> What do you think is happening?
>
> What would happen in the _____th case?

In *Thinking Mathematically*, Carpenter, Franke, and Levi (2003) recommended two powerful instructional routines to teach students to conjecture and generalize: *Open Number*

Sentences and *True/False Number Sentences*. They go into depth describing both routines, and I highly recommend you read their discussion. A quick synopsis:

Open Number Sentences

Number sentences such as $67 + 83 = \square + 82$ encourage students to figure out what's missing by reasoning and looking for relationships rather than calculating. Because students likely don't want to compute $67 + 83$, they can reason that 82 is 1 *smaller* than 83, so the other number must be one *bigger* than 67. If the teacher presses students to justify their thinking, students will often state a generalization. In this case, students might say:

> *If you are adding two numbers, you can take some from one of the numbers and give it to the other number, and it won't change your answer.*

Or

> *When you're adding, you can break apart the numbers, rearrange them, and put them back together.*

Or

> *If you're adding two numbers, you can add some amount to one of the numbers and subtract the same amount from the other number and the sum will be the same.*

And just like that, elementary school students are discovering the algebraic properties of the operations! By choosing open number sentences carefully, teachers can encourage students to uncover these important properties. For example, Carpenter, Franke, and Levi shared a classroom example in which the teacher asked the students to solve $56 + 75 + 25 = \square$ (2003, 106). This problem is beautifully designed to encourage students to explore the associative property of addition:

$$(a + b) + c = a + (b + c) \text{ for all numbers } a, b, \text{ and } c.$$

$56 + (75 + 25)$ is much easier than $(56 + 75) + 25$, but it is not at all obvious to children that "you can do that." This teacher wrote an open number sentence to elicit the important mathematical question *Can you add in any order?* In response, students grew curious, explored the mathematics, produced a general conjecture, and eventually convinced one another of its truth.

True/False Number Sentences

Like *Open Number Sentences*, *True/False Number Sentences* encourage students to think about underlying structures and relationships, rather than rushing into calculations. The idea is you post a number sentence that is likely to reveal properties of the operations, such as:

$$34 + 27 = 36 + 25, \text{ or}$$
$$5 \times 70 = 10 \times 35, \text{ or}$$
$$49 - 26 = 50 - 25$$

You then pose the question, "Is it true or false? Why?" Often, the discussion leads to a generalization, starting with language like "When you multiply, . . ." or "If one of the addends . . ." To get a sense of the power of *True/False Number Sentences*, I recommend viewing a marvelous classroom clip of a fourth-grade class discussing this provocative sentence:

$$80 \div 4 = (80 \div 2) + (80 \div 2)$$

Is it true or false? Why? Enjoy the students' thinking at tedd.org, where there is also a valuable collection of resources, information, planning tools, examples, and video about *True/False Number Sentences*, or at the Teaching Channel: teachingchannel.org/videos/common-core-teaching-division.

Number Talks and Number Strings

In addition to *Open Number Sentences* and *True/False Number Sentences*, *Number Talks* and *Number Strings* are flexible instructional routines that can lead to conjecturing and generalizing. As teachers, we can design specific sets of problems that encourage students to investigate general truths about numbers and operations. In *Making Number Talks Matter*, Cathy Humphreys and Ruth Parker (2015) called these *Number Talks* that lead to "Will It Always Work? And Why?" investigations:

> Investigations offer the gift of time for those most basic of mathematical pursuits: tinkering with ideas, sniffing around for patterns, and making conjectures and testing them out . . . Many investigations arise from particular strategies used in Number Talks and give students the opportunity to think about why a strategy works . . . [The investigations] have the same primary purpose: to help students realize that when something happens over and over again in mathematics, *there has to be a reason*. So what is that reason? And will that something *always* happen? Why? Could I prove it? If not, when will it happen and when won't it? (2015, 133–134)

Humphreys and Parker suggest building *Number Talks* around common strategies:

- Constant difference (a.k.a. same difference) in subtraction (shifting $63 - 29$ to $64 - 30$)
- Switching the digits within place value in addition ($93 + 29 = 99 + 23$)
- Doubling and halving when multiplying ($8 \times 13 = 4 \times 26$)

Will they always work? Why?

In addition to Humphreys and Parker, I also recommend Fosnot and Dolk's Young Mathematicians at Work (2001), Sherry Parrish's *Number Talks* (2010), Kathy Richardson and Ruth Parker's "Number Talks Toolkit" at www.mathperspectives.com/num_talks.html, and, again, tedd.org for further learning about *Number Talks* and *Number Strings*.

Games: "If Player 1 starts with two cubes, Player 1 will always . . ."

At the 2014 National Council of Teachers of Mathematics conference, I went to a fascinating session led by Toni Cameron, Melissa Singer, and their colleagues in the New York City public schools. During the session, the presenters argued convincingly that we could use games to teach conjecturing and generalizing. Reflecting on their session later, I thought about how much I've learned from watching Marilyn Burns (2009) teach mathematical reasoning through games like *Four Strikes and You're Out!* I also researched how important games have been in the history of mathematics. The more I thought about it, the more I saw how games of strategy could provide a terrific context for generalizing, conjecturing, and crafting claims. When my colleague Aimee Krauss asked me to guest-teach conjecturing to her third- and fourth-grade students, I jumped at the chance to design a three-day, mini-investigation built around a game.

I started by drawing a blank *Tic-Tac-Toe* board and asked students, "What are your winning strategies for *Tic-Tac-Toe*?" Within a few minutes, we had several different strategies on the board:

- Get three corners so you can control the board.
- Start with the central square and then move toward the corners.
- Work two lines of attack simultaneously so you can't be defeated by a block.

Once they understood what I meant by *winning strategies*, I told them they'd be playing a new game today, a *Nim* variation called *Train*, and we were all going to work together to figure out winning strategies. The rules:

- There are ten loose cubes.
- Players must take turns adding cubes on until the cubes form a train ten cubes long.
- In a turn, the players can add one, two, or three cubes.
- The player who places the tenth cube on the train wins that round of the game.

As always, if you can spend a few minutes playing, the following discussion will make a lot more sense to you. It's also an enjoyable game! The rules may be simple, but it carries surprises.

In Aimee's class, I told students, "I am going to give you a little time to play it in pairs so that you understand it, and you're going to try to win. After a couple of go-rounds, I want you to worry a little bit less about winning and a little bit more about working together to see if you can figure out what's a winning strategy. If you start to notice, 'The person who does _____ always wins' or 'I think the person who goes (first, second) always loses,' you're starting to make conjectures about what's going on in this game. That's something we do in mathematics!"

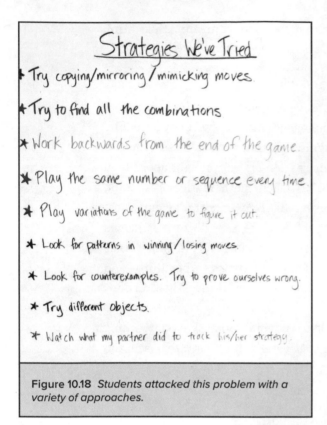

Figure 10.18 *Students attacked this problem with a variety of approaches.*

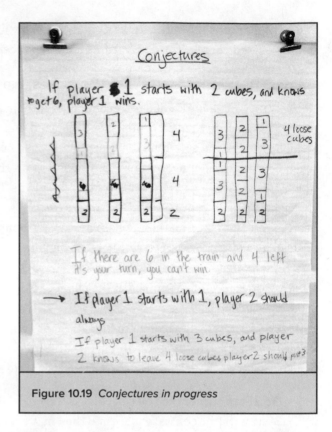

Figure 10.19 *Conjectures in progress*

Students paired up and started playing. Within about ten minutes, students had a sense of the game and were starting to figure out strategies. I paused and gave them two focus questions:

- Is this game fair?
- Would you rather go first or second?

We also passed out paper and suggested they start trying to put words to what they noticed and what they tried. I said, "You might start to write your strategy by saying, 'Player 1 should always . . .'" Students found it challenging to articulate what they'd noticed, but it was a productive struggle, and all students were engaged. Aimee and I observed that their approaches were broad and interesting, so we started a chart to keep track of how they attacked this problem (Figure 10.18). We added to it over the course of the next few days.

After a bit more play, our first conjecture emerged. Jenna and Gregory said, "If Player 1 starts with two cubes, Player 1 is guaranteed to win and Player 2 cannot win." I asked students whether they agreed or disagreed and why. Students picked up their cubes and tested it out. After a few minutes, Joseph and Edward had broken the conjecture with a counterexample, showing it was possible for Player 1 to lose even if he started with two cubes. I turned back to Jenna and Gregory and asked whether they wanted to revise their conjecture. They did. They wanted to be more specific about the strategy Player 1 should use for the full game.

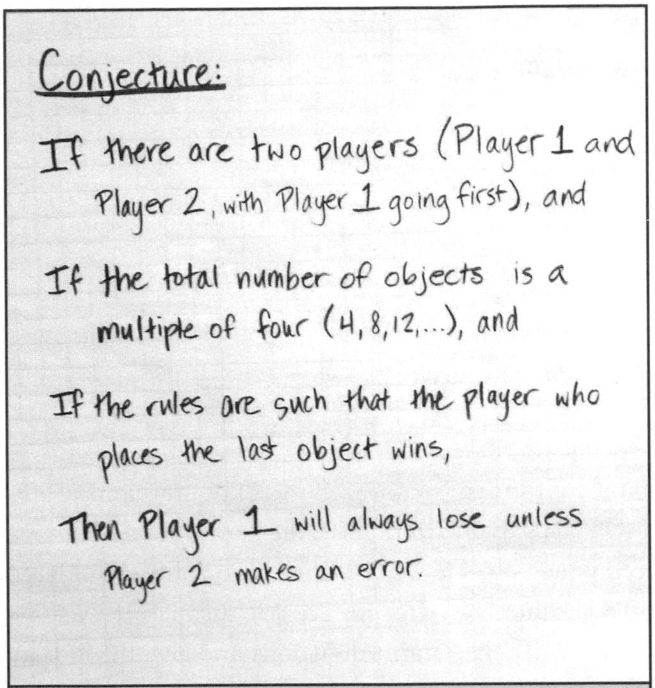

Conjecture:

If there are two players (Player 1 and Player 2, with Player 1 going first), and

If the total number of objects is a multiple of four (4, 8, 12, ...), and

If the rules are such that the player who places the last object wins,

Then Player 1 will always lose unless Player 2 makes an error.

Figure 10.20 *As we worked, students started to nail down the language.*

So began a lovely process of making conjectures, trying to break them with counterexamples, and revising them so they were more precise. Writing conjectures is difficult, and we started with bumpy conjectures such as those in Figure 10.19. Over the course of the three days, however, we made a lot of progress. For example, students discovered nobody in their community understood what they meant when they used the word *you*, so they agreed to define and use terms such as Player 1 and Player 2. They started to specify the conditions of their conjectures to preempt counterexamples. Together, we began to generate more complete and clear mathematical conjectures (see the draft in Figure 10.20).

After the second day, we asked students what they were wondering about the game. I grouped their questions into categories to help us plan how to use our final day together.

Questions about the rules/number of cubes/number of players:

- How many cubes can you use? Could we use twenty for *Train*?
- I wonder if you can play the game with more than ten Unifix cubes?
- Do six and four always work?
- I wonder if more (than two) people can play Train?

Questions about what objects we play with:

- I wonder if you have to have the Unifix?
- I wonder why it is blocks and not something else like dice?
- I wonder if you can use any other objects besides cubes?

Questions about the name and the game:

- Why is it named *Train*?
- I wonder if there is more than one name for *Train*?
- How did *Train* ever become a game?

Questions about strategy:

- I wonder who will win? How did you know?
- I wonder if there are any more strategies to win?

I knew I could address their questions about the name of the game quickly. Mathematically, I wanted to take up the questions about strategy and variations of the game, but almost one third of the class wondered if it mattered which objects we were using! At first, I wondered if this question would be mathematically productive. After thinking it through with some colleagues on Twitter, I decided I should honor their genuine questions and give the kids an opportunity to find out. I hoped we'd also have time to take a whack at game variations.

The third day, students played with keys, dice, plastic bugs, tiles, and whatever else we could find. After a while, they decided that changing the objects used in the *game* did not affect the *strategy*. To my delight and relief, we found the extra playtime this question took was invaluable because it required several more rounds of play. Students who were quietly not yet convinced about certain conjectures played the game enough times to have their own aha! moments, and started playing more strategically. I was glad their question led to extra practice.

In addition, the extra playtime led to more wondering about and experimentation with variations of the game. What would happen if we played with nine cubes? Eleven? Twelve? Twenty? What if students could add only one or two cubes, rather than one, two, or three? What if more than two players played? They spent much of the third day testing out these different variations and trying to write conjectures about them. Aimee e-mailed me the work in Figure 10.21 two days after the investigation ended. Students' enthusiasm and focus were still high, and they continued to articulate their ideas. Aimee and I were pleased with how much her kids had learned to think generally, formulate conjectures, and start to learn the communication skills needed to discuss their ideas with their communities.

After this mini-investigation, I became more convinced that strategy games are a fruitful context for cultivating general thinking and conjecturing. Classic games such as *Tic-Tac-Toe*, *Nim*, *Dots*, *Mancala*, *Mastermind*, *Fifteen*, and *Race to Twenty* are motivating, accessible, and full of mathematical opportunities. *Thinking Mathematically* by John Mason, Leone Burton, and Kaye Stacey (2010) is chock-full of wonderful games and questions to try. I've also included several linked blogs, videos, games, and resources at stenhouse.com/becomingmathteacher.

Numberphile.com deserves special mention: they feature charming videos of mathematicians generalizing, conjecturing, reasoning, and proving winning strategies for everyday games such as *Rock, Paper, Scissors*; *Dots and Boxes*; and *Tic-Tac-Toe*. If your students doubt that this work is math, it might help to show them mathematicians doing this work!

Whatever game you choose, the first step is for students to play several rounds and to see what they notice. Keep an ear out for that beautiful shift in language from specific to general, when "I won" or "I lost again" gives way to "I won because" or "The player who _____ always loses." Mathematical reasoning and general conjectures emerge naturally in the face of a good puzzle.

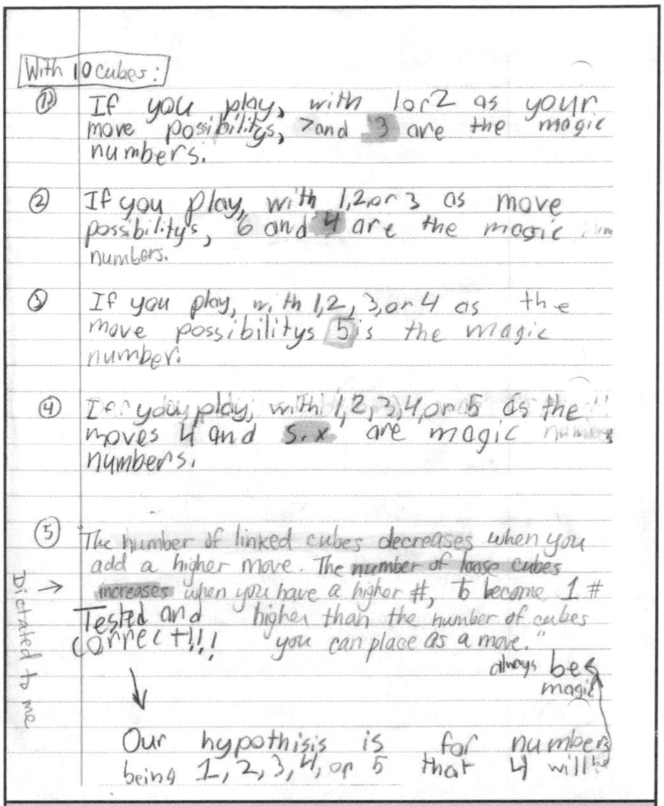

Teaching Strategies for Crafting Claims

Articulating general claims is essential to investigating generalizations. As students put their ideas into words, they clarify their ideas, develop common language, and come to a common understanding of exactly what their general claim is. Once they have agreed what it is they are trying to prove, they can work together to justify their claim.

—Susan Jo Russell, Deborah Schifter, and Virginia Bastable,
Connecting Arithmetic to Algebra

Figure 10.21 *Students continued to explore variations and make conjectures several days after the lessons.*

As Aimee and I saw in the games investigation, at some point during a prolonged period of tinkering with, generalizing about, and investigating a conjecture, students become convinced of its mathematical truth. When students feel certain about a mathematical idea but haven't proved it yet, they are ready to make a claim to their peers. In this way, stating conjectures and making claims are social activities: students will feel a genuine *need* to state their thinking clearly so their classmates understand. Communication is the driver here, and it's a powerful one (Harel 2013). Clear language and precise, common vocabulary will provide relief to students struggling to get their ideas across. As teachers, we can take advantage of the opening to press for well-crafted, specific, clear claims.

Articulating and Revising Claims

We've all been in the situation in which we think we know something, but when we try to

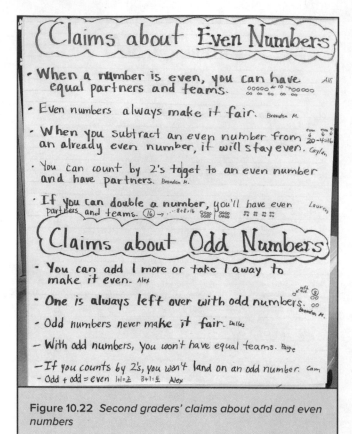

Figure 10.22 *Second graders' claims about odd and even numbers*

articulate our thought—to make it explicit—we fumble. Trying to put our ideas into words exposes what we understand and what we lack. In mathematics, finding the words, symbols, and representations to articulate a claim is an essential part of forging and sharing understanding. We teachers need to give students the opportunity and time it takes to articulate their claims, work out the kinks, and then test, revisit, and revise them as needed.

For example, after several days of exploring, conjecturing, and generalizing about odd and even numbers, Linda Melvin's second-grade students in Traverse City, Michigan, generated a list of claims they were pretty sure about (Figure 10.22).

The following day, Linda paired off her students and assigned a claim to each pair. Linda knew that, as her students tried to prove or disprove claims, they would run into vague language and terms that needed to be clarified. She encouraged students to revise claims as needed.

In Figure 10.23, we see students' work on the claim, "If you count by twos, you won't land on an odd number." The students testing this claim realized the claim didn't specify where the count started: if they started counting by twos from an odd number, all the numbers in the series would be odd. The partners provided the counterexample 1, 3, 5, 7, . . . , and then revised the language in the claim from *won't* to *may*:

"If you count by twos you *may* land on an odd number."

In Figure 10.24, we see a different group's work. They tackled the claim "even numbers always make it fair." This is a fascinating claim that grew from students' thinking about splitting groups into teams. The first student wrote in support of the claim, arguing that an odd number of players would result in one player being left out. The other two students, however, found flaws in the claim. They each generated an example in which four people shared three objects (candy or basketballs) and

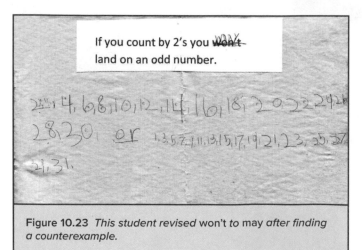

Figure 10.23 *This student revised* won't *to* may *after finding a counterexample.*

pointed out the sharing did not work out fairly, even when starting with an even number.

My favorite detail about this example is that the student who poked holes in the claim with the candy example is the same student who wrote the claim! Through this process of trying to disprove his claim, he realized there was a big gap between what he *meant* and what he actually *said*. Now he had a chance to clarify his claim. This is exactly the thought process we want to make explicit and ultimately have students internalize. Linda told her class, "Just like in writing when we revise our writing, we make changes and make it meaningful. Mathematicians do the same thing. They revise their claims." Teachers sometimes need to model and guide students to look for counterexamples or to test the vague aspects of the claim, but we don't want to take over the revising or the disproving. That's the kids' job. That's the reasoning we're trying to teach.

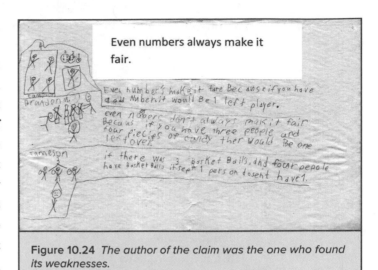

Figure 10.24 *The author of the claim was the one who found its weaknesses.*

The work of revising, refining, and clarifying claims happens in a big flurry at the outset but continues over time. Kristin Gray has students post their claims on a *Claims Wall* so they are available for revision on a longer time scale. Figure 10.25 shows some example claims her students have made and posted about the strategy of doubling and halving. Her students have really taken this claim out for a test-drive! They've looked at whether it works with other operations, odd and even numbers, single or multiple times, and so on.

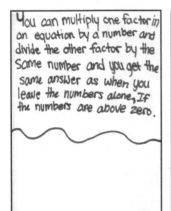
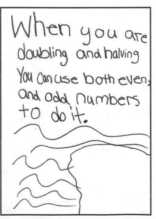

Figures 10.25a, b, c, and d (left to right) *Examples from Kristin Gray's* Claim Wall

As students learn about new sets of numbers or different properties of the operations, they may want to revisit their claims: *I wonder if that claim I made about multiplication holds true for fractions and decimals? I was only thinking about whole numbers then.* In addition, students may continue to accumulate evidence and experience that influence their thinking about a claim over time. Therefore, the *Claim Wall* isn't a display of finished work; it's a living document that should be revisited now and then.

A few key points about teaching students to craft claims:

- Challenge students to nail down their language. The only way to be sure everyone is talking about the same thing is to use precise, shared language. *It*, *this*, and *that* need to be replaced with nouns. Vocabulary should come as a relief to students trying to communicate.

- If one student says a claim clearly, don't assume other students understand. Crafting claims is hard work, and each student needs a chance to make sense. Turn-and-talks and individual writing time are especially important when crafting and making sense of claims.

- Build in opportunities for revisiting and revising claims at all stages of the process. When students are drafting claims, they need to take multiple passes to get the language clear. Even after claims are stated clearly and posted on the wall, they should remain open to revision.

Whatever the math content you are teaching, keep your ears attuned to opportunities for students to articulate their claims. Claims often come in the middle of the work—after students have noticed patterns, generalized them, and become curious if there's an overall rule that governs the patterns and strategies they're using.

Conditions, Constraints, and Leaving the Door Open

Once a claim has been stated, there are two big questions on the table:

> *Whether* the statement is true, and, if so,

> *When* is the statement true?

When mathematicians make mathematical statements, they always specify the conditions of or constraints on the statement so other mathematicians know whether and when it is valid. For example, let's look at how mathematicians describe the inverse property of multiplication:

$$\text{For every real number } a, a \neq 0, \text{ there is a real number } \frac{1}{a} \text{ such that } a \times \frac{1}{a} = 1.$$

Why have that introductory clause? Why not just jump right to $a \times \frac{1}{a} = 1$, or use language such as "any number multiplied by its reciprocal equals one?" Because we need to know *when* this statement is true or false, and part of formalizing the claim is specifying those conditions. The phrase, "For every real number" tells us that we are working with the set of all numbers except imaginary ones. That means we can use this inverse property with positive numbers, negative numbers, fractions, decimals, irrational numbers such as pi (π), exponents, square roots, and so on. There is one notable exception, however, so it's specified. We can't use this property with zero because it's not true: $0 \times \dfrac{1}{0} \neq 1$.

Whenever students explore conjectures and make claims, we need to encourage them to think about the sets of numbers or objects they are talking about. Kristin Gray constantly asks her fifth graders:

- What types of numbers have you tried?
- Does this always work?
- Tell me about the numbers you are trying here.
- Why did you choose those numbers to test? How do they relate to your conjecture?
- Does this work for all numbers?

Over time, her students internalize this type of thinking, and try to pin down sets themselves. For example, Kristin recorded her students discussing mathematical statements in small, independent groups. The students at one table were considering the statement, "When multiplying, the product is always greater than the factors," and deciding whether they agreed or disagreed. One student, Kayla, said, "I think I disagree, because what if you were multiplying negatives?" The students jumped into this exciting idea together, even though they hadn't yet studied negative numbers and weren't sure what actually happens when multiplying them. Nevertheless, they pressed on! I love this exchange between Amy and Kayla:

Amy: I'm kind of unsure because I was going to say I agree because, a product, when you're multiplying, like if I had 40 times 5, that would be 200, so it's going to be bigger than both (factors). But then again, you said negatives, so now I'm kind of unsure.

Kayla: I actually have something to add on to yours. So when you're multiplying whole numbers the product is going to be higher, but when you're multiplying negatives, it's going to be lower.

Well, sometimes. There's plenty of time to address the content of operations with negative numbers later. What's exciting, though, is these students are thinking about different sets of numbers in the context of a mathematical claim. Figure 10.26 shows another student's work on this same statement.

Wow! She's thinking about several sets, including whole numbers, decimals greater than 1, and decimals between 0 and 1. She makes no claim about whether the statement is true with negative numbers,

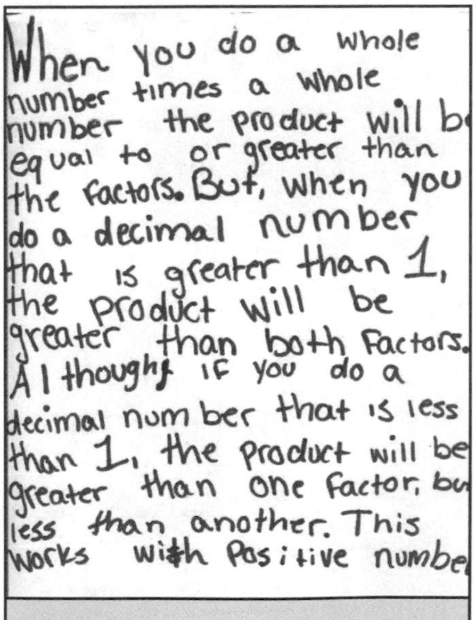

When you do a whole number times a whole number the product will be equal to or greater than the factors. But, when you do a decimal number that is greater than 1, the product will be greater than both factors. Although if you do a decimal number that is less than 1, the product will be greater than one factor, but less than another. This works with positive numbe[r]

Figure 10.26 *A fifth-grade student's thinking about the conditions on her claim*

but she acknowledges their existence and leaves the door open to further revision. This is beautiful thinking from a fifth-grade student and brings up an important idea for us.

It's essential that students, together, decide what is mathematically true. At the same time, they don't know what they don't yet know. Many times, students will decide a claim is valid because it's valid for all the operations, shapes, or sets of numbers they know so far, but unbeknownst to them, their claim will fall apart when they learn about fractions or negative numbers or decimals. For example, students often conjecture about what makes things bigger or smaller, such as, "The product will always be greater than the factors" or "The more digits a number has, the bigger it is." If we're talking about the natural counting numbers, sure. Once we consider negative numbers, fractions, or decimals, though, these claims implode.

As teachers, we can handle moments like this by supporting the good work our students are doing while explicitly acknowledging that they may want to revise their work down the road. Sample language, *which we should use whether their claims will last or expire*:

> "I wonder how your thinking might change as you learn about other types of numbers? Make sure to revisit this claim again then."

> "So you're feeling pretty confident about this claim because it seems to be true for all the types of numbers you know about so far? You're convinced for now? OK. Let's remember to look at it again later in the year and see if we still agree."

> "We might need to think about different arguments or different representations when we're working with different sets of numbers. Something to keep in mind."

> "You've done great thinking today and made a lot of sense. I'm so curious how your thinking might change as you learn more mathematics. You'll have to come back and tell me!"

The goal here is to respect students as arbiters of truth while recognizing that their thinking should evolve as they gain experience and learn new content.

Evaluating Claims and Conditions: Always, Sometimes, Never

Always, Sometimes, Never is a lovely instructional routine that gives students experience articulating, evaluating, and constraining claims. This is a flexible activity you can use as a warm-up, a formative assessment, or as the basis of a lesson with lots of partner or small-group discussions. The basic structure of *Always, Sometimes, Never* is you provide students with one or more mathematical statements and ask them to determine whether the statements are true in all cases, true in some cases, or true in no cases. Some of the statements are always true: "All four sides of a square have the same length." Some of the statements are never true: "1.5 feet equals 1 foot, 5 inches." Most of the statements are ambiguous, however, meaning they are true under some conditions and false under others, which is precisely what makes *Always, Sometimes, Never* such a valuable teaching strategy for mathematical reasoning.

Let's look at three examples to get a sense of how they can work:

1. *"In fractions, the number on the bottom can't be bigger than the number on the top."*

Students can generate many examples that follow the statement: $\frac{1}{4}, \frac{3}{8}, \frac{99}{100}$. Nevertheless, as soon as students generate one counterexample, for example, $\frac{5}{3}$, they have disproved the claim. Depending on your goals, students could classify it as never true and work on a new claim or revise it into a better statement.

2. *"One-third is one of three pieces."*

Student conversation could develop like this:

"It's true, because the thirds fraction circle has three pieces, and one of them is one-third."

"What if the pieces aren't the same size, though? Like, I could cut a cake into three pieces but make one piece really big, one piece medium, and one piece tiny. That's not fair."

"Also, one-third can be other things, too. If a brownie were cut into six equal pieces, one-third would be two of six pieces. Is that part of the claim?"

"But, you guys, think about the fraction circles. There *are* three pieces, and one-third is *one* of them."

"I think it's sometimes true. It's true if the pieces are equal size, but it's not true if they're not."

3. *"Altogether" means add.*

In searching for a counterexample, students may develop a story problem in which *altogether* doesn't mean add at all. For example: *Monica has 3 boxes of toy cars. There are 10 cars in each box. How many toy cars does Monica have altogether?*

She doesn't have 13, does she? Teachers often set "rules" or teach "keywords" that generally hold for numbers and operations students know but fall apart as students move through school. If all a student knows is addition or subtraction, *altogether* often does mean add. Once multiplication is an option, however, all bets are off. Keywords eventually confuse children and create the impression that math is an indecipherable code to calculate. Older students have told me they felt betrayed when they discovered what their earlier teachers told them isn't really true. It's always better to teach students to reason through problems, rather than use shortcuts that expire. If your students have learned tricks and keywords, *Always, Sometimes, Never* can help students reconnect to their internal sense making as they figure out what is or isn't true mathematically.

Some ideas for using *Always, Sometimes, Never* statements in your classroom:

- Choose three to six statements appropriate for your current investigation and have students discuss them in pairs or groups. Choose the statement you see sparking the most interesting discussions and debrief it as a class.
- Choose three to six statements appropriate for your current investigation and have students work on them in pairs or groups. Ask students to revise *Sometimes* statements into *Always* or *Never* statements.
- Print statements and cut them so each statement is on a slip of paper. Give students poster paper and ask them to sort statements into *Always*, *Sometimes*, and *Never* columns. Post their work, and have students do a *Gallery Walk* with journals. Ask them to find choices with which they agree and disagree and then have students discuss.
- Have groups of four students work on a statement with a large whiteboard divided into "placemat" format. Each student takes a corner for individual work. When they've worked for a bit, they talk and come to consensus, which they write in a box in the middle.
- Choose one statement and have students work on it individually, in pairs, or in groups and then discuss. This might be a weekly routine. If you have the space, post a three-column chart on a wall with *Always*, *Sometimes*, and *Never* as category headers. Each time your class reaches consensus about where a statement should go, post it in the appropriate place.
- Choose some statements to explore in your next faculty meeting! Five or ten minutes of discussion in table groups can stimulate rich professional learning about mathematical content, practices, and teaching. More heads are better than one because other people will have different perspectives and approaches, which will help you and your colleagues make new connections and build deeper understanding.

As for the mathematical statements themselves, it's useful to include a variety of types. Some are mathematical claims meant to encourage students to think about conditions and constraints. Some are ambiguously worded statements meant to push students toward precision. Some are designed to expose typical student misconceptions. Some are number sentences that can serve as springboards to generalization. Some encourage students to clarify definitions. Some statements push at shortcuts, tricks, and keywords. All statements should provoke interesting conversations about mathematics!

In 2014, several teachers in the Math-Twitter-Blog-o-Sphere (#MTBoS) brainstormed an elementary version of *Always, Sometimes, Never* statements: tinyurl.com/K6ASN. Feel free to share and use it. I have also posted the link as well as several blogs and examples at stenhouse.com/becomingmathteacher so you can see *Always, Sometimes, Never* in action.

We need to give students ample practice evaluating claims so they develop healthy skepticism, mathematical precision, and logical thinking. We are building a powerful foundation on which proof can be built. *Always, Sometimes, Never* can help.

Example *Always*, *Sometimes*, *Never* Statements

Geometry

All four sides of a square have the same length.

All three sides of a triangle have the same length.

Two triangles put together make a square.

Triangles have to have the point on top.

A square is a rectangle.

A rectangle is a square.

Measurement and Data

A tall glass holds more water than a short glass.

1.5 foot = 1 foot 5 inches

Something measured in centimeters is smaller than something measured in inches.

When you've done something for 30 minutes, the minute hand is on the 6.

All shapes with the same perimeter have the same area.

All shapes with the same area have the same perimeter.

Number and Operations in Base 10/The Number System

A number that begins with 9 is greater than a number that begins with 2.

Zero is the smallest number.

300,70 = three hundred seventy

1,010 < 1,009

There are 3 tens in 130.

There are 13 tens in 130.

Operations and Algebraic Thinking

Subtract means take away.

The sum of three numbers is bigger than the sum of two numbers.

You can switch the order of addends and the sum will be the same.

Any number multiplied by zero equals zero.

$42 \times 6 = (40 \times 6) + (2 \times 6)$

$99 - 35 = 100 - 36$

> **Operations and Algebraic Thinking: Fractions**
>
> Fractions are between 0 and 1.
>
> One-third is one of three pieces.
>
> Equal-sized pieces have the same shape.
>
> In a fraction, the number on top can't be bigger than the number on bottom.
>
> The bigger the denominator, the bigger the pieces.
>
> $1.2 \times 10 = 1.20$

Intuition, Mathematical Reasoning, and Sexism

In the previous chapter, I made the case that using intuition is an essential element of thinking mathematically, even though the myth of mathematics is logical, deductive, and objective. Public perception is that intuition and creativity belong in art, music, and poetry and are not valued in mathematics, which is a realm of pure, absolute, cognitive thought. Think for a moment about the gender implications of this myth:

> There is a whole network of associations typically identified with mathematics: rational, objective, a focus on the mind. But this same set of traits is also traditionally identified with men. Moreover, the counterparts of these traits—intuitive, subjective, a focus on the body—are typically identified with women. Though women may reject these cultural associations, they are nonetheless subject to them . . . One example of this is intuition. We are accustomed to hearing phrases such as "women's intuition." Yet there is no evidence that women mathematicians are any more intuitive or less logical than their male counterparts. And as we have seen, both intuition and logic are critical in doing mathematics. (Henrion 1997, 261)

Despite widespread myths and junk science about left- and right-brained thinkers, we are *all* both intuitive and rational. Despite the tropes about feminine intuition, women are designed for logical reasoning. Despite the pervasive socialization that teaches boys to ignore their feelings, men are perfectly capable of visceral insight. What powerful changes we could bring to our kids and society-at-large if we taught all our students to be their complete selves and use all their faculties—creative, logical, intuitive, rational, emotional, cognitive—when doing mathematics!

Therefore, expect your boys to be intuitive. Expect your girls to be logical. Let all kids know that mathematicians are both creative and rational. Teach them that one of the most enticing aspects of this discipline is that we get to use every square inch of ourselves.

11

MATHEMATICIANS PROVE

A proof should be an epiphany from the gods, not a coded message from the Pentagon.

—Paul Lockhart, *A Mathematician's Lament*

What Is Proof?

Proof has multiple meanings to mathematicians, and those meanings have evolved over time. The most formal usages emphasize objective, airtight, written arguments in which each step follows logically from the one before it, yielding deductive certainty. While modern mathematicians certainly strive for flawless arguments, many have pushed back against traditional, formal definitions, arguing they are reductive and do not convey the essence, experience, or reality of what mathematicians do. For example, Ian Stewart wrote:

> A proof, they tell us, is a finite sequence of logical deductions that begins with either axioms or previously proved results and leads to a conclusion, known as a *theorem* . . . This definition of "proof" is all very well, but it is rather like defining a symphony as "a sequence of notes of varying pitch and duration, beginning with the first note and ending with the last." Something is missing. Moreover, hardly anybody ever writes a proof the way the logic books describe. (2006, 89)

After wondering about a richer, fuller description, Stewart decided on this one:

> A proof is a story. It is a story told by mathematicians to mathematicians, expressed in their common language . . . If a proof is a story, then a memorable proof must tell a ripping yarn . . . When I can really feel the power of a mathematical storyline, something happens in my mind that I can never forget. (2006, 89–94)

Oxford mathematician Marcus du Sautoy explained proofs using a different analogy, but with a similarly enticing description of the audience's experience:

> A successful proof is like a set of signposts that allow all subsequent mathematicians to make the same journey. Readers of the proof will experience the same exciting realization as its author that this path allows them to reach the distant peak. Very often a proof will not seek to dot every *i* and cross every *t*, just as a story does not present every detail of a character's life. It is a description of the journey and not necessarily the re-enactment of every step. The arguments that mathematicians provide as proofs are designed to create a rush in the mind of the reader. (2015)

"A *rush* in the mind of the reader!" What a lovely way to describe a moment of insight! What a wonderful goal for a writer!

Mathematician Paul Lockhart takes rushes one step further:

> A proof, that is, a mathematical argument, is a work of fiction, a poem. Its goal is to *satisfy*. A beautiful proof should explain, and it should explain clearly, deeply, and elegantly. A well-written, well-crafted argument should feel like a splash of cool water, and be a beacon of light—it should refresh the spirit and illuminate the mind. And it should be *charming*. (2009, 68)

Proofs, it turns out, are far more interesting than dry, step-by-step verifications, although mathematicians certainly verify by proving. They also use proofs to convince, explain, justify, illuminate, systematize, check, discover, communicate, argue, teach, and explore (e.g., CadwalladerOlsker 2011; de Villiers 1990; Hanna 1989, 2000; Harel and Sowder 2007; Hersh 1993, 1997; Strogatz 2012; Stylianides 2007). There are both subtle and substantive differences among these meanings of proof, and scholars have been discussing them for decades. There is broad consensus, however, that "convince" and "explain" are the most important functions of proof for students and teachers in educational settings, so let's look at those meanings more closely.

To Prove Is to Convince Colleagues That a Claim Is True

When a mathematician submits his work to the critical eyes of his colleagues, it is being tested or "proved." With few exceptions, mathematicians have only one way to test or "prove" their work—invite everybody who is interested to have a shot at it.
—Reuben Hersh, "Proving Is Convincing and Explaining"

Mathematicians verify the truth of a plausible mathematical statement through convincing arguments. First, they must convince themselves, so they analyze their own work with as much skepticism and criticism as they can muster. After they have doubted their own reasoning and emerged fairly sure they are right, they try to convince other mathematicians. The mathematical community accepts important proofs after knowledgeable peers have scrutinized them and been convinced.

To Prove Is to Explain Why a Claim Is True

It is not enough to believe that something works, that it is a good way to proceed, or even that it is true. We need to know why it's true. Otherwise, we don't know anything at all.
—Ian Stewart, *Letters to a Young Mathematician*

Through the process of proving, mathematicians build new knowledge for themselves and their peers. Mathematicians use visual images, gestures, analogies, logic, symbols, equations, and written text to explain their ideas. The most valued proofs—the "ripping yarns" that "create a rush in the mind" or "feel like a splash of cool water"—are those that illuminate an aspect of mathematics such that readers gain new insight and intuition.

How shall we define proof for use in school settings, then? My friend and colleague Avery Pickford uses this elegant definition of proving for his middle school students: "convincing your skeptical peers that a mathematical statement is true" (2013). I would keep his definition, but add one more element to emphasize *explain* as much as *convince*:

Proving is convincing your skeptical peers that a mathematical statement is true in a way that helps them understand why.

We have two major reasons to teach proving: (1) it's what mathematicians do, and (2) it's an educational tool to build deep understanding. So how do we teach students to convince, to explain, and to promote new understanding in their peers and themselves? How do we teach students to create powerful arguments that justify their mathematical statements? How do we teach students to try to understand why their claims are true and communicate that thinking to the rest of their mathematical community?

The short answer is we need to focus on *exploring why* in all aspects of our math teaching and learning. We need to press students to consider why strategies work, why patterns hold, why statements are true (Kazemi and Stipek 2001). We shouldn't be satisfied with procedural explanations, and neither should our students. In this chapter, we'll look at a classroom structure that encourages students to be skeptical and demand justifications. We will then turn our attention to student thinking: What are the types of arguments and justifications students tend to make in response to the question *Why?* What types of arguments and justifications do mathematicians use? Can we close the gap between them?

A Structure for Exploring Why: Convince Yourself, Convince a Friend, Convince a Skeptic

Mason, Burton, and Stacey developed a beautiful, three-stage process for creating arguments compelling enough to convince and explain, which they call *Convince Yourself, Convince a Friend, Convince a Skeptic:*

> The first step is to convince yourself. Unfortunately that is all too easy! The second step is to convince a friend or a colleague. This forces you to articulate and externalize what may seem obvious to you, so that the friend is provided with convincing reasons for why what you say is true . . . Examples are, of course, not enough by themselves. They may convince your friend that your statements are plausible, but you must justify every step of your argument . . . The third step is to attempt to convince someone who doubts or questions every statement you make. I like to add force by using the word "enemy." Learning to play the role of enemy to yourself is an extremely important skill, if only because other suitable enemies may be hard to find! (2010, 87–88)

I love this structure and find it to be an incredibly useful mental framework. That said, I've noticed it's hard to implement in the classroom for one big reason: students aren't sufficiently skeptical. They're too easily convinced.

We need to make it clear to students that standards for *mathematical* arguments are much more rigorous than standards for arguments about whose turn it is to take out the trash. The difference is not because math teachers are "picky": it's because our goal in a mathematical argument is different than our goal in an argument with brothers or sisters. When we argue about chores or politics or who started it, we're trying to get the other person to agree with us. When we argue for a mathematical claim, we're trying to establish the truth (Balacheff 1991).

Similarly, in everyday life, we rarely seek a complete understanding of why something works; it's usually sufficient to know just enough to work it. I don't need to understand the details of a catalytic converter to drive myself to work, and I don't need to specify the chemical reactions in the sauté pan in order to make a delicious dinner. In mathematics, however, we have the means and desire to figure out why something works with complete certainty. We can know truth.

Therefore, our peers, colleagues, and partners in producing knowledge, understanding why, and establishing truth have a different role than our counterparts in everyday arguments. We need skeptical, thinking collaborators to help us find the strengths and flaws in our arguments. We need people who will keep acting skeptical even if they are secretly convinced. Someone who rolls over easily—who is swayed by confident presentations and big vocabulary words—is not a useful sounding board in mathematics. As teachers, we must stress the importance of effective, pointed critiques; model productive, skeptical, focused listening and questioning; and encourage our students to become critical friends to one another.

At first, students may find this kind of interaction uncomfortable. Many students like to be agreeable above all else, and girls especially have been socialized to be "nice" and suppress their natural tendency to argue. With practice, however, students can become increasingly comfortable finding holes in mathematical thinking, whether it's someone else's thinking or their own. As we establish the norms of our mathematics classrooms, it's essential we teach students how to disagree respectfully. Critiquing an argument is not the same as criticizing a person, and we must make the difference clear. These sentence frames are especially useful for refutations, critiques, and constructive criticism:

"I respectfully disagree with _____ because _____."

"I don't think _____ is true because _____."

"I found a gap in this argument. _____ doesn't follow logically from _____."

"I found a counterexample to _____'s claim."

"I can prove _____'s claim is not true because _____."

"I'm not convinced by _____'s argument because _____."

"Alternatively, _____."

"Another possibility is _____."

"I think this is true sometimes but not always because _____."

"I think the language in this step needs to be tightened because _____."

"Can you clarify _____ part of your argument? I find it confusing because _____."

"Can you be more precise about _____? I'm not sure what _____ means."

The teacher's role in cultivating skepticism and critiquing arguments is an essential and tricky one. On the one hand, we must model skepticism. Students will learn how to convince a skeptic by convincing us, and how to play a skeptic by watching us, provided we are sufficiently skeptical. We can show students how to find holes in thinking and point them out in respectful terms. On the other hand, if we're the house skeptic, students won't have any incentive to serve as active, skeptical peers. They'll just wait to hear what we say instead, and students will learn to analyze our reactions instead of analyzing the mathematical arguments (Pickford 2013).

There's no pat answer I can give that resolves this tension. Teaching is hard. My general advice:

- Model respectful skepticism early and often.
- Encourage students to take on the role of skeptical peers, and when they do, clam up.
- Make sure to press against arguments that are both true and false so students won't look to you for answers, cues, and hints.
- Practice your poker face and keep it on when students are arguing. In other words, listen to all students with genuine and obvious interest without revealing what you think is "right."
- Give students opportunities to reflect on skeptical exchanges: What question would have helped us find the flaws in this argument early on? How can we remember to ask questions like that?
- Teach students to try to defeat claims, not just confirm them. Ask, "How can we break it?" It's human nature to look for evidence that confirms our hypotheses rather than disproves them. This is called confirmation bias, and mathematicians must train themselves to overcome it. For example, Jennifer Clerkin Muhammad told her students, "Go back tonight and look at it after you've been doing other things so your mind is a little fresher. Rethink through it. See if you still agree with yourself. Remember that it's hard to find mistakes when you assume that you're right. So go back into it assuming something went wrong."
- Use and teach language like "Prove it" or "Convince me" rather than "right" or "wrong" (Petti 2009).
- If students are convinced a false claim is true, it's true, at least for a bit. Write it on the board, post it on the wall, and let it stand. Then think about what problems you can give students so they will find the flaw in their claim for themselves.
- Above all else, maintain your focus on developing young mathematicians who listen to and refine their internal truth detectors. Encourage them to be skeptical and allow them to remain in doubt until they are genuinely convinced. Do not apply pressure to concede, even if you'd like to move on. When you give students the time and respect to decide what's convincing for themselves, you are making a tremendous investment in our young people.

What Counts as Proof?

So what should we find convincing? Every academic discipline has its own version of how to defend claims, with criteria for what constitutes support and evidence. What's considered credible and convincing in mathematics? How does that compare to what counts as sufficient support in other academic disciplines and everyday life? Equally important, what types of arguments are students likely to make? What have we learned by listening to students as they reason about math? What convinces them, and how does that change over time? How can we honor their thinking while encouraging their standards for proof to become increasingly mathematical, sophisticated, and rigorous?

In this section, we'll look at different types of reasoning you're likely to hear. Throughout, we'll consider instructional strategies that help students seek out increasingly compelling and mathematical justifications and refutations. This discussion has its origins in Harel and Sowder's seminal study of "proof schemes" (Harel and Sowder 1998; Sowder and Harel 1998) and was further informed by descriptions of what some of these proof schemes look like with younger students in Lannin, Ellis, and Elliot (2011); Russell, Schifter, and Bastable (2011); and Carpenter, Franke, and Levi (2003).

External Proof Schemes: Appeals to Outside Authorities

Older students will believe a claim is true because, "That's what it says in the textbook." When evaluating a claim, they'll say, "It looks right," if it's formatted and presented in the formal way their teachers value. Students of all ages will assert a claim is true because, "_____ said so." And students are easily swayed by the opinion of the class. If the majority thinks a statement is true, most kids will go along with the crowd. While we're all more likely to accept things asserted by those we respect, it's important that we teach students that "My fourth-grade teacher told us that last year" or "That's what it said online" or "Jamal said so, and he's good at math" do not count as mathematical proof.

Each time students appeal to outside authorities, especially us, to find out whether an answer is right or a claim is true, we have an opportunity to teach students to seek a different, higher standard. As Magdalene Lampert described: "Instead of looking to me to judge whether their 'answers were right,' I wanted students to look to themselves and to their conversations with one another, and learn how to shape these interactions into 'proofs' of their assertions" (2001, 79). Yes. Exactly. A few examples of teacher language to try:

Linus: Is this right?

Debbie Nichols: I can't tell you that. You have to tell me that.

❀   ❀   ❀

Maggie: If it crosses the negative y-axis, do we write $-b$ or just b?

Shawn Towle: (With a smile.) I don't know. Give it a try.

❀   ❀   ❀

Jen Clerkin Muhammad: Is eight a prime number?

Students: No!

Jen: Are you sure?

Students: Yes!

Jen: (Wrinkled her nose and made a skeptical face.) Are you sure?

Students: Mix of yeses and nos.

Jen: Wait. Now some students aren't so sure now that I'm saying it that way. Who is really confident one way or the other?

Shawn Towle: We have heard from both sides and have a good dispute going here. I want you to consider each other's point of view. Think about it overnight. And then we'll talk some more and we'll see if they have changed their mind, or if maybe you have changed your mind. But we change our minds in mathematics based on proof and good reasoning, not the popular vote.

During my classroom observations, I've seen many exchanges like these ones. These teachers are intentionally casting off the role of validator, verifier, arbiter of correctness, answerer-in-chief. Instead, they redirect questioning students to much better, more lasting authorities:

1. The mathematics
2. Their inner sense-making processes
3. Each other

This work is essential. "As long as students rely on the teacher to decide on the validity of a mathematical outcome of their activity, the word 'proof' will not make sense for them" (Balacheff 1991, 179).

Empirical Thinking and Inductive Reasoning

Empirical evidence is support we gather through experience, experiment, and observation, rather than through theory or logic. Empiricism plays an important role in science, data collection, statistics, applied mathematics, and most important, everyday life. When a baby drops food out of her high chair—over and over—and watches it fall to the floor—over and over—she isn't just driving her parents bonkers and feeding the family dog. She's also gathering evidence about how objects behave on Earth. Eventually, she'll accumulate enough empirical evidence to expect that objects will fall downward toward Earth, everywhere and always. This leap—assuming what we've observed in specific cases is generally true—is called inductive reasoning.

Examples of Inductive Reasoning

- Every time I drop something, it falls to the ground. Therefore, dropped things will always fall to the ground.

- Every time I visit England, it is raining. Therefore, it is always raining in England.
- 11 × 2 = 22. 11 × 6 = 66. 11 × 9 = 99. Anything multiplied by 11 will be that number, repeated twice.
- All the birds I've seen have feathers and fly. Therefore, birds have feathers and fly.

In science and everyday life, the more we have confirmatory evidence gathered from a wide range of trials, the more convincing the argument. But here is where mathematics and science part ways. Reams of experimental evidence carry a lot of weight in science. If scientists reproduce results in a variety of controlled experiments, they become increasingly convinced their hypotheses are probably true. Over time and with a preponderance of evidence, scientists come to accept these hypotheses and call them theories and laws. But scientists are clear: there is no such thing as proof based on empirical evidence or induction. Evidence can be consistent with a hypothesis, but no amount of evidence can guarantee that it is true. Furthermore, there always lurks the possibility of finding counterevidence—some unforeseen example—that proves a hypothesis false.

In mathematics, however, guarantees *do* exist. Mathematicians can use another type of thinking called deductive reasoning, in which they begin with general, universally accepted truths and then deduce specific, logical consequences of those rules.

Examples of Deductive Reasoning

- All squares are rectangles. All rectangles have four sides. Therefore, all squares have four sides.
- All mammals have hair. Mice are mammals. Therefore, mice have hair.
- If it is a beagle, it is a dog. It is not a dog, so it is not a beagle.

With logical, deductive reasoning, a mathematician *can prove something true for all time with certainty*, at least insofar as she convinces her skeptical peers of her argument. This tantalizing prospect has all kinds of implications for how mathematicians think. They often use inductive reasoning to figure out what they think is true and then ironclad deductive reasoning to try to prove it. When they're reasoning inductively, they gather empirical evidence as part of making sense, but they recognize the limitations of this process as well as its strengths. Empirical evidence and inductive reasoning can make mathematicians pretty sure they're on the right track. It can get them close enough to reduce some doubts. It can help them figure out what happens with different sets. It can even disprove. But no amount of empirical data can prove a mathematical statement to be true with certainty. For proof, they need deductive reasoning.

Proof is a challenging idea for students and teachers alike because it flies in the face of our everyday experience (Fischbein 1982). We are convinced the sun will come up tomorrow because it has come up in the past. Most of us haven't learned how to think about the gap between what's good enough for daily use and what's possible with the tools of mathematics. It's exciting to consider that we could learn a new way to think that holds such power! Armed with empirical evidence, inductive reasoning, and deductive reasoning, we can think empirically when it's productive, appreciate its limitations when appropriate, and go beyond it when we are ready. Empiricism is square one for students, so let's dig into it more.

Empirical Thinking: Measurement and Computation

Let's think about the *True or False* question:

$$7 \times 6 = 7 \times 5 + 7$$

An empirical answer might be: "7 times 6 is 42, so that's what's on the left side. On the right side, 7 times 5 is 35, and 35 plus 7 is 42. Both sides are 42, so I know it's true."

Similarly, consider this justification for "The interior angles of a triangle sum to 180 degrees":

"I drew a triangle and measured the angles, and they were 71°, 19°, and 90°. 71 + 19 + 90 = 180. So the angles sum to 180°."

If students answer the question "How do you know?" by saying, "I measured," or "I solved it," they are thinking empirically, using only what they observe. Obviously, computation and measurement are essential skills, and we need students to be proficient at them. And to be clear, nothing these students have said is wrong. The downside to their approach, however, is they are thinking only about the specific problem that's right in front of them. By thinking in this narrow way, they are missing out on the opportunity to build deeper understanding about multiplication, or triangles, or whatever concepts, relationships, and logic underlie their current problem.

Helpful questions to nudge students toward more general thinking:

"Can you figure it out without calculating?"

"What about for *any* triangle? Is there a way we can figure it out for *any* case?"

"What if you didn't have a protractor (ruler, calculator, etc.)?"

Empirical Thinking—Perception

Students tend to be convinced by what a problem *looks like*. Sometimes, our visual sense of a problem can lead to intuitive, correct solutions, and we shouldn't waste time proving things we can clearly see are true. Perception can be misleading, however, and students need to back up dubious statements with better evidence than perception. For example, Mary Beth Schmitt's eighth-grade students were overly focused on orientation when discussing whether the rectangles in Figure 11.1 were similar. To disrupt their perception-based thinking, Mary Beth simply rotated the chart, as shown in Figure 11.2. Now students had to look at the properties of the rectangles, think about scale factor, and reason.

With younger students, it's important to address issues around perception when counting. For example, students will say there are more cubes in a line if the cubes are spaced farther apart. The size of the objects can also make it look like there are more or less than there are. For elementary and middle students, geometry, fractions, and concepts such as area, perimeter, surface area, and volume provide excellent opportunities to address the difference between perception and mathematical reasoning. For example, many students initially think fractions have to have the same shape in order to be equal pieces. Most students would divide a rectangle into fourths in the ways shown in Figure 11.3. But what happens when a student splits the rectangle as shown in Figure 11.4? The pieces no longer look the same, but are they congruent? Can you prove it without measuring? Do the lines in Figure 11.5 help?

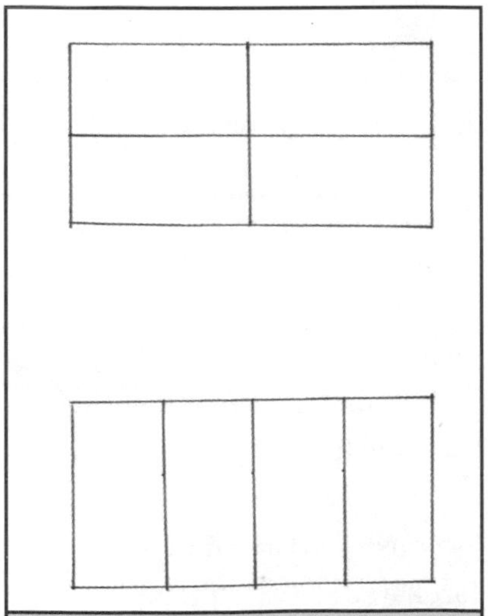

To push her students beyond arguments based on perception, Jennifer Clerkin Muhammad regularly

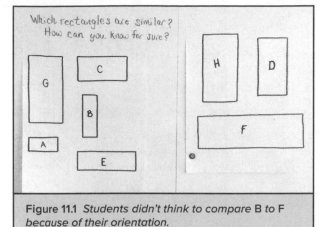

Figure 11.1 *Students didn't think to compare B to F because of their orientation.*

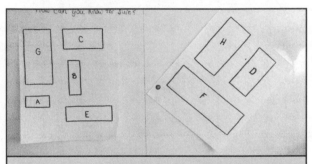

Figure 11.2 *Once Mary Beth rotated the paper, students stopped focusing on orientation and started thinking about similar rectangles.*

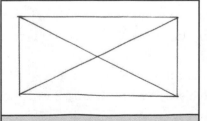

Figure 11.3 *Students typically draw fourths so each piece is the same shape.*

Figure 11.4 *Are the pieces fourths? Are they the same size?*

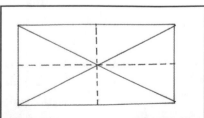

Figure 11.5 *Do the dotted lines change your perception?*

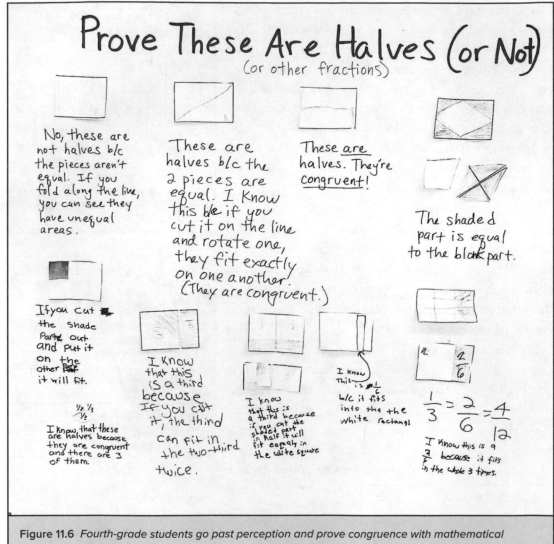

Figure 11.6 *Fourth-grade students go past perception and prove congruence with mathematical arguments.*

asks students to reason this way. Consider students' reasoning about halves in Figure 11.6. Jen's students aren't content with "looks like." They are transforming these shapes by folding, cutting, and rotating pieces around as they construct arguments based on symmetry, number, and area. This is a wonderful example of how younger students can justify based on reasoning rather than perception. We'll look at this type of thinking further when we discuss representation-based proofs.

When you hear your students saying "It looks like . . ." to answer "How do you know?" questions, it's time to disrupt their thinking. Sowder and Harel argued that optical illusions such as the classic question "Which line segment is longer, $\overline{AB}$ or $\overline{CD}$?" in Figure 11.7 can be helpful when teaching students the limits of perception (1998).

Generalizing Empirical Evidence: Arguing from Cases and Examples

When students are encouraged to prove whether a general claim will always work, they usually start by trying a few cases. For example, to test the claim *order doesn't matter when adding*, students will start picking pairs of numbers and adding them in different orders. If they're new to mathematical reasoning, students will probably try random pairs of numbers: 1 + 3 and 3 + 1; 7 + 8 and 8 + 7; 100 + 59 and 59 + 100. If they've thought about sets of numbers, they might choose their cases more systematically and thoughtfully: "Does it matter if the numbers are even or odd? What about fractions? Does it work for decimals? I should try zero. Does it work for negative numbers?" Either way, most of the time, if students find several examples that work, they think their claim is always true (Stylianides 2009).

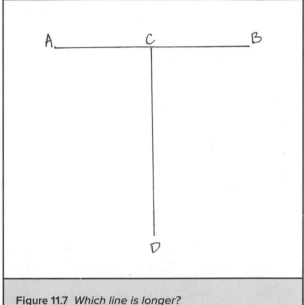

Figure 11.7 *Which line is longer?*

The problem is, proving a claim holds for three, five, or ten examples is not the same thing as a mathematical proof, which must hold for all cases within the sets specified by the constraints. What if a case exists that disproves our claim, and we didn't happen to try it? A single counterexample is enough to prove the claim doesn't work and needs to be revised or discarded. How can we know there isn't a counterexample lurking out there somewhere?

If this question comes from us, students will likely think their teachers are being pedantic and hypothetical and fail to see that proof fills a real need. A better scenario is for us to create conditions in which students will realize the limitations of inductive, case-based arguments for themselves. In other words, we need to throw students into doubt so they feel a genuine need for proof (Meyer 2015; Stylianides 2009).

The optimal way for students to feel doubt and the need for proof is for them to get tangled up in problems that will create this situation naturally. "Problems that invite an examples-based approach, with the resulting patterns breaking down, can alert students to the dangers of such reasoning . . . Students who place full faith in examples should at least find out that examples can betray them and that patterns found in several examples are not completely trustworthy" (Sowder and Harel 1998, 672–674). For example, consider this lovely problem my daughter, Maya, asked me: "What will be the next palindrome year?"

She'd read about the question in Marilyn Burns's *The I Hate Mathematics! Book* (1975). This book is one of the Brown Paper School Book series, all of which are filled with juicy problems. Maya reads them frequently and sprang this problem on me when we were driving. I turned on my phone and started recording.

Tracy: What's a palindrome year?

Maya: When the numbers are the same backwards and forward, like 1991.

Tracy: Oh, I see. What do you think?

Maya: Well, 2002 was a palindrome year. So I'm trying to figure out what the next one will be.

We drove along in silence for a while, each of us thinking about this question. Take a minute to think about this problem yourself. When is the next palindrome year? And how do you know that it will be the next one, and that there are none in between now and then?

After a little while, Maya piped up from the back seat.

Maya: 2112 will be a palindrome year.

I thought she'd probably figured out a good mathematical pattern, but I wasn't sure. I needed to know more, so I asked a question.

Tracy: Are there any others between 2002 and 2112? Is 2112 the *next* one?

Maya: I'm not sure.

She fell into quiet thinking again, and several minutes passed by. I was curious what was happening back there, so I asked.

Tracy: Can you tell me how you're thinking about it?

Maya: Well, different numbers pop into my head, and then I try them and see. Like I just thought of 2034, but that doesn't work, because backwards, it's 4302.

Whoa! When she first suggested 2112, I thought she was thinking more generally and perhaps she was. But now, she was trying cases in an unorganized way. As a teacher, I was excited about this situation. There are *a lot* of palindrome years and even more nonpalindrome years, so I thought the problem might help Maya see the limits of *proof by exhaustion*. Trying every possible case is a drag, and mathematicians both young and old try to avoid this brute-force method. I wanted to stay out of her way and let the problem do the heavy lifting, so I kept quiet.

After a few minutes, she said: "If it starts with 2, it has to end with 2. So, two-zero-zero-two. Two-one-one-two. Two-two-two-two! That's funny. Two-three-three-two. Oh! I see the pattern!"

Because she was talking about the symmetry of the first and last number, I thought she had seen the pattern would follow an ABBA structure. Once again, I assumed something that wasn't true. She went on: "The pattern is that it adds 110 each time."

Think back to our discussion of visual patterns and growing patterns. Maya was thinking additively, recursively, right? Because of the nature of this particular problem, though, I had a beautiful opportunity to let her see her pattern breaks.

Tracy: Does it? Will that pattern always be true?

Maya: I think so. Because 2222 plus 110 is 2332. And 2332 plus 110 is 2442. It just changes the hundreds and the tens place, but by the same amount. That's why it works.

Tracy: Keep going.

Maya: 2552, 2662, 2772, 2882. See? It works every time!

Tracy: Keep going.

Maya: I don't know why. OK. I was at 2882, right? So 2992 . . . (long pause.) Uh oh.

This was the moment I'd been waiting for! After a while, she continued:

Maya: Um, so 2992 plus 110 is 3102. I think the pattern changes when you get to the next thousand. So it works all the way through the two-thousands, and then you have to start again at 3003. But then it works again. So 3003 plus 110 is 3113. And then 3223, 3443, and you'd have threes at the beginning and at the end. And then you keep going until you get to the next thousand.

Tracy: How do you feel about that? Are you satisfied by a pattern that changes every thousand?

Maya: Well, kind of yes and kind of no.

I was hoping to appeal to Maya's natural sense of aesthetics. The idea of a pattern that keeps resetting itself at certain numbers is ugly. Maya has great mathematical taste, which I thought would motivate her to find a more elegant solution. Several hours later, at home, she pulled out some paper and created the chart shown in Figure 11.8, setting it up like a choral count.

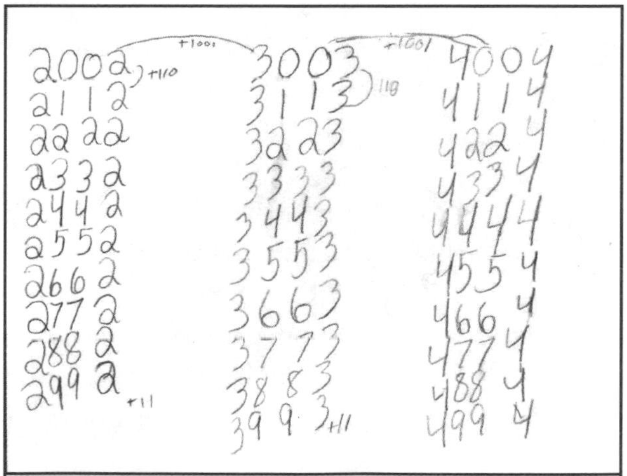

We sat with it together for a long time, looking at patterns. It turned out to be very interesting. The differences between palindromes were either 11, 110, or 1001, which makes lots of sense if you think about it for a bit.

Figure **11.8** *Maya's count of palindrome years. What do you notice?*

After playing around some, it seemed like she was ready to think about these numbers in a new, nonadditive way, so I opened up the conversation.

Tracy: What other patterns do you see?

Maya: The middle numbers are the same in each one. Like 00, 11, 22, 33, 44, 55, 66, 77, 88, 99. And the first and last numbers are the same in each one, like 2, 2 or 3, 3 or 4, 4.

Tracy: When we were first thinking about the problem, you were thinking about a date like 2034, and you were trying to figure out if that was going to work. What do you think now?

Maya: Well, it's a different kind of palindrome.

Tracy: What do you mean?

Maya: Well, it's not a palindrome now, but if you mirrored it, it would be. It would have eight digits though.

Tracy: Can you show me what you mean?

She wrote 20344302. Aha! *If you mirrored it* was the beginning of something delightful. Now she was looking at structure, symmetry, and form of numbers, not just individual cases at random. She had begun using analytical reasoning. We'll pick this story back up again in just a bit.

Thinking about students, empirical thinking, cases, and examples more broadly, I want to emphasize that working with cases is still extremely valuable. Maya used cases to create, extend, test, and disprove her theories. Students need to test a range of examples and revise conjectures based on the results of their testing throughout the process of generalizing, conjecturing, and justifying. Trying a variety of cases can help the broader patterns and generalizations emerge. As Lannin, Ellis, and Elliot argued, "We can use specific examples as entry points into general reasoning" (2011, 7). Choosing a random case to serve as a generic example can help us get a feel for the mathematical terrain around that example. We need that grounded insight and intuition while we're searching for proof. Therefore, encourage your students to try cases and test their conjectures out. Play! Just make sure to clarify that a list of cases is just that: a list of cases. It can never prove.

Empirical Thinking: The Powerful Role of Counterexamples

Mathematicians train themselves to look for counterexamples—cases that will disprove claims. This type of thinking takes discipline because we tend to look for evidence that confirms our theories, rather than breaks them. Therefore, mathematicians have to build the mental habit of hunting for counterexamples. They also have to develop the emotional courage to look for ways to be wrong. The payoff for this rigor and skepticism is enormous:

> The mathematician is interested in extreme cases—in this respect he is like the industrial experimenter who breaks lightbulbs, tears shirts, and bounces cars on ruts. How widely does a reasoning apply, he wants to know, and what happens when it doesn't? What happens when you weaken one of the assumptions, or under what conditions can you strengthen one of the conclusions? It is the perpetual asking of such questions that makes for broader understanding, better technique, and greater elasticity for future problems. (Halmos 1968, 380)

Children need to be taught to value the illumination and insight that comes from proving themselves wrong and figuring out *exactly when and why a claim fails*. Useful questions include:

- Is there a set of numbers for which this *won't* work?
- Now that we understand the pattern, let's try to break it. Can anyone find a counterexample?
- Hmm. So far we have confirming evidence. Let's doubt the claim. How can we try to prove it wrong?
- Let's try our hardest to disprove this claim. Can we find an example to prove it's *not* true?

When students come up with counterexamples, make sure to value rather than bemoan them. "Well done, Alexis, you found the hole in our argument!" and "Excellent work, Lavonne, you tried to find a case that broke the pattern!" will encourage students to *try to be wrong in order to understand the mathematics more deeply*. This habit is essential because we learn as much from our failed conjectures and claims as we do from our proven ones, and we can always learn from the process of looking for flaws, even if we don't find any:

> Distrusting your conjectures is not just lip-service to fallibility. There may indeed be an error, but it may also be that by trying to pick holes in a conjecture you begin to see **why** it cannot be beaten and so must be true. It is curious that belief and disbelief carry quite different perspectives. Looking for why something is true may yield nothing, when seeking to disprove it may reveal what is going on. (Mason, Barton, and Stacey 2010, 90)

Children might come to you afraid to be wrong, but they do arrive as masters of finding counterexamples and flaws in arguments, and we can build on their experience. For example, my family frequently drives by the billboard shown in Figure 11.9. It's posted over a factory. One morning, Maya asked, "Why does it say, 'Made here. Enjoyed *everywhere*'? It's not true! We don't eat their food in our house, so that automatically means it is *not* enjoyed *everywhere*." What a great use of a counterexample! I was thrilled. Then again, as a parent, I find it less charming when my kids turn their technical, literal, litigious argumentativeness on me:

Figure 11.9 *"We don't eat their food in our house, so that automatically means it is* not *enjoyed everywhere."*

Tracy: I'm on the phone. Please go downstairs.

(Maya left and returned one minute later.)

Tracy: What are you doing? I told you to go downstairs!

Maya: I did go downstairs. I touched my toe to the floor and then I came back. You said *go* downstairs; you didn't say *stay* downstairs!

Me: Oh, for crying out loud, you knew what I meant!

Next time I feel exasperated, I'll try to remember that my kids are sharpening their use of examples, counterexamples, and argument. Maybe.

Analytical, Logical, and Deductive Reasoning: Knocking on Proof's Door

We've dabbled a bit in the strengths and limits of empirical and inductive reasoning and how identifying those limits can help us feel the need for logical or deductive reasoning. It's certainly beyond the scope of this book to get into different types of proofs for older students, but I hope to introduce some ideas for using prooflike reasoning with younger students. With a foundation in reasoning and arguments, our students will be ready to learn different proof strategies later.

As discussed above, it's human nature to prefer inductive or empirical thinking (creating general arguments from specific, observable examples), to deductive thinking (constructing general arguments based on logical extensions of known truths). Deductive reasoning feels foreign and uncomfortable for everyone at first:

> *The concept of a formal proof is completely outside the main stream of behavior.* A formal proof offers an absolute guarantee to a mathematical statement. Even a single practical check is superfluous. This way of thinking, knowing and proving, basically contradicts the practical adaptive way of knowing which is permanently in search of additional confirmation . . . A new completely non-natural "basis of belief" is necessary . . . a new intuitive approach must be elaborated which will enable the pupil not only to understand a formal proof but also *to believe* (fully, sympathetically, intuitively). (Fischbein 1982, 17)

For our students to understand, intuit, and accept proof, they need lots of experience making general arguments supported by mathematical reasoning. So what does that look like with younger kids?

Figure 11.10, taken from Stylianides (2009, 9), gives us helpful guidance about what can count as proof in school. He showed three ways students could make a general argument that satisfactorily proves "the sum of any two odd numbers is an even number" for the set of whole numbers. When I look at this chart through an elementary lens, I see proofs using "words, symbols, numbers, and pictures." That's familiar language to me and to students. We've long had students explain their mathematical thinking using these methods. The next logical step is for us to extend their use into general arguments.

In practice, younger students will use a mixture of words, symbols, numbers, pictures, models, and gestures when they explain why a mathematical statement is true. This blending of techniques and mixing of methods should be encouraged. In other words, please don't take this chart to mean that we should teach lessons on *proof using everyday language,* as compared to *proof using algebra* or *proof using pictures.* While there's certainly value in discussing

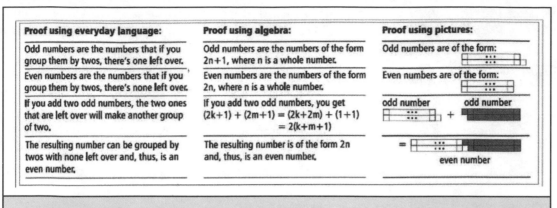

Figure 11.10 *Stylianides (2009) showed three possible proofs (on the set of whole numbers) for "odd + odd = even."*

the different techniques and reflecting on their strengths, there is no need to formalize or standardize proof with school-aged kids. Proving is a *process*, and it would be a shame to focus too much on *products*: "prematurely dealing with formal proof can lead students only to attempts at memorization and to confusion about the purpose of proof" (Battista and Clements 1995, 50).

The students' arguments *are* the proofs, as they are. Students will naturally reach for different methods and representations such as drawings, manipulatives, story contexts, number lines, written explanations, spoken arguments, and actions in an effort to "convince their skeptical peers of the truth of a mathematical statement in a way that helps them understand why." Our job is to facilitate students' thinking as they learn how to explain and convince. We can ask probing questions, introduce students to different representations, model skepticism, expose gaps in reasoning, emphasize the words *why* and *because*, and press students to structure arguments where each step follows logically from the one before it. We can seek several explanations and encourage students to make connections among them (Beckmann 2002). Mathematician Ian Stewart argued, "The essence of a proof is not its 'grammar,' but its *meaning*" (2006, 90). As we equip students with techniques for proving, we must keep that focus on *meaning* paramount.

Words as a Way to Prove

Although I find Stylianides's framework helpful, I have to admit he and I disagree on our definition of *everyday language*. Most kids I've met don't use *thus* in their everyday language! Conjectures often start more like this one about area and dimensions from one of Kristin Gray's fifth graders: "The smaller the first number like the 1 in 1 × 14, however small it is the area will be smaller than a first number that is higher."

Kristin is a skilled kid-listener, and she was able to recognize the deep mathematical thinking inside all those jumbled-up words. As discussed in Chapter 10, through a lot of discussion, clarifying questions, individual written work in student journals, and shared

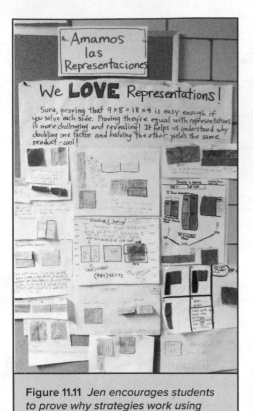

Figure 11.11 *Jen encourages students to prove why strategies work using representation-based proofs.*

writing, Kristin helps students learn how to craft their claims and arguments into something someone else can follow. In this particular lesson, Kristin consolidated students' claims into a list and then started the next day by giving students time to ask each other clarifying questions in pairs. Students synthesized their work, writing new claims using more mathematical language. For example, one student wrote the concise claim: "The sum of the dimensions of a rectangle is half the total perimeter." Now that he has an organized claim, he can develop the rest of his written argument. You can see more examples in Kristin's blog: mathmindsblog.wordpress.com/2015/01/14/developing-claims-through-rectangles-with-equal-perimeters/.

This type of guidance is essential work. Students trying to make an argument will find precise vocabulary, common language, and clear sentences a relief because they can more easily communicate their thinking to their mathematical community. We don't need templates or formulas to teach young kids how to author paragraph proofs. We do need to listen closely to students, supply vocabulary as it's needed, and help students figure out how to write their statements and reasons in clear, logically sequenced language.

Representations as a Way to Prove

Jennifer Clerkin Muhammad says, "I want to make it clear why you need a representation. It's for two big reasons. One, it helps you think. Two, it helps you prove your thinking to other people." More often than not, mathematicians young and old will need some form of picture, representation, or model to make their argument. Jen's fourth-grade students used a mixture of representations, language, cutting, folding, and arranging to prove doubling and halving in Figures 11.11 and 11.12.

In this case, Jen's students used 4 × 18 = 8 × 9 as a *generic example* of doubling and halving. When students are thinking generally but grounding their work in a generic example, they'll say things like:

- "It doesn't matter what numbers you choose."

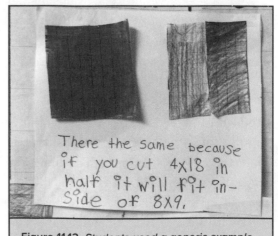

Figure 11.12 *Students used a generic example to prove this strategy works.*

- "I just picked these numbers. But for any numbers ..."
- "This array could be as long as you want. It doesn't matter. You can still cut it in half and the pieces will fit."
- "It doesn't matter how many cubes I have here. I just grabbed some to show how it works for any number."
- "You could pick any part of the number line. It will be the same."
- "Pretend I was adding *any* two odd numbers."

In other words, students will construct a representation based on a specific example, but then describe how that image can represent many examples. This is just the mental process we're after: abstract, logical thinking. Russell, Schifter, and Bastable give lots more detail about representation-based proofs in *Connecting Arithmetic to Algebra: Strategies for Building Algebraic Thinking in the Elementary Grades* (2011). I can't recommend it highly enough.

Symbolic Notation as a Way to Prove

Depending on the mathematics involved, words and representations might be unwieldy and difficult. Young students may develop the same need for variables that led mathematicians to invent them: variables are concise, elegant ways to describe a general case. When this need arises, it's perfectly appropriate to introduce variables to students of any age. Like precise language, variables will come as a relief to students struggling to describe their arguments.

For example, I thought variables might help Maya think about her palindrome year question (pages 291–294). Once Maya started "mirroring" the numbers and looking at their symmetric structure, I thought variables would help her think more generally:

Tracy: Mathematicians have a tool that makes conversations like this easier, and I want to introduce you to this tool that mathematicians use all the time. I'm going to write down the name here. (Wrote *variable*.) Do you know this word at all?

Maya: I've heard it once or twice, but I don't know what it means.

Tracy: OK. So *vary* means change. So a variable is—

Maya: Changeable?

Tracy: Yes. A variable is where we can put a letter in instead of a number and say it could—

Maya: Oh, like x could represent 26 or something.

Tracy: That's not a variable. If x is 26, it's not a variable; it's not changing. That might be a solution or that might be an answer, but it's not a variable. It's only a variable if we say something like, *a* could be *any odd number*.

Maya: Oh ...

Tracy: So we can pick a group of numbers and say, "We're going to think about *these numbers*. We don't care *which number*, but we want to understand the structure of *all* of them, so we're going to say that *a* could be any fraction between 1 and 2. Or *a* could be any number between 1,000 and 2,000. Or we could say *a* could be *any* number: whole number, fraction, irrational number, any number we want. We get to decide."

Maya: So like *q* could be any number from 10 to 20.

Tracy: Right. So when you looked at the middle numbers of these palindrome years and you said, "0, 1, 2, 3, 4, 5, 6, 7, 8, 9," I thought it would be useful for you to use variables. So, I'm going to write a palindrome year like this: *abba*. And I'm going to set the rules. It's our problem, so we get to set the rules. So I am going to let *a* be any digit from 1 through 9. And I'm going to let *b* be any digit from 0 through 9. We can talk about why I picked different ones in a minute. So, if that's the case, then I'm going to say that any number in the form *abba* is going to be a palindrome year. So, for example, let's let *a* equal 3. Let's pick that one. And let's let *b* equal—pick another number.

Maya: Eight.

Tracy: So if *a* is 3 and *b* is 8, what year is it?

Maya: It would be three thousand, eight hundred, eighty-three.

Tracy: Exactly. So when you were trying to figure out the palindrome years, what I noticed listening to you is that you were struggling a little until you started saying "two-one-one-two." When you were thinking "two thousand," it was hard. When you started thinking about them as digits, you were able to do it. You started saying "two-one-one-two, two-two-two-two, two-three-three-two." So you were thinking about these first pairs. You were picking your first pair, your *ab*. Once you had your *ab*, all you had to do was—

Maya: Switch it around!

Tracy: Switch it around, so it was *ba*.

Maya: So it was like a mirror image. So here's a mirror . . . (She drew *32* and *23* reflected in a mirror.)

Tracy: So here's a question. Can we have an odd number of digits in a palindrome?

I asked a new question here for a couple of reasons. I wanted to tug at Maya's notions of symmetry, and I wanted to give her an opportunity to practice with variables. Throughout, as she decided how to construct her numbers, I told her, "You're setting the rules. You're the author of this problem." After she'd created a few examples, I pulled our conversation back to using variables to generalize:

Tracy: So, could you look at any number in this form, *acwpopwca,* and do it the same way, where we say, "Let *a* be any digit from 1 through 9, let *c* be any digit from 0 through 9, let *w* be any digit from 0 through 9, let *p* be any digit from 0 through 9, let *o* be any digit from 0 through 9," and if they're written in this form, can you *promise* that the person would get a palindrome?

Maya: I don't think you could promise, because even if you checked 98 percent of the numbers in the world, there would still be 2 percent that you didn't check. If people all over the world checked 98 percent of the numbers, there could be twenty-eight of them or something in that 2 percent, and you were just unlucky that you didn't get any of them. So people would need to check 100 percent of the numbers to know exactly and that would take a *long* time, and I don't think people are going to do that.

I love this excerpt so much. In a couple of sentences, Maya shows how learners' thinking is complex, in flux, and developing. She's using empirical thinking to look at the limits of empirical thinking. She's becoming skeptical. She acknowledges the possibility of a counterexample, sees that checking every case is practically difficult, but doesn't yet have the new "basis of belief" to trust the general argument. Beautiful. I was in no hurry to resolve any of that. Developing these ideas takes time. I did want to help her develop a feel for variables, though, and I thought a more familiar problem might help me there. I wrote:

$$a + 0 = a$$

Tracy: This is *a* plus zero equals *a*. We don't usually use *o* as a variable because it looks too much like a zero. So this is a zero. And I'm going to say that you can let *a* equal *any number*. No limits. It can be any number you can think of in the world. Fraction, decimal, percent, whole number, negative number, any number. And I'm going to say that $a + 0 = a$. And I *can't* check them all. But I'm *sure* of it.

Maya: What does that last *a* mean?

Tracy: Oh, that's important. This *a* is the same as the first *a*. Within each problem, you can pick any number you like for *a*, and *a* equals that number wherever you find it in the problem. So pick a number.

Maya: 998.

Tracy: 998 + 0 = 998. Pick another number.

Maya: 543.

Tracy: 543 + 0 = 543.

Maya: OK, so 16 + 0 = 16.

Tracy: Now, I can't try every case. So how can I prove this to you?

Looking at Maya, I could see she wasn't convinced. She was my skeptical peer, and I had not persuaded her of the truth of my mathematical statement. So I did what we want our students to do: I tried another approach. I used another method. I went and got a jar of toothpicks from the kitchen and tried a representation-based proof.

Tracy: I'm going to try to prove this to you using a representation. I'm going to put some toothpicks down. Four toothpicks. And then I'm going to add zero toothpicks. Four

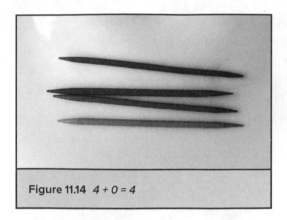

Figure 11.14 *4 + 0 = 4*

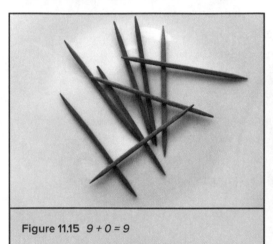

Figure 11.15 *9 + 0 = 9*

Figure 11.16 a + 0 = a

toothpicks plus zero toothpicks . . . (I gestured adding zero toothpicks; see Figure 11.14.)

Maya: Is four toothpicks.

Tracy: (Adding more toothpicks, so we now had Figure 11.15.) OK. That many toothpicks. That many toothpicks plus zero—

Maya: You have nine toothpicks.

Tracy: OK. Nine toothpicks plus zero is . . .

Maya: Nine toothpicks.

Tracy: (Dumping out the jar of toothpicks in a pile, shown in Figure 11.16.) All these toothpicks plus zero equals . . .

Maya: All these toothpicks. The same number.

Tracy: Do we need to count them to know?

Maya: No.

Tracy: Why?

Maya: Because we know that if you add zero to anything, it's still the same number. Even if it's the largest number on Earth, it's still the same number.

Tracy: We can write what you just said in this general form, $a + 0 = a$.

Maya: Oh!

Now she was starting to get a feel for this new symbolic language. We returned to the palindrome years and played around for quite a bit. We discussed why I'd set *a* as any digit from 1 through 9 but included 0 in all the rest. We tried several examples with different numbers of digits. I made sure to ask her about cases where *a* happened to equal *b*, such as 2,222, 3,333, and 4,444. And then I asked her a question I hoped would help her see the usefulness of thinking this way.

Tracy: When we were in the car and you were saying, "Numbers are popping into my head and I'm trying each one," I thought "Holy cow, there are *thousands* of numbers."

Maya: (Laughing.) Yeah. I probably only checked five or six.

Tracy: And then you started looking for a pattern because there are too many numbers to try them.

Maya: Yeah.

Tracy: For me, if I know it's going to be a four-digit number and it has to be a palindrome, it has to be in this form *abba*.

So then I can think about all the possibilities. You were at 2002 and you were wondering what the next one was, and you figured out it was going to be 2112. I asked if there were any in between and you said, "I don't know." Looking at this rule of *abba*, I wonder if that helps us with that question? Could there be any between 2002 and 2112?

(Long think time.)

Maya: No.

Tracy: Why?

Maya: Because the two would stay the same. And then for these two numbers (pointing to *bb*), there's no number between zero and one unless you go to fractions, and we're not going to fractions because we don't do that when we count years. So there's no number in between zero and one, so there are no palindromes in between 2002 and 2112.

I'm convinced and I understand why! Maya crafted a lovely general argument using words, built on understanding she developed through use of symbolic notation and a representation-based proof.

Tracy: Now you know that for sure because you've thought about it in this more general way rather than just saying, "Let me check 2097. Let me check 2018. Let me check 2051."

Maya: (Cracking up.) That's exhausting!

Tracy: (Laughing.) Exactly! And that strategy is even called *proof by exhaustion* because you're trying to exhaust all the cases!

I hope this example illustrates the organic process of generalizing and proving. Maya and I moved in and out of general and specific language. We used representations, words, symbols, actions, and numbers. There was nothing linear about our conversation, although there was an overall progression from original question through exploration, empirical thinking, and logical reasoning. As we wandered around that terrain, Maya began to see the limits of inductive reasoning—of generalizing from cases. The usefulness of variables and the benefits of general thinking appeared on the horizon for her. This is the kind of messy, fruitful investigation that captures students' thinking while introducing them to true mathematics.

The Tracks of Thinking and Formal Proofs

A distinction should also be made between proving and proof. Proving is a process, which may include arguments and trains of thought which ultimately lead nowhere. The proof, which is the result of this process, will not include such dead ends.
> —Todd CadwalladerOlsker, "What Do We Mean by Mathematical Proof?"

In formal proofs, mathematicians erase the traces of their real process. They gloss over the role of intuition; they leave out their dead ends, guesses, and mistakes. In keeping with the conventions of formal mathematics, they create a sense of inevitability about their proofs, as if they really started with the first axiom and proceeded in a linear, deductive, objective fashion until they arrived at their theorem. In reality, we know mathematicians often start with a guess about a possible theorem—a conjecture—and then engage in a disordered, human, flawed, interesting process of trying to figure out whether and why it's true. At the very end of that process, if they're successful, they pare out their process and create a product—a mathematical proof.

> Mathematics—this may surprise you or shock you some—is never deductive in its creation. The mathematician at work makes vague guesses, visualizes broad generalizations, and jumps to unwarranted conclusions. He arranges and rearranges his ideas, and he becomes convinced of their truth long before he can write down a logical proof. The conviction is not likely to come early—it usually comes after many attempts, many failures, many discouragements, many false starts. It often happens that months of work result in the proof that the method of attack they were based on cannot possibly work, and the process of guessing, visualizing, and conclusion-jumping begins again. A reformulation is needed—and this too may surprise you—more experimental work is needed . . . I mean thought-experiments . . . he often tries out a particular numerical case, and he hopes that he will gain thereby an insight that pure definition-juggling has not yielded. The deductive stage, writing the result down, and writing down its rigorous proof are relatively trivial once the real insight arrives; it is more like draftsman's work, not the architect's. (Halmos 1968, 380)

In educational settings, we have a different purpose than mathematicians, and we should not feel the need to be bound by the same conventions. Students who go on to become mathematicians will have plenty of time to learn "the draftsman's work" of how to write impersonal proofs if they have the "architect's" solid foundation in mathematical reasoning. In school, we need to focus on building that foundation for all our students by making mathematical thinking visible so we can examine, discuss, and learn from it. Rather than erase the tracks of human thought, we need to zoom in on them, to emphasize and highlight them. Our goal is not to have students produce formal proofs; our goal is to nurture and develop skeptical, logical, rigorous, insightful mathematical thinkers. This is not a process to rush.

Reason and *Prove* Are Verbs

Learning mathematics also means getting better at the action verbs that are often used to describe the thinking habits mathematicians routinely employ: looking for patterns, conjecturing, justifying, analyzing, wondering, and so on. Everyone can learn these ways of thinking if given the opportunity.

—Cathy Humphreys,
Connecting Mathematical Ideas

We have a strong tendency in schools to value nouns: things, papers, projects, products that we can collect, grade, and send home in a folder. We emphasize long lists of nouns—*fractions, decimals, ratios, divisibility rules, exponents, quadratics*—when we think about math as a collection of content knowledge. If we step back and think about the process of reasoning mathematically and proving, however, verbs carry the meaning.

notice	relate	disprove
identify	articulate	argue
explore	claim	support
apply	test	refute
play	ascertain	justify
conjecture	revise	verify
wonder	refine	explain
guess	question	convince
generalize	check	persuade
connect	doubt	prove

When we teach mathematical reasoning, we have a wonderful opportunity to teach students that math is much more than a collection of stuff to learn. Making mathematics is an action. It's a verb.

Assessing verbs is an entirely different process than assessing nouns. To assess how our students do mathematics, we need to be there with a class list and a clipboard, watching, listening, and recording snippets of dialogue and students' strategies. If you have it, technology can be quite helpful here. There are a number of apps that students can use to record their representations with actions and narrated arguments so teachers can hear from everyone. After listening carefully, teachers can decide where to go next with students' claims. Or teachers might save some students' work, put it to the side during other mathematical investigations, and then bring it back out later. "What do we think about this claim now?" is a powerful question. Sometimes, students have thought of a complete argument and will consider the claim proven. Other times, students might have learned new mathematics that throw the claim into doubt, and they'll want to revise or refute.

The action of proving is fluid in an educational setting: partially formed, incomplete, and incorrect claims play a vital role. As we explore different aspects of mathematics, students need opportunities to engage in these verbs—to notice, generalize, test, claim, revise, explain, prove, and so on. In one unit, we might spend quite a bit of time sniffing out and playing with patterns and leave it at that. In another unit, we might focus on nailing down claims so students learn how to communicate with their peers. In a third unit, we might find ripe opportunities for students to make and revise representation-based arguments, so we develop that skill. We can teach an element here and an element there, strengthening students' mathematical reasoning throughout. Occasionally, there might be an opportunity for young students to journey all the way from noticing a pattern to proving the mathematics that underlie it. That's exciting, but it's not the expectation, and formal proofs are certainly not the goal.

Math Celebration: An Idea for Sharing the Process with Families

If the heart of what we're doing in math class involves process and actions, how do we communicate what we're doing so families understand? It's difficult to convey the spirit and culture of an active, dynamic mathematics class to families through newsletters, written work, and one back-to-school night a year. It's not so easy to put verbs in a homework folder.

Some teachers use video, screencasts, and blogs to show families their kids in action. A series of Family Math Nights can be an effective way to give families a sense of our math classrooms. And, as the following example shows, we can invite families into our classes during the school day.

Mark Pettyjohn, fourth grade, Athens, Ohio

Mark Pettyjohn, a fourth-grade teacher in Athens, Ohio, visited his teaching partner's Writing Celebration. He watched students share their writing work with families and was inspired to figure out a math corollary. With the counsel of his teaching partner, Susan Matters, and his math coach, Nina Sudnick, Mark and his students planned a special event that would include families in the doing and learning of math. They invited parents, siblings, friends, relatives, and a class of kindergarten buddies so all students would connect with the audience (medium.com/@m_pettyjohn/math-celebration-6a12dc563f88).

Because Mark's students spend so much time noticing patterns, conjecturing, crafting claims, and justifying their thinking, quite a bit of the celebration involved mathematical reasoning. For example, Mark's class had worked hard on this student-created claim:

> *If you multiply a number by a factor less than 1, then the product will be less than the first factor.*

They had tested it using *Always, Sometimes, Never*; tried it with every type of number they knew; and even extended it by asking if it would "work opposite with division." At the Math Celebration, students were excited to share how their thinking developed with their families.

Students had tremendous ownership over their claims and arguments, and parents were deeply impressed with the caliber of thinking they saw.

Mark and his students engaged families in authentic mathematical sense making through *Number Talks*, writing and testing claims, and sharing models that explain why procedures work. Given that *proving* is a verb—and that we shouldn't get wrapped up in creating proofs as products—Math Celebration is a creative way to communicate with families and give them insight into the powerful thinking and working their children are doing in school each day. Mark said the most common response he heard from family members was, "I wish I had learned math this way!"

Proof and Equity

Proving is a social process, situated in social contexts. Mathematicians use their reasoning and knowledge to prove mathematical ideas to one another at conferences, on chalkboards, over coffee, and in journals. We've seen that young mathematicians can also use their reasoning and knowledge to prove mathematical ideas to one another, with our guidance. Because people do all of this proving in social contexts, we can be sure that they—*we*—are influenced by fads, assumptions, and preferences. Pólya said, "Mathematics in the making resembles any other human knowledge in the making" (1954b, vi). The human act of proving is complex, and so it shall be in our classrooms!

But there's a downside, too. For far too long, we have been biased toward a certain type of mathematical thinking, couched a certain way, from a certain type of student. We hold deeply ingrained stereotypes about ideal math students: typically, white and Asian boys, "logical" thinkers, fast memorizers, confident calculators. How many students are we pushing out of mathematics because of these stereotypes? Far too many, as evidenced by the persistent underrepresentation of African American, Latino/a, and Native American students; of emergent bilingual students; and of girls of all ethnicities in advanced math classes, mathematics majors, and STEM professions.

We have an especially long and ugly history of discriminating against African American children in math class; of "having low expectations for African American children"; of allowing "the identity of African American children to be publicly disparaged"; of seeing African American children as "in need of being rescued from their Blackness, on one hand, or worthy of being cast off as expendable from society, on the other"; of assuming "the intellectual inferiority of African American children as the starting point" (Martin 2009, 13, 17). As part of this systemic racism, we've set values on what kind of knowledge and thinking "counts" in math class, and what doesn't:

> Very little consideration is given to exploring patterns in the ways that low-income and African American children *do* engage in abstraction, representation, and elaboration . . . It is clear that school mathematics knowledge is privileged over children's out-of-school knowledge and that low-income children's out-of-school math knowl-

edge is valued even less. Given such a restrictive view of mathematics knowledge, it is very likely that mathematical competencies linked to the cultural contexts and everyday life experiences of African American children are under-assessed and under-valued because these competencies do not fall within dominant views of what counts as mathematics knowledge. (Martin 2009, 16–17)

I recently experienced an example of the inequity Martin described. I blogged about exploring number lines and intervals with a mostly white group of students from a small, country town. A teacher from a major city wrote that she couldn't expect her mostly black and Latino/a students to have prior experience with number lines and intervals because they didn't grow up with the fence lines, measuring tools, and thermometers that my more rural students had. Meanwhile, I'd been secretly wishing my small-town students had the background knowledge of her urban students! Regular experience with blocks laid out in a grid, sequentially numbered streets, apartment buildings with odd and even door numbers, elevators, subways, and bus lines gives students tremendous knowledge and intuition for number lines, intervals, area, perimeter, distance, coordinate grids, and negative numbers. As Martin argued, however, we often don't recognize or value this lived experience as a mathematical advantage.

I find myself wondering, what if the racial makeup of our two classes had been reversed? If I'd been working in a predominately black rural school, would I have recognized my students' strengths and lived experiences, or been blind to them? If she had been teaching in a white urban neighborhood, would she have assumed her students' prior knowledge was deficient? I sent her Dr. Martin's provocative quote, and she found the questioning of her assumptions as powerful as I did. We both realized we have work to do.

All teachers need to reflect on what we value and where authority lies in the math classroom. Think back to our definition of proving: "Convincing skeptical peers of the truth of a mathematical statement in a way that helps them understand why." The authority for deciding what's convincing and what's true lies within each mathematical community, and within each mathematician. If we want all students to engage with mathematics and be empowered by mathematics, then all students must feel that authority reside within themselves and be honored as judges of the truth. Because our students bring a wide variety of cultural and life experiences, they will bring a valuable multiplicity of perspectives, ideas, questions, and evidence.

Over six years of taking data, David Henderson, a white professor from Cornell University, found that 31 percent of his novice students taught him new mathematics, and those students were disproportionately women, students of color, or both (1996). The *Why?* questions these students asked were different from Henderson's *Why?* questions. The arguments they found convincing were different from the arguments Henderson had been taught to value. The proofs these students shared were creative and novel to Henderson, who had been schooled only in formal, Eurocentric, textbook mathematics. As he learned to listen carefully and respectfully to his students' unfamiliar lines of thought, he noticed his students risked and learned more, and that their innovative approaches to mathematics were often beautiful and exciting.

By expanding his notions of what mathematical thinking "counts," Henderson increased his students' access to meaningful mathematics. Most of us need to undergo a similar process because most of us have internalized a Eurocentric view of math teaching, learning, and history, even though it's not historically accurate:

> A culturally responsive mathematics education needs to acknowledge the pan-human origins and presence of mathematics in all its diverse forms. The myth, long foisted by traditional texts and philosophies, that mathematics is a European creation, needs to be refuted . . . Essential elements of mathematics derive from non-European cultures, like zero (India and Central/South America), place value (Middle East and India), geometry (North Africa as well as Greece), and algebra (Islamic civilization in North Africa/Spain and Middle East). Incorporating elements of the history of mathematics into school mathematics enables all students . . . to feel a pride in the contributions of their ancestors as well as an ownership of mathematics. (Ernest 2009, 56)

It is the human right of every student to have a culturally responsive, high-quality math education and to graduate with all the opportunities a foundation in STEM provides. All students are entitled access to intellectually stimulating mathematics. The converse is true as well: mathematics needs the perspectives, questions, and ideas from a culturally, ethnically, linguistically diverse group of thinkers, because the only way to crack unsolved problems is with new thinking.

In other words, don't look for a singular, established answer key for proofs. Just ask yourself, your colleagues, and, most important, your students: *Is it convincing? Does it explain? Are you satisfied?*

12

MATHEMATICIANS WORK TOGETHER AND ALONE

*I*n 1948, a twenty-nine-year-old mathematician named Julia Robinson completed her PhD and began working on the great unsolved problem known as Hilbert's Tenth. Robinson wrestled with it on and off for decades, both on her own and in collaboration with others. She made an important conjecture and other significant contributions but still the answer eluded her:

> When it came time for me to blow out the candles on my cake, I always wished, year after year, that the Tenth Problem would be solved—not that I would solve it, but just that it would be solved. I felt that I couldn't bear to die without knowing the answer. (Reid 1996, 69)

Twenty-two years later, in 1970, Julia got her birthday wish. She learned that a twenty-two-year-old Russian mathematician, Yuri Matijasevich, had a proof that built upon her work. She wrote him, "If you really are 22, I am especially pleased to think that when I first made the conjecture you were a baby and I just had to wait for you to grow up!" (Reid 1996, 73).

Matijasevich wrote back to Robinson, emphasizing the essential role her work had played, including how the "fresh and wonderful idea" she'd published in 1969 had paved the way for his final breakthrough (Reid 1996, 104). So began a fruitful collaboration that lasted until Robinson's death in 1985.

To call Robinson and Matijasevich an unlikely duo is a gross understatement: they were an American woman and a Russian man working together during the height of the Cold War. They had political, gender, generational, and language barriers between them and had to collaborate using slow, unreliable, overseas mail checked by Soviet censors. Nevertheless, they had each found a collaborator who cared about this problem with the same level of passion, and they overcame every obstacle to work together.

Matijasevich and Robinson listened to each other's ideas and pushed back on each other's thinking. They critiqued each other's work, finding both small errors and big mistakes in reasoning. They built on each other's thinking to forge new solutions together. And they rooted each other on, always. As Robinson wrote Matijasevich in one of her many letters, "I am very pleased that working together (thousands of miles apart) we are obviously making more progress than either one of us could alone" (Reid 1996, 116).

Working Together and Alone in Mathematics and Working Together and Alone in Math Class

Mathematicians are not told to work in isolation or to work together. They are never instructed to get in groups with specified roles and assigned problems; yet, like Robinson and Matijasevich, mathematicians engage in both independent and collaborative work.

When mathematicians interact, their exchanges range from supportive to competitive, from structured to casual, from playing devil's advocate to serving as closest confidant and cheerleader, depending on the nature of the relationship and the desired outcome of the interaction. For example, a mathematician who wants to think aloud about a fledgling idea with someone is looking for a more nurturing interaction than a mathematician who needs a skeptical colleague to read his or her proof line by line, hunting for gaps and flaws. A mathematician who has some developing ideas might engage a sparring partner to help him or her ascertain the truth, while a group of mathematicians who share a common purpose might blend their ideas and work collectively. In other words, as mathematicians' goals and needs vary, so do their interactions.

If a major part of doing mathematics involves interacting with other mathematicians, then a major part of teaching students mathematics must be to teach students how, why, and whether to interact with one another mathematically. Students need to learn how to *ask for what they need from each other* and to *be what they need for each other*. In other words, we need to teach students how to be good colleagues, in math and in life.

Let me be clear at the outset: it's important we honor individual thinking and working time. It's not reasonable to expect students to collaborate at every moment, and that's not how mathematicians work. We all need time to immerse fully in our own thoughts without distraction, and it's vital we teach students how to say, "I need to work on this problem on my own for a while before I can talk about it." At the same time, collaboration is essential to doing mathematics, and we must teach students how to ask a peer, "Can we think through number four together?" or hear a peer who asks, "Are you ready to discuss this question, because I'm out of ideas."

In this chapter, we'll explore how to teach four of the most essential, pedagogically productive kinds of mathematical interactions. Throughout, I hope you'll think about how to support your students' social and emotional growth, as well as their interpersonal and communication skills, all in the context of rich mathematics learning. This isn't "group work" for the sake of group work. If we want students to make more progress together than they can alone—like Robinson and Matijasevich—we need to give them good, mathematical reasons to work together, and we need to teach them how.

Productive Mathematical Interactions
- Thinking Partnerships: Making sense together by talking through ideas and problems
- Cross-Pollination: Listening to and building on other people's ideas
- Math Disputes: Discovering the truth by debating each other
- Peer Feedback: Sharpening each other's arguments through constructive critiques

Thinking Partnerships: Making Sense Together by Talking Through Ideas and Problems

Students should spend most of their math time gathered around rich problems, flowing naturally among thoughtful dialogue, periods of quiet thinking and individual work, and bursts of active chatter as they make sense of mathematics. I call this type of collaboration a thinking partnership, and its tone is encouraging, dynamic, and productive (Figure 12.1).

Consider this account from mathematician Paul Halmos:

Figure 12.1 *Thinking partnerships: making sense together by talking through ideas and problems*

> The best seminar I ever belonged to consisted of Allen Shields and me. We met one afternoon a week for about two hours. We did not prepare for the meetings and we certainly did not lecture at each other. We were interested in similar things, we got along well, and each of us liked to explain his thoughts and found the other a sympathetic and intelligent listener. We would exchange the elementary puzzles we heard during the week, the crazy questions we were asked in class, the half-baked problems that popped into our heads, the vague ideas for solving last week's problems that occurred to us, the illuminating problems we heard at other seminars—we would shout excitedly, or stare together at the blackboard in bewildered silence—and,

whatever we did we both learned a lot from each other during the year the seminar lasted, and we both enjoyed it. (1985, 73)

Halmos described several key traits of thinking partners: the side-by-sideness of their collaboration; the absence of competition and judgment; the casual, low-pressure interactions; their eagerness to serve as sounding boards for each other; the safe space for risk taking; the emphasis on process; and, always, the free-flowing mutual respect.

Thinking partnerships are the kind of interaction we seek when we're grappling with an engaging question. In fact, we *only* seek thinking partnerships when we're working on a rich problem or question. If we can solve it on our own without much trouble, we don't need the power of other people's thinking, and it's easier to finish the problem solo than to tangle with group dynamics. If the problem is complex and thought provoking and we feel we'd genuinely benefit from putting multiple heads together, then we look for a productive collaboration.

The inherent nature of putting our heads together—of stumbling, talking, listening, and sharing while we're still in the midst of the problem—has important ramifications for classroom discourse. We must teach and remember that thinking partnerships do not sound like coherent, organized summaries after the fact. When students serve as thinking partners, they jump around and stop short. They share their confusion, questions, wonderings, and kernels of ideas in real time. Their language isn't finished, polished, or ready for presentation. It is raw. And therein lies the power of the collaboration.

This rawness presents a challenge as well. If students (and teachers) have internalized the idea that we should wait to talk until we are sure we have the right answer in math class, it will take a little work to get thinking partners off the ground. As Magdalene Lampert taught us, "It requires courage and modesty to expose one's exploratory thinking to others in the hopes that by engaging in the exchange of ideas in classroom discourse, one might end up with better ideas in the end" (1990, 54). You'll need to make it clear that, in this class and in mathematics, partially formed, incomplete, and incorrect ideas are essential and valued.

For example, if a student tosses an idea out to her group and it helps get the ball rolling, be sure to highlight how great that was. Be explicit. "I noticed table five didn't seem sure how to get started, but then Loren said, 'Well, one thought I had was . . .' Jack was able to add on to Loren's idea, and then heads were nodding and Diasia started writing on their group whiteboard. They were off. In the end, Loren found a flaw in her original idea, but that's part of doing mathematics. We zigzag around and change our minds in response to new ideas. That's exactly the sort of collaboration I want to see when we're being thinking partners. Great job."

Jennifer Clerkin Muhammad, fourth grade

"I can't wait to get confused!"

I've seen thinking partnerships every single time I've visited Jen's classroom. On this particular day, Jen's students were working on multistep story problems, which are always challenging for fourth graders. There's a lot to keep track of. At the beginning of the lesson, she asked students, "What are some good habits to have when you are solving multistep problems?" Her students made comments like these:

- "It's too much to try to keep track if you don't write down while you're working. So I think that sometimes, you should stop and write down what you know so far."
- "Estimate. Then you know if your answer makes sense."
- "Label as you go. Otherwise, it gets too confusing. You don't remember what number represents what."
- "Put your answer back into the equation and see if it makes sense."
- "When you're reading the problem and it seems long and confusing, just stop and read it one piece at a time."
- "It helps to stop and wonder if my answer makes sense. I try to think about that a bunch of times while solving."

At the end of the discussion, Jen asked, "So who is excited for multistep problems?" Her class actually cheered, and then students asked if they were working together or on their own. Jen knew that all students would benefit from some quiet thinking time to get them invested and engaged with the problems. She also knew that most students would benefit from working in thinking partnerships on problems this complex. She said, "Let's start off for the first five or six minutes alone to get ourselves going, and then, those of us who want to find a partner can. I'll move to the green rug, and students who want a little support can join me over there. But let's all take five or six minutes to think on our own first."

After students worked silently on their own, most of them chose to put their heads together for the rest of the session. I heard these comments in conversation as I walked around:

- "Dude, that doesn't make sense!"
- "Wait. Why did I subtract?"
- "Let's read it again."
- "Where should we start?"

I placed a small recording device near a group of three girls so I could hear how they communicated when no teachers were nearby, and then I moved away. They were working on this problem:

> *Before her birthday, Christy had some books. She got 25 more books for her birthday. She put her books into piles with 35 books in a pile and made 10 piles of books. How many books did Christy have before her birthday?*

Make sure to solve this problem on your own before reading the transcript, especially because what follows is nonlinear, raw, active student thinking.

Noemi: (Begins by reading the problem aloud, slowly.) Before her birthday, Christy had some books. She got 25 more books for her birthday. (Pause.) She got 25 *more* books for her birthday. OK. She put her books into piles with 35 books in a pile and made 10 piles of books. How many books did Christy have before her birthday?

Mihaela: She got 25 books for her birthday and she put books into piles of 35 books in a pile.

Noemi: In a pile. So there's 35 books in 10 piles. So 35 divided by 10?

Mihaela: No. Multiplying.

Emily: There's 10 piles of books and there's 35 books *in each* pile.

Noemi: Oh, yeah, yeah. So that means . . . she has . . .

Emily: I think I'm starting to get it now.

Mihaela: Um. Wait, so it's 35 times 10 minus 25?

Emily: Maybe we should read it again.

Mihaela: Before her birthday, Christy had some books. She got 25 more books for her birthday. She put her books into piles with 35 books in a pile and made 10 piles of books.

Jen was moving around the room, stopping at different groups. At this point, she came by and asked: "How are you doing, girls?" The students didn't even look up because they were so engrossed in their conversation, which they continued:

Noemi: Wait. I feel like we're reading it wrong.

Emily: I think I get it.

Mihaela: I think it's 10 times 35, which equals 350, *plus* 25.

Noemi: She put 35 books into a pile . . .

Mihaela: Let's read it again.

Jen: (Smiling, before moving on.) You guys are doing an awesome job.

Note that Jen did not stick around to make sure they understood the problem and answered it correctly. She was happy with the thinking these students were doing and had confidence they could make sense together.

Noemi: Before her birthday, Christy had some books. She got 25 more books for her birthday. She put her books into piles with 35 books in a pile and made 10 piles of books.

Mihaela: Oh, so she put it into *a* pile of 35 books, and made 10 piles.

Noemi: Oh, so she made *a* pile of 35.

Emily: And there were 10 piles!

Mihaela: That's what I just said!

Noemi: So she made 10 piles of books. And there were 35 books in a pile. So it's 35 times 10 plus 25. No! Minus 25, because we want to know what she had *before* the 25.

Mihaela: So it's 35 times 10 minus 25 books.

Emily: Yeah.

Noemi: Let's do this.

After reading the problem aloud *four times* and discussing it, the girls each quieted down and worked on their own. All three of them were able to solve the problem successfully. When they were done, they put their heads back together and talked through the next problem. I especially admired their ability to flow back and forth between independent and group work, depending on their needs. Their communication with one another was honest and productive.

Jen invests quite a bit of time in teaching students how to work together and to listen to each other as well as Emily, Noemi, and Mihaela did. She frequently facilitates discussion around social issues that come up when we work in groups:

- What does respectful listening look like?
- What should you do if someone takes over?
- How can you state your needs, for example, "I need a little more time to think before I'll be ready to talk" or "Could you explain that again, please, but go a little slower?"
- What should a group do to make sure everyone in the group understands?
- What should you do if someone in the group isn't pulling his or her weight?
- What can you do if someone is being left out of the conversation? What if you are being left out of the conversation?
- How can we disagree respectfully?

Jen opens these conversations throughout math class. Sometimes she pauses students while they're working to highlight what groups are doing well or to address issues that have come up, and then lets them resume. She often launches group work with a discussion about collaboration or closes a lesson by asking students to reflect on how they worked together. For example, later in this same lesson on multistep problems, Jen's students took up *The Cat Challenge*:

> *There are 7 girls on a bus.*
>
> *Each girl has 7 backpacks.*
>
> *In each backpack there are 7 big cats.*
>
> *For every big cat, there are 7 little cats.*
>
> *Question: How many legs are on the bus?*

This is an extremely difficult problem for fourth graders, and Jen's kids were eager to rise to the occasion. As soon as Jen cut her students loose, Santina turned to her group and said, "Let's start! I can't wait to get confused!"

As they worked, students made great use of their thinking partnerships. For example, I recorded one group having this conversation after about five minutes of focused effort:

Maribel: "There are 7 girls on a bus. Each girl has 7 backpacks. In each backpack there are 7 big cats." So there were 49 backpacks, and each backpack has 7 cats, so that's 49 times 7.

Tania: So estimating, that's pretty close to 50 times 7, which is 350, right?

Janaya: What if we did 50 times 7 and then minus a 7, which is ... 350 minus 7 ... 343.

(Tania and Janaya wrote and thought. Maribel didn't write, but was clearly thinking.)

Maribel: We could do, like we could do 7 times 40 is 280. And 7 times 9 is 63. 280 plus 63 is ...

Janaya: But we rounded to 50 and went back down.

Maribel: You did. It's easier for me to do it this way. So 280 plus 63 is 343. Is that what you found?

Tania: Yeah. We got the same thing two ways.

Janaya: Cool. That was a good way to check.

Maribel: So it equals 343. 343 *what*?

Tania: 343 ...

(Long pause.)

Maribel: Let's reread the problem.

(They each reread the problem, and then thought quietly for about a minute.)

Janaya: Three hundred and forty-three cats. I think it's 343 cats.

Maribel: Oh my god. Each of the cats has 4 legs!

(Everybody laughed.)

Tania: Oh my god. That means 343 divided by 4 to figure out the legs.

Janaya: No, 343 times 4.

Maribel: Should we start over because we forgot we were thinking about legs?

Tania: Yes.

Here's the same group, several minutes later:

Maribel: So 7 big cats. No! 7 times 7 big cats. We have to do 7 times 7 again.

Tania: I'm just so confused. Too many sevens!

Janaya: When we get the answer of how many cats, we just need to multiply by 4 to find the number of legs.

Maribel: But humans have 2 legs!

Janaya: We're not counting the humans.

Maribel: We're not? Why not?

These bits of discourse are truly representative of the conversations happening around the room. Jen and I floated from group to group, jotting notes, listening in, and supporting students, and this is the caliber of conversation we heard from all groups. After twenty-five minutes of intense, active work, Jen stopped the class over howls of protest.

Jen: What do you think I'm going to say about how you did today?

Ethan: I think we did well because we were persevering on a hard problem.

Jen: Good word.

Eduardo: This is so hard, but I like it. I like getting confused!

Several students: Me, too!

Monique: I think we did very good because we were communicating with our partners and saying what we thought.

Jen: There was a lot of communication, and it wasn't about stuff we're not supposed to be talking about, right? In fact, sometimes it got kind of loud in here, but I didn't mind because I would say, like 98 percent of it was math talk, wouldn't you say?

Class: Yeah.

Joseph: You're going to say Joseph did awesome.

(Laughter.)

Jen: That's totally what I was going to say. Why am I going to say that?

Joseph: Because I didn't get frustrated when I didn't know the answer.

Jen: It's normal to get frustrated, but it's what you do when you get frustrated, right? You don't just give up!

Noemi: We were working really well with our partners because we were doing a really good job with each other when we disagreed. We didn't get up and leave. We stayed and talked it through.

Jen: You would sit there and defend yourself and say this is *why* I believe what I believe.

Jake: We've been working on this for like twenty minutes and we've gotten like five different answers, and we disagreed about all of them but we're still going.

Manuel: We've gotten like twelve different answers, and we still don't know which is right!

Class: Us, too!

Eric: We had like 9,576 and 9,814 and we got tons of different answers and my answer of 1,582, well I sort of think it's wrong but I sort of think it's right.

Maribel: Can we *please* keep working?

Jen: One last comment first.

Leon: I tried to hop in with them and try and defend my answer even though it was 37,530 and they said I was wrong, but I tried to defend my answer.

Max: He did defend his answer.

Manuel: You did a good job defending your answer.

Jen: I saw that you guys were getting a little frustrated over here, and I think what happened was—if you are still trying to solve something and you're not sure about what you think yet and someone says, "Here's what I think!" you might not be *ready* to hear yet because you're still trying to think about what *you* think. I get like that. If someone tries to talk to me about something I haven't thought about yet, I get like, "No! Don't talk to me!" (Jen covered her ears as a gesture. Lots of kids nodded at this.)

Jen is teaching students that empathy, communication, reading social cues, disagreement, building shared norms, and collaboration are part of doing mathematics. They are not add-ons or lessons that we only do during morning meeting or as part of an antibullying curriculum. They are not for September only, and they are not indulgences. Socialization into the collaborative culture of mathematics is, in fact, part of learning mathematics. It's what mathematicians do and is as important content as fractions.

The Educational Payoff, Especially for Marginalized Students

In the 1970s and 1980s, Robert Fullilove and Uri Treisman conducted a seminal study of college students at University of California, Berkeley, that showed another reason why we need to teach students to work together mathematically. The researchers were seeking explanations for why, in calculus class at Berkeley, "African American students were disproportionately represented among the ranks of the weak students" and "Chinese Americans were disproportionately represented among the strong students" (Fullilove and Treisman 1990, 465). In the decade before the study, 60 percent of black students who took calculus at Berkeley received grades of D or F. Why?

Their study quickly revealed that the researchers' stereotypes and assumptions about black students at Berkeley were unfounded. Black students were highly motivated, had been adequately prepared for college math, and had strong family support for higher education. Income levels didn't correlate either. So what was really causing the gap?

Fullilove and Treisman studied all the variables they could generate and found the major difference lay in how the two groups studied: the African American students diligently studied as many hours as the professor suggested, but they *studied alone*. The Chinese American students studied independently as well for about the same amount of time but also spent several, additional hours each week *studying together*. In other words, they studied more, and they studied more together:

> In the evenings [the Chinese-American students] would get together. They might
> make a meal together and then sit and eat or go over the homework assignment. They
> would check each others' answers and each others' English . . . They would edit one an-
> other's solutions. A cousin or older brother would come in and test them. They would
> regularly work problems from old exams . . . They had constructed something like a
> truly academic fraternity. (Treisman 1992, 366)

In response to these findings, Fullilove and Treisman formed honors mathematics workshops to teach students how to work together—to make studying mathematics social. They organized students into groups that worked together, twice per week, two hours per session, on "carefully constructed, unusually difficult problems" (Fullilove and Treisman 1990, 468) and encouraged students to discuss their thinking. Students in the math workshop spent about half the time working together, and the other half working independently.

The results were stunning. Over twelve years of study and hundreds of participants, researchers documented that students who worked together in the math workshop "substantially outperformed not only their minority peers, but their White and Asian classmates as well" (Treisman 1990, 369). In other words, students who had been failing in large numbers were now at the top of the class. Students in the workshop were also far more likely to enroll and persist in mathematics-based majors compared to their nonworkshop peers.

I believe it. I took several physics courses in college, and I never would have made it through without my study group. Every Wednesday night, we met at our regular table with our weekly problem set for as long as we needed, anywhere from two to eight hours. We listened to each other. We went down dead ends together and then found our way back. We shared different representations, analogies, connections, and references from our different majors (geology, mathematics, physics, chemistry, and premedicine). If one of us was stumped while the rest had something figured out, we all worked together to help our peer who was stuck. Often, the conversations that were ostensibly to help someone else were what sparked relational thinking and deeper understanding or solidified what had been shaky. We were all the stuck one now and then, and we knew our peers would slow down and address our confusion fully and respectfully. We were generous with each other. My study group happened to include one black woman, two Asian women, two white women, and one Latina woman, and I'm proud to say we all aced physics together.

Creating Physical Space for Thinking Partnerships

I approach this topic with humility, given that I taught thirty fourth-grade students in a tiny portable classroom with carpeted walls. We all have real constraints on the size and layout of our teaching spaces. Nevertheless, it's worth thinking about how we can work within those constraints to provide students workspaces that promote thinking partnerships.

Canadian researcher Peter Liljedahl spent ten years studying how to build what he called "Thinking Classrooms," and students' workspaces were an essential element (2016). He and his team looked at whether it was better for students to stand and write on vertical surfaces or sit and write on horizontal surfaces. They also studied what those surfaces were. Did it make a difference whether students worked on poster board, chart paper taped to the wall, chart paper on desks, blackboards, mounted whiteboards, mini-whiteboards, or individual notebooks?

It turned out that, yes, where students work and on what surfaces made an enormous difference. Liljedahl found that nonpermanent, erasable surfaces like whiteboards trumped permanent surfaces like paper, by a lot. Groups were more eager to start a problem if they were using a whiteboard. They had more discussion, more participation, and more persistence on the whiteboard. Their work was authentically nonlinear because they wrote as they thought on a whiteboard, rather than trying to create a perfect, organized, nice-looking product. They also made their first mathematical notation much more quickly when they worked on a whiteboard: an average of 20.3 seconds on vertical whiteboards compared to 2.4 minutes on vertical paper. That is a stunning difference. Liljedahl says:

> This can be attributed to the non-permanent nature of the whiteboards. With the ease of erasing available to them *students risk more and risk sooner*. The contrast to this is the very permanent nature of a felt pen on flipchart paper. For students working on these surfaces it took a very long time and lots of discussion before they were willing to risk writing anything down. (2016, 370; emphasis added)

Liljedahl also found that, in each case, vertical surfaces are preferable to horizontal surfaces. Students standing and writing on vertical whiteboards, chalkboards, or windows instead of sitting around horizontal whiteboards had markedly better participation, were more engaged, and were much more eager. Liljedahl reflected:

> When students stand around a whiteboard or a window they are all visible. There is nowhere to hide. When students are at their desks, it is easy for them to become anonymous, hidden, and safe—from participating and from contributing. It is not that all students want to be hidden, to not participate, but when the problems get difficult, when the discussions require more thinking, it is easy for a student to pull back in their participation when they are sitting. Standing in a group makes this more difficult. Not only is it immediately visible to the teacher, but it is also clear to the students who is pulling back. To pull back means to step towards the centre of the room, towards the teacher, towards nothing. There is no anonymity in this. (2016, 376)

Furthermore, researchers observed that standing groups working on whiteboards engaged with other standing whiteboard groups, increasing collaboration by another degree. Sitting groups never checked in with other sitting groups and hardly looked at the vertical whiteboards, despite their visibility. Standing groups working on paper rarely interacted with other groups either, probably because there wasn't nearly as much written on paper as there was on whiteboards.

After gathering these results, Liljedahl gave several workshops for teachers in which he taught them how to use vertical, nonpermanent surfaces. Six weeks after the workshops, 98 percent of the 200 elementary, middle, and secondary teachers were still using vertical, nonpermanent surfaces and planned to continue to do so (2016, 374). I can't get over that number. I've never heard of 98 percent of teachers agreeing on anything! Liljedahl described teachers thrilled with the transformational effects of this simple, powerful change in their teaching practice.

When I first read Liljedahl's research, a whole series of narratives and images from the history of mathematics buzzed through my brain. Mathematicians frequently talk about standing around blackboards or whiteboards together, thinking and talking. Remember Halmos's description of his seminar with Shields: "We would shout excitedly, or stare together at the blackboard in bewildered silence" (1985, 73)? This particular kind of collaboration—standing, talking, thinking, and writing—is so inherent to doing mathematics that many math buildings are designed around it. Consider the architecture of the Isaac Newton Institute in Cambridge:

> The building is especially designed to encourage the academics to concentrate on collaboration and brainstorming. There are no dead-end corridors in which to hide and every office faces a central forum. The mathematicians are supposed to spend time in this open area, and are discouraged from keeping their office doors closed. Collaboration while moving around the institute is also encouraged—even the elevator, which travels only three floors, contains a blackboard. In fact, every room in the building has at least one blackboard, including the bathrooms. (Singh 1997, 4)

Now, I won't go so far as to encourage putting whiteboards in school bathrooms, especially not in middle school, but I love the image of vertical boards up everywhere so mathematicians can jot their thinking, even while they're riding the elevator from the first to the third floor. Given that mathematicians work this way, and that educational research has revealed there are tremendous benefits to vertical, nonpermanent surfaces in classroom settings, it seems we have ample reasons to set them up.

How? Many classrooms have limited wall space, so getting enough boards up requires some innovation and pluck. Vis-à-vis markers on the windows are a great option, and kids love using them. Many teachers hang whiteboards on hooks so they can post papers and posters directly on the walls and then hang whiteboards over top during mathematics, thereby increasing the amount of usable wall space. Teachers have hung whiteboards on cabinet, closet, or classroom doors, or the casings of heaters or air conditioners. Teachers have even hung shower curtains from folding classroom walls or found ways to lean large whiteboards up against them. I have listed several teacher's blogs about their use of vertical nonpermanent surfaces on the companion website. With a little poking around, you'll find teachers who face the same logistical challenges you do, and you can learn how they worked around them to defront their classrooms and get affordable whiteboards up around the room.

Grouping

A quick word on grouping, before we leave thinking partnerships and Liljedahl's research. He conducted similarly robust studies about different ways to group students: teachers grouping students strategically, students grouping themselves, teachers grouping students randomly ahead of time, teachers grouping students randomly during class, and so on. He found that there was little difference in effectiveness between student-selected groups and either strategic or random teacher-created groups *if* the teacher composed the groups out of view of the students. The kids, astute as ever, didn't believe random groups were truly random if they didn't see the grouping for themselves. They figured the fix was in, and assumed teachers secretly adjusted their "random" groups to keep friends separated, deal with problem behaviors, and meet other social and pedagogical goals. Let's admit it: they were almost certainly right.

Liljedahl found that when teachers created truly random groups every day—via shuffling cards, drawing names from a hat, organizing by birthdays—publicly, visibly, in front of students, there were profound changes in the effectiveness of group work. After a few weeks, the time it took for students to trust that each day's groups were both *temporary* and truly *random*, teachers and researchers noticed powerful changes:

> Students very quickly shed their anxieties about what groups they were in. They began to collaborate in earnest. After three weeks a *porosity* developed between group boundaries as both intra- and inter-group collaboration flourished. With this heightened mobilization of knowledge came a decrease in the reliance on the teacher as the *knower* in the room. In the end there was a marked heightening of enthusiasm and engagement for problem solving in particular, and in mathematics class in general. (Liljedahl 2016, 377)

Ninety-three percent of the 200 elementary, middle, and secondary teachers in the study were so pleased with the results they continued to use visibly random grouping after the study was over. Some experimented with a return to student-selected partnerships but found visibly random grouping was more effective, so they resumed using their popsicle sticks, playing cards, or randomizer apps.

Liljedahl conducted much of this research in a school where there were significant cultural barriers between students of different ethnicities, as well as the typical social hierarchy among adolescents. Through visibly random groups in math class, those barriers began to come down (Liljedahl 2014, 10–11).

I find this research fascinating. We often put so much work and thought into crafting groups we think will function well. How interesting to find that we're better able to teach mathematics by expecting that every student can and will work with every other student in the class. I don't mean "expecting" in the feel-good sense of the word; rather, I mean actually expecting our students to work together in ever-changing, random groups, no matter which sticks we pull out of the can.

Cross-Pollination: Listening to and Building on Other People's Ideas

I hope you're developing an image of what your math classes could look and feel like most of the time: groups of students gathered around (hopefully vertical) whiteboards, engaged with rich mathematical problems, in successful, productive thinking partnerships. Some groups are having animated discussions; some groups are standing and staring at their boards, processing; and other groups are quietly writing, thinking, and drawing representations. As you walk around, you can easily see how the groups are working together and what each group has written. You notice which strategies have emerged and which have yet to show up. You can see which groups are stuck and which groups are making progress. You have a pretty good read on how communication is going. Students have been working for about twenty minutes, so everyone has had a chance to fumble around with the problem and make headway. You feel like it's time to pause your groups and let them see what you see. It's time to diversify students' thinking by spreading and cross-pollinating ideas (Figure 12.2).

Building Number Lines in Kindergarten: "That group gave me an idea!"

My primary colleagues at the Rollinsford Grade School and I had just this experience together. Four of us were in veteran

Figure 12.2 *Cross-pollination: listening to and building on other people's ideas*

teacher Becky Wright's kindergarten class in the spring, coteaching a lesson about number lines. We wanted to give students an opportunity to build number lines for themselves, so we put long pieces of painter's tape on the floor around the room. We wondered what would it look like if we stretched their familiar number chart out into a line. Becky and I asked groups of students to work together to choose a sequence of ten numbers from the chart and then write those numbers on ten sticky notes and place them on their line.

Much of teaching kindergarten math is teaching kids how to work together in thinking partnerships, so the teachers and I were moving from group to group, listening to children share ideas, agree or disagree, and eventually come to consensus. All our groups eventually wrote their ten numbers and placed them on their number line. That's when things got really interesting. We noticed that every single group placed their sticky notes side by side, written and sequenced correctly, but all scrunched up at one end (Figure 12.3). The teachers had a quick huddle and decided to ask students, "Can you use more of your line?" There was nothing wrong with what kids had done, but we wanted to get the idea of *intervals* on the table.

Most groups didn't know where to start. One group, however, got the idea to put a space in between each of their numbers. They started with a finger space, like they use between words in their writing, which is a brilliant and beautiful connection. After adding all the finger spaces, they saw they still had a lot of empty space

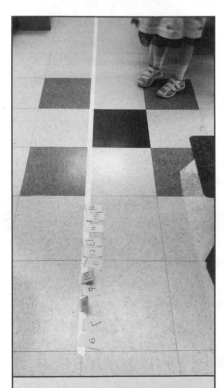

Figure 12.3 *All students initially placed their numbers right next to one another at one end of their line.*

Figure 12.4 *"Look, we could use these lines where the tiles are!"*

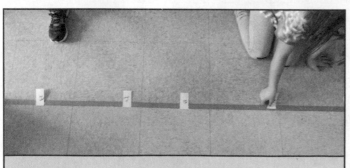

Figure 12.5 *Students began adding spaces between their numbers but didn't make the spaces regular.*

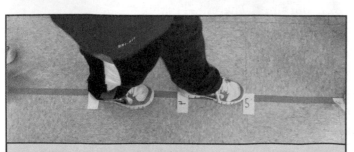

Figure 12.6 *"This one is bigger than this one. See, on this one, my toe touches. But on this one, there's all this extra space."*

left. Next, they decided to use a hand space between each number. They were making some headway now but still had plenty of line leftover. (The lines were eleven feet long.) One of the students in the group noticed the tiles on the floor were spaced evenly, and she suggested they put a sticky note at each tile seam (Figure 12.4). Now we were getting somewhere!

When we looked around the room, we saw that other students were still stumped how to answer our question, "Can you use more of your line?" We wanted the idea of spacing to spread throughout the class, but we wanted the idea to move *directly from students to students*. There was no need to insert ourselves, and plenty of reasons not to. We decided to pause the groups for one minute, ask them to walk around the room to see what other groups were trying and gather some new ideas, and then return to their groups. Aside from those directions, we kept quiet.

It worked! One boy gasped when he saw the numbers spread out, turned on his heel, and ran across the room to his group. He jumped up and down as he told them, "That group gave me an idea! I know what we can do! We can put spaces in between the numbers!"

We teachers smiled and thought we were on our way. Then something fascinating happened. The other groups all took up this idea of spacing the numbers out, but none of the other groups thought about spacing the numbers out with *equal intervals*. Number lines began to look like Figure 12.5, with irregular spaces between numbers.

We watched and waited and then noticed something new. One student used his sneakers to prove to his group that the spaces on his number line weren't even, and he was troubled by the difference in length (Figure 12.6). A girl in his group used cubes to show the same thing (Figure 12.7).

Now we had two new ideas we wanted to spread: *thinking about the length of the spaces* between the numbers and *using tools to measure those spaces*. Once again, we paused students and had them walk around to get ideas from one another's work. The idea of tools caught on quickly, and we saw other groups think about what they could use in the classroom to spread their intervals more evenly. One group loved the sneaker idea so much they replicated it with success.

It's important to note that not all groups were ready to pick up these ideas. Many kids barely glanced at other kids' work and then resumed taping their numbers down without equal intervals. Exposing children to an idea doesn't mean they'll take up that idea or even notice it. With repeated opportunities to cross-pollinate, however, students will learn how to pause their own thinking long enough to consider other people's approaches. They will have direct experience inspiring a peer with their own work or being inspired by

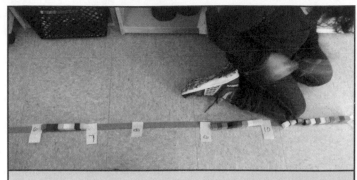

Figure 12.7 *"This one is 8 cubes long and this one is 10 cubes long."*

someone else's work. In other words, over time, they will learn how to learn from one another.

Classroom Structures That Encourage Cross-Pollination

Cross-pollination can take several forms, and you've seen it in many of the examples throughout this book. The two essential ingredients for cross-pollination are

- Expose students to other people's thinking to add variety to the ideas they're considering.
- Give students time and opportunities to react to, to engage with, or to build on those ideas for themselves.

Here are a few especially useful structures for cross-pollination, often used as a mid-workshop break.

Take a Lap: The *Walk-Around*

In the number line example, we interrupted thinking partnerships, gave them a few minutes to walk around and gather ideas from other groups, and then return to their own groups:

> *I know you're right in the middle of thinking hard about this problem, but I want to give you a chance to see some other ideas. Let's take one minute for you to walk around the classroom and notice what other kids are trying. Then you'll return to your work.*

After the *Walk-Around*, you can simply let students resume working or you can have a brief discussion to highlight what students can get out of seeing other people's ideas:

> *Let's hear from a few people who got a new idea from another group. What did you notice? What are you thinking about trying now?*

With or without a public airing, it's essential students have time to work with the ideas they picked up on their *Walk-Around*. New ideas only influence students' work if students resume working after being exposed to the new idea. Otherwise, those fleeting thoughts won't penetrate.

Gallery Walks

Gallery Walks are similar to *Walk-Arounds*, but they're a little more structured and longer. Often, teachers will ask students to create a poster or a whiteboard representing their work and then give students time to look at each poster. Guiding questions can make *Gallery Walks* much more effective and interactive. For example, I've heard Jennifer Clerkin Muhammad give these directions:

- "As you walk around, I want you to find someone who used a similar strategy to yours. And then I want you to find someone who used a different strategy than you did. Take your notebook with you and jot them both down."
- "As you look at other groups' posters about prime, square, and composite numbers, I want you to keep track of what you notice, which claims you agree with, and which claims you disagree with" (Figure 12.8).
- "On your whiteboard, I want you to choose a strategy to solve the problem 4872 ÷ 12. But I only want you to do the first couple of steps and then stop. In a few minutes, you'll move to someone else's whiteboard. Can you figure out how they're approaching the problem? What do you think they would do next? Can you complete the problem using their strategy? Try!"

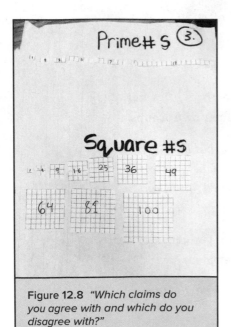

Figure 12.8 *"Which claims do you agree with and which do you disagree with?"*

Again, it's essential that students have a chance to explore and use what they picked up during their *Gallery Walks*. Just posting or seeing the ideas isn't enough. Students need a chance to wrestle with, incorporate, or push back against the new ideas in their own work. It's common to end lessons with *Gallery Walks*, and they can be a nice way to feel some closure, but if kids only walk around, look, and leave, they're missing out on the opportunity to cross-pollinate. If there's no time for them to apply what they've learned at the end of the lesson, then a good solution is to give them time at the start of the next lesson. Let them sleep on it!

Open Strategy Shares

Several math-teaching routines rely on *Open Strategy Shares*. For example, *Quick Images, Number Talks, Pattern Talks,* and discussions of open-ended or open-middle problems often start with these questions:

"How did you do it?"

"How do you know?"

"How did you see it?"

"Did anyone use a different strategy?"

The goal of an *Open Strategy Share* is to get lots of ideas on the table (Figure 12.9). We want students to see a range of possibilities and to build their repertoire of strategies (Kazemi and Hintz 2014, 18). Once the strategies are public, we can create opportunities for students to try a problem "Grant's way" or use "Kenya's strategy." We can encourage students to think relationally about the strategies and representations by choosing a few strategies and facilitating *Connect and Compare* or *What's Best and Why?* discussions (Kazemi and Hintz 2014). We can also nurture cross-pollination with these questions:

- "Who learned a new strategy from a peer today?"
- "Who saw an approach they'd like to try?"
- "Did anyone admire someone else's way to keep track of a problem and think they might use that organizational strategy in their own work next time?"
- "Is anyone planning to stick with their strategy but maybe incorporate an element of someone else's work? Tell us about that."
- "I'm curious if any of these representations spoke to you. See anything you want to try for yourself?"
- "I'm going to give you a new problem. You might want to use the strategy you used last time and refine it, or you might take an idea from someone else's approach and experiment with it."

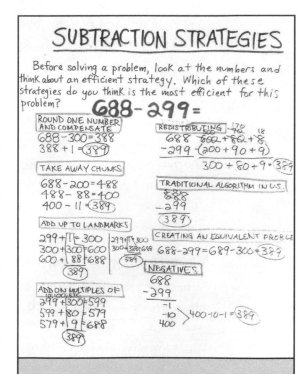

Figure 12.9 *"Which of these strategies do you think is the most efficient for this problem?"*

Even five minutes with a new problem and journals or whiteboards can help students try out ideas they heard in the *Open Strategy Share* and make a mental note of what they want to explore further.

Cross-Pollinator as a Group Role

I was once a participant in a Jo Boaler workshop in which she taught us a bit about *Complex Instruction* (CI), which is a structure for collaborative group work. (For more about CI, see Cohen and Lotan [2014], Horn [2012], and Featherstone et al. [2011]). Teachers who use CI are especially focused on disrupting typical social hierarchies and perceived status in the math classroom through meaningful group work in which all students' contributions are valued. To this end, CI teachers sometimes assign students cooperative group roles.

In our workshop, Jo Boaler designated one member of each group as a spy of sorts. Each spy was granted one (and only one) time to leave his or her group workspace, circulate around the room, and eavesdrop on other groups while they worked. The spy's goal was to gather new ideas, approaches, questions, or strategies that might help his or her own group.

Our group had a rich conversation about when our spy should venture out. Should we wait until we were stuck? Or until we were almost sure of our answer and wanted to check it? This chance to cross-pollinate felt valuable, and we wanted to use it strategically. I happened to be our group's spy, and I was able to gather a useful new idea for representing our problem. I was glad to learn this technique from Boaler and thought it was an innovative way to get ideas spreading around a class.

That said, I'm not sure I would use the name *spy*. It's certainly fun and mysterious and adds a bit of intrigue to math class. If we're working hard to create a culture of open, honest communication and collaboration, however, I'm not sure we want to introduce the furtive feel of spying and secrecy, and we certainly don't want to create competition among groups while they're working in thinking partnerships. Perhaps this role could be renamed the idea gatherer, the cross-pollinator, the ambassador, the envoy, the emissary, the sponge, the bee, the pollen collector, or the researcher? Perhaps you'll think of a better name yet!

Turn-and-Talks or Think-Pair-Share

I would be remiss if I didn't include *Turn-and-Talks* here. Looking at them through the lens of cross-pollination, *Turn-and-Talks* provide opportunities for students to share their ideas and listen to peers' thinking in intimate, accessible conversations peppered throughout large-group instruction. A student who is only thinking about her own approach will double the ideas she's considering if she listens to her neighbor's perspectives regularly.

Credit, Ownership, and Collaboration

Whatever cross-pollination classroom structure you use, your purpose is to give students a chance to diversify the ideas they're considering. Students' notions about ownership and kids' worries about stealing from or insulting a friend can interfere with effective cross-pollination unless we address the issue of *credit*.

On the one hand, an idea belongs to the person who hatched it. In their play, children use language like, "I have an idea!" or "No fair, that was *my* idea!" because they feel ownership over their ideas, and they should. Ideas are valuable! Therefore, it's important to teach students to give credit to individuals and groups when and where it's due.

On the other hand, ideas flow and evolve in a collaborative group, and there's no point in keeping track of whose idea brought about each minor change. In fact, too much focus on individual credit in a group setting can deeply undermine the collective effort of the group. If a group comes to an understanding through joint effort, then that understanding is the property of every member of that group. Their participation needn't have been measurably equal for group members to feel shared ownership of the thinking, and they shouldn't try to tally up contributions. As Halmos teaches us, "The count must not be made."

> Once a conversation that might lead to a collaborative result is begun, then anything it leads to, for better, for worse, is a collaborative result. The contributions of the partners to the final result might be numerically equal—the same number of definitions, the same number of theorems, the same number of proofs—or they might not; it must not matter, the count must not be made. Perhaps one partner contributes the insight and the other the technique; perhaps one partner asks the questions and the other knows the literature well enough to avoid the waste of time that comes from trying to re-discover already known answers; or, possibly, one is active and the other is the foil needed to keep up his morale and inspiration. No matter—once a collaboration is begun . . . anything that comes out of it is, must be, called a collaborative product. (Halmos 1985, 98)

This tension between credit and collaboration can peacefully exist in our mathematics classrooms if we bring it out into the open and deal with it honestly. We want students to know these truths:

- Hearing someone else's idea can get our thinking going or get us started on a challenging problem. Whether that idea ultimately turns out to be right or wrong, that idea is valuable because it serves as a catalyst to mathematical thinking.
- Sometimes someone else's idea will catch on and spread through the class. This productive exchange of ideas is part of doing mathematics, and we value it. We should all feel free to use this idea and eventually own it, but we should give credit to the idea's originator by saying, "I used Keisha's strategy," or "I was inspired by Malcolm's idea, and then I added on to it."
- Sometimes people disagree with a peer's idea in a way that helps us find mathematical truth. This disagreement is productive, and the idea's originator made a significant contribution to our collective effort.
- Considering other people's ideas can help clarify our own thinking. We need to listen to one another's ideas carefully and respectfully so we all feel safe sharing our thinking.
- One of the goals of our math class is for all students to understand deeply. Sharing ideas within our mathematical community is an important part of that effort. We are on the same team.
- When we rub ideas up against each other and share thinking with others, our thinking evolves. Ideas can take on a life of their own that's out of control of the person who originated the idea. Rather than try to keep ideas static and frozen, we enjoy that they are dynamic and evolving. We can't predict the ripple effects of our own ideas, but we can celebrate them.

Cross-Pollination in the Mathematics Community

Mathematicians live with this tension between credit and collaboration as well. Theorems, questions, and conjectures are named for the people who thought of them (or sometimes the people who published them). It's an honor to have your name attached to a good piece of mathematics: Riemann's hypothesis, Noether's theorem, or Ramanujan's prime. At the same time, mathematicians value collaboration so much they have institutionalized the free and open exchange of ideas.

For example, university mathematics departments across the world share a common tradition: afternoon tea. Daily or at least weekly, mathematics departments have tea, cookies, and games set out in a common meeting area. Graduate students, professors, and visitors mingle and talk about their work. Often, colloquia, seminars, or symposia are scheduled immediately following tea, and everyone is encouraged to attend and learn about what their colleagues are doing. Mathematics professors are expected to go to these teas and sessions, travel quite a bit, participate in conferences, and circulate among different universities, talking, sharing, listening, and cross-pollinating ideas. Deborah Heiligman's picture book biography *The Boy Who Loved Math: The Improbable Life of Paul Erdős* gets this idea across in a wonderful way (2013). She described Erdős as a "math matchmaker" who spent his life introducing mathematicians to one another and connecting their ideas.

The cultural norm is that mathematicians engage in this social flow of ideas regardless of whether the topic of conversation relates to their research in an obvious way or seemingly not at all. Mathematics is so interconnected, and connections sometimes pop out of surprising places. The history of math is filled with stories of mathematicians politely learning about someone else's work over coffee and then realizing with a thunderclap that this colleague's work—in a completely different area of mathematics—is the missing piece of a puzzle they've been trying to solve for ages. Glory goes to the solver; credit goes to the contributor. Even if that magic moment doesn't happen, the chat over coffee is still beneficial if the parties involved learn some new mathematics and build community in a friendly, social exchange of ideas.

Perhaps we should pour tea in math classes sometimes?

Going Further with Cross-Pollination

These favorite titles will help you dig more deeply into the sharing of ideas through productive mathematical discourse in the classroom. All are fabulous resources for cross-pollination.

- Kazemi and Hintz's *Intentional Talk: How to Structure and Lead Productive Mathematical Discussions*, especially the *Connect and Compare* targeted discussions (2014)
- Smith and Stein's *5 Practices for Orchestrating Productive Mathematics Discussions* (2011)
- Chapin, O'Connor, and Anderson's *Classroom Discussions, Second Edition: Using Math Talk to Help Students Learn, Grades K–6* (2009)

- Descriptions of "Math Congresses" from any book in Fosnot and Dolk's Young Mathematicians at Work series (2001)

Math Disputes: Finding the Truth by Debating Each Other

When two members of the Arts Faculty argue, they may find it impossible to reach a resolution. When two mathematicians argue—and they do, often in a highly emotional and aggressive way—suddenly one will stop, and say, "I'm sorry, you're quite right, now I see my mistake." And they will go off and have lunch together, the best of friends.

　　　　　　—Ian Stewart, *Letters to a Young Mathematician*

Figure 12.10 *Math disputes: discovering the truth by debating each other*

Argument is central to mathematics. We assert what we think is true, defend our arguments with reasons and logic, and challenge arguments we think are false. As Stewart's quote shows, however, these arguments are not personal. In mathematics, we argue about ideas with people we respect (Figure 12.10). And here's the key: the purpose of mathematical arguing is not to win; the purpose is to figure out what's true. Therefore, when we engage in a mathematical argument with someone else, we are, in a very important sense, partnering together to determine the truth through this process of making claims, supporting them, disputing them, and then revising our thinking as needed.

Let's turn to specific classroom strategies to teach students how to engage in math disputes.

Shawn Towle, eighth grade

Take a Position

Shawn often urges students to take a position and defend it. In this case, Shawn's class was working on a spinners problem during their study of probability. For homework, Shawn had asked students to look at the three-spinner problem in Figure 12.11 and to think about whether it's fair, and if it's not, whom does it favor? What do you think?

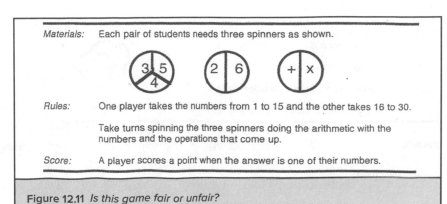

Materials:　Each pair of students needs three spinners as shown.

Rules:　One player takes the numbers from 1 to 15 and the other takes 16 to 30.

Take turns spinning the three spinners doing the arithmetic with the numbers and the operations that come up.

Score:　A player scores a point when the answer is one of their numbers.

Figure 12.11 *Is this game fair or unfair?*

Shawn asked everyone to stand.

Shawn: Barbara, what was your prediction?

Barbara: I think it's unfair and it favors Player 2.

Shawn: If you agree with Barbara, go stand near her. (Some students moved accordingly, and then Shawn called on Joey, who had not moved.)

Joey: I also think it's unfair, but I think it favors Player 1.

Shawn: If you agree with Joey, go stand by him.

(The remaining students thought the game was fair. Shawn grouped them up.)

Once students had voted with their feet and assembled in like-minded groups, Shawn told them to put their heads together and clarify their arguments. Why did they think the game was fair or unfair? For what reasons? During this discussion, a few students left their groups and walked across the room to take different positions. Shawn asked why, and students said, "I was listening to what they were saying and I realized I disagree because . . ." or "I looked at the problem more closely and noticed that the third spinner . . ." Students were already revising their positions based on mathematical arguments.

Shawn listened in as students discussed their thinking in groups and then asked a few representatives to share their reasoning with the large group. Example reasons included:

- "It's fair because each spinner has equal opportunities, so there are an equal number of possible outcomes."
- "Player 2 has a better chance of winning because there was both addition and multiplication. That would increase the chance to have numbers more than fifteen."
- "It favors Player 1 because addition of these numbers will always be less than fifteen, and you have to multiply by six to get sixteen or more."

Once the main arguments were on the table, it was time to play.

Shawn paired students off thoughtfully. Students who thought the game would favor Player 1 became Player 1. Likewise, students who thought the game would favor Player 2 became Player 2. Students who thought the game was fair played against students who thought it was unfair.

Shawn constructed this lesson so students already had at least two in-depth conversations: one with classmates who agreed with their position, and one with a classmate who disagreed with their position. Through this mixing and remixing, Shawn pushed all students to look at their reasons and arguments from at least two sides.

We listened while students played. Many students changed their minds during the game. Because students had taken a position, they were especially invested in figuring out whether their original position was correct or incorrect and *why*. We heard the happy buzzing sound of the word *because* coming from every pair. We also heard these comments:

- "I'm pretty sure, if you get plus, there's no way for it to be over fifteen."
- "Hey! This isn't fair!"
- "I think it flavors Player 1 because there are twelve possible outcomes, but there are only three that come out above fifteen."

When each pair had played twenty rounds of the game, they posted their results in the class tally (Figure 12.12). Pairs spent time looking over this larger data set and refining their arguments about the game. Students naturally began wondering about finding a pattern or rule that would allow them to figure out if a game was fair or unfair by looking at the possible outcomes, without having to gather data.

This particular lesson occurred during the last few weeks of the school year with graduating eighth graders. Senioritis was rampant throughout the school. As I observed several sections of eighth-grade math, however, I saw all students on task and engaged in deep mathematical thinking. Games are fun, certainly, and Shawn is wise to close his year with a probability unit. The structure of *Take a Position* is such an engaging one, though, that all students needed to pay attention and think, and they did.

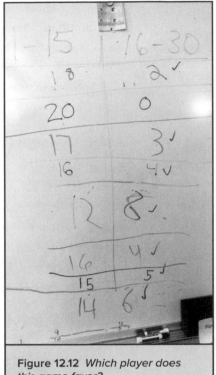

Figure 12.12 *Which player does this game favor?*

In fourth grade, I often used a variant of this strategy called *Vote with Your Feet*, which I learned from language arts teacher Barry Hoonan. We'd set up a continuum across the room. If students agreed with Position *X*, they were on one end. If they agreed with Position *Y*, they were on the other end. Kids who were undecided or leaning one way or the other positioned themselves somewhere in the middle. My question for them was always, "Students in the middle, what information would you need to make up your mind?" Undecided students would ask questions of classmates who were firmly decided. As they heard more arguments, students often revised their thinking and changed their positions accordingly.

Where in our math teaching could we ask students to stake out mathematical claims, vote with their feet, or take a position? What makes for an interesting mathematical dispute? To learn more about how to set up high-quality mathematical disputes, I called secondary math teacher and debate coach Chris Luzniak for advice.

Chris Luzniak

Making Math Debatable

Chris has been experimenting with using debate structures in his math classroom for several years. PBS Boston affiliate WGBH featured Chris in their argumentation and critique series, *Making the Case*, so you can watch Chris and his students in action in a terrific, brief video at mass.pbslearningmedia.org/resource/mtc13.pd.math.deb/encouraging-debate/. I've included links to all the videos as well as Chris's blog and website at stenhouse.com/becomingmathteacher, and I encourage you to see the power of these techniques for yourself.

For those of us who are new to debate in math class, I want to highlight two essential points from Chris's work: (1) ask debatable questions and (2) teach argumentation.

Ask Debatable Questions

For students to engage in productive mathematical debate, they need to work on debatable questions. Students can't have interesting debates about a closed problem with a single solution path and one clear answer because there is nothing to debate! Therefore, we need to ask questions with mathematically rich ambiguity or multiple interpretations. We want students debating about the key concepts and methods, not insignificant details.

With practice, Chris has become skilled and quick at converting closed questions into debatable ones. He finds question structures like these particularly helpful:

- What's the best/worst way to _____?
- Which is bigger/smaller?
- What is the most efficient/effective/elegant/weirdest/coolest method/solution for this problem?
- Do you agree, somewhat agree, or disagree with this claim: _____?
- A student said this: _____. Is he right or wrong? Always, sometimes, or never?

Consider the differences among the questions shown here:

CLOSED QUESTIONS VS. DEBATABLE QUESTIONS	
Solve 18 × 32.	What is the easiest way to solve 18 × 32 using mental math?
Solve 7,426 ÷ 2.	What's the least efficient way to solve 7,426 ÷ 2?
Amanda has five shirts and three skirts. Make a table that shows all the outfits she can make.	Amanda has five shirts and three skirts. What's the best problem-solving strategy to use to figure out how many outfits she can make?
Calculate the area and perimeter of the polygon.	Consider this claim from one of Mr. Luzniak's students: *When you cut a piece off a polygon, you reduce its area and perimeter.* Agree, somewhat agree, or disagree?

When students work on debatable questions, they are still solving math problems. Debatable questions have an inherent advantage, however, which is that constructing and critiquing arguments are built right into their structure. Students form opinions based on mathematical reasons while they work, and they emerge ready to debate their peers. The next step is to teach them how to debate.

Argument = Claim + Warrant

Starting from Day 1, Chris teaches his class that *answers always have two parts,* a claim and a warrant, defined as (Luzniak 2011):

> *Claim = a controversial statement*
>
> *Warrant = reason why your controversial statement is true*

These terms come right from debate, and Chris finds they translate beautifully to math classroom use. He drums this sentence structure into his students from the first day and posts it on every wall of his classroom:

> *My claim is _____, and my warrant is _____.*

Chris has established a lovely trajectory that starts small but builds up to full debates. The following table shows a brief outline of the sequence he uses each fall.

Soapbox Debates (stating arguments)	Each student takes a turn to stand and say, *"My claim is _____, and my warrant is _____."* Chris starts with nonmath contexts, such as "What's the best movie?" or "Who's the most powerful superhero?" As students internalize the rhythm of these two-part answers, he shifts the topic to mathematical questions.
Circle Debates (listening to and summarizing arguments)	Chris teaches students to listen to others by asking them to summarize the prior person's position before stating their own claims and warrants. Students say, *"I heard _____ say that _____. My claim is _____ and my warrant is _____."*
Point/Counterpoint Debates (responding to arguments)	Chris teaches students how to respond to other people's arguments by requiring students to argue the opposite of whatever has just been stated. Students now need further rhetorical structures like: *I concur with _____ because _____. I can clarify _____ with _____. I agree/disagree with _____ because _____. On the contrary, _____. To add on to what _____ was saying, _____. To supplement that, _____.*

Table Debates (debating opposite positions)	Students are assigned to play Side A or Side B of an argument. Chris passes out their positions, and students have to construct arguments for whichever side they are assigned.
Full Debates	Students are now ready to have mathematical debates as a class.

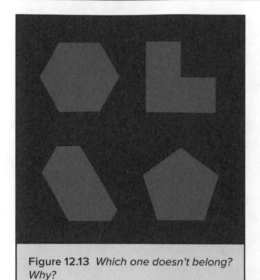

Figure 12.13 *Which one doesn't belong? Why?*

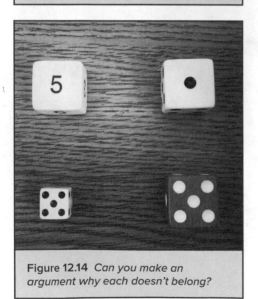

Figure 12.14 *Can you make an argument why each doesn't belong?*

Through debate, Chris's students learn to construct arguments and critique mathematical reasoning. They internalize the habit of providing a justification for every statement they make: Chris hardly has to ask, *Why?* because students automatically back up their claims with reasons both orally and in writing. Students grow comfortable having lively mathematical discussions without taking dissent personally. And they learn how to sharpen their thinking through disagreement with and pushback from their peers.

On top of all of that, students who routinely debate in math class destroy society's myths about math being completely objective and always having one right answer. When they take positions, state opinions, construct arguments, critique reasoning, and have passionate debates, students experience mathematics as it's actually practiced by mathematicians.

Here are some additional resources to get you and your students debating mathematics:

• Christopher Danielson's marvelous book, *Which One Doesn't Belong?* (Figure 12.13; 2016), and the website he inspired, wodb.ca, are wonderful tools to spark debate in mathematics class. Each image has four objects, numbers, pictures, or graphs, and the question to ponder is "Which one doesn't belong?" The loveliest bit is that each of the objects can be eliminated for some reason or reasons. Can you find a reason why each of the four doesn't belong in Figures 12.13 and 12.14?

• *Would You Rather?* (wouldyourathermath.com) is a website that pits two choices against each other, so it's perfect for debating. For example, "Would you rather drive to the airport and pay for parking or take a taxi?" or "Would you rather have a pound of quarters or a pound of dimes?"

• Chris uses the game KenKen, which is available in many places, including free from the National Council of Teachers of Mathematics at illuminations.nctm.org/activity.aspx?id=4184. Before each move, students have to state a claim about what number must go in the box, along with a warrant explaining why.

Peer Feedback: Sharpening Each Other's Thinking Through Constructive Critiques

The final type of interaction we're going to explore is peer feedback (Figure 12.15). Mathematicians frequently seek out critiques from peers they respect for several reasons:

- They need the fresh perspective outside eyes can bring.
- They want input from someone with different expertise.
- They want to clarify and tighten their arguments.
- They need someone else to referee their work—to read it line-by-line and check for correctness.

If students are doing mathematics, these same reasons for critique will arise naturally in our classrooms. For students to seek and give useful feedback, however, we must teach them how to critique so students move beyond, "It's good. I liked it." We need to socialize them into a culture in which feedback is normal, expected, and valued. Ron Berger's powerful video, *Austin's Butterfly*, at vimeo.com/38247060 demonstrates how teaching students to give "kind, specific, and helpful" feedback equips them to produce beautiful quality work (Berger, Rugen, and Woodfin 2014, 138).

Critiques also teach mathematics! Jen will show us how.

Figure 12.15 *Peer feedback: sharpening each other's arguments through constructive critiques*

Jennifer Clerkin Muhammad

"This is the type of feedback you're going to give."

When teaching fractions to her fourth-grade students, Jen invests lots of classroom time developing deep conceptual understanding. To this end, Jen constantly requires students to shift among representing fractions on the number line, with area models, and numerically. Creating and using these multiple representations helps students make connections, develop powerful visual models, and think relationally about fractions.

For the representations to be effective as teaching and learning tools, however, they need to be accurate, thoughtful, clear, and informative. In this lesson, Jen used two different teaching structures to establish her high standards for representations and to teach students how to give and receive useful critiques. She started with a whole-class mini-lesson in which they critiqued three different representations of the same problem. Fresh off the modeling and instruction of the group critique, Jen's students worked in pairs to give each other individual feedback on their fraction cards.

Group Critique: "What do we think about this representation?"

Jen's students had worked independently on a series of word problems involving addition and subtraction with fractions. For the group critique, Jen focused on one problem:

Before breakfast there were $\frac{7}{12}$ of a gallon of milk in the refrigerator. The family used $\frac{3}{12}$ of a gallon of milk during breakfast. How much of a gallon of milk remained after breakfast?

How would you represent this problem in an area model? On a number line? It's worth jotting down your representation in order to think about the mathematics and to anticipate what students might do.

Jen started the discussion by helping everyone visualize the fraction:

Jen: I'm just curious, before we start this. So, what do they start with again?

Students: Seven-twelfths of a gallon.

Jen: Who could talk about the fraction seven-twelfths and how much is seven-twelfths in terms of a whole gallon? Is it *more than* a whole gallon? Is it *less than* a whole gallon? Who could sort of visualize what seven-twelfths of a gallon would look like? (Jen walked over to her bin of different containers—pints, liters, 2-liter bottles, cups—and pulled out a gallon jug. She held it up.) Here's a gallon. So who can picture what seven-twelfths would look like? William?

William: Just a little bit more than one-half.

Jen: Just a little more than one-half. Can you explain to me why you think that?

William: I think that because six-twelfths is equivalent to one-half. Seven-twelfths is only one more twelfth than one-half or six-twelfths, so it's a little more than half.

Jen: You're saying if you broke this up into twelve equal parts, if you had six of them, that would be half. So he says seven-twelfths must be a little more than that. How much more?

Students: One-twelfth.

Jen: One-twelfth more. Okay, so we're all sort of picturing a gallon of, it's maybe this full, would you say? (Jen gestured with her hand on the gallon jug and students nodded when she showed a little more than half.)

At this point, Jen had reactivated her students' thinking about this particular problem and helped them visualize the scenario. It was time to begin critiques:

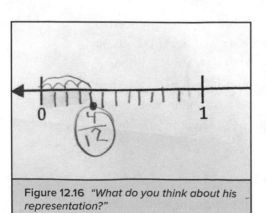

Figure 12.16 *"What do you think about his representation?"*

Jen: So who would like to be brave and show their representation of this problem? The rest of the class is going to critique it for how clear it is. (Antoine volunteered, so Jen placed his work under the document camera as shown in Figure 12.16.) Make sure you have the story problem in front of you so you can refer back to it. Take a look at his representation. OK, what do you think about it? Why don't you talk at your tables? What do we think about his representation?

As Jen walked around, she listened in as students talked about Antoine's representation. She encouraged them to think about whether he had made an accurate representation and if he showed the action of the problem. She asked, "Does this representation show what's happening in the story?" After a few minutes, she pulled everyone back together and asked students to share out.

Adam: I don't think you showed the whole of the problem, because, well, he did do the four-twelfths out of the twelve-twelfths of a gallon, but I think he's missing something. It said they started out in the morning, before breakfast, at seven-twelfths. You should probably make a mark at seven-twelfths *and* four-twelfths.

Jen: It sounds like you think there should be something indicating the seven-twelfths that they started with?

Adam: Yeah, maybe mark it at the seven-twelfths point. They didn't start with twelve-twelfths. They started with seven-twelfths.

Jen: And all we see is that one over there at the start. So it almost looks like it started off with a whole gallon?

Adam: Yeah.

Rita: I agree with his answer, but I don't agree with how he got it. Like Adam said, it doesn't really show you—like if you walked in you wouldn't really know what the problem was.

Jen: Oh, if Ms. Soto (the principal) walked in right now and saw this, she wouldn't know that this had been a subtraction problem involving fractions?

Rita: She would know it's a fraction problem, but she wouldn't know where it starts. She'd think it started with a whole gallon.

Jen: Well, would she even know it's about gallons?

Rita: No, and she'd think it started at zero or one.

Karl: I don't really get where the answer comes from. I don't see the three-twelfths or the seven-twelfths.

Jen: Mmm, I heard a lot of other kids saying that too, Karl. Thank you.

Jen turned to Antoine to see what he thought about the feedback.

Jen: What do you think about what the class has said? Do you agree with them, are you confused by what they're saying? What do you think?

Antoine: Well, I was just putting the answer. I didn't think about putting what was happening in the problem. Next time, I'll show what's happening.

Antoine said all of this in an appreciative way. He took his work back and wrote some notes to himself about what to change. In the meantime, Jen invited Meryl to post her representation so students could discuss a different piece of work (Figure 12.17).

Jen: So let's take a look at this. This'll be interesting to look at a different representation. Let's take twenty seconds, twenty-five seconds to really look at this and see what we think. (Think time.) Comments about this? Comments, questions, agree, disagree? What do you think? This is very different. Tammy?

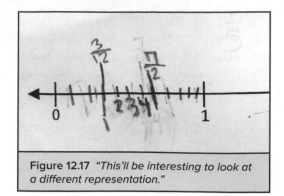

Figure 12.17 *"This'll be interesting to look at a different representation."*

Tammy: I'm a little confused because if you take the hops to the three-twelfths from seven-twelfths it wouldn't be where the 4 is, 'cause you have to start on the line where three-twelfths is. And *that* would be 1. *That* would be 2, *that* would be 3 and then *that* would be 4.

Jen: Can you come up? I think I understand your confusion, but I'm a little confused while you're explaining it.

Tammy: So this should be 1, where the 2 is, and 3 should be 2, and 4 should be 3. And under seven-twelfths, it should be 4. (Meryl nodded while Tammy was talking.)

Jen: So you're saying, if we're hopping, this would be one jump, two jumps, three jumps, four jumps. And Meryl, do you agree with that? (Meryl nodded.)

Tammy: Yeah. And it's not written as fractions. It's only written as 1, 2, 3, 4.

Jen: What does she mean when she's writing these 1, 2, 3, 4? What do those mean?

Nathan: Those are the twelfths. Like one-twelfth, two-twelfths, three-twelfths, four-twelfths.

Jen: Interesting. What more can we say about this?

William: So I can say that she must have taken some time to do this 'cause I see a lot of erasing marks. So I would say that there are twelfths, and she marked pretty clearly where the seven-twelfth mark was. And then so at three-twelfths she marked that too 'cause that's what they used. And then that part in the middle must be what they still have. They still have four-twelfths.

Jen: So, this (gesturing from zero to seven-twelfths), would be the whole amount of milk. This is *all* of the milk. And then this (gesturing from zero to three-twelfths) is the *part that they used*. And this (gesturing from three-twelfths to seven-twelfths), is the *part that's left*. Is that what you're saying?

William: Yeah.

Jen: What do people think about that? Do you agree with that? And it's OK not to know. You can ask a question right now. You don't have to have any answers.

Jen spent a good amount of wait time here, looking to see whether students who had not yet spoken up were ready to talk. As she gently checked in with individual students, it became clear they were on shaky ground. William had done a great job identifying the different parts of the problem in Meryl's representation, but most of the students were having difficulty seeing what he saw or talking about it yet. Jen decided to introduce one more representation in the hopes it might help students see the action, parts, and wholes on the number line, so she chose to project Stella's work (Figure 12.18).

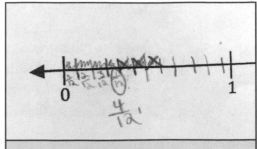

Figure 12.18 *"Talk to people at your table about what you notice about this representation."*

> Jen: Let's take a moment to look at this. This is a little different. Talk to people at your table about what you notice about this representation.

Jen walked around and listened in while students talked. She asked students questions like, "Do you see seven-twelfths in this representation?" "Where is the part they used?" "What do those *x*'s mean?" and "Do you see the action in this story problem?" After a few minutes, she pulled the class together for one more analysis and critique.

> Jen: So what do you think about Stella's representation?
>
> Anielies: I don't see the seven-twelfths, and where does she get the numbers? She only showed the answer.
>
> Jen: So Anielies says where's the seven-twelfths? She says, "I only see the answer." She doesn't see the seven-twelfths and she doesn't see the—what other than fractions do you want to see?
>
> Anielies: I don't understand how she got the answer.
>
> Jen: OK, and I see Tammy agreeing. (Stella raised her hand to comment.) Let's see if someone else can explain it for you. Who else understood this?
>
> Aidan: Those *x*'s right here are the rest of the seven-twelfths, and this shaded part is the four-twelfths. She just didn't mark the numbers.
>
> Jen: So you're saying that whole part that's sort of dark up there represents the seven-twelfths? Including the *x*'s?
>
> Aidan: Yeah.
>
> Jen: What are those *x*'s for? Why is she putting *x*'s on there? Is she cray?
>
> Students: No!
>
> Jen: Tell me, what are the *x*'s?
>
> Adam: They're the three-twelfths that she used.
>
> Jen: Why is she x-ing them out?
>
> Students: "She drank them!" "They're gone!" "They don't exist anymore!" "They're digested!"
>
> Jen: (Laughing.) Oh!

Jen: What I think is kind of cool about this, and I think yes, Stella, it might be helpful—for someone who is just coming in and has no idea what's happening—maybe it would have been helpful to mark seven-twelfths. But I like how you're showing how you're *getting rid* of a twelfth, another twelfth, and another twelfth. By "getting rid of" I mean they're actually drinking it, right? Meryl?

Meryl: What are the squiggly lines for?

Stella: (Rising and going to the projector.) These little ones? Well, there's actually a key. (She zoomed out the projector and showed her key, seen in Figure 12.19.)

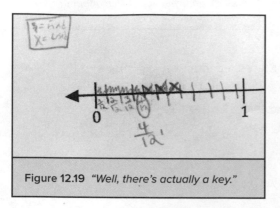

Figure 12.19 *"Well, there's actually a key."*

Jen: (Laughing.) Oh, I missed the key! And we were trying to figure it out without the key! Silly us. Silly me.

Students: "Oh!" "Cool!" "Great idea!"

Stella: So the squiggly lines is how much they *had*, and the *x*'s are how much they *used*.

Jen: Oh, so is that why underneath the *x*'s it's dark? This whole part was dark originally 'cause that was the milk? (Stella nodded.) Maybe it's chocolate milk? So, this whole part was dark at first because that was the *total amount of milk*. And then she *x*'ed out *the part that they drank*, that they used, and the four-twelfths was *what was left*.

Students: "Oh!" "I see!" "I get it!"

Jen: Oh . . . it's starting to become much clearer! Thank you, Stella.

By now, students had been sitting for a long time, and Jen knew she needed to make a transition from the group critique to more independent work and individual feedback. Before asking students to put this piece of work away and join her on the rug, though, Jen asked students to back up and think more broadly about the importance of the representations they'd been analyzing:

Jen: We're going to shift gears just a little bit. I just want you to keep in mind that you make representations for two big reasons, probably even more. One really important reason you want a representation is that, a lot of times, it helps you think. I know that sometimes I try to do these problems, and I'm like "Oh, I don't know what to do." But as soon as I start making a representation, it's like, "Oh, I get it!" But there's a second reason to make representations. They help you prove your thinking to other people, right?

Whenever I am in Jen's class, I am struck by the level of scrutiny and respect her fourth-grade students give their peer's representations. Critiques and discussions about students' work last a fairly long time: this particular critique lasted twenty-three minutes, which is typical. During critiques, students are intense and focused, really studying their classmates' work and getting down to the nitty-gritty details.

How might it change the quality of our students' mathematics if they were accustomed to having their work taken this seriously? To feel their work was worthy of this level of attention? In all the visits I've made to Jen's room, I've never seen a student turn in a piece of slapdash mathematics, and her use of critiques is a big reason why her students take such pride. It's one thing to say we want thoughtful work or ask for quality work or tell kids to take their time. It's quite another thing to spend large amounts of class time analyzing students' work so they really understand what it means to produce accurate, informative, clear, thorough mathematics. And, as this vignette demonstrates, students have to engage deeply with the mathematical objective (in this case, subtracting fractions on the number line) to make sense of and critique the representations. Win-win.

Individual Critiques: "You didn't sugarcoat things, did you?"

Jen had students move their bodies to the rug area so she could give them a new set of directions. As per Jen's curriculum, *Investigations in Number, Data, and Space,* the students had spent several lessons creating a set of fraction cards. Working from a list of fractions, students used unlined index cards to represent one fraction per card: numerically, with an area model, on a number line, and in a series of equations. After the group critique of the gallon of milk problem, Jen gave students the opportunity to give and receive individual feedback about their fraction cards:

> Jen: What you're going to do is you're going to look through the cards and you're going to give feedback to each card. You're going to write your feedback on a sticky note. This is the type of feedback you're going to give:
>
> - You could ask a **question** of them, like, for example, on that last one you could say "Where's the seven-twelfths?" Right? Or, "Why did you make that part dark?" Which she explained in the key, right? (Laughing.)
> - You could say **what impressed you**. And you'll see what I mean when you see some of the equations that people came up with and some of the representations.
> - You can write **something that you disagree with and why**. There are some mistakes, which is OK. If you find them, you can say what you disagree with and hopefully you can explain why.
> - You can also make a comment about **something that you hadn't thought of** but you agree with.
> - And last but not least, if you have **any advice**. So maybe you notice that a kid is having a really hard time making eighths and you want to give them a tip on how to make eighths really easily, you can write that on a sticky note.
>
> Capisce? So you're kind of being like a teacher right now. Can we handle that?

Students got right to work. As I walked around, Jen and I were struck by the specificity and usefulness of their feedback (Figures 12.20 and 12.21).

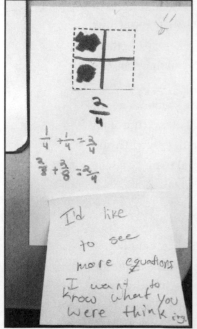
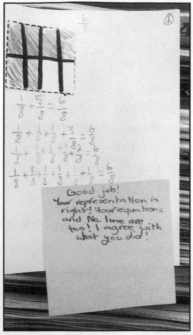

Figures 12.20 (Left), 12.21 (Right) *"You gave people compliments when you thought they deserved them, but you didn't sugarcoat things, did you?"*

As I looked over the class set of fraction cards, I was struck by how many of the students gave kind, specific, and helpful feedback, as recommended by Berger, Rugen, and Woodfin (2014, 138). Students were honest—there was no empty praise—but they critiqued from the expectation that their classmates were capable of excellent work. For example, a student who hadn't taken the time to divide his whole carefully into four equal parts was told, "Your area models are not accurate." Students who hadn't written enough equations or challenged themselves adequately were told, "I'd like to see more equations. I want to know what you're thinking!" Students were encouraging, clear, and direct with one another.

As is her way, Jen pulled the class back together to reflect on their process at the end:

Jen: Quick question that I want you to talk about with your group. What was one of the main mistakes or things that you didn't quite agree with that you found in the cards that you looked at? I'm going to kind of listen around as you talk to your groups. What was one of the main issues that you found?

Students discussed what they noticed in their classmates' work, pointing out strengths and room for improvement. After a few minutes, Jen pulled them back together.

Jen: I have to say, I have to give you a compliment. I thought you did a really nice job inspecting each other's cards, wouldn't you say? You didn't just say, "Yeah, yeah, yeah, this looks good. Blah, blah, blah." You really took your time. You gave people compliments when you thought they deserved them, but you didn't sugarcoat things, did you?

Students: No.

Jen: You were very honest, which is great. And I think the kids are going to appreciate it when they see the feedback that they're getting.

Jennifer collected all the cards so she could give a round of feedback as well. The following day she returned the cards to their owners, and students had time to act on the feedback they'd received. We often skip this step, which, unfortunately, negates all the advantages of feedback! For critiques to be effective, students must have time to take the feedback into account and improve their work.

By this point in the year, Jen's students were used to these cycles of drafting, receiving feedback, revising, critiquing, and revising again. They learn in a culture of continuous improvement. For them, multiple drafts and revisions are as much a part of doing mathematics as they are a part of writing workshop. No wonder the quality of their mathematics is so high!

Be Explicit: What Kind of Mathematical Interaction Do You Need Right Now?

We've considered four different types of mathematical interactions: (1) thinking partnerships, (2) cross-pollination, (3) math disputes, and (4) peer feedback. We've looked at different teaching techniques and structures that will teach students how to engage in each type of communication as they do mathematics. If students are going to initiate and engage in these interactions spontaneously, however, not just when we orchestrate them, we need to teach students how to identify what type of interaction they need and seek it out. At the same time, we need to teach students how to hear what their peers are asking for and reply appropriately.

If we look closely at collegial interactions, we can see how people convey their expectations and desires to each other. For example, when I am grappling with an engaging problem or concept, I oscillate between working independently and needing to think aloud with someone. When it would help me process through talk, I look for a thinking partner. I reach out to another teacher, a colleague on Twitter, or my spouse, and ask, "Would you think something through with me?" or "Can I think aloud with you for a minute?" or "Can you help me make sense of something?" By beginning with those questions, I've conveyed my needs. I've set the tone and expectations for a thinking partnership. My partner knows that what's coming will be thinking-in-the-rough, not a finished product, and that I need a friend to help me by serving as a sounding board. If, instead, I start by saying, "I think I've proven this. Can you find the weak spots in my argument? What'd I miss?" I'm signaling that I want a totally different interaction.

We need to teach students to recognize and use these cues in both our spoken language and in unspoken messages, summarized in the table that follows. Role playing, modeling, and debriefing are particularly fruitful ways to teach communication skills. If you see a student ask for an interaction and her peers respond appropriately, make sure to highlight their communication to the class and discuss it. What about it worked? How did the student ask to work together so her intentions and needs were clear? How did the other students respond? What sort of interaction were they able to have? When a student needs help from a peer, it's fair game to ask, "What kind of mathematical interaction do you need right now?" If you've taught students different ways to work together, they will have the language to express, "I could use some feedback on how to make my work better" or "I'm stuck. I'd like to work with someone who is approaching it in a different way because that might help."

	EXAMPLE REQUESTS	UNSPOKEN MESSAGES	HOW TO HEAR THE REQUEST
THINKING PARTNERSHIPS	"Would you help me think something through?" "Can I bounce an idea off you?" "Can I think out loud with you for a second?" "Hey, look what I noticed. What do you think about it?" "Can we work on number 5 together? It would really help me to talk it through with somebody."	I need to talk through this problem while I am trying to figure it out. I want to do more than solve it; I want to use this problem to learn. I'm looking for a sympathetic listener and a supportive partner who will join with me. We will both say things that are right and things that are wrong, and that's part of making sense. We'll create a safe space to share raw, partial, and unedited thinking with each other. By the end, I hope we'll both learn a lot.	This person needs someone to work alongside him in a collaborative way. We'll probably go back and forth between working independently and sharing ideas together. I need to listen carefully, be honest, and make it safe for us both to make mistakes and revise our thinking as we go. I should be encouraging and join with him. If he doesn't understand something, I'll ask him questions that will help him figure it out for himself. He'll do the same for me. We'll both make sure we're both learning, and we'll take the time we need to understand.
CROSS-POLLINATION	"I'm stuck. It would help me to hear what some other people have tried." "I'm thinking about this problem in one way, but it would help me to hear some other perspectives." "Can we walk around and look at other people's work? I need some new ideas." "What have you been thinking about in your group?"	I feel like I've run through my ideas and I'm not getting where I want to go. I need some input from other people. Maybe somebody else's perspective will help me figure out where to go next. I will give credit to other people for their ideas, of course, and share my ideas with them, too. Their reactions to what I've done might help them or me.	This person needs to hear some different ideas to spark her thinking. She's not copying or stealing; she's looking for inspiration. That's a good thing! I will share my ideas in the hopes they help her, and in the hopes that people's reactions to what I've done will help me. I'll listen to everyone carefully because I've learned that my peers are amazing sources of mathematical ideas.
MATH DISPUTES AND DEBATES	"I'm not sure what's true here. If we argue opposite positions, we might be able to figure it out together." "Would you debate this with me?" "I need someone to argue this through with me." "OK. I'm going to act like I accept this claim. Can I argue it with you?"	The process of constructing and critiquing arguments will help me clarify my thinking about this concept. I need a partner who will listen carefully and engage in productive debate with me. We can use the structure of debate to help us both figure out what's true. Even though we're positioning ourselves on opposite sides of an argument, we are working together to determine the truth, understand mathematics, and articulate our thinking.	This person needs to debate in order to figure out the math. We'll disagree or agree with each other's ideas, remembering that our debate isn't personal. Through the process of debating, I'm sure my arguments will get sharper, and I'll help her make her arguments better also. I hope our debate will be lively, and we'll make sure it is respectful.

	EXAMPLE REQUESTS	UNSPOKEN MESSAGES	HOW TO HEAR THE REQUEST
PEER FEEDBACK	"I need a critical friend to look at my work." "Would you read my argument and see if you can find any weaknesses to attack?" "I made this as clear as I can, but I'm not sure it's clear to a new reader. Would you read it for me and give me feedback?" "Could you critique this for me?"	We all need outside eyes to make our work better. I need someone to critique what I've done and help me improve it. When someone criticizes my argument, they are not criticizing me. They are helping me strengthen my mathematical work, and I won't take it personally. I want to hear what they thought I did well so I can keep doing it, and identify and improve the parts that need work.	This person needs me to be skeptical and critical and look for flaws in his argument so he can make it better. In my own work, I value meaningful feedback I can act on, rather than empty praise, so I'll try to give him thorough, constructive comments. I'll make sure to give some positive feedback about the strengths, and then useful suggestions about areas that could be improved.

When students have internalized these different interactions and essential habits of mathematical practice, they flow from one type of interaction to another, organically, as their needs vary and evolve. They act and think like the young mathematicians they are.

"FAVORABLE CONDITIONS" FOR ALL MATH STUDENTS

Clarence F. Stephens is the best educator we teachers have never heard of. He developed such successful math teaching methods that his work from 1969 to 1987 as department chair at State University of New York (SUNY) Potsdam has been called the Potsdam Miracle.

At the time, mathematics degrees constituted 1 percent of all bachelor's degrees granted in the United States nationwide. During Stephens's tenure at SUNY Potsdam—a typical, liberal arts state school—the number of mathematics majors grew to a whopping 25 percent of the school's student body, and mathematics majors made up more than 40 percent of the honor roll (Datta 1993). Between 1980 and 1987, seven of eight valedictorians were math majors. The Potsdam math department didn't just cater to high-achieving students, however. More than half of all incoming freshmen took calculus as an elective course, largely because of the positive reputation of the department. Many students went on to take additional elective math classes, regardless of their majors. Perhaps most remarkable is that, year after year, women outnumbered men among SUNY Potsdam's math majors (Datta 1993).

Several researchers and college math professors visited SUNY Potsdam over the years to figure out just what the math department was doing. Lowering standards? No, by all accounts, no. The math they taught was rigorous. Changing the curriculum? No, they used the same texts as other universities. Using one particular teaching style? No, different professors maintained their individual styles. Remediating and intervention? No, in fact Stephens eliminated all remedial math classes and raised expectations. "Ability" grouping? Absolutely not. He got rid of placement exams altogether and recognized the SATs as discriminatory toward students of color and women.

So what did he do? Stephens wrote, "My primary goal as Chair was to help establish the most favorable conditions I could for students to learn and teachers to teach" (Datta 1993, 65). Here was the mission statement of the department:

> The major program in mathematics is based on the premise that the study of pure mathematics can be undertaken successfully by a large number of students if they are provided with a supportive environment including: careful and considerate teaching by a well-trained and dedicated faculty, continual encouragement, successful (student) role models, enough success to develop self-esteem, enough time to develop intellectually, recognition of their achievement, and the belief that the study is a worthwhile endeavor. We are dedicated to providing this supportive environment. (Spencer 1995, 860)

I've read all the papers and books I can find about the Potsdam method and Clarence Stephens. He is, by all accounts, a remarkable person. He was a black man born in the Jim Crow South in 1917. He was orphaned young and subject to covert and overt racism throughout his schooling. He persevered and became the ninth black American to earn a PhD in mathematics. He spent his teaching life at Morgan State College, SUNY Geneseo, and SUNY Potsdam. At each college, he distinguished himself by welcoming students into his beloved mathematics, especially those from underrepresented groups such as black students and women, and creating a humanistic, supportive, challenging environment in which they could learn.

It worked.

Students at SUNY Potsdam were greeted with the motto "Students Come First." Stephens constantly told his staff, "Believe in your students, everyone can do mathematics." He encouraged teachers to know their students well, including their hopes and fears and lives outside of mathematics, and to treat them with love and respect. He taught teachers to take special pride in lifting students from above, to say, "We know our students are not well prepared, our job is to teach and prepare them" (Datta 1993, 20). He insisted that all physical spaces—classrooms, faculty offices, the math lab and common areas—should be comfortable and foster interaction among students and teachers. Doors were open, literally and figuratively. Faculty taught students to work together in study groups, and teachers joined those groups as members. Relationships mattered.

Stephens emphasized developing independence in students by teaching them how to read mathematics and make sense of it for themselves. His entire stance was one of empowering students, of believing in and supporting them. He instructed professors to give students all the time they needed to learn a new concept, to figure out what students understood and build from there, to engage students deeply in mathematical reasoning, and to teach students how to prove rather than memorize proofs. At a time when most mathematics departments were focused on weeding out all but the very best students, Stephens and his colleagues at Potsdam taught mathematics as an essential component of a liberal arts education to as many students as possible.

I came across Clarence Stephens's work early in the research for this book, and his emphasis on creating "the most favorable conditions" for students to learn and teachers to teach mathematics has been something of a guiding light for me. How can we create such nurturing, responsive, challenging climates for all students, at any age, at scale? How can we create supportive, dynamic, aspirational, sustained professional development for teachers so we are equipped to create favorable conditions? These are the questions that occupy me.

Throughout this book, I've been sharing the work of teachers who have generously invited me into their classrooms and taught me how they cultivate the most favorable conditions for their students to learn mathematics. I've been lifting the veil on their instructional decisions to make their reasoning as transparent as possible. My approach has been to offer you a buffet of techniques and strategies to choose from, in the hopes you'll find several ideas to try in your own teaching and thereby create more favorable conditions for students to learn mathematics in your context. I'm eager and curious to hear what works for you and hope you will share your successes, challenges, and questions with me so we can keep learning together.

Before I go, however, I must share one more classroom story with you. I'm hoping to show how the different ideas we've talked about combine in a glorious, spontaneous, nonlinear mash-up of delightful math teaching and learning. As you read it, what examples of risk taking, mistake making, striving toward precision, rising to a challenge, questioning, connecting, intuitive thinking, reasoning, proving, working together, and working independently do you notice? What do you notice about how students who are empowered to make sense of mathematics move among these practices and habits of mind? Finally, what do you notice about Ann's role as teacher and learner-in-chief? How is she creating the most favorable conditions for this mathematical community?

Enjoy.

Ann Gaffney, seventh grade, Londonderry, New Hampshire

"I don't think it's right, but I want to put it up just so people can say stuff about it."

I met Ann at a regional conference. We hit it off, and she invited me to visit her seventh-grade classroom at Londonderry Middle School. She knew I was writing a book, so you can imagine she was a little nervous and excited to have me observe and record her teaching. She let me know that her students had been working on probability for a few weeks, and she had planned a synthesis lesson to help them review for the test the following day.

Ann asked her students to figure out the odds of winning the state lottery in New Hampshire, called the Powerball. Students dug right into the task. Ann was circulating and listening to students' thinking when two students told her they'd observed something that didn't make sense to them. By their math, the odds of winning $1,000,000 were better than the odds of winning $10,000.

Ann looked over their work and found no errors. They'd approached the problem differently than she had, but their work seemed coherent and correct. Ann pulled out her notes and scanned them. She couldn't make sense of what was going on. The clock was ticking toward the end of class, my camera was rolling, and she had a decision to make. She pulled the students together and asked what they were thinking about the Powerball problem. Several students shared their observations, and then Ann turned toward the students with the curious solution and asked them to share:

Ann: Listen up. This is cool.

Edward: There is a better chance of winning $1,000,000 than winning $10,000.

Ann: Huh! Look at your numbers!

Students: "What?" "Huh?" "Whoa!"

Ann: What's going on there?

Students: It's because the Powerball throws everything off!

Ann: Could that be right? I mean, why would they have done the prizes that way then?

(Students talked to one another, trying to figure out what was going on. Ann pulled them back together.)

Ann: Does anybody think that maybe the statisticians who figured it out for the state of New Hampshire might have done a better job than we did? (Ann raised her hand.) Do you think the people who figure out statistics for a living might have done a better job than we did? Maybe we made a mistake! Maybe we made a mistake! Right? That doesn't seem to make sense that they would give a higher dollar amount for a more likely thing! Right?

Ann quickly changed her plans. She put off the test and promised to e-mail students a new homework assignment that might shed some light on what was going on. Her students headed out, and Ann headed to her office to construct a new plan.

The next day, Ann and I walked to the classroom and found students already engaged in heated discussions about the problem in the hallway. They had their work out and were leaning on lockers and one another's backs to write and talk. Ann opened the door and her students piled in, talking about combinations and permutations all the way. Several minutes later, Ann asked them to come together and share their thinking from the homework. Student after student raised hands and offered ideas. They used language like, "I'm thinking it might be . . ." or

"Maybe what's happening is . . ." or "I tried to figure out if order matters and . . ." or "Jack's work is making me wonder if it matters if numbers can repeat or not? I hadn't thought of that." They shared formulas they had derived and tables of data they'd generated the night before. They compared solutions and were influenced by their classmates' approaches. It was beautiful. And then Ann stood up and said something that made me break into an even wider grin:

> Ann: I'm not asking these questions because I want to say things to you. I'm asking these questions because *I really have them. I have no idea what we were doing wrong yesterday. I don't get it yet! I haven't figured it out.*

We have all had a moment in which a student's question or comment makes it obvious that we don't understand the mathematics. Maybe we learned something procedurally and don't know why it works. Perhaps we haven't yet dug into a concept deeply enough or ever considered the student's question. Most teachers feel exposed, vulnerable, or insecure at this moment. We tell students it's great for them to not-know, but we keep our own not-knowing hidden under our authority.

Ann did the opposite. She took advantage of this genuine, unplanned opportunity to model how she handles it when she doesn't understand a piece of mathematics. She jumped into her not-knowing with both feet, making as big and public a splash as she could.

> Ann: I created a problem that I thought would spark a discussion about something that I thought might help us figure out what's going on with the real Powerball problem. OK? Because how we're attacking the Powerball problem is different than the answer key I found online.
>
> Students: What?

Ann explained that she'd gone online to study the Powerball problem and she'd found a solution that used a different approach. She had yet to reconcile the two.

> Ann: So now I'm looking as another mathematician and you're looking as other mathematicians and coming up with a different way to solve the problem. We *should* get the same answer. But we didn't. So something must be up! And *I've decided to doubt my own answer* rather than their answer. I could have decided to doubt theirs, and try and figure out the mistake in theirs. Instead, I've decided to doubt my own and try and figure out the mistake in my own. We might go through this and find that we didn't make a mistake at all; the one posted online made the mistake. But I think by examining ours and understanding ours, we'll come to determine which of those is correct and why . . . So that's what we're going to do. And when we figure it out, then we'll do our test. And you'll know more than you knew yesterday and today.
>
> Lisa: OK, so I've been sitting here doing some thinking. I don't think it's right, but I want to put it up just so people can say stuff about it.

Ann: Please do, please do.

Lisa: I don't think this makes much sense at all, but it made sense when I did it.

Ann: Good! OK. Let's talk about it.

If I had to pick favorite moments I've ever witnessed in a math classroom, this one would be high on the list. Ann boldly and clearly used her leadership position to create a safe space for taking risks, making mistakes, and making sense of mathematics. Through her actions and words, she defined this messy, exciting, investigative work as what it means to do mathematics. The words were hardly out of Ann's mouth when Lisa stood up and stepped into the safe space her teacher created. Lisa walked over to the document camera and projected her work, knowing it was at least incomplete and probably wrong, but confident that she, her classmates, and her teacher could make sense of it together.

And they did! It took several days, but Ann's students solved the Powerball problem. Ann told me students were e-mailing her in the middle of the night with ideas, texting each other about math, and generally bursting at the seams to work on this problem until they cracked it. When they figured it out, proved why their math worked, and made sense of what they'd been doing wrong, they felt the delight and satisfaction that comes with solving a worthy puzzle. And they were closer as a class, bonded by this shared experience of making sense of challenging mathematics all the way at the frontiers of their understanding.

Becoming the Math Teacher You Wish You'd Had

So we come to an end where we began, with the acknowledgment that our attitudes, beliefs, experiences, and knowledge impact our teaching and our students, for good or ill. Reuben Hersh and Vera John-Steiner wrote, "People aren't born disliking math. They learn to dislike it in school" (2011, 305). Yes, and many of us did. But Ann, Jen, Heidi, Shawn, Debbie, and every other teacher herein have shown us that math class doesn't have to be that way anymore. Our math classes can and should be vibrant social communities, full of curiosity and questions, perplexity and joy, seriousness and passion, because that's what it means to do mathematics.

Our students arrive in kindergarten with powerful mathematical ideas, observations, and wonderings. If we create the most favorable conditions we can for all students, we'll equip them to enjoy mathematics all their lives.

The icing on the cake? We get to witness and support their thinking and learn ever more interesting and beautiful mathematics right alongside them.

REFERENCES

Arcavi, Abraham. 2003. "The Role of Visual Representations in the Learning of Mathematics." *Educational Studies in Mathematics* 52 (3): 215–241.

Ashcraft, Mark H. 2002. "Math Anxiety: Personal, Educational, and Cognitive Consequences." *Current Directions in Psychological Science* 11 (5): 181–185.

Ashcraft, Mark H., and Alex M. Moore. 2009. "Mathematics Anxiety and the Affective Drop in Performance." *Journal of Psychoeducational Assessment* 27 (3): 197–205.

Balacheff, N. 1991. "The Benefits and Limits of Social Interaction: The Case of Mathematical Proof." In *Mathematical Knowledge: Its Growth Through Teaching*, ed. Alan J. Bishop, Stieg Mellin-Olsen, and Joop van Dormolen. Dordrecht, The Netherlands: Kluwer Academic Publishers.

Ball, Deborah Loewenberg. 1992. "Magical Hopes: Manipulatives and the Reform of Math Education." *American Educator* 16 (2): 14–18, 46–47.

Battista, Michael T., and Douglas H. Clements. 1995. "Geometry and Proof." *Mathematics Teacher* 88 (1): 48–54. http://investigations.terc.edu/library/bookpapers/geometryand_proof.cfm.

Beatty, Ruth. 2014. "Exploring the Power of Growing Patterns." What Works? Research into Practice Series of Monographs from Student Achievement Division and Ontario Association of Deans of Education (55).

Beckmann, Sybilla. 2002. "Mathematics for Elementary Teachers: Making Sense by 'Explaining Why.'" http://www.math.uoc.gr/~ictm2/Proceedings/pap174.pdf.

Behrend, Jean. 2001. "Are Rules Interfering with Children's Mathematical Understanding?" *Teaching Children Mathematics* 8 (1): 36–40.

_____. 2003. "Learning-Disabled Students Make Sense of Mathematics." *Teaching Children Mathematics* 9 (5): 269–273.

Berger, Ron, Leah Rugen, and Libby Woodfin. 2014. *Leaders of Their Own Learning: Transforming Schools Through Student-Centered Assessment.* San Francisco, CA: Jossey-Bass.

Boaler, Jo. 1999. "Open and Closed Mathematics: Student Experiences and Understandings." *Journal for Research in Mathematics Education* 29 (1): 41–62.

_____. 2008. *What's Math Got to Do with It? How Parents and Teachers Can Help Children Learn to Love Their Least Favorite Subject.* New York: Penguin.

_____. 2012. "Timed Tests and the Development of Math Anxiety." *Education Week,* July 3. http://www.edweek.org/ew/articles/2012/07/03/36boaler.h31.html.

_____. 2014. "Research Suggests That Timed Tests Cause Math Anxiety." *Teaching Children Mathematics* 20 (8): 469–473.

Boaler, Jo, and Cathy Humphreys. 2005. *Connecting Mathematical Ideas: Middle School Video Cases to Support Teaching and Learning.* Portsmouth, NH: Heinemann.

Bronson, Po, and Ashley Merryman. 2009. *NurtureShock: New Thinking About Children.* New York: Twelve.

Brown, Stephen I., and Marion I. Walter. 2005. *The Art of Problem Posing.* 3rd ed. New York: Routledge.

Burns, Marilyn. 1975. *The I Hate Mathematics! Book.* A Brown Paper School Book. Covelo, CA: Yolla Bolly Press.

_____. 2000. *About Teaching Mathematics: A K–8 Resource.* 2nd ed. Sausalito, CA: Math Solutions.

_____. 2009. "4 Win-Win Math Games." *Instructor,* March/April, 23–29. http://www.mathsolutions.com/wpcontent/uploads/winwin_mathgames.pdf.

Burton, Leone. 1999. "Why Is Intuition So Important to Mathematicians but Missing from Mathematics Education?" *For the Learning of Mathematics* 19 (3): 27–32.

CadwalladerOlsker, Todd. 2011. "What Do We Mean by Mathematical Proof?" *Journal of Humanistic Mathematics* 1 (1): 33–60. doi:10.5642/jhummath.201101.04.

Carpenter, Thomas P., Elizabeth Fennema, Megan Loef Franke, Linda Levi, and Susan B. Empson. 1999. *Children's Mathematics: Cognitively Guided Instruction.* Portsmouth, NH: Heinemann.

_____. 2014. *Children's Mathematics: Cognitively Guided Instruction.* 2nd ed. Portsmouth, NH: Heinemann.

Carpenter, Thomas P., Megan Loef Franke, and Linda Levi. 2003. *Thinking Mathematically: Integrating Arithmetic & Algebra in Elementary School.* Portsmouth, NH: Heinemann.

Chapin, Suzanne H., and Art Johnson. 2006. *Math Matters: Understanding the Math You Teach, K–6.* Sausalito, CA: Math Solutions.

Chapin, Suzanne H., Catherine O'Connor, and Nancy Canavan Anderson. 2009. *Classroom Discussions: Using Math Talk to Help Students Learn, Grades K–6.* 2nd ed. Sausalito, CA: Math Solutions.

Chen, Qixuan, and Jingguang Li. 2014. "Association Between Individual Differences in Non-symbolic Number Acuity and Math Performance: A Meta-analysis." *Acta Psychologica* 148:163–172.

Cherniwchan, Chrystal, Azita Ghassemi, and Jon Keating. 2009. "Are Mathematicians Creative?" *Mathematical Ethnographies Project.* https://www.youtube.com/watch?v=9QeUYyecjZ0.

Clements, Douglas H., and Julie Sarama. 2000. "Young Children's Ideas About Geometric Shapes." *Teaching Children Mathematics* 6 (8): 482–488.

Cohen, David K. 1990. "A Revolution in One Classroom: The Case of Mrs. Oublier." *Educational Evaluation and Policy Analysis* 12 (3): 311–329.

Cohen, Elizabeth G., and Rachel A. Lotan. 2014. *Designing Groupwork: Strategies for the Heterogeneous Classroom.* 3rd ed. New York: Teachers College Press.

Corwin, Rebecca B., Judith Storeygard, and Sabra L. Price. 1996. *Talking Mathematics: Supporting Children's Voices.* Portsmouth, NH: Heinemann.

Dacey, Linda Schulman, and Rebeka Eston Salemi. 2007. *Math for All: Differentiating Instruction, K–2.* Sausalito, CA: Math Solutions.

Danielson, Christopher. 2012. "The Hierarchy of Hexagons." *Overthinking My Teaching,* October 12. http://christopherdanielson.wordpress.com/2012/10/12/the-hierarchy-of-hexagons/.

———. 2013. "What Did You Learn?" *Overthinking My Teaching,* August 23. http://christopherdanielson.wordpress.com/2013/08/23/what-did-you-learn/.

———. 2014. "Spirals." *Talking Math with Your Kids,* May 6. http://talkingmathwithkids.com/2014/05/06/spirals/.

———. 2016. *Which One Doesn't Belong? A Shapes Book.* Portland, ME: Stenhouse.

Daro, Phil [SERP Media]. 2013. *Against "Answer-Getting."* November 20. https://vimeo.com/79916037.

Datta, Dilip. 1993. *Math Education at Its Best: The Potsdam Model.* Framingham, MA: Center for Teaching/Learning of Mathematics.

de Villiers, Michael. 1990. "The Role and Function of Proof in Mathematics." *Pythagoras* 24 (1): 17–24.

Duckworth, Eleanor. 1987. *"The Having of Wonderful Ideas" and Other Essays on Teaching and Learning.* New York: Teachers College Press.

du Sautoy, Marcus. 2015. "How Mathematicians Are Storytellers and Numbers Are the Characters." *The Guardian,* January 23. http://gu.com/p/456x9/sbl.

Dweck, Carol. 2006. *Mindset: The New Psychology of Success.* New York: Random House.

Empson, Susan, and Linda Levi. 2011. *Extending Children's Mathematics: Fractions & Decimals: Innovations in Cognitively Guided Instruction.* Portsmouth, NH: Heinemann.

Edward, Rathmell C., and Anthony J. Gabriele. 2011. "Number and Operations: Organizing Your Curriculum to Develop Computational Fluency." In *Achieving Fluency: Special Education and Mathematics,* ed. Francis Fennell. Reston, VA: National Council of Teachers of Mathematics.

Ernest, Paul. 2009. "New Philosophy of Mathematics: Implications for Mathematics Education." In *Culturally Responsive Mathematics Education*, ed. Brian Greer, Swapna Mukhopadhyay, Arthur B. Powell, and Sharon Nelson-Barber. New York: Routledge.

Featherstone, Helen, Sandra Crespo, Lisa M. Jilk, Joy A. Oslund, Amy Noelle Parks, and March B. Wood. 2011. *Smarter Together! Collaboration and Equity in the Elementary Math Classroom.* Reston, VA: National Council of Teachers of Mathematics.

Fennema, Elizabeth, and Barbara Scott Nelson. 1997. *Mathematics Teachers in Transition.* Mahwah, NJ: Lawrence Erlbaum.

Fischbein, Efraim. 1982. "Intuition and Proof." *For the Learning of Mathematics* 3 (2): 9–18.

Fosnot, Catherine, and Maarten Dolk. 2001. *Young Mathematicians at Work: Constructing Number Sense, Addition, and Subtraction.* Portsmouth, NH: Heinemann.

Fullilove, Robert E., and Philip Uri Treisman. 1990. "Mathematics Achievement Among African American Undergraduates at the University of California, Berkeley: An Evaluation of the Mathematics Workshop Program." *Journal of Negro Education* 59 (3): 463–478.

Geist, Eugene. 2010. "The Anti-anxiety Curriculum: Combating Math Anxiety in the Classroom." *Journal of Instructional Psychology* 37 (1): 24–31.

Gutstein, Eric, and Bob Peterson. 2013. *Rethinking Mathematics: Teaching Social Justice by the Numbers.* 2nd ed. Milwaukee, WI: Rethinking Schools.

Halberda, Justin, Michèle M. M. Mazzocco, and Lisa Feigenson. 2008. "Individual Differences in Non-verbal Number Acuity Correlate with Maths Achievement." *Nature* 455: 665–668.

Halmos, Paul R. 1968. "Mathematics as a Creative Art." *American Scientist* 56: 375–389.

———. 1985. *I Want to Be a Mathematician: An Automathography in Three Parts.* Washington, DC: Mathematical Association of America.

Hanna, Gila. 1989. "More Than Formal Proof." *For the Learning of Mathematics* 9 (1): 20–23.

———. 2000. "Proof, Explanation and Exploration: An Overview." *Educational Studies in Mathematics* 44: 5–23.

Harel, Guershon. 2013. "Intellectual Need." In *Vital Directions for Mathematics Education Research*, ed. Keith R. Leatham. New York: Springer.

Harel, Guershon, and Larry Sowder. 1998. "Students' Proof Schemes: Results from Exploratory Studies." *Issues in Mathematics Education* 7:234–283.

———. 2007. "Toward Comprehensive Perspectives on the Learning and Teaching of Proof." In *Second Handbook of Research on Mathematics Teaching and Learning*, ed. Frank K. Lester. Reston, VA: National Council of Teachers of Mathematics.

Heiligman, Deborah. 2013. *The Boy Who Loved Math: The Improbable Life of Paul Erdős.* New York: Roaring Book Press.

Henderson, David W. 1996. "I Learn Mathematics from My Students: Multiculturalism in Action." *For the Learning of Mathematics* 16 (2): 46–52. http://flmjournal.org/Articles/5A730AB6D45226E38BEF5A8F9AA1A9.pdf.

Henrion, Claudia. 1997. *Women in Mathematics: The Addition of Difference.* Bloomington: Indiana University Press.

Hersh, Reuben. 1993. "Proving Is Convincing and Explaining." *Educational Studies in Mathematics* 24: 389–399.

———. 1997. *What Is Mathematics, Really?* New York: Oxford University Press.

Hersh, Reuben, and Vera John-Steiner. 2011. *Loving + Hating Mathematics: Challenging the Myths of a Mathematical Life.* Princeton, NJ: Princeton University Press.

Hiebert, James, Thomas P. Carpenter, Elizabeth Fennema, Karen C. Fuson, Diana Wearne, Hanlie Murray, Alwyn Oliver, and Piet Human. 1997. *Making Sense: Teaching and Learning Mathematics with Understanding.* Portsmouth, NH: Heinemann.

Hilbert, David. 1932. Preface to *Geometry and the Imagination*, by David Hilbert and Stephan Cohn-Vossen. Translated by P. Nemenyi. Originally published 1952, New York: Chelsea Publishing. Reprinted 1999, Providence, RI: American Mathematical Association.

Hilton, Peter, Derek Holton, and Jean Pederson. 1997. *Mathematical Reflections: In a Room with Many Mirrors.* New York: Springer Science-Business Media.

Horn, Ilana Seidel. 2012. *Strength in Numbers: Collaborative Learning in Secondary Mathematics.* Reston, VA: National Council of Teachers of Mathematics.

Hsu, Eric, Judy Kysh, and Diane Resek. 2007. "Differentiated Instruction Through Rich Problems." *New England Mathematics Journal* 39: 6–13.

Humphreys, Cathy, and Ruth Parker. 2015. *Making Number Talks Matter: Developing Mathematical Practices and Deepening Understanding, Grades 4–10.* Portland, ME: Stenhouse.

Hyde, Arthur. 2006. *Comprehending Math: Adapting Reading Strategies to Teach Mathematics, K–6.* Portsmouth, NH: Heinemann.

———. 2014. *Comprehending Problem Solving: Building Mathematical Understanding with Cognition and Language.* Portsmouth, NH: Heinemann.

Hyde, Daniel C., Saeeda Khanum, and Elizabeth S. Spelke. 2014. "Brief Non-symbolic, Approximate Number Practice Enhances Subsequent Exact Symbolic Arithmetic in Children." *Cognition* 131: 92–107.

Imm, Kara Lousie, Despina A. Stylianou, and Nabin Chae. 2008. "Student Representations at the Center: Promoting Classroom Equity." *Mathematics Teaching in the Middle School* 13 (8): 458–463.

Jackson, Carol D., and R. Jon Leffingwell. 1999. "The Role of Instructors in Creating Math Anxiety in Students from Kindergarten Through College." *The Mathematics Teacher* 92 (7): 583–586.

Jackson, Robyn, and Claire Lambert. 2010. *How to Support Struggling Students.* Mastering the Principles of Great Teaching. Alexandria, VA: ASCD.

Kamii, Constance, and Leslie Baker Housman. 2000. *Young Children Reinvent Arithmetic: Implications of Piaget's Theory.* 2nd ed. New York: Teachers College Press.

Kapur, Manu. 2010. "Productive Failure in Mathematical Problem Solving." *Instructional Science* 38 (6): 523–550.

———. 2014. "Productive Failure in Learning Math." *Cognitive Science* 38: 1008–1022.

Kazemi, Elham, Megan Franke, and Magdalene Lampert. 2009. "Developing Pedagogies in Teacher Education to Support Novice Teachers' Ability to Enact Ambitious Instruction." In *Crossing Divides: Proceedings of the 32nd Annual Conference of the Mathematics Education Research Group of Australasia* 1: 12–30.

Kazemi, Elham, and Allison Hintz. 2014. *Intentional Talk: How to Structure and Lead Productive Mathematical Discussions.* Portland, ME: Stenhouse.

Kazemi, Elham, and Deborah Stipek. 2001. "Promoting Conceptual Thinking in Four Upper-Elementary Mathematics Classrooms." *The Elementary School Journal* 102 (1): 59–80.

Knuth, Eric J. 2002. "Fostering Mathematical Curiosity." *Mathematics Teacher* 95 (2): 126–130.

Kohl, Herbert. 1992. "I Won't Learn from You! Thoughts on the Role of Assent in Learning." *Rethinking Schools* 7 (1): 16–17, 19. Revised and republished in Kohl, H. 1994. *"I Won't Learn from You" And Other Thoughts on Creative Maladjustment.* New York: The New Press.

Lampert, Magdalene. 1990. "When the Problem Is Not the Question and the Solution Is Not the Answer: Mathematical Knowing and Teaching." *American Educational Research Journal* 27 (10): 29–63.

———. 2001. *Teaching Problems and the Problems of Teaching.* New Haven, CT: Yale University Press.

Lannin, John K., Amy B. Ellis, and Rebekah Elliot. 2011. *Developing Essential Understanding of Mathematical Reasoning for Teaching Mathematics in Pre-K–Grade 8.* Reston, VA: National Council of Teachers of Mathematics.

Lappan, Glenda, James T. Fey, William M. Fitzgerald, Susan N. Friel, and Elizabeth Difanis Phillips. 2009. *Looking for Pythagoras.* 2nd ed. Connected Mathematics Project. Boston, MA: Pearson.

Libertus, Melissa E., Lisa Feigenson, and Justin Helberda. 2011. "Preschool Acuity of the Approximate Number System Correlates with School Math Ability." *Developmental Science* 14 (6): 1292–1300.

———. 2013. "Is Approximate Number Precision a Stable Predictor of Math Ability?" *Learning and Individual Differences* 25:126–133.

Libertus, Melissa E., Darko Odic, and Justin Halberda. 2012. "Intuitive Sense of Number Correlates with Math Scores on College-Entrance Examination." *Actua Psychologia* 141 (3): 373–379.

Liljedahl, Peter. 2004. "Repeating Pattern or Number Pattern: The Distinction Is Blurred." *Focus on Learning Problems in Mathematics* 26 (3): 24–42.

———. 2014. "The Affordances of Using Visibly Random Groups in a Mathematics Classroom." In *Transforming Mathematics Instruction: Multiple Approaches and Practices*, ed. Yeping Li, Edward A. Silver, and Shiqi Li. New York: Springer.

———. 2016. "Building Thinking Classrooms: Conditions for Problem Solving." In *Posing and Solving Mathematical Problems: Advances and New Perspectives*, ed. Patricio Felmer, Erkki Pehkonen, and Jeremy Kilpatrick. New York: Springer.

Lockhart, Paul. 2009. *A Mathematician's Lament: How Schools Cheat Us out of Our Most Fascinating and Imaginative Art Form.* New York: Bellevue Literary Press.

———. 2012. *Measurement.* Cambridge, MA: Harvard University Press.

Lortie, Dan C. 1975. *Schoolteacher: A Sociological Inquiry.* Chicago: Unversity of Chicago Press.

Luzniak, Christopher. 2011. "The Basics of Mathdebating." *CLopen Mathdebater*, August 17. https://clopendebate.wordpress.com/2011/08/17/the-basics-of-mathdebating/.

Ma, Liping. 1999. *Knowing and Teaching Elementary Mathematics: Teachers' Understanding of Fundamental Mathematics in China and the United States.* New York: Routledge.

Martin, Danny Bernard. 2009. "Liberating the Production of Knowledge About African American Children and Mathematics." In *Mathematics Teaching, Learning, and Liberation in the Lives of Black Children,* ed. Danny Bernard Martin. New York: Routledge.

Mason, John, Leone Burton, and Kaye Stacey. 2010. *Thinking Mathematically.* 2nd ed. Harlow, England: Prentice Hall.

Mazzocco, Michèle M. M., Lisa Feigenson, and Justin Halberda. 2011. "Preschoolers' Precision of the Approximate Number System Predicts Later School Mathematics Performance." *PloS one* 6 (9): e23749. doi:10.1371/journal.pone.0023749.

McAnallen, Rachel R. 2010. "Examining Mathematics Anxiety in Elementary Classroom Teachers." PhD diss., University of Connecticut. http://www.gifted.uconn.edu/siegle/Dissertations/Rachel%20McAnallen.pdf.

Meyer, Dan. 2010. *"Math Class Needs a Makeover." Ted Talk*, March. https://www.ted.com/talks/dan_meyer_math_curriculum_makeover?language=en.

———. 2014. *"Video Games and Making Math Class More Like Things Students Like." dy/dan*, December 16. http://blog.mrmeyer.com/2014/video-games-making-math-more-like-things-students-like/.

———. 2015. "If Proof Is Aspirin Then How Do You Create the Headache?" *dy/dan*, July 30. http://blog.mrmeyer.com/2015/if-proof-is-aspirin-then-how-do-you-create-the-headache/.

Montague, Marjorie, and Delinda van Garderen. 2003. "A Cross-Sectional Study of Mathematics Achievement, Estimation Skills, and Academic Self-Perception in Students of Varying Ability." *Journal of Learning Disabilities* 36 (5): 437–448.

The National Council of Teachers of Mathematics. 2000. *Principles and Standards for School Mathematics.* Reston, VA: National Council of Teachers of Mathematics.

———. 2014. *Principles to Actions: Ensuring Mathematical Success for All.* Reston, VA: National Council of Teachers of Mathematics.

Nguyen, Fawn. 2013. "When I Let Them Own the Problem." *Finding Ways,* May 8. http://fawnnguyen.com/let-problem/.

Nunes, Terezinha, Analúcia Dias Schliemann, and David William Carraher. 1993. *Street Mathematics and School Mathematics.* Cambridge, UK: Cambridge University Press.

Nunes Carraher, Terezinha, Analúcia Dias Schliemann, and David William Carraher. 1985. "Mathematics in the Streets and in Schools." *British Journal of Developmental Psychology* 3: 21–29.

O'Connell, Susan, and John SanGiovanni. 2011a. *Mastering the Basic Math Facts in Addition and Subtraction: Strategies, Activities, and Interventions to Move Students Beyond Memorization.* Portsmouth, NH: Heinemann.

———. 2011b. *Mastering the Basic Math Facts in Multiplication and Division: Strategies, Activities, and Interventions to Move Students Beyond Memorization.* Portsmouth, NH: Heinemann.

Omohundro Wedekind, Kassia. 2011. *Math Exchanges: Guiding Young Mathematicians in Small-Group Meetings.* Portland, ME: Stenhouse.

Papert, Seymour. 1980. *Mindstorms: Children, Computers, and Powerful Ideas.* New York: Basic Books.

Park, Joonkoo, and Elizabeth M. Brannon. 2013. "Training the Approximate Number System Improves Math Proficiency." *Psychological Science* 24 (10): 2013–2019.

Parrish, Sherry. 2010. *Number Talks: Helping Children Build Mental Math and Computation Strategies*. Sausalito, CA: Math Solutions.

Petti, Wendy. 2009. "Convince Me." *Education World*. May 12. http://www.educationworld .com/a_curr/mathchat/mathchat017.shtml.

Pickford, Avery. 2013. "Proof Doesn't Begin with Geometry: Redefining Proof." *Without Geometry, Life Is Pointless*. November 4. http://www.withoutgeometry.com/2013/11/proof-doesnt-begin-with-geometry.html.

Pólya, George. 1954a. *Induction and Analogy in Mathematics*. Princeton, NJ: Princeton University Press.

_____. 1954b. *Mathematics and Plausible Reasoning*. Princeton, NJ: Princeton University Press.

_____. 1963. *Mathematical Methods in Science*. Studies in Mathematics Series 6. Washington, DC: Mathematical Association of America.

Rathmell, Edward C., and Anthony J. Gabriele. 2011. "Number and Operations: Organizing Your Curriculum to Develop Computational Fluency." In *Achieving Fluency: Special Education and Mathematics*, ed. F. Fennell. Reston, VA: National Council of Teachers of Mathematics.

Ray, Max. 2013. *Powerful Problem Solving; Activities for Sense Making with the Mathematical Practices*. Portsmouth, NH: Heinemann.

Raymond, Anne M. 1997. "Inconsistency Between a Beginning Elementary School Teacher's Mathematics Beliefs and Teaching Practice." *Journal for Research in Mathematics Education* 28 (5): 550–576.

Reid, Constance. 1996. *Hilbert*. New York: Springer.

Richardson, Kathy. 2012. *How Children Learn Number Concepts: A Guide to the Critical Learning Phases*. Bellingham, WA: Math Perspectives Teacher Development Center.

Russell, Susan Jo, Deborah Schifter, and Virginia Bastable. 2011. *Connecting Arithmetic to Algebra: Strategies for Building Algebraic Thinking in the Elementary Grades*. Heinemann: Portsmouth, NH.

Schifter, Deborah. 1996. *What's Happening in Math Class? Reconstructing Professional Identities*. Vol. 2. New York: Teachers College Press.

_____. 1999. "Learning Geometry: Some Insights Drawn from Teacher Writing." *Teaching Children Mathematics* 5 (6): 360–366.

Schifter, Deborah, Virginia Bastable, Susan Jo Russell, Danielle Harrington, and Marion Reynolds. 2001. *Geometry: Examining Features of Shape Casebook*. Developing Mathematical Ideas. Upper Saddle River, NJ: Dale Seymour.

Schifter, Deborah, and Catherine Twomey Fosnot. 1993. *Reconstructing Mathematics Education: Stories of Teachers Meeting the Challenge of Reform*. New York: Teachers College Press.

Schoen, Harold L., Glendon Blume, and Eric Hart. 1987. "Measuring Computational Estimation Processes." Paper presented at the Annual Meeting of the American Educational Research Association, April 20–24, 1987, Washington, DC.

Seeley, Cathy L. 2009. *Faster Isn't Smarter: Messages About Math, Teaching, and Learning in the 21st Century.* Sausalito, CA: Math Solutions.

Seethaler, Pamela M., and Lynn S. Fuchs. 2006. "The Cognitive Correlates of Computational Estimation Skill Among Third-Grade Students." *Learning Disabilities Research & Practice* 21 (4): 233–243.

Shumway, Jessica F. 2011. *Number Sense Routines: Building Numerical Literacy Every Day in Grades K–3.* Portland, ME: Stenhouse.

Siena, Maggie. 2009. *From Reading to Math: How Best Practices in Literacy Can Make You a Better Math Teacher.* Sausalito, CA: Math Solutions.

Singh, Simon. 1997. *Fermat's Enigma: The Epic Quest to Solve the World's Greatest Mathematical Problem.* New York: Anchor Books.

Skemp, Richard R. 1976. "Relational Understanding and Instrumental Understanding." *Mathematics Teaching* 77: 20–26. Reprinted 2006. *Mathematics Teaching in the Middle School* 12 (2): 88–95.

Smith, Margaret S., and Mary Kay Stein. 2011. *5 Practices for Orchestrating Productive Mathematics Discussions.* Reston, VA: National Council of Teachers of Mathematics.

Sowder, Larry, and Guershon Harel. 1998. "Types of Students' Justifications." *The Mathematics Teacher* 91 (8): 670–675.

Spencer, Armond. 1995. "On Attracting and Retaining Mathematics Majors—Don't Cancel the Human Factor." *Notices of the American Mathematical Society* 42 (8): 859–862. http://www.ams.org/notices/199508/spencer.pdf.

Stewart, Ian. 2006. *Letters to a Young Mathematician.* New York: Basic Books.

Stigler, James W., and James Hiebert. 1999. *The Teaching Gap: Best Ideas from the World's Teachers for Improving Education in the Classroom.* New York: Free Press.

Storeygard, Judy. 2009. *My Kids Can: Making Math Accessible to All Learners, K–5.* Portsmouth, NH: Heinemann.

Strogatz, Steven. 2012. *The Joy of X: A Guided Tour of Math, from One to Infinity.* Boston: Houghton Mifflin Harcourt.

Stylianides, Andreas J. 2007. "Proof and Proving in School Mathematics." *Journal for Research in Mathematics Education* 38 (3): 289–321.

———. 2009. "Breaking the Equation." *Mathematics Teaching* 213: 9–14.

Taimina, Daina. 2009. *Crocheting Adventures with Hyperbolic Planes.* Wellesley, MA: A. K. Peters.

Tanton, James. 2012. "How to Think Like a School Math Genius: Five Principles." *Thinking Mathematics!* May 1. http://www.jamestanton.com/?p=1097.

Tao, Terrence. 2007. "There's More to Mathematics Than Rigour and Proofs." *What's New,* May 6. http://terrytao.wordpress.com/careeradvice/there%E2%80%99s-more-to-mathematics-than-rigour-and-proofs/.

TERC. 2008. *Investigations in Number, Data, and Space.* 2nd ed. Glenview, IL: Pearson Scott Foresman.

Thurston, William P. 1994. "On Proof and Progress in Mathematics." *Bulletin of the American Mathematical Society* 30 (2): 161–177.

Treisman, Uri. 1992. "Studying Students Studying Calculus: A Look at the Lives of Minority Mathematics Students in College." *The College Mathematics Journal* 23 (5): 362–372.

Tripathi, Preety N. 2008. "Developing Mathematical Understanding Through Multiple Representations." *Mathematics Teaching in the Middle School* 13 (8): 438–445.

Usiskin, Zalman. 1986. "Reasons for Estimating." In *Estimation and Mental Computation, 1986 Yearbook*, ed. Harold L. Schoen and Marilyn J. Zweng. Reston, VA: National Council of Teachers of Mathematics.

Van de Walle, John A., Karen S. Karp, and Jennifer M. Bay-Williams. 2013. *Elementary and Middle School Mathematics: Teaching Developmentally*. Boston: Pearson.

Van de Walle, John A., LouAnn H. Lovin, Karen S. Karp, and Jennifer M. Bay-Williams. 2014. *Teaching Student Centered-Mathematics: Developmentally Appropriate Instruction for Grades*. 2nd ed., Vols. 1 and 2. Boston: Pearson.

Van Hiele, Pierre M. 1984. "A Child's Thought and Geometry." In *English Translation of Selected Writings of Dina Van Hiele-Geldof and Pierre M. Van Hiele,* ed. David Fuys, Dorothy Geddes, and Rosamond W. Tischler. Brooklyn, NY: Brooklyn College. http://files.eric.ed.gov/fulltext/ED287697.pdf.

Warren, Elizabeth, and Tom Cooper. 2008. "Generalising the Pattern Rule for Visual Growth Patterns: Actions That Support 8 Year Olds' Thinking." *Educational Studies in Mathematics* 67: 171–185.

Whitin, David J., and Robin Cox. 2003. *A Mathematical Passage: Strategies for Promoting Inquiry in Grades 4–6*. Portsmouth, NH: Heinemann.

Wittmann, Erich. 1981. "The Complementary Roles of Intuitive and Reflective Thinking in Mathematics Teaching." *Educational Studies in Mathematics* 12 (3): 389–397.

Yau, Shing-Tung, ed. 1988. *S.S. Chern: A Great Geometer of the Twentieth Century*. Singapore: International Press.

INDEX

Page numbers followed by *f* indicate figures.